Praise for *Baseball in the Ga...*

"If you love history or baseball, you will enjoy Thorn's impeccably researched tome; if you love both, you will be mesmerized."

—Dave Sheinin, *The Washington Post*

"Among the many books that have educated us about the birth and infancy of baseball, John Thorn's extraordinarily detailed and well-documented *Baseball in the Garden of Eden* is the advanced seminar."

—Bruce Weber, *The New York Times Book Review*

"John Thorn is a historian who delights in scandals and debunking popular myths. Which makes baseball his perfect subject."

—Bob Minzesheimer, *USA Today*

"Thorn writes with authority, precision, and humor. . . . *Baseball in the Garden of Eden* will give you perspective on any other baseball book you ever read."

—Allen Barra, *San Francisco Chronicle*

"John Thorn's *Baseball in the Garden of Eden* reveals a secret history of the early game that is more fantastical (and funny) than any concocted story."

—Jim Bouton, author of *Ball Four*

"No one, absolutely no one, knows more about the history of our national pastime than John Thorn, and this new book ought to settle once and for all many of the questions fans have about baseball's origins. Superb."

—Ken Burns

"Fresh and fascinating . . . Will become the benchmark for future chroniclers of our national pastime. . . . His scholarship, eloquence, and wit permeate each page. Grade: Home run."

—Mark Hodermarsky, *The Plain Dealer*

"The One True Game's old creation myths are nowhere near as interesting and as much fun as the truths that Thorn digs up about the conspiracies, vices, and raucous behavior of baseball's earliest innings."

—Robert Lipsyte, author of *An Accidental Sportswriter*

"*Baseball in the Garden of Eden* takes us on a fascinating journey through baseball's rise and flowering in nineteenth-century America. . . . This book is the masterwork we would expect from baseball's foremost historian."

—David Block, author of *Baseball Before We Knew It*

"With elegance, wit, and precision, John Thorn traces the lineage of baseball. . . . *Baseball in the Garden of Eden* is a must-read for anyone who claims to know the game."

—Jane Leavy, author of *The Last Boy: Mickey Mantle and the End of America's Childhood* and *Sandy Koufax: A Lefty's Legacy*

"Baseball's creation myth—Abner Doubleday in a Cooperstown pasture in 1839—has the merit of being enchanting but the defect of being false in every particular. Now comes another of John Thorn's many contributions to our understanding of baseball, proof that the game is even older and more interesting than most fans know."

—George F. Will, author of *Men at Work: The Craft of Baseball*

"What a garden of delight! John Thorn takes us through the tangled history of the game's origins with great good humor and flair. He accepts nothing on face value, but gives all sides their due. A pleasure for fans, but also for anyone with an interest in history and myth."

—Kevin Baker, author of *Strivers Row*

"No one knows baseball history as well as John Thorn or writes about it more ably. And there is no one better suited to record—with affection, amusement, and sometimes hilarity—the chicanery, misrepresentation, and downright lies that have obfuscated the fascinating story of the origins and development of our national game."

—Robert W. Creamer, author of *Babe: The Legend Comes to Life* and *Stengel: His Life and Times*

"No sport clings to its myths like baseball, which means it takes a baseball historian of the first rank like John Thorn to turn those myths upside down and inside out. *Baseball in the Garden of Eden* offers enlightenment for every fan. It is also a joy to read."

—Michael Shapiro, author of *Bottom of the Ninth* and *The Last Good Season*

"An invaluable, enduring, and unique history of the early game and how it swiftly changed, in some ways for the worse, and yet survived and thrived."

—David Nemec, author of *The Great Encyclopedia of Nineteenth-Century Major League Baseball*

"Thorn thrillingly illustrates how baseball exemplified, reflected, and even molded American history."

—Glenn Speer, *The Star-Ledger*

"Recognized as perhaps the country's most noteworthy historian of baseball, John Thorn throws the final bucket of ice water on the apocryphal origins of America's not-so-much-anymore national pastime. . . . The myths are colorful but not half as intriguing as the truth."

—John Pantalone, *The Providence Journal*

"John Thorn's *Baseball in the Garden of Eden* is what you expect from one of the sport's most authoritative historians: definitive analysis and myth debunking."

—Gene Sapakoff, *The Post and Courier*

"Splendid . . . Thorn is that rare archaeologist who can dig in ancient civilizations and then elegantly describe what he has found. . . . Brilliant."

—Stan Hochman, *Philadelphia Daily News*

"A vital addition to any devoted fan's bookshelf."

—Dick Kreck, *The Denver Post*

"Whether describing New York's Knickerbockers of 1845 baseball, the Gotham Baseball Club, the game in New England, or on Hoboken's Elysian Fields, Thorn shows his chops as a primary-source researcher."

—*Library Journal*

"Baseball history tends toward the mythical, pastoral, and fuzzy. Renowned baseball historian John Thorn takes all of that head on in what will likely stand as the definitive book on baseball's roots . . . fascinating stuff for students of baseball, the nineteenth century, or how institutions are made."

—Joe Gross, *Austin American-Statesman*

"*Baseball in the Garden of Eden* took John Thorn nearly three decades to complete. . . . The result is a fascinating tale that will help inform discussion of the sport's founding in years to come."

—James Bailey, baseballamerica.com

"A prominent baseball historian's delightfully literate take on the mythmakers who shaped the story of the game's creation."

—*Kirkus Reviews*

"[Thorn] is an innovator in statistical analysis and a witty writer who takes nothing at face value."

—Jeff Baker, *The Oregonian*

ALSO BY JOHN THORN

New York 400: A Visual History of America's Greatest City with Images from the Museum of the City of New York

The Glory Days: Baseball in New York City 1947–1957 (with the Museum of the City of New York)

Total Baseball, Eighth Edition (with Phil Birnbaum and Bill Deane)

Total Football, Second Edition (with Bob Carroll, Michael Gershman, and David Neft)

Total Browns (with Bob Carroll, Michael Gershman, and David Neft)

Total Steelers (with Bob Carroll, Michael Gershman, and David Neft)

Total Packers (with Bob Carroll, Michael Gershman, and David Neft)

Total Cowboys (with Bob Carroll, Michael Gershman, and David Neft)

Total 49ers (with Bob Carroll, Michael Gershman, and David Neft)

Treasures of the Baseball Hall of Fame

Total Baseball Catalog (with Bob Carroll, David Pietrusza, and Lloyd Johnson)

Total Mets (with Pete Palmer, Michael Gershman, David Pietrusza, and Matt Silverman)

Total Braves (with Pete Palmer, Michael Gershman, David Pietrusza, and Dan Schlossberg)

Total Indians (with Pete Palmer, Michael Gershman, David Pietrusza, and Paul Hoynes)

Baseball: Our Game

Ted Williams: Seasons of the Kid (with Richard Ben Cramer, Dan Okrent, and Mark Rucker)

The Official Major League Baseball Record Book (with Pete Palmer)

The Football Abstract (with Pete Palmer and Bob Carroll)

The Hidden Game of Football (with Bob Carroll and Pete Palmer)

The Armchair Traveler (with David Reuther)

The Pitcher (with John Holway)

The Armchair Book of Baseball II

The National Pastime

The Armchair Book of Baseball

The Hidden Game of Baseball (with Pete Palmer)

The Armchair Mountaineer (with David Reuther)

The Armchair Aviator

The Armchair Quarterback

Pro Football's Ten Greatest Games

Baseball's Ten Greatest Games

The Relief Pitcher

A Century of Baseball Lore

BASEBALL *in the* GARDEN *of* EDEN

The Secret History of the Early Game

JOHN THORN

SIMON & SCHUSTER PAPERBACKS
NEW YORK LONDON TORONTO SYDNEY NEW DELHI

Simon & Schuster Paperbacks
1230 Avenue of the Americas
New York, NY 10020

First Simon & Schuster paperback edition March 2012

SIMON & SCHUSTER PAPERBACKS and colophon are registered trademarks of Simon & Schuster, Inc.

For information about special discounts for bulk purchases, please contact Simon & Schuster Special Sales at 1-866-506-1949 or business@simonandschuster.com.

The Simon & Schuster Speakers Bureau can bring authors to your live event.
For more information or to book an event contact the Simon & Schuster Speakers Bureau at 1-866-248-3049 or visit our website at www.simonspeakers.com.

Designed by Level C

Manufactured in the United States of America

10 9 8 7 6 5 4 3 2 1

The Library of Congress has cataloged the hardcover edition as follows:
Thorn, John
Baseball in the Garden of Eden : the secret history of the early game / John Thorn.
p. cm.
Includes bibliographical references and index.
1. Baseball—United States—History—19th century. I. Title.
GV863.A1T458 2011
796.357097309034—dc22 2010045155

ISBN 978-0-7432-9403-4
ISBN 978-0-7432-9404-1 (pbk)
ISBN 978-1-4391-7021-2 (ebook)

Some of the material herein first appeared in *Base Ball: A Journal of the Early Game*, published by McFarland & Co. It is reprinted here in substantially modified form with the kind permission of the publishers.

"Without speculation there is no good and original observation."

—Letter from Charles Darwin to Alfred Russel Wallace,
December 22, 1857

CONTENTS

INTRODUCTION

Reflecting on the appeal of history in Jane Austen's *Northanger Abbey*, heroine Catherine Morland comments, "I often think it odd that it should be so dull, for a great deal of it must be invention."

Indeed. And in no field of American endeavor is invention more rampant than in baseball, whose whole history is a lie from beginning to end, from its creation myth to its rosy models of commerce, community, and fair play. The game's epic feats and revered figures, its pieties about racial harmony and bleacher democracy, its artful blurring of sport and business—all of it is bunk, tossed up with a wink and a nudge. Yet we love both the game and the flimflam because they are both so . . . American. Baseball has been blessed in equal measure by Lincoln and by Barnum.

Miss Austen's novel, written in 1798, but published posthumously twenty years later, is today well known in baseball-history circles not for the passage above but for this one:

> Mrs. Morland was a very good woman, and wished to see her children everything they ought to be; but her time was so much occupied in lying-in and teaching the little ones, that her elder daughters were inevitably left to shift for themselves; and it was not very wonderful that Catherine, who had nothing heroic about her, should prefer cricket,

> base ball, riding on horseback, and running about the country at the age of fourteen, to books—or at least books of information. . . .

Yet before April 1937, when Robert W. Henderson of the New York Public Library called public attention to this Austen reference to baseball, and to an even earlier woodcut of the game in John Newbery's *A Little Pretty Pocket-Book* (1744), few Americans knew that English boys and girls had played a game called *baseball*, whatever its rules may have been. Magnanimously, we had granted the Brits their primacy in cricket; some American cosmopolites might go so far as to acknowledge a playing-fields link between their national game and ours—perhaps, as the early sportswriter Henry Chadwick claimed, through rounders—but baseball, well, that was *our game*.

A special commission constituted by sporting-goods magnate Albert Goodwill Spalding affirmed in 1908, after nearly three years' purported study of the game's true origin, that baseball was assuredly American for it had been created from the fertile brain of twenty-year-old Abner Doubleday in Cooperstown, New York, in 1839. Critics of the commission's methods and conclusions soon made an alternative case for the genius of Alexander Cartwright and the Knickerbocker Base Ball Club, founded in New York in 1845. Weary after decades of America's jingoistic rodomontade, the British gallantly departed the field, never having comprehended what the whole fuss was about ("it's just rounders, you know").

Responding to Henderson's conclusion that baseball was "made in England," John Kieran wrote in his April 11, 1937, column for the *New York Times:*

> Oh, Abner of the Doubledays in far-off fields Elysian,
> Your claim to fame is called a foul by later-day decision.
> Some prying archeologists have gone and found some traces
> Of baseball footprints ages old in sundry English places.

Dryly, Kieran proposed that "in view of the enjoyment which we in this country derive from baseball, it would be a sporting gesture to let the English inventors know that we are very much obliged to them."

However, with publication of the commission's report in the spring of '08, followed shortly by Chadwick's death from complications of a cold aggravated by his ill-advised attendance at a drizzly Opening Day, the contest as to who invented baseball had ceased to be one of national origin. It soon boiled down to a two-man affair, both contestants American. Doubleday, whose dossier bore an official stamp, took the lead over the late-to-the-fair Cartwright and has held it, except among knowledgeable fans, to the present day.

Like Henderson's report (the forerunner of his 1947 book *Ball, Bat and Bishop*), Kieran's commentary amounted to a howl in the wilderness, for the Baseball Hall of Fame had already been designated for Cooperstown as consecration of Doubleday's ingenuity. Recent scholarship, especially that of David Block in *Baseball Before We Knew It*, has swung origins interest back to the mother country while affirming Henderson's view that bat-and-ball games are of great variety, antiquity, and geographic diversity, tangled up in the same evolutionary bramble bush from which baseball emerged. In this book we may touch upon some of these variant games, from the banks of the Nile (*seker-hemat*) to the meadows of medieval England (stoolball) to twentieth-century Finland (*pesäpallo*), but the story of baseball that fills these pages takes place in America.

Decades ago, when I became convinced that the well-worn tales about the rise and flower of the game were largely untrue, I determined to set matters straight . . . in other words, to fashion a history based upon excavation of fresh documentary evidence and to expose the truth. However, as time wore on I found myself more engaged by the lies, and the reasons for their creation, and have sought here not simply to contradict but to fathom them. And the liars and schemers in this not so innocent age of the game proved to be far more compelling characters than the straight arrows: In the Garden of Eden, after all, Adam and Eve are bores; it is the serpent who holds our attention.

Why, I wondered, had so many individuals expended so much energy in trying to shape and control the creation myth of baseball: to return to an Edenic past, real or imagined; to create the legend of a fall from grace, instigated by gamblers? That became the driving question behind this book. Baseball nostalgia, which I had always dismissed as curdled history for the soft of heart and head, now began to have an edge to it.

It has turned out that Spalding and Chadwick—like the calculating exponents of Doubleday and Cartwright—were not mere liars and blowhards. They were conscious architects of legend, shapers of national identity, would-be creators of a useful past and binding archetypes (clever lads, noble warriors, despised knaves, sly jesters, wounded heroes, and so on). In short, they were *historians* as that term once was understood. They were trying to create a national mythology from baseball, which they identified as America's secular religion because it seemed to supply faith for the faithless and unify them, perhaps in a way that might suit other ends. If in the process of crafting this useful past, certain individuals, events, ball clubs—even competing versions of the game, like those played in New England or Pennsylvania—had to be left along the road in the name of progress, so be it.

In *The Death of the Past*, J. H. Plumb described this earlier model for history as the establishment of "a psychological reality, used for a social purpose: to stress the virtues of courage, endurance, strength, loyalty and indifference to death." If we substitute "injury" for "death" in that formulation, we have a fair definition of the virtues of sport: providing for its players sublimated, graduated danger in preparation for national service, and for its spectators a salutary exposure to risk, through dashed hopes or unsuccessful wagers. The analytical impulse that marks modern historiography is, in Plumb's view, nothing less than an assault on the created ideology, or myths, by which people have given meaning to their institutions and societies. Large narratives and small pieties are swept away, replaced by skepticism and sometimes the bright if not warming light of truth.

The modern reader may ask: *Apart from why it may have mattered to so many in the past, why do the origins of baseball matter today?* Why does each announcement of a new find—an advertisement for a game of baseball in New York City from 1823, a prohibition against playing it in Pittsfield from 1791, a diary mention of the game in Surrey in 1755—land on the front page of major newspapers? Because baseball provides us with a family album older and deeper, by many generations, than all but a relative handful of Americans can claim for their own lineage; because the charm of baseball today is in good measure its echo of a bygone age; and because it is gratifying to think we have something lighthearted in common with the harsh lives of our forefathers, going back to the nation's earliest period and likely beyond. Parson Weems created the tale about a boyish George Washington and a cherry tree ("I cannot tell a lie, I did it with my little hatchet"), but it is no creation myth to report that the Father of Our Country played a bat-and-ball game called *wicket,* now vanished but long concurrent with baseball, with the troops at Valley Forge.

"The best part of baseball today," Larry Ritter, author of *The Glory of Their Times,* was fond of saying, "is its yesterdays." The old marketing adage is that in any field there are two positions worth holding: the first and the best. And it is because of baseball's success—the game on the field today is unquestionably superior to that of a century ago—that a special quality of interest pertains to its early years; for it is with institutions as with men, as Mrs. Schuyler Van Rensselaer wrote a century ago in another context, "the greater their importance in adult life the greater is the interest that attaches to their birth and antecedents, the incidents of their youth, and the influence that molded their spirit and shaped their destinies."

More recently, the paleontologist Stephen Jay Gould observed, "Most of us know that the Great Seal of the United States pictures an eagle holding a ribbon reading *e pluribus unum.* Fewer would recognize the motto on the other side (check it out on the back of a dollar bill): *annuit coeptis*—'he smiles on our beginnings.' "

All the same, I recognize that I may not presume my readers' familiarity with the themes and plots and players that make baseball's paleolithic period so fascinating to me. Prudence prompts the provision of a scorecard and a bit of a road map, too. As the book's title indicates, this is a serpentine tale, winding from ancient Egypt to Cooperstown on June 12, 1939, with present-day concerns regularly peeping through.

This book honors baseball's road not taken: the Massachusetts version, which was, in many ways, a better game of baseball than the New York game, although the latter triumphed through superior press agentry. Also coming in for examination will be the Philadelphia game, which like its New England sibling disappeared in an instant, more mysteriously than the dinosaurs. Gambling will be seen not as a latter-day pestilence brought upon a pure and innocent game, but instead the vital spark that in the beginning made it worthy of adult attention and press coverage.

Among the organized groups that played baseball before the ostensibly original Knickerbockers were the Gotham, New York, Eagle, Brooklyn, Olympic, and Magnolia clubs. The last named came into view only recently, as a ball club composed not of white-collar sorts with shorter workdays and gentlemanly airs but sporting-life characters, from ward heelers to billiard-room operators and bigamists. Why did the game's earliest annalists forget to include this club in its histories? One might venture to guess that the Magnolias were too unseemly a bunch to have been covered by a fig leaf, so they were simply written out of the Genesis story, which when presented less messily became the stuff of legend.

In the words of psychiatrist George E. Vaillant, "the passage of time renders truth itself relative. . . . It is all too common for caterpillars to become butterflies and then to maintain that in their youth they had been little butterflies. Maturation makes liars of us all." And so it was with the rough and ready game of baseball, constructing a legacy in support of its social and business models.

Among those lost in the shuffle of Cartwright and Doubleday and Chadwick and Spalding in the first decade of the twentieth century were four other men, each of whom had a better claim to "inventing" the game than any of those named. Of these little-known four fathers only one, a mysterious Mr. Wadsworth, was accorded even a bit part in the drama of the 1908 Special Commission's findings. We will soon enough catch up with him and with the others—Daniel Lucius Adams, William Rufus Wheaton, and William H. Tucker.

Although Doubleday did not start baseball, it may be said that he started the Civil War: The first Confederate shot at Fort Sumter "penetrated the masonry and burst very near my head," he wrote, after which "we took breakfast leisurely"; thus fortified, he "aimed the first gun on our side in reply to the attack." A Sanskrit-reading mystic who corresponded on esoteric matters with Ralph Waldo Emerson, Doubleday never thought to place himself on baseball's pedestal: A bookish sort as a boy, with no taste for athletics, he died more than a decade before anyone thought to credit him with baseball's design.

It was Doubleday's unusual credibility as a warrior and as a spiritualist that made him seem, to those with a grand plan, the perfect instrument by which an exogenous religious sect might thoroughly Americanize itself and become a major player in the promised land for all mankind. Doubleday had been named president of the Theosophical Society in 1879 after the departure for India of its founder, Madame Helena Petrovna Blavatsky. His apotheosis as father of baseball was engineered with Theosophical Society assistance, particularly that of Spalding's second wife. They were aided immeasurably by the rabbit-out-of-the-hat appearance of elderly mining engineer Abner Graves, whose 1905 testimony to having witnessed Doubleday's brainstorm in 1839, when Graves was five years old and the future military hero was twenty, sealed the deal for generations to come.

Like Doubleday, Cartwright did not know he had invented baseball when he died in 1892, one year before his unwitting rival. The muscle massed behind the Doubleday story after the commission report of 1908 prompted grandson Bruce Cartwright Jr. to launch an equally propagandistic plot that yielded for the Knickerbocker Cartwright a plaque in the Baseball Hall of Fame on which every word of substance is false. (Alex Cartwright did not set the base paths at ninety feet, the sides at nine men, or the game at nine innings.) And, as has recently been demonstrated, in Monica Nucciarone's biography, grandson Bruce inserted fabricated baseball exploits into a typescript of Alex Cartwright's handwritten Gold Rush journal, which contains no baseball remarks and itself has been judged a forgery.

Unraveling this twisted yarn in which various players hoped to shape America's future by imagining its past, we travel to the Theosophical Society compound at Point Loma, California, strategically selected by the society because it was the westernmost part of the continental United States, and thus nearest the Aryan (i.e., ancient Asian) motherland. Along the way we pick up a motley crew of Cuban refugee children, American millionaires and statesmen, utopian dreamers, and the newlywed Spaldings.

Baseball historians have treated Albert Spalding as a combination of Daddy Warbucks and Mr. Micawber because of his penchant for both profit and fustian. ("Baseball," he once declared, "is the exponent of American Courage, Confidence, Combativeness; American Dash, Discipline, Determination; American Energy, Eagerness, Enthusiasm; American Pluck, Persistency, Performance; American Spirit, Sagacity, Success; American Vim, Vigor, Virility.") But Spalding was something of an idealist, too, one who loved the game for its pure amateur spirit, for its joy, for its uplifting qualities. It has been easy to make him out as the architect of the scheme, by turns evil and comic, but at some point during his Point Loma years he may have become its unwitting victim, afflicted with early-onset dementia that left him in thrall to others. Two of his sons thought so, and sued Spalding's widow for twisting his mind and his assets toward the interests of the Theosophists. The plot to steal baseball started with Doubleday and Spalding and a utopian paradise in America's Golden West; it ended with the Theosophists suing each other into near extinction and a Spalding family feud that made headlines for years after the magnate's death in 1915.

"Who controls the past," George Orwell wrote, "controls the future: who controls the present controls the past." So it has been with baseball.

1
ANOINTING ABNER

By Monday, December 30, 1907, sixty-four-year-old Abraham Gilbert Mills, chairman of the Special Base Ball Commission on the game's origins, knew he could put off his final report no longer. The investigative mandate of the group, commenced in the spring of 1905, would cease at year's end, and the responsibility to summarize its findings fell to him.

Upon his return from an extended stay in Europe, Mills had been greeted by a bulging packet of edited statements and news clippings—a condensation of the material that had been provided to each member of the seven-man commission over the past two years. Upon riffling through the documents he instantly perceived that he had been boxed in. "From the nature of the case," Commission Secretary James E. Sullivan had written to Mills and the other commissioners in a covering letter, "and from the preponderance of the evidence submitted it would seem that there is but one decision that can be made as to [baseball's] American or foreign origin."

In a letter that Mills received that morning, Sullivan repeated what he had said a few days earlier when they met on the subway: that he had heard from all the others except him. Mills had been waiting to receive some additional information, but now he knew that "if I got anything off on the subject this year I would have to hustle." Accordingly, that afternoon he dictated a draft letter that "the star stenographer of our staff quickly presented . . . in such perfect typographical form that I fired it off as it was." And so this hurried first draft, still wanting data, became baseball history.

Constrained by the lack of evidence pointing in another direction, Mills, trained as an attorney, knew he would have no choice as the commission chair but to anoint as baseball's inventor young Abner Doubleday, said to be a resident of Cooperstown, New York, in 1839 or 1840, the attested period of invention. As a youth Doubleday had cared nothing for games. "I was brought up in a book store and early imbibed a taste for reading," he wrote to a New York *Sun* editor who had inquired about his boyhood habits. "I was fond of poetry and art and much interested in mathematical studies. In my outdoor sports, I was addicted to topographical work . . ."

Although he could not imagine the celebrity that would attach to him in death as baseball's Edison, Doubleday was no stranger to fame and good fortune. On April 12, 1861, after a Confederate assault upon Union troops at Fort Sumter with cannon fire at daybreak, Captain Doubleday positioned the first Union salvo in response; in his memoir he acknowledged that it "bounded off from the sloping roof of the battery opposite without producing any apparent effect." All the same, he was in later years pleased to be referred to in print as "the old Sumter hero": the man who, by engaging the Rebellion, had "started" the glorious Civil War.

Complicating Doubleday's posthumous coronation as the man who had invented baseball was the fact that he and Mills had been friends for twenty years. A. G. Mills (the press rarely cited his given names) had first met the major general in 1873 at a gathering of the Lafayette Post of the Grand Army of the Republic. When Doubleday died in 1893, it was Mills who organized his memorial service at New York's City Hall and arranged for his burial at Arlington. Yet not once in the intervening two decades of their friendship had Doubleday mentioned to Mills, who was widely known to be a past president of the National League, anything about the game he had supposedly dreamt up one fine summer day in Cooperstown.

Over the past century, historians have positioned Mills as an architect of the Doubleday myth, his friendly feelings overriding his reason. But close review of the commission documents reveals him to have been a dupe of what appears to have been a conspiracy. Particularly galling to Mills was his belief, which he held for the rest of his long life, that he had been manipulated to boost one old friend by another old friend, Albert Goodwill (like Mills, generally referred to as "A. G.") Spalding. At the National League's fiftieth anniversary dinner in New York on February 2, 1926, reporters asked the eighty-one-year-old Mills what conclusive evidence he had for Cooperstown as the birthplace of the national pastime. "None at all," Mills answered, "as far as the actual origin of baseball is concerned. The committee reported that the first baseball diamond was laid out in Cooperstown. They were honorable men and their decision was unanimous. I submit to you gentlemen, that if our search had been for a typical American village, a village that could best stand as a counterpart of all villages where baseball might have been originated and developed—Cooperstown would best fit the bill."

Mills and Spalding had known one another since the mid-1860s, when the latter was an up-and-coming pitcher with the Forest City Club of Rockford and the former presided over and played ball for the Olympic Club of Washington, D.C. In 1876 the two men had joined forces with William A. Hulbert in Chicago, where Spalding had gone to join Hulbert's White Stockings and Mills had gone to practice law and assist in the formative period of the new National League.

After Hulbert died in 1882, he was replaced as head of the league by an interim chief, but his permanent successor in the office of National League president was Mills. Spalding succeeded Hulbert in his ownership of the White Stockings and by turns became a force in league affairs, a sporting-goods magnate, and a world-touring missionary for the game that had given him everything. It was Spalding who recruited his old allies, including Mills, to the commission to decide whether baseball was of American or foreign origin. Spalding knew his own mind beforehand, but the matter needed to be settled with seeming respect for due process and honest inquiry.

The direct irritant that spurred Spalding to scratch this itch might have been jingoism, or greed, or overweening ego, or it may have been mere pique with the octogenarian editor of his self-branded yearly *Guide*. *Spalding's Guide* was the annual bible of the game, reporting on league matters, championship races, player performances, and official year-end statistics for every club in Organized Baseball, including the dozens of minor leagues. It was also the centerpiece of Spalding's American Sports Publishing empire, which provided guides for other sports and games and instructional manuals for youngsters wishing to become the next idols of the nation. English-born writer Henry Chadwick, who had edited *Spalding's Guide* each year since 1881, had been declaring in print for as long as anyone could remember—since before Spalding himself first set foot on a ball field—that the grand old game, which all the early players believed to be purely American, in fact derived from an older English schoolboy game called *rounders*. Spalding and others countered that no American could be found who would testify to having played a game of that name, even if the rules of some scrub (shorthanded) versions of baseball, particularly "old cat," seemed similar to the English game. Let Spalding describe the game of cat:

> "One old cat" was played by three boys—a thrower, catcher and batsman. The latter, after striking the ball, ran to a goal about thirty feet distant, and by returning to the batsman's position without being put out, counted one run or tally. Two old cat was played by four or more boys with two batsmen placed about forty feet apart. Three old cat was played by six or more boys with three batsmen, the ground being laid out in the shape of a triangle. Four old cat was played by eight or more boys with grounds laid out in the shape of a square. . . . Individual scores or tallies were credited to the batsman making the hit and running from one corner to the next. Some ingenious American lad naturally suggested that one thrower be placed in the center of the square, which brought nine players into the game, and which also made it possible to change the game into teams or sides, one side fielding and the other side batting. This was for many years known as the old game of town ball, from which the present game of base ball may have had its origin.

When professional baseball players first traveled to England in 1874, to exhibit their game in the home of cricket, they were informed that it was simply rounders, made duller by the dominant role of the pitcher. We will look at rounders more closely in chapter 3.

The long simmering if good-natured argument between Spalding and Chadwick came to a head after the latter used the 1903 *Spalding's Guide* as his bully pulpit to dust off his rounders theory, first aired in 1860 in the premier issue of *Beadle's Dime Base-Ball Player*, the handbook of the game when Albert was a pup. In the 1904 *Guide*, Old Chad went on further to discuss the game's evolution in America, in the form of "town ball," which he viewed as nothing more or less than American rounders.

How rounders, town ball, cat, and other early games of bat and ball—especially those played in Massachusetts and Pennsylvania—were related we will examine. Chadwick had it largely right when he observed, "Like Topsy, baseball never had no 'fadder'; it jest growed." But so did Spalding. Baseball grew to become an American institution not entirely by chance—it had not one father but several, though none named Doubleday.

Later in 1904, Spalding, patriotically and entrepreneurially galled at having yet again provided space to Chadwick's Anglophile bias, began writing to colleagues from bygone days, pointedly soliciting evidence that would support his belief that the games of cat and town ball, which he saw as unquestionably American, gave rise to baseball. On November 5, 1904, he wrote to John Lowell, a major figure in Boston baseball of the 1860s:

> I am preparing an article on the early history of Base Ball in this country, and I want some information as to the old Massachusetts game of ball, and how the New York and Massachusetts games were merged into the latter [sic; surely what he meant to write was how those two quite different games resolved into what became a national pastime]. I would appreciate any information you could give me on this subject, or any printed matter pertaining thereto, and I would also like your theory as to the origin of the present game of base ball [the one-word spelling was not yet the universal standard]. I have become weary of listening to my friend Chadwick's talk about base ball having been handed down from the old English game of "Rounders," and am trying to convince myself and others that the American game of Base Ball is purely of American origin, and I want to get all the facts I can to support that theory. My patriotism naturally makes me desirous of establishing it as of American origin, and as the same spirit will probably prompt you, I would like your ideas about it.

One may see in these remarks Spalding's bald intent to obtain precisely the outcome he intended. Spalding had grown up in baseball but he knew little of its history before the Civil War, so it is probably unfair to say "the fix was in" for Doubleday at this time. Later in the month, Spalding delivered a major speech about the national origin of the game at the Springfield, Massachusetts, YMCA. This was also the basis of articles that appeared in newspapers nationwide, arranged through Spalding's able secretary James E. Sullivan. In March of 1905, Spalding challenged Chadwick's position in the pages of his *Guide*, declaring his intention to settle the matter by means of an elite panel, what was to become the Special Base Ball Commission.

The members of the commission were, like Spalding, baseball luminaries of an earlier day: Morgan G. Bulkeley, titular president of the National League in its inaugural season of 1876, although Hulbert made all the decisions; Nick Young, the league's first secretary and fifth president; Al Reach and George Wright, star players of the era before the advent of the League, whose successful sporting-goods businesses had been quietly purchased by Spalding and permitted to continue in business under their old names; and Mills himself, fourth president of the National League and author of the landmark reserve clause, which bound a player to one club for life, while the club obligation to the player was for ten days only, over which players and owners would battle for nearly a century. United States Senator Arthur P. Gorman of the amateur Maryland club of the 1860s, another commission appointee, would die in midterm and not be replaced. Sullivan, president of the Amateur Athletic Union as well as Spalding factotum, gathered and, to a significant degree, filtered the evidence.

Over the next two years, the commissioners attended to their charge in desultory fashion, although Sullivan did receive hundreds of interesting letters and documents. "Space in the *Guide*," he wrote in the 1908 edition, "will not permit the publication of all the data and evidence that was collected and submitted to the Commission, but it is the intention of the publishers of Spalding's Athletic Library to add to that series a special book on the 'Origin of Base Ball,' which will contain the whole matter in detail."

Such a publication never emerged. But Sullivan's "data and evidence," long thought to have burned in the American Sports Publishing conflagration of July 5, 1913, miraculously turned up intact in

1999, part of a donation to the Baseball Hall of Fame of boxloads of humdrum Spalding publications. The source of this largesse was the family of John Doyle, a Spalding employee who had, for whatever fortunate reason, taken the originals home with him at some point before the fire. In prior years, researchers into the commission's process had had to make do with a selection of Sullivan-edited carbon copies that survived in the papers of A. G. Mills. The 1999 find revealed that Sullivan, as he said, had in fact done a lot of work. Spreading his net wide, with Spalding providing the leads, Sullivan had drawn forth amazingly clearheaded reminiscences by aged ballplayers and scribes. His raw, unedited files of original correspondence offer many treasures not present in the summaries that scholars accessed prior to 1999 and, with their marked excisions, make for interesting speculation as to motive.

When on October 12, 1907, Sullivan delivered to the commission members "the gist of the information so far received," with its startling claims by Abner Graves, a seventy-three-year-old mining engineer from Denver, about his boyhood recollections of Abner Doubleday and Cooperstown, no one registered surprise, perhaps because in his covering letter to the commissioners Sullivan had urged restraint: "There is considerable public interest in this question, and to avoid premature publication and discussion I would suggest that this whole matter be treated in confidence until a decision is finally reached, and then it can be promulgated in some systematic way that will be satisfactory."

But Graves had already expressed himself, beginning with his letter to the editor of the *Akron Beacon Journal*, published on April 4, 1905, under the headline "Abner Doubleday Invented Base Ball." The letter, which described in vivid detail how his childhood friend orchestrated the first game of baseball in Cooperstown in or around 1839, was a response to Spalding's article on the origins of baseball published the previous Saturday. That article had invited readers to send to Sullivan, at 15 Warren Street in New York, "any proof, data, or information" about baseball's true origin "with the hope that before another year rolls around this vexed question . . . may be settled for all time." The *Beacon Journal* article began thus:

> Abner C. Graves, mining engineer of Denver, Co., claims to know all about the origin of the game of base ball. He is stopping at the Thuma

> hotel, and reading the article in Saturday's Beacon Journal from the pen of A. C. [sic] Spalding prepared the following article and submitted it to the Beacon Journal for publication. . . .
>
> "The American game of base ball [Graves wrote] was invented by Abner Doubleday of Cooperstown, N. Y., either the spring prior or following the 'Log Cabin and Hard Cider' campaign of General Harrison for president, the said Abner Doubleday being then a boy pupil of Green's Select School in Cooperstown, and the same, who as General Abner Doubleday won honor at the battle of Gettysburg in the Civil War. . . ."

Graves' letter, which was the whole of the article except for the perfunctory introduction, went on at some length to describe the game of town ball and the improvements to it offered by young Doubleday, principally in limiting the number of players.

For reasons unknown, miner Graves ("Consulting Engineer to 'The Big 5,' " his business card read) was staying at the Hotel Thuma in Akron, a city not noted for its mineralogical opportunities. His letter, dated April 3 and typed on his personal stationery with its Denver address of 32 Bank Block, was likely hand-delivered to the newspaper in carbon copy, for the original was mailed to "J. E. Sullivan, 15 Warren Street, New York City, N.Y." in a Hotel Thuma envelope postmarked "Akron, Ohio, Apr 4, 1905, 4 PM." It has survived, along with the business card clipped to it and the envelope addressed to Sullivan, in the Doyle papers uncovered in 1999.

Sullivan promptly (on April 5!—either mail truly flew in those days before airmail or Sullivan knew what was coming) wrote Graves a perfunctory acknowledgment of receipt. At some point, he shared the letter with Spalding, who asked probing (or disingenuous) questions of Graves in a letter dated November 10, 1905.

> I am very much interested in your comments about Abner Doubleday and I would like to ask you a few questions bearing on this subject:
>
> Who was Abner Doubleday?
>
> About how old was he when the incident occurred to which you refer?
>
> Can you positively name the year in which this incident happened?

You say it was either the spring prior to or following the 'Log Cabin and Hard Cider Campaign of General Harrison.' If my memory serves me right that campaign took place in 1840, consequently it would make Doubleday's invention in 1839 or 1841. If it can be proven that this game was named by Doubleday in 1839, and really invented by him as your letter intimates, that in itself will have a good deal of influence in fixing its birth, and at present I do not know of any one who has really attempted to establish Base Ball before 1839.

You say this game of Base Ball as invented by Doubleday was undoubtedly the first starter of Base Ball and quickly superseded Town Ball. Your remark would indicate that while Doubleday made some changes in the game, which he called Base Ball, it really was an improvement or evolution of Town Ball, and if this is so, it directly confirms the contention that I have made that Base Ball was the direct evolution of Town Ball or Four Old Cat.

Could you give me the name and address of any persons now living in Cooperstown, New York City, or elsewhere, that could substantiate your recollections of Doubleday's invention or his first introduction of the game of Base ball? I am very much interested in this matter and will very much appreciate any information you can give me on the entire subject, and if there are any side lights that you can throw on the circumstance, not contained in your 'Beacon Journal' letter, I would be pleased to have it.

Hoping to hear from you as soon as possible, as the whole matter and the evidence collected will go to the Special Base Ball Commission appointed a year ago for the purpose of considering and, if possible, deciding on the origin of Base Ball, I remain,

Yours very truly, [signature]

Long before Spalding's response, however, the Graves letter had been quoted in full in the *Otsego Farmer* of Cooperstown, New York, and in part in an article in the *Wilkes-Barre Times* of Tuesday, July 18, 1905, as "When Was Base Ball Organized," and then in a handful of Sunday newspapers five days later (including the *Fort Wayne Journal-Gazette* and the *San Antonio Sunday Light*) under the heading "The Origin of Base Ball." All articles featured a section on Cooperstown that began the same way, but the Wilkes-Barre paper devoted less space to the rules of "Doubleday's game":

> Another man who disputes the statement that the Knickerbockers were the first players of bona fide baseball is Abner Graves, a mining engineer of Denver, Col.
>
> [Quoting Graves] "The pupils of Otsego academy and of Green's select school were then playing the old game of town ball in the following manner:
>
> "A 'tosser' stood close to the 'home goal' and tossed the ball straight upward about six feet for the batsman to strike at on its fall, the latter using a four-inch flat board bat. All others wanting to play were scattered about the field, far and near, to catch the ball when hit. The lucky catcher took his inning at bat. When a batsman struck the ball he ran for a goal fifty feet distant and returned. If the ball was not caught or if he was not 'plunked' by a thrown ball, while running, he retained his innings, as in old cat.
>
> "Doubleday then improved town ball to limit the number of players, as many were hurt in collisions. From twenty to fifty boys took part in the game I have described. He also designed the game to be played by definite teams or sides. Doubleday called the game 'base ball,' for there were four bases in it. Three were places where the runner could rest free from being put out, provided he kept his foot on the flat stone base. The pitcher stood in a six-foot ring. There were eleven players on a side. The ball had a rubber center overwound with yarn to a size somewhat larger than the present day sphere, and was covered with leather or buckskin. Anyone getting the ball was entitled to throw it at a runner between the bases and put him out by hitting him with it."

As the article quoted not only the Graves letter but also those of other correspondents to the commission, there can be no doubt that Sullivan was its source.

When Sullivan had delivered their packets in October 1907, the commissioners were fatigued by the attenuated two-year process. Their attentions had drifted to their more important personal or business matters. They were not now inclined to take issue with Sullivan's findings or how they were to be presented; they would leave that to Mills. The Graves revelation had been little more than a sideshow, and no one expected Spalding to champion it, at least not to the exclusion of other evidence.

Mills, too, was frankly tired of the debate. Within a month after

Spalding had sent his letters of invitation to the commission from his home at Point Loma in March 1905, all those who would go on to serve had accepted. Mills wrote, however, "while I am not inclined to take up the baseball question [i.e., its origin] again in any of its aspects, I will not be the one to break the chain, in other words, if all the others will serve I will." As has been alluded to, he had served Spalding's interests previously, and nobly.

On April 8, 1889, Mills had chaired the banquet held at Delmonico's hall in New York to welcome Spalding's "World Tourist" baseball players upon their return home. In attendance were Mark Twain, Chauncey Depew, Theodore Roosevelt, De Wolf Hopper, the globetrotting ballplayers and other worthies but, perhaps pointedly, not Henry Chadwick. On that memorable evening Mills revealed to the assemblage that baseball was, "in its present perfected state, an evolution of American genius," adding that "patriotism and research alike vindicate the claim that it is American in its origin." This elicited staccato table thumping and foot stomping in the hall, accompanied by cries of "No rounders!"

The patriotism Mills cited was evident everywhere in the flag draped hall and had been the underlying theme of the frankly promotional world tour. But the research he mentioned was not that of Chadwick or Mills or Spalding, but the published work of John M. Ward, star shortstop of the New York Giants and captain of the All-America team that had circumnavigated the globe with Spalding's White Stockings. Ward was a compelling figure—at first an outstanding pitcher (he had thrown a perfect game in 1880) and, after hurting his arm, a fine center fielder before settling in at shortstop. Studying law at Columbia in the offseason, he earned his degree and passed the bar while still an active player; this circumstance heightened his sensitivity to the injustices players suffered at the hands of owners, with the reserve clause agreed by players to be the root of all such evil. In 1885, Ward had been the prime mover in organizing the Brotherhood of Professional Base Ball Players, the first players' union; his opposition to Spalding and the magnates made his participation in the World Tour seem the signal of a rapprochement between labor and management, but this proved to be merely a feint.

The *New York Times* reported on Ward's speech at Delmonico's thus: "Mr. 'Johnny' Ward seemed glad of the opportunity given him to display his singularly correct knowledge of the English language." In fact, his speech was terse, for he had attended the banquet only grudgingly. Erudite, tough-minded, and not a little vain, Ward had succumbed to Spalding's appeal to captain the touring all-star squad. However, the impresario's covert plan may well have been to get the dangerous Ward out of the country while the club owners enacted a plan for the 1889 season to classify players by their presumed abilities, then cap their salaries within those classifications. Learning of the plot upon landing in England on the final leg of the tour, Ward left his mates behind and returned to New York, but it was too late to reverse the owners' course. Next year, he would lead a rebellion that produced a separate Players' League and ushered in the most disastrous decade in baseball history, in which the three leagues of 1890 were reduced by 1892 to one.

Ward was also a sturdy writer with a historical bent, and in the months before he went on tour with Spalding and the boys, he penned a small book, *Base-Ball: How to Become a Player, with Origin, History and Explanation of the Game.* Ward's take on baseball's origins was succinctly expressed by the World Tour banqueters as "no rounders," but his reasoning was more elegant. He interviewed several veterans of baseball's amateur era and supplied an analytical coolness that would have served the Mills Commission well had he been asked to serve on it; instead, with a nod to his legal expertise, he was invited merely to supply a brief for the American origin of the game.

SO, ON DECEMBER 30, 1907, with his commission's mandate set to expire, Mills prepared to "take up the baseball question again," but for the last time. He had considered the legalistic briefs supplied by Spalding and Ward for the American side and Chadwick for the British. He had reviewed the news clippings and personal communications from old-timers, especially in New England, although what Mills saw had been redacted by Sullivan. As a persistent rain pelted the windowpanes of his office at the Otis Elevator Company at 7 Battery Place in Manhattan, he reflected upon his distaste for both the patriotism and the research that had characterized this commission's efforts as well as its conclusion that baseball had been invented by his old army friend sometime before (or after) the campaign of Tippecanoe and Tyler Too.

Mills crafted an artfully equivocal summation, in which he simultaneously reported the commission's documentary findings yet retained for himself a skeptical distance. It is presented in full here, but much lies between the lines. Indeed, this circuitous document was initially so confusing to Sullivan that, receiving it the day after it was written, he dashed off a note to Mills: "as I glance over the first page, I am disappointed in your decision. I really had convinced myself that Base Ball was of American origin." Reading Mills' letter in full, one may see how Sullivan was dismayed upon first glance:

Mr. James E. Sullivan, Secretary.
Special Base Ball Commission
21 Warren St.
New York City.

Dear Sullivan:

On my earliest opportunity, after my recent return from Europe, I read—and read with much interest—the considerable mass of testimony bearing on the origin of Base Ball which you had sent to my office address during my absence. I cannot say that I find myself in accord with those who urge the American origin of the game as against its English origin as contended for by Mr. Chadwick, on "patriotic ground." In my opinion we owe much to our Anglo-Saxon kinsmen for their example which we have too tardily followed in fostering healthful field sports generally, and if the fact could be established by evidence that our national game, "Base Ball," was devised in England, I do not think that it would be any the less admirable nor welcome on that account. As a matter of fact, the game of ball which I have always regarded as the distinctive English game, i.e., cricket, was brought to this country and had a respectable following here, which it has since maintained, long before any game of ball resembling our national game was played anywhere. Indeed, the earliest field sport that I remember was a game of cricket, played on an open field near Jamaica, L. I., where I was then attending school. Then, and ever since, I have heard cricket spoken of as the essentially English game, and, until my perusal of this testimony, my own belief had been that our game of Base Ball, substantially as played to-day, originated with the Knickerbocker club of New York, and it was frequently referred to as the "New York Ball Game."

While "Father" Chadwick and I have not always agreed (I recall that he at first regarded as revolutionary the "Full Team Reserve Rule" and the alliance between professional Base Ball associations, both of which I devised in 1883, and I later modeled after the latter the Alliance feature of the A.A.U. reorganization), yet I always have had respect for his opinions and admiration for his inflexible honesty of purpose; and I have endeavored to give full weight to his contention that Base Ball is of English origin. It does seem to me, however, that, in the last analysis, his contention is based chiefly upon the fact that, substantially, the same kind of implements are employed in the game of Base Ball as in the English game of "Rounders" to which he refers; for if the mere tossing or handling of some kind of ball, or striking it with some kind of a stick, could be accepted as the origin of our game, then "Father" Chadwick would certainly have to go far back of Anglo-Saxon civilization—beyond Rome, beyond Greece, at least to the palmy days of the Chaldean Empire! Nor does it seem to me that he can any more successfully maintain the argument because of the employment, by the English schoolboy of the past, of the implements or materials of the game.

Surely there can be no question of the fact that Edison, Frank Sprague and other pioneers in the electrical field were the inventors of useful devices and processes whereby electricity was harnessed for the use of man, although they did not invent electricity, nor do they, nor does anybody, know to-day what electricity is! As I understand it, the invention or the origination of anything practical or useful, whether it be in the domain of mechanics or field sports, is the creation of the device or the process from pre-existing materials or elements; and, in this sense, I do not, myself, see how there can be any question that the game of Base Ball originated in the United States and not in England—where it certainly had never been played, in however crude a form, and was strange and unfamiliar when an American ball team first played it there.

As I have stated, my belief had been that our "National Game of Base Ball" originated with the Knickerbocker club, organized in New York in 1845, and which club published certain elementary rules, in that year; but, in the interesting and pertinent testimony for which we are indebted to Mr. A. G. Spalding, appears a circumstantial statement by a reputable gentleman [Abner Graves], according to which the first known diagram of the diamond, indicating positions for the players, was drawn by Abner Doubleday in Cooperstown, N. Y., in 1839. Abner Doubleday subsequently graduated from West Point and entered the regular army, where, as Captain of Artillery, he sighted the first gun fired on the Union side (at Fort Sumter) in the Civil War. Later still, as Major General, he was in command of the Union army at the close of the first day's fight in the battle of Gettysburg, and he died full of honors at Mendham, N. J., in 1893. It happened that he and I were members of the same veteran military organization—the crack Grand Army Post (Lafayette), and the duty devolved upon me, as Commander of that organization, to have charge of his obsequies, and to command the veteran military escort which served as guard of honor when his body lay in state, January 30, 1893, in the New York City Hall, prior to his interment in Arlington.

In the days when Abner Doubleday attended school in Cooperstown, it was a common thing for two dozen or more of school boys to join in a game of ball. Doubtless, as in my later experience, collisions between players in attempting to catch the batted ball were frequent, and injury due to this cause, or to the practice of putting out the runner by hitting him with the ball, often occurred.

I can well understand how the orderly mind of the embryo West Pointer would devise a scheme for limiting the contestants on each side and allotting them to field positions, each with a certain amount of territory: also substituting the existing method of putting out the base runner for the old one of "plugging" him with the ball. [This last innovation was nowhere substantiated in the Graves letters to the Commission.]

True, it appears from the statement that Doubleday provided for eleven men on a side instead of nine, stationing the two extra men between first and second, and second and third bases, but this is a minor detail, and, indeed, I have played, and doubtless, other old players have, repeatedly with eleven on a side, placed almost identically in the manner indicated by Doubleday's diagram, although it is true that we so played after the number on each side bad been fixed at nine, simply to admit to the game an additional number of those who wished to take part in it.

I am also much interested in the statement made by Mr. [Duncan F.] Curry, of the pioneer Knickerbocker club, and confirmed by

Mr. [Thomas] Tassie, of the famous old Atlantic club of Brooklyn, that a diagram, showing the ball field laid out substantially as it is to-day, was brought to the field one afternoon by a Mr. Wadsworth. Mr. Curry says "the plan caused a great deal of talk, but, finally, we agreed to try it." While he is not quoted as adding that they did both try and adopt it, it is apparent that such was the fact; as, from that day to this, the scheme of the game described by Mr. Curry has been continued with only slight variations in detail. It should be borne in mind that Mr. Curry was the first president of the old Knickerbocker club, and participated in drafting the first published rules of the game.

It is possible that a connection more or less direct can be traced between the diagram drawn by Doubleday in 1839 and that presented to the Knickerbocker club by Wadsworth in 1845, or thereabouts, and I wrote several days ago for certain data bearing on this point, but as it has not yet come to hand I have decided to delay no longer sending in the kind of paper your letter calls for, promising to furnish you the indicated data when I obtain it, whatever it may be.

My deductions from the testimony submitted are:

First: That "Base Ball" had its origin in the United States.

Second: That the first scheme for playing it, according to the best evidence obtainable to date, was devised by Abner Doubleday at Cooperstown, N. Y., in 1839.

Yours very truly,
A. G. Mills [signed]

Predictably, the other commission members fell into line. To Mills' final decision they subsequently appended this statement for publication: "We, the undersigned members of the Special Base Ball Commission, unanimously agree with the decision as expressed and outlined in Mr. A. G. Mills' letter of December 30."

WHEN, ON MARCH 20, 1908, the commission conclusions, along with the briefs supplied by Spalding, Chadwick, and Ward, were revealed in the *Guide*, Spalding emerged triumphant. Chadwick had been trounced, his rounders theory thrown into the bin of historical curiosities. Those whose noses wrinkled at the Doubleday tale held to their belief, in accord with the private view of Mills, that the Knickerbocker

Base Ball Club pioneered the "New York Game." In this innovation a modern eye might discern *baseball* as opposed to the Massachusetts variant, which old John Lowell proclaimed "was no more like the National Game of Base Ball than a horse is like a mule."

Once upon a time even Chadwick, whose long life permitted him the luxury of many self-contradictions, had appeared to agree. In the *New York Clipper* of October 26, 1861, in a report of a game played at the Elysian Fields of Hoboken, he had written:

> The game of base ball is, as our readers are for the most part aware, an American game exclusively, as now played, although a game somewhat similar has been played in England for many years, called "rounders," but which is played more after the style of the Massachusetts game. New York, however, justly lays claim to being the originators of what is termed the American Game, which has been so improved in all its essential points by them, and its scientific points so added to, that it does not stand second either in its innate excellencies, or interesting phrases, to any national game of any country in the world, and is every way adapted to the tastes of all who love athletic exercises in this country.

However, in the heady days of mock combat with Spalding, Chadwick had tossed this view aside or forgotten it. On the day the *Guide* was published, the eighty-three-year-old Chadwick, whose palsied handwriting was by this time barely legible, feebly pecked a typewritten note to Mills:

> 106 Howard Av Brooklyn Mar 20th 08
>
> My Dear Mr Mills
>
> I read you[r] decision in the case of Chadwick Vs Spalding, contained in Spalding'[s] Guide—just out to day—with great interest, and I want to say to you that it is a masterly piece of special pleading, which lets my dear old friend Albert escape a bad defeat.
>
> I notice that the italicised paragraph, which closes your dictum in the case, dates your strongest witnesses's [sic] evidence at 1839, whereas it is well known that the old Philadelphia Town Ball Club played under the "rounders" rule in Town Ball in *1831*, eight years earlier. How about that?

I was so sure of my case that I failed to present more detailed evidence. The fact is, The whole matter was a Joke between Albert and myself, for the fun of the thing.

As for the Judges Reach and Wright, "They Mean well but they don't know."

Some day or other, in the near future, I'll drop in on you and talk it over. Let me know by letter what you think of my Guide of this year.

Yours sincerely,
Henry Chadwick (Twenty-eight Years editor of the Guide)
Excuse my awful typing.

They never did talk it over. Chadwick died precisely one month later, having recklessly exposed himself to the damp and cold of an Opening Day game. For his burial plot at Brooklyn's Green-Wood Cemetery, the National League would supply an ornate monument to which was affixed an engraved plaque declaring him "Father of Base Ball." He was correct that the Olympic Club of Philadelphia began playing town ball in 1831, although this fact presents interesting taxonomic questions about what is baseball and what is not.

By this time, the spring of 1908, Graves had long since returned to Denver, Spalding to Point Loma, Ward to his New York practice of law, and Mills to his vice presidency with the Otis Elevator Company.

Mills' "final decision" for more than a century has proven to be anything but conclusive. Original Knickerbocker president Duncan F. Curry had told reporter Will Rankin, a cantankerous sort with a hatred of Chadwick, quite a story about a summer's day in 1877. In the presence of Thomas Tassie of the Atlantic Base Ball Club, Curry told Rankin that "a diagram, showing the ball field laid out substantially as it is to-day, was brought to the field one day by a Mr. Wadsworth." Rankin had written about his interview with Curry in a letter to the Commission on January 15, 1905. Spalding replied eleven days later, three months before Abner Graves wrote his epistle to the *Akron Beacon Journal*:

Your interview with Mr. Tassie is very interesting and tends to corroborate Mr. Curry's statements. Would it be possible to find the Mr. Wadsworth he refers to. If not living perhaps we can find some of his heirs. He is the man we are looking for. I return herewith [early baseball editor William] Cauldwell's article. Yours, A. G. Spalding.

On February 8, 1905, Spalding wrote again to Rankin, speaking more directly here than perhaps anywhere else to his motivation for establishing the Special Base Ball Commission:

> The fact that my business firm has been engaged in the manufacture and sale of base ball implements, has always been a [sic] more or less of an embarrassment to me in my base ball legislation work in the past, for my enemies could see nothing but business motives in my efforts regardless of what might have been my real sentiments toward the game itself. I confess to a sincere love and affection for the game itself, loved it as a boy.

Despite Mills averring in his report that "I wrote several days ago for certain data bearing on this point [the possible connection between a diagram drawn by Doubleday and one brought to the Knickerbocker playing field by Wadsworth]," no more was heard about Wadsworth until 1973, when Harold Peterson published a book entitled *The Man Who Invented Baseball*—about Alexander Joy Cartwright of the Knickerbockers. By this time scholarly research had demolished the Doubleday claim. However, in the binary approach to baseball's origins established by Chadwick and Spalding, a new anointee was called for, and if Doubleday was not the man for the job, then Cartwright had to be. Reviewing the flawed work of the Commission, Peterson noted: "Mr. Wadsworth, whose Christian name, occupation, residence, and pedigree remained secreted in Mills' bosom, was never heard of before or until long after that fateful afternoon [in 1877, when former Knickerbocker president Curry spoke with reporter Rankin]."

Other writers besides Peterson have assumed that Mills' promised search for Wadsworth was a ploy designed either to keep them off Cartwright's scent or to deflect attention from the absurdity of the Doubleday claim. However, rummaging through carbon copies of Mills' letters, I came upon a few notes indicating that Mills was a man of his word. On December 20, 1907, ten days before composing his "final decision," he wrote a letter to Col. Edward S. Fowler, Collector of Customs:

[. . .] The Extracts show that a Mr. Curry (who was a President of the Knickerbocker, the first baseball club organized in New York) said that some one—he did not remember who—presented a plan drawn up on paper, showing the ball field, etc.

Then Mr. Tassie (who was one of the organizers of the old Atlantic club of Brooklyn), stated who this person was, i.e., Mr. Wadsworth, 'not the one who played ball, but a gentleman and a scholar, who held an important position in the Custom House. He was one of the best after-dinner speakers of the day.' Now, I have a notion that there is quite a colony of Wadsworths in the part of the State where Abner Doubleday spent his early life before going to West Point, that the Mr. Wadsworth referred to by Mr. Currie [sic] and named by Mr. Tassie was one of that family, and that, therefore, very likely he got the plan of the game from Abner Doubleday.

Should this prove to be fact, the connecting link between Doubleday at Cooperstown and the beginning of the game in New York would be established, and, perhaps, in the years to come, in view of the hundreds of thousands of our people who are devoted to baseball, and the millions who will be, Abner Doubleday's fame will rest nearly, if not quite as much, upon the fact that he was its inventor in the United States, as upon his brilliant and distinguished career as an Officer of the Federal Army.

You can see from the foregoing what I wish your help in is to ascertain who this Mr. Wadsworth was, who held a high position in the Custom House about 1843, 1844, or 1845—his name and what part of the State he came from. Possibly the records in your office would furnish this data, but if not, I am sanguine that you will be able to get it for me, as this kind of information must exist somewhere in the Government records.

With kindest regards and the compliments of the season, I am

Yours very truly,
(Signed) A. G. Mills.

On January 6, 1908, Mills received a reply from Col. Fowler's associate Curt Preggers:

Mr. Mills,-

Col. Fowler's secretary . . . states that they have made a most exhaustive examination of the records way back, but can find no trace of Wadsworth. He suggested that possibly you could get on the track of Wadsworth, by writing to someone in Livingston County, NY, as "the Wadsworths own that place." He thought probably Speaker Wadsworth may in some way be connected with the family. Col. Fowler's Sec'y apologized for delay. [James W. Wadsworth Jr. of Geneseo, in Livingston County, had been named Speaker of the New York State Assembly in 1905, serving until 1910.]

On that same day Mills, who seemed to have drawn new energy once the commission's duties were officially closed, wrote to Will Rankin:

In the mass of correspondence in regard to the origin of Base Ball, that was submitted to me, as a member of the Commission, by its Secretary, Mr. J. E. Sullivan, are copies of two very interesting letters written by you, under date of Jan. 15th and Feb. 15th, '05. In the first of the three [*sic*] letters you quote Mr. Curry as stating that "some one had presented a plan showing a ball field," etc., and, in the second letter, Mr. Tassie told you that he remembered the incident, and that he "thought it was a Mr. Wadsworth who held an important position in the Custom House," etc. Taking this as a clue I wrote sometime ago to the Collector of Customs, asking him to have the records searched for the years '40 to '45, for the purpose of ascertaining from what part of the State the Mr. Wadsworth, in question, came. I am today advised that a thorough search has been made without disclosing the name of any Mr. Wadsworth as having been connected with the Custom House during the decade of the '40s.

If you have the opportunity to do so, I wish you would see or communicate with Mr. Tassie, to try to clear this point up, as I would very much like to get on the track of the party who actually presented the plan of the ball field at the time and place indicated. The fact that Mr. Tassie remembered Mr. Wadsworth as the man who presented the plan inclines me to believe that his memory in this respect is likely to be correct, whereas it might well happen that he was a Custom House broker or had some relation other than that of being an employee of the Government in the Custom House. However that might be, if you can get me any further information upon the point indicated I would be very glad to have it.

Yours very truly,
(Signed) A. G. Mills.

Herein lay a crucial misunderstanding. Tassie's Atlantic Base Ball Club did not organize until the mid-1850s and his contact with "Mr." Wadsworth—whose given name was Louis and whose occupation was that of a Custom House attorney—could not have come in the mid-1840s. Tassie was a Scottish immigrant from Forres, born in 1835. He served on a crucial rules committee in 1857 in which Wadsworth moved that the length of the game be set at nine innings rather than the seven that his fellow Knickerbockers had proposed. (Most fans think the nine man, nine inning, ninety foot base path game was established with the Knickerbocker rules of 1845; not so. More on this later.)

Rankin, who in early 1905 had recounted his story of Curry, Tassie, and Wadsworth from the summer of 1877, subsequently recanted, telling Mills that he had erred in recording Wadsworth's name; upon reflection he was sure that Curry had said *Cartwright*. When this repressed memory dawned upon Rankin in mid-1905, Curry was no longer available for confirmation, having died in 1894; like Chadwick after him, he had been buried at Brooklyn's Green-Wood Cemetery under the graven rubric "Father of Base Ball."

But Tassie still lived. Rankin went to his home and bullied the old fellow into allowing that perhaps he too recalled not Wadsworth but Cartwright . . . though Tassie had been ten years old when the Knickerbockers formed in 1845, and Cartwright had left New York in the Gold Rush year of 1849, before Tassie became involved in baseball. Moreover, as a Brooklyn resident, it was unlikely that Tassie ever set eyes upon Cartwright, who lived in Manhattan and played ball in Hoboken.

Reacting to Rankin's reversal, no matter how implausible, some writers then shifted their glance to Cartwright, who had been uncredited in Mills' final decision and barely mentioned in the hundreds of pages of commission documents. Cartwright would now serve as the un-Doubleday, assisted by the publicity drumming of his son Bruce, who got the ear of Will Irwin, a journalist about to launch upon a four-part history of baseball for *Collier's*. In the opening installment, on May 8, 1909, Irwin became the first man ever to credit Cartwright with inventing anything. "General Doubleday certainly did not invent the name 'baseball,' " Irwin wrote, "and in 1839 he was at West Point. However, Mr. Cartwright may have got his game from Cooperstown and not out of his head." Mills' double-play-combo idea still lived.

Today, Cartwright's name is known to baseball fans because he was inducted into the Baseball Hall of Fame while Abner Doubleday was not (although Abner clearly won the bigger prize). Perhaps Mills didn't think to name Cartwright because Alex had lived in sunny Hawaii for such a long time. In fact, the game's replacement inventor was so thoroughly forgotten in the annals of the game that when Spalding's World Tourists went ashore at Honolulu for a banquet with King Kalakaua in November 1888, no Hawaiian thought to invite him, and no tourist thought to inquire after him. Despite the once-in-a-lifetime opportunity that brought Spalding to Cartwright's doorstep, there is no evidence that they met. When Mark Twain spoke about Hawaii and baseball at the Delmonico's banquet, where some gray heads in the audience might have been expected to recall Cartwright, no mention was made of "the man who invented baseball."

To be fair, in his report as published in the *Spalding Guide* on March 20, 1908, Mills also did not mention William Rufus Wheaton or Daniel Lucius Adams, recently revealed to be larger figures in baseball's factual beginnings than either Cartwright or Doubleday. And Mills also did not know that baseball was played before the Knickerbockers in 1845, before the Gothams in 1837, and before the Olympics in 1831 to 1833. In England we have references to baseball in Jane Austen's *Northanger Abbey* (written in 1798, though published in 1817, after the author's death) and in Mary Russell Mitford's *Our Village* (1824); in an English novel by John Kidgell (*The Card*) and a diary by William Bray, both from 1755; in a miniature children's book by John Newbery (*A Little Pretty Pocket-Book*) from 1744 . . . but these references are to games played in a spontaneous manner, by children, young women, and in the Bray diary, young people of both sexes. Regarding the earliest citation for baseball played in America by precisely that name, a prohibition against its play in Pittsfield, Massachusetts, in 1791, that game too was played on a pickup basis, probably by boys rather than young men.

And Mills certainly did not know that only one week after the public issuance of his report, the mysterious Mr. Wadsworth, whom he was never able to locate, died in a poorhouse in Plainfield, New Jersey.

2
FOUR FATHERS, TWO ROADS

Two roads diverged in a yellow wood,
And sorry I could not travel both
And be one traveler, long I stood
And looked down one as far as I could
To where it bent in the undergrowth.

—Robert Frost, "The Road Not Taken"

In baseball history, two versions of the early game have come down to us, known as the New York game and the Massachusetts game, but that nomenclature simplifies much and explains little. The former was the straight path to the future, America's cricket; the latter, richer in variation and possibility, an evolutionary dead end. It is by no means certain that the survivor was the superior version.

An organized American game that we will have reason to call *baseball* starts in several places, more or less simultaneously. If Abner Doubleday is today seen by scholars and sophisticated fans not to have invented baseball, Alexander Cartwright has likewise been celebrated excessively: At best he may be credited with recruiting players for a club he, along with fellow baseball devotees, wished to form. But some other individuals, including the mysterious Louis Fenn Wadsworth, may lay particular claim to innovations that made the New York game the one we recognize in the baseball of today. By examining these key players in the rise and flowering of a national pastime we see how the New York game split off from versions of the game played by Young America since colonial times. Additionally, two nameless clubs were advertised to play a match at Jones' Retreat in New York in 1823, but we do not know anything about them, nor are we certain that the game was actually played, as no account of its outcome survives. Identifying the innovators associated with the more venerable Massachusetts game of "round ball" (no mere redundancy, the old name describes a ball game played in the round) is more difficult, and the reason for that game's disappearance harder to pinpoint.

Historians have long credited the Knickerbockers with the invention of baseball for these reasons: First, they were organized as a ball club; second, they created a written set of by-laws and rules for play; third, they eliminated the practice of retiring a runner by plugging him with the ball between bases; and fourth, they devised the important feature of foul territory. It appears today, however, that they were neither the first club to organize nor the first to write down their rules, and that the concepts of tagging, forced outs, and boundaries were likewise not original with them. John Ward had it right when he stated in his 1888 book *Base Ball: How to Become a Player* that the Knicks were consolidators rather than innovators:

> They drew up a Constitution and By-laws, and scattered through the latter are to be found the first written rules of the game. They little thought that that beginning would develop into the present vast system of organized base-ball. They were guilty of no crafty changes of any foreign game; there was no incentive for that. They recorded the rules of the game as they remembered them from boyhood and as they found them in vogue at that time.

In 1858, a Philadelphia correspondent with the pen name "Excelsior" wrote to the *New York Clipper*, the dominant sporting weekly of the day, about early ball play in New York and called town ball, the Philadelphia favorite, "comparatively unknown in New York." Three old cat, with its three bases plus a striker's point and its six or seven players to the side, was the game that New Yorkers of the 1820s termed "*baseball*" and played at places evocatively named retreats or gardens. This version of baseball included the old-fashioned way of throwing the ball *to* the batter and *at* the runner.

In a letter to William S. Cogswell dated January 10, 1905, A. G. Mills, just beginning to accumulate data for his Commission's report, wrote:

> Among the vivid recollections of my early life at Union Hall Academy [where Knickerbocker William R. Wheaton had trained] is a game of ball in which I played, where the boys of the side at bat were put out by being hit with the ball. You made a splendid shot at me at quite a long distance, and put me out fairly and squarely while [I was] running from second base to home. My recollection is that we had a first base near the batsman's position; the second base was a tree at some distance, and the third base was the home base, also near the batsman's position. This . . . at least, as I remember it, we played at Union Hall Academy for some years.

To which Cogswell replied on January 19:

> My recollection of the game of base ball as we played for years at Union Hall, say from 1849 to 1856, is quite clear. You are quite right about the three bases, their location and the third base being home. When there were few players there was a rule against screwing, i.e., making strikes that now would be called "foul." We used flat bats, and it was considered quite an art to be able to "screw" well, as that sent the ball away from the bases.

Cogswell further supplied a précis of the game's rules: a batsman is out if the ball is caught on the fly or the bound, the ball must strike the runner or touch him between bases to record an out, all must be retired before the side is out, and three home runs by the last batter would restore his side to the bat.

This New York game of three-cornered cat, whose players called it *baseball,* had already been modified for adult players a decade earlier, as Wheaton would recollect in the *San Francisco Examiner* in 1887. The mention of foul territory, intuitively sound for occasions when there were too few players to cover a broad expanse, is of particular interest, as the only other early game that distinguished between fair and foul ground was likewise a modification of a game played in the round by full sides of eleven: cricket. That modification was single-wicket cricket, which when played by fewer than five to the side rendered foul those balls hit behind the wicket or beyond a sixty-six-foot distance on either side of it.

As to ninety feet, nine men, and nine innings, the accomplishments engraved on Alexander Cartwright's plaque in the Baseball Hall of Fame, it may be said with certainty that neither he nor the Knickerbockers originated any of those central features in 1845. "Carried baseball to Pacific Coast and Hawaii in pioneer days," the plaque goes on to read, but recent scholarship has debunked that too. Hawaii resident William Castle returned home after attending Oberlin College in Ohio from 1864 to 1866, at which time, he wrote in his autobiography, he found "that no one knew how to play baseball, although several had read of the new game and were curious to try it. The only game of ball played in Hawaii at that time was exactly the same as when I had gone away two years before, that is, 'two o-cat' or 'three o-cat.' " A few years after his 1866 return Castle called upon Cartwright in a business context. "He surprised me by saying that he was an old ball player but added that he hardly recognized the game 'as played now.' "

We can better understand Castle's remark once we know that Cartwright also did not create certain other features sometimes credited to him: the fixed pitching distance that endured as forty-five feet until 1880, or the requirement that a ball be caught on the fly to register an out, or a system for calling balls and strikes. In short, the creation of modern baseball awaited a distant day, long after "the man who invented baseball" had made Hawaii his permanent home.

So, what may we reliably say that Cartwright did? In 1866, Charles A. Peverelly credited him thus in his *Book of American Pastimes*: "In the spring of 1845 Mr. Alex. J. Cartwright, who had become an enthusiast in the game, one day upon the field proposed a regular organization, promising to obtain several recruits. His proposal was acceded to, and Messrs. W. R. Wheaton, Cartwright, D. F. Curry, E. R. Dupignac Jr., and W. H. Tucker, formed themselves into a board of recruiting officers, and soon obtained names enough to make a respectable show." Up to and including the Mills Commission, this was the full reported extent of Cartwright's ingenuity.

The Knickerbocker game during Cartwright's tenure (he departed for the Gold Rush early in 1849) was almost never played with nine men to the side, but instead by as few as seven or as many as eleven. The number of innings was unspecified, as victory went to the side that was first to score twenty-one runs in equal turns at bat. The length of the baselines was imprecise, although latter-day pundits have credited Cartwright with divine-inspired prescience in determining a distance that would yield so many close plays at first. Sometimes referred to in histories of the game as an engineer even though he was a bank teller, and then a book seller, Cartwright was further credited with laying out the game on a diamond rather than a square. Yet even this was no innovation in 1845.

Cartwright may have umpired what was handed down to posterity as the "first match game" by Knickerbocker rules, June 19, 1846, which the Knicks lost to the New York Ball Club by a score of 23–1 in four innings. (He did not play in it.) As early as 1889, a writer for the *New York Sunday Mercury* observed the irony that baseball's "first team" had no trouble in finding a rival club experienced enough to give it a thrashing.

Nineteenth-century histories of baseball gave credit to the Knickerbockers for devising the New York game that would win out over the competing Massachusetts game but did not identify Cartwright as a principal force, let alone a sole inventor. In 1860, in the premier edition of *Beadle's Dime Base-Ball Player*, Henry Chadwick acknowledged the existence of the New York Ball Club prior to the organization of the Knicks, but stated, "we shall not be far wrong if we award to the Knickerbocker the honor of being the pioneers of the present game of base ball." Presumably he admired their level of organization—a formal club with formal rules. All the same, he almost never swerved from his assertion, in that same essay, that it was rounders, the game of his English childhood, "from which base ball is derived."

Cartwright won his plaque in the Baseball Hall of Fame initially through the efforts of his son Bruce and, more importantly, those of grandson Bruce Jr. These efforts extended even to crafting the senior Cartwright's Hawaii "recollections" of baseball's invention and to inserting fabricated baseball exploits into a purported typescript of Alexander Cartwright's Gold Rush journal, which survives as a handwritten book devoid of any remark about baseball. (Amusingly bogus among the grandson's stilted emendations: "It is comical to see the mountain men and Indians playing the new game" and "During our week's stay here I unpacked the ball we used in forming the Knickerbockers back home and we have had several satisfactory contests. My original copy of the rule book has come in handy and saves arguments.")

Cartwright became, no less than Doubleday, a tool of those who wished to establish baseball as the product of an identifiable spark of American ingenuity, without foreign or evolutionary taint. In fact, until the Mills Commission volunteered Abner Doubleday, it was Chadwick himself—champion of the "rounders" origin—who had most frequently been called the "Father of Baseball," not for any powers of invention but for his role in popularizing and shaping the game.

But there are four men with legitimate claims to baseball's paternity. They were all present at the creation, although no lightning bolt attaches to any given date, and all played with the Knickerbocker Base Ball Club of New York. Three of these men posed for a half-plate daguerreotype in late 1845 that portrayed six original Knickerbockers; miraculously it survives in a private collection and is reproduced in the photo insert: William Rufus Wheaton, Daniel Lucius "Doc" Adams, and William H. Tucker, whose names until recent years had been largely forgotten. The fourth Knickerbocker father is the aforementioned Wadsworth, whom Will Rankin at first identified, with Mills' concurrence, as the man behind the diagram of the playing field.

D. L. Adams was the younger of two sons of Daniel Adams, a noted scholar, medical doctor, orator, and author whose mathematics textbook, *The Scholar's Arithmetic; or, Federal Accountant*, was constantly published and revised from 1801 to the Civil War. The junior Adams, after first attending Amherst College and then graduating from Yale in 1835, progressed to a medical degree of his own from Harvard in 1838. He went into general practice in New York City, coupled with an active involvement with treating the poor at the New York Dispensaries.

Known to all as "Dock" (as the nickname for doctor was then spelled), Adams began to play baseball in New York in 1839. "I was always interested in athletics while in college and afterward," he recalled at the age of eighty-one:

> . . . and soon after going to New York I began to play base ball just for exercise, with a number of other young medical men. Before that there

> had been a club called the New York Base Ball Club, but it had no very definite organization and did not last long. Some of the younger members of that club got together and formed the Knickerbocker Base Ball Club, September 24, 1845 [actually September 23]. The players included merchants, lawyers, Union Bank clerks [like Cartwright], insurance clerks and others who were at liberty after 3 o'clock in the afternoon. They went into it just for exercise and enjoyment, and I think they used to get a good deal more solid fun out of it than the players in the big games do nowadays.
>
> About a month after the organization of this club, several of us medical fellows joined it, myself among the number. The following year I was made President and served as long as I was willing to retain the office.

According to Adams, the New York Base Ball Club not only preceded the Knickerbocker, as we have seen, but *formed* it: for example, some of its early members became prominent Knickerbockers in the 1845–46 season. From 1839 forward, Adams played a game in New York that he understood to be baseball, no matter what its rules and field configuration may have been. When only a handful of participants gathered for play, the game was likely a version of cat. Three old cat, for example, had a triangular base layout—and thus was also known as three-cornered cat—and three strikers.

With as many as seven or eight to the side, however, the game likely to be played was not four-cornered cat but baseball, just as it was played by the Knickerbockers' antecedents in New York and Brooklyn. At least five such clubs preceded the Knickerbockers, who for a century and a half have received too much credit. These five were the original Gotham, also known as the Washington for their primacy among New York ball clubs; the New York Ball Club, whose membership seemed for some time to be interchangeable with that of the Gotham; the Eagle, which formed as a ball-playing club in 1840 but did not adopt all points of the Knickerbocker-style game of baseball until fourteen years later; the Brooklyn Base Ball Club, which was a subset of the Union Star Cricket Club; and the recently discovered Magnolia Ball Club, a workingman's aggregation formed in 1843, which has been written out of all the histories. Beyond these five there was the Olympic Ball Club of Philadelphia, formed by incorporating other clubs from 1831 to 1833 to play a game that is today understood as town ball but to the end of the nineteenth century was regarded by many as a prototype form of baseball. Town ball rules varied by region but in Philadelphia it was marked by plugging, overhand throwing to the bat, and the requirement that one entire side be put out in batting before taking their places in the field.

The game played in New York, always called *baseball* and never rounders or town ball, had been documented in the city under that name as early as 1823, when the playing of a match was staged to draw patrons to a saloon known as Jones' Retreat, at what is today roughly Broadway and 8th Street. The New York game may also have been played as "bace" in 1805 by two clubs linked with Columbia College, and surely was played earlier than that.

TIME HURTLES BACK TOO rapidly; as Melville described historical writing, one form is strictly chronological, while in the other "circumstances, facts, and events . . . are only to be set down as the general stream of the narrative shall dictate; for matters which are kindred in time, may be very irrelative in themselves." For now, let's look not into an ever-retreating past but only to the direct antecedents of the Knickerbockers. It is reported in an 1867 book by William Wood that baseball was played in New York as early as 1832 by two clubs, one composed of residents of the first ward (the lowermost part of the island, from the Battery to Maiden Lane), the other of residents of the ninth and fifteenth wards (both located between Houston and 14th Streets, the whole of which was then called Greenwich Village).

It is perhaps noteworthy that the influx of wealthy New Yorkers into rural Greenwich Village, originally contained within the ninth ward, was so great after the yellow fever epidemic of 1822 that an additional ward, the fifteenth, was created from the ninth in 1832, a year ahead of the great cholera epidemic. By 1843, when the men who would become Knickerbockers were playing at their original site in Madison Square, the optimal sides had been figured at eight, which included a "pitch," a "behind," three infielders, and three men positioned in the outfield.

In fact, baseball as played by the Knicks in the years from 1845 to 1849 (Cartwright played his last game with the club in 1848) was almost never a nine-man game; as late as 1855, an unsigned columnist for the *New York Clipper* indicated how fluid the structure of the game still was: "Base Ball can be played by any number from five upwards; nine, however, being the usual number of each side." Play was conducted in accord with the original baseball model of only three basemen (the game had emerged, after all, out of three-cornered cat) and on the rare occasions when nine or more fielding positions might have arisen due to a surfeit of players, the "extras" were put into the outfield, or a second catcher was added, or the surplus men were held in reserve. In an intramural game in May 1847, for example, when eleven men were available to each side, the Knickerbockers' response was to play with nine, including four outfielders, while holding two men out as substitutes.

The advent of the short fielder, or shortstop—a position created in 1849 or 1850 by Adams—was a radical development, and a distinct innovation of the Knickerbocker club, unlike so much else that is claimed for them. "I used to play shortstop," he reminisced, "and I believe I was the first one to occupy that place, as it had formerly been left uncovered." However, when Adams first traipsed out to a spot between and beyond second and third bases, it was not to bolster the infield but to assist in relays from the outfield. The early Knickerbocker ball was so light that it could not be thrown even two hundred feet, thus the need for a short fielder to send the ball in to the pitcher's point. It was also soft enough to permit barehand play, which was the standard well into the 1880s.

"We had a great deal of trouble in getting balls made," Adams recalled, "and for six or seven years I made all the balls myself, not only for our club but also for other clubs when they were organized. [He also supervised the turning of the bats during this period.] I went all over New York to find someone who would undertake this work, but no one could be induced to try it for love or money. Finally I found a Scotch saddler who was able to show me a good way to cover the balls with horsehide, such as was used for whip lashes. I used to make the stuffing out of three or four ounces of rubber cuttings, wound with yarn and then covered with the leather. Those balls were, of course, a great deal softer than the balls now [1896] in use."

When the ball was wound tighter, gaining more hardness and resilience, it could be hit farther and, crucially, thrown farther. This permitted the shortstop to come into the infield, which Adams did. It also made the old practice of plugging, still in favor among baseball players in the hinterlands, potentially hazardous, for until then being struck with a thrown ball between the bases merely stung; there is no record of anyone ever being seriously hurt in this way.

Even more important, the introduction of the hard ball permitted a change in the dimensions of the playing field. The Knickerbocker rules of 1845 had specified no pitching distance and no baseline length: all that was indicated was from home to second base, forty-two paces; from first to third base, forty-two paces, equidistant. It has been presumed by journalists that when a three-foot distance for the pace is plugged in, the resulting baselines of eighty-nine feet, by application of the Pythagorean theorem, are close enough to the present ninety so that we could reasonably proclaim Cartwright's genius. In fact, the pace in 1845 was an imprecise and variable measure, used to gauge distances by "stepping off," or if it was intended as a precise measure, it would have had to have been two and a half feet (for reasons detailed below), in which case the forty-two-pace distance from home to second would have been 105 feet and the "Cartwright base paths" would have been a hair shy of seventy-five feet.

The pace of 1845 could not have been interpreted as the precise equivalent of three feet. This alternate definition of a pace as a three-foot measure, while offered up singularly in a Horace Mann arithmetic textbook of 1850, was not then the standard meaning. Here is the definition of a *pace* from Noah Webster's *American Dictionary of the English Language*, 1828: "1. A step. 2. The space between the two feet in walking, estimated at two feet and a half. But the geometrical pace is five feet, or the whole space passed over by the same foot from one step to another." This latter definition was not changed for *Webster's* 1853 revised edition, and in fact was the definition that had obtained since ancient Rome (the Roman expression for 1,000 paces was *milia passuum*; from this came our mile, which was originally 5,000 feet in length).

I have come to believe that seventy-five-foot base paths were the norm into the mid-1850s and were the standard for youth play well into the next decade. In describing the rules of baseball in 1864, by which time the base paths had been fixed at ninety feet and the pitching distance at forty-five, Dick and Fitzgerald's *The American Boy's Book of Sports and Games* states, "We give the rules and principles of the game, as played by grown players, remarking that boys should reduce the distances there set down about one-sixth." The practical implementation of this advice was to retreat to the distance befitting inexperienced players: base paths of seventy-five feet and a pitching distance of thirty-seven and a half feet. "Inexperienced players" in the 1830s and '40s, when the ball was soft and light and games were few and far between, meant everyone.

In 1848, Adams, as Knickerbocker president, headed the Committee to Revise the Constitution and By-Laws. His interest in refining the rules of the game, already evident, was further piqued by the formation of additional clubs, beginning with the Washington Base Ball Club in 1850, which like the Knickerbockers was constructed around several former New York and Gotham Ball Club members (these men had surely continued to play among themselves since 1846, although there is no newspaper record of their games). In 1852, the Washingtons took up the old name of Gothams and embraced additional players, while the venerable Eagle Ball Club, which dated to 1840, reconstituted itself as the Eagle Base Ball Club. "The playing rules remained very crude up to this time," Adams said, "but in 1853 the three clubs united in a revision of the rules and regulations. At the close of 1856 there were twelve clubs in existence, and it was decided to hold a convention of delegates from all of these for the purpose of establishing a permanent code of rules by which all should be governed. A call was therefore issued, signed by the officers of the Knickerbocker Club as the senior organization, and the result was the assembling of the first convention of baseball players in May 1857. I was elected presiding officer."

At this meeting, eight years after Cartwright's western expedition, the winner of a game was for the first time defined as the club that was ahead at the conclusion of a set number of innings, rather than the first team to score twenty-one runs. Adams recalled in his *Sporting News* memoir:

> In March of the next year [i.e., 1858] the second convention was held, and at this meeting the annual convention was declared a permanent organization, and with the requisite constitution and by-laws became the "National Association of [Base] Ball Players."
>
> I was chairman of the Committee on Rules and Regulations from the start and so long as I retained membership. I presented the first draft of rules, prepared after much careful study of the matter, and

> it was in the main adopted. The distance between bases I fixed at 30 yards, the only previous determination of distance being 'the bases shall be from home to second base 42 paces, from first to third base 42 paces equidistant,' which was rather vague. In every meeting of the National Association while a member, I advocated the fly-game, that is, not to allow first-bound catches, but I was always defeated on the vote. The change was made, however, soon after I left, as I predicted in my last speech on the subject before the convention.
>
> The distance from home to pitcher's base I made 45 feet. Many of the old rules, such as those defining a foul, remain substantially the same today [i.e., at the time of the interview in 1896] while others are changed and, of course, many new ones added. I resigned in 1862, but not before thousands were present to witness matches, and any number of outside players standing ready to take a hand on regular playing days.

The widespread success of the game was a marvel to Adams and the old-time players. During the 1840s, players could not be relied upon to show up for practice. Adams recalled that the Knickerbockers frequently went to the Elysian Fields of Hoboken to find only a few members present. On such occasions, he recalled, they were obliged to take their exercise "in the form of 'old cat,' 'one' or 'two' as the case might be."

When Adams withdrew from the Knickerbocker Base Ball Club in the spring of 1862 (he would retire from his New York medical practice not long thereafter and move with his new wife to Connecticut), his associates awarded him an honorary membership and passed a resolution naming him the "Nestor of Ball Players." Knickerbocker comrade James Whyte Davis, who had joined the club in 1850, wrote in a letter to Adams, "I indulge the hope that the 'spirit' you express of being with us always, may be accompanied by the *body* on the old Play Grounds." Adams indeed returned to Hoboken one last time to play his final formal game of baseball on September 27, 1875, in an old-timers' contest (the first such recorded) that was staged in conjunction with Davis' twenty-fifth anniversary of Knickerbocker membership.

At the time Adams was invited to join the nascent club in the fall of 1845, about a month after its formation, William R. Wheaton was the most important Knickerbocker. He was a lawyer who, like five of the 1845 Knicks in addition to Cartwright, would leave New York as a "Miner '49er" but he was the only one to make his permanent home in California. Settling in the Bay Area, he made his reputation and his fortune as a merchant, an attorney, a vigilante, a legislator, and more.

Born in 1814 like Adams, Wheaton attended Union Hall Academy, as A. G. Mills would a generation later, a pioneering institution of higher learning founded in Jamaica, Long Island, in 1791. He read law with the notable attorney John Leveridge, passed the bar in 1836, was active in the New York 7th Regiment, and in 1841 was admitted to practice in the Court of Chancery and the Supreme Court of New York. His legal training, more than that of any other original Knick mentioned as a "father of baseball," equipped him to codify the venerable playing rules. Of the five others portrayed in the 1845 Knickerbocker daguerreotype, Cartwright was a bank teller, Curry an insurance broker, Adams a doctor, William H. Tucker a tobacconist, and Henry T. Anthony a future daguerreotypist.

Wheaton was a solid cricketer as well as a baseballist. He umpired two pre-Knickerbocker baseball games played between the New York and Brooklyn clubs on October 21 and 24, 1845, both of which were reported in the press. He recruited members for the Knickerbocker Base Ball Club, as Peverelly noted. He was the club's first vice president (Duncan F. Curry initially presided, but by 1847 he yielded to Adams). Wheaton umpired the first recorded Knickerbocker game at Hoboken's Elysian Fields, an intramural affair on October 6, 1845. And although paired with Tucker as the entirety of the Knickerbocker Committee on By-Laws, Wheaton appears to have been the one who truly wrote the rules formalized on September 23, 1845. Before that, he had drawn up the rules for the Gotham club of the 1830s, which he later asserted the Knickerbockers adopted with little, if any, change.

By the spring of 1846, barely six months after their founding, Wheaton had resigned from the Knickerbockers—we do not know the circumstances—and returned to active play at cricket, going on to win a trophy bat for highest score in a match of the New York Cricket Club in October 1848. Three months later, on January 28, 1849, a month before Cartwright's departure, he embarked for California in a speculative venture called the New York Mining Company, in which he was one of a hundred gold-besotted souls who purchased and outfitted a ship, the *Strafford*, for what would be a 213-day journey to San Francisco around Cape Horn.

It is possible that Wheaton played baseball as a member of San Francisco's Knickerbocker Association in Portsmouth Square in February 1851: Baseball was played there then and we cannot know for sure by whom, but seven members of the Knickerbocker Base Ball Club of New York were in or around San Francisco at this time.

Less than a year before his death in Oakland, California, in 1888, at age seventy-four, Wheaton spoke with a *San Francisco Examiner* reporter. In a story titled "How Baseball Began: A Member of the Gotham Club of Fifty Years Ago Tells About It," he provided a fascinating window on baseball in the period from 1837 to 1845; his name is not provided in the article but there can be no doubt as to the narrator's identity:

> In the thirties I lived at the corner of Rutgers street and East Broadway in New York. I was admitted to the bar in '36, and was very fond of physical exercise. . . . There was a racket club in Allen street with an inclosed [sic] court. Myself and intimates, young merchants, lawyers and physicians, found cricket to[o] slow and lazy a game. We couldn't get enough exercise out of it. Only the bowler and the batter had anything to do, and the rest of the players might stand around all the afternoon without getting a chance to stretch their legs. Racket was lively enough, but it was expensive and not in an open field where we could have full swing and plenty of fresh air with a chance to roll on the grass. Three-cornered cat was a boy's game, and did well enough for slight youngsters, but it was a dangerous game for powerful men, because the ball was thrown to put out a man between bases, and it had to hit the runner to put him out. . . .
>
> We had to have a good outdoor game, and as the games then in vogue didn't suit us we decided to remodel three-cornered cat and make a new game. We first organized what we called the Gotham Baseball Club. This was the first ball organization in the United States, and it was completed in 1837. Among the members were Dr. John Miller, a popular physician of that day; John Murphy, a well-known hotel-keeper; and James Lee, President of the New York Chamber of Commerce. . . . The first step we took in making baseball was to abolish the rule of throwing the ball at the runner and order that it should be thrown to the baseman instead, who had to touch the runner with it before he reached the base. During the regime of three-cornered

> cat there were no regular bases, but only such permanent objects as a bedded boulder or an old stump, and often the diamond looked strangely like an irregular polygon. We laid out the ground at Madison square in the form of an accurate diamond, with home-plate and sand-bags for bases. You must remember that what is now called Madison square, opposite the Fifth Avenue Hotel, in the thirties was out in the country, far from the city limits. We had no short-stop, and often played with only six or seven men on a side. The scorer kept the game in a book we had made for that purpose, and it was he who decided all disputed points. The modern umpire and his tribulations were unknown to us. . . .
>
> After the Gotham club had been in existence a few months it was found necessary to reduce the rules of the new game to writing. This work fell to my hands, and the code I then formulated is substantially that in use to-day. We abandoned the old rule of putting out on the first bound and confined it to fly catching. The Gothams played a game of ball with the Star Cricket Club of Brooklyn and beat the Englishmen out of sight, of course. That game and the return were the only two matches ever played by the first baseball club.

That scorebook, along with the Gotham by-laws and playing rules, was not a figment of Wheaton's aged imagination. Gotham shortstop Charles Commerford wrote to Henry Chadwick in 1905 that the first baseball game he saw (he played in the 1840s and 1850s) was played by the New York Club, which "had its grounds on a field bounded by 23rd and 24th streets and 5th and 6th avenues." Commerford would have seen this game prior to the fall of 1843, when the New York Ball Club moved its playing grounds to Hoboken, a fifteen-minute ferry ride across the North (Hudson) River. "There was a roadside resort nearby and a trotting track in the locality. I remember very well that the constitution and by-laws of the old Gotham club, of which I became a member in 1849, stated that the Gotham Club was the successor of the old New York City Club."

To provide additional gloss on Wheaton's startlingly contrarian reminiscence—that is, contrary to the story as told in every baseball history—the games cited above, in which the Gothams "beat the Englishmen out of sight," were the very same games recorded in the press as pitting New York against Brooklyn on October 21 and 24 of

1845. One might call these games home-and-home, although neither was played in New York. The first match was played at the Elysian Fields of Hoboken, by then already New York's favorite "place of general resort for citizens, as well as strangers, for health and recreation," wrote its proprietor, John Stevens, in 1824. "So easily accessible, and where in a few minutes the dust, noise, and bad smells of the city may be exchanged for the pure air, delightful shades, and completely rural scenery. . . ." By the 1830s, Stevens' ferries transported 20,000 passengers a day to his riverfront Eden on summer weekends. Today the Elysian Fields are long gone, but their proprietor's name is preserved in the Stevens Institute of Technology.

The return match between the New York and Brooklyn clubs was played at the grounds of the Union Star Cricket Club at the intersection of Myrtle and Portland avenues in Brooklyn, near Fort Greene. Both baseball games were played eight to the side.

On June 5, 1846, the Knickerbockers, not yet one year old, elected their first honorary members, forty-nine-year-old James Lee and fifty-three-year-old Abraham Tucker, both of whom had played with Wheaton on the Gothams. (Wheaton was never accorded such an honor, which raises suspicion that the terms of his resignation may have been acrimonious.) At the same meeting Curry, Adams, and William H. Tucker were appointed a committee to arrange the preliminaries for a match with the New York Base Ball Club. Peverelly, writing twenty years later, declared, "From all the information the writer has been able to gather, it appears that this was not an organized club, but merely a party of gentlemen who played together frequently, and styled themselves the New York Club." With this dismissive slap, echoing Chadwick's remark in the 1860 *Beadle's Guide*, the original Gotham and New York Clubs were consigned to the back pages of baseball history.

Wheaton concluded his 1887 reflections about that primal aggregation:

> The new game quickly became very popular with New Yorkers, and the numbers of the club soon swelled beyond the fastidious notions of some of us, and we decided to withdraw and found a new organization, which we called the Knickerbocker. . . .
>
> We were all mature men and in business, but we didn't have too much of it as they do nowadays. There was none of that hurry and worry

> so characteristic of the present New York. We enjoyed life and didn't wear out so fast. In the old game when a man struck out[,] those of his side who happened to be on the bases had to come in and lose that chance of making a run. We changed that and made the rule which holds good now. [The Massachusetts game continued its rule of "one out, all out" rather than three outs to the side.] The difference between cricket and baseball illustrates the difference between our lively people and the phlegmatic English. Before the new game was made we all played cricket, and I was so proficient as to win the prize bat and ball with a score of 60 in a match cricket game in New York of 1848, the year before I came to this Coast. But I never liked cricket as well as our game.

Most of the recent study of baseball's evolution has been structural—focusing on rules of play, field arrangements, regional variants, and of course national origins, and this writer is not immune to the lures of such analysis. Yet in the remarks above we may have our best clue about the origins on which the Mills Commission focused: those of the New York game. No one cared where the old games of round ball and town ball came from, for they, unlike the vibrant game of baseball at the turn of the twentieth century, were dusty museum pieces. Indeed, those abandoned versions of baseball appeared to go back so far that they might as well have been played by Adam and Eve.

Despite Wheaton's obligatory bashing of John Bull, he approved of baseball because it was quicker and livelier than cricket, while retaining that game's fastidiousness about who might play. When baseball's early players could believe themselves to be fashioning a new game fit for their social and class aspirations—in the ethos of the day, time spent on play had to be good for something more than escapism—it could grow alongside cricket, which had been played in the city since at least 1751. When the new game attracted the wrong sort of people, like the saloonkeepers and billiard-hall men of the Magnolia Club, then it threatened to veer back toward the country variants of baseball that were populist and undignified. (We will say more about the Magnolia in another chapter.)

WHEATON'S STORY OF THE Gotham contributions to baseball takes us back to 1837, the year in which the thirteen-year-old Henry Chadwick arrived on these shores, already a veteran player of rounders and steeped in the tradition of cricket. In his teens, he played England's national game and in his twenties he reported on it, for a variety of newspapers, including the *Long Island Star* and the *New York Times*. With his subsequent recording and promoting the American game of baseball, however, no figure was more important to the game's attaining full flower. Chadwick claimed occasionally to have played baseball, too, as a young man in the 1840s. He wrote that he was not favorably impressed, having received "some hard hits in the ribs," which if true would testify to the lingering practice of plugging. He also claimed to have played shortstop at Hoboken in 1848, a year or two before Adams' invention of the position. Not until 1856, however, when he had been a cricket reporter for a decade, were Chadwick's eyes opened to the possibilities in the American game, which had improved dramatically since his youth.

Writing in 1868:

> On returning from the early close of a cricket match on Fox Hill, I chanced to go through the Elysian Fields during the progress of a contest between the noted Eagle and Gotham clubs. The game was being sharply played on both sides, and I watched it with deeper interest than any previous ball game between clubs that I had seen. It was not long before I was struck with the idea that baseball was just the game for a national sport for Americans . . . as much so as cricket in England.

Like A. G. Mills in 1908 ("if the fact could be established by evidence that our national game, 'Base Ball,' was devised in England, I do not think that it would be any the less admirable nor welcome on that account"), Chadwick saw nothing unpatriotic in stating the obvious truth that many fine American institutions could trace their roots to the mother country. He declared in *Beadle's Guide* of 1860 that baseball began with a game he knew as rounders, and he would stick to this story until his death, although with some puzzling variations along the way. Sometimes he would opine further that while the New York game began in 1840, baseball did not truly take shape until 1857, when area clubs met, in the conclave initiated by Doc Adams, to conform the rules of play.

Chadwick *also* declared, on the fiftieth anniversary of the Olympic Ball Club of Philadelphia in 1883, that this body of *town*-ball players was unquestionably the first *base*-ball club, a belief he would repeat twenty years later, just prior to the formation of the Mills Commission. Particularly galling to Spalding may have been Chadwick's implied syllogism that because town ball was modified rounders, and town ball was baseball, then the two held a common English parentage.

The Olympic game of ball in the 1830s was termed *town ball* by later writers but we do not know what it was called at the time the Olympics were formed, except that the term "playing ball" was in the air. References in current historical works to an Olympic Town Ball Club are a misnomer, but the Olympics were reported to be playing town ball by that name in 1838. While the surviving 1838 Olympic Ball Club constitution offers no hint of how their game might have been played, we may surmise from other evidence that the bases were five stakes (four bases plus the striker's point) arranged in a circle of approximately thirty feet in diameter, yielding, to modern eyes, exceedingly small base paths of some twenty feet. (The New York game went from seventy five foot base paths to ninety feet; the Massachusetts game ranged from forty feet to sixty.) When the Olympics gave up their game in favor of the New York style of play in 1860, some older members retired, for as Peverelly wrote, "three hundred and sixty feet, compared with the old town ball circle of eighty feet, was enlarging the sphere of action with a vengeance." An Olympic Ball Club inning ended only when every player on the side had been put out, as in cricket. The bat was either a paddle or a billy-club truncheon, swung with one hand rather than two. This Olympic game seems indeed to have been rather like Chadwick's rounders, except for the latter's rule permitting a new turn at bat for the whole side if the final batter were to hit "for the rounder," that is, a home run.

Should the Philadelphia game even be in the baseball family alongside the New York and Massachusetts games? I am persuaded that the childhood games of England and western Massachusetts are indeed baseball when they involve: a bat; a ball that is pitched or thrown to the bat; two sides alternating innings; multiple safe havens, whether bases or stones or stakes; and a round circuit of the havens that scores a run. One might object that this generous definition embraces not only the New York game, which survives, and the Massachusetts game of round ball and the Philadelphia game of town ball, which do not, but also four old cat, very nearly extinct, and English rounders, which David Block, in *Baseball Before We Knew It,* has shown to be a rather late western England synonym for a game that in the east had been called . . . baseball.

The origin of ball play by young men in an organized club may well be accorded to Philadelphia in 1833, but let's go back a few years earlier. In September 1905 the Mills Commission learned from John W. Oliver, ninety-year-old editor of the *Yonkers Statesman*, of baseball play in Baltimore in 1825. His family had arrived there from England in about 1819. Oliver's friend and interviewer C. H. McDonald reported:

> He remembers very distinctly having played the game of Base Ball when a boy, both before and after becoming an apprentice. He states that his earliest recollection of the playing of the game was when he was about ten years of age, and at that time the game was played in this manner: The batter held the ball in one hand and a flat stick in the other, tossed the ball into the air and hit on the return, and then ran to either one, two, or three bases depending on the number of boys playing the game. If the ball was caught on the fly or the batter hit with the ball while running the bases, he was out. These bases, so called, at that time, were either stones or pieces of sod was removed [sic], or bare places where grass was scraped off. He remembers seeing the game played frequently while an apprentice boy, but always in this manner, never with a pitcher or a catcher, but sometimes with sides. . . . [Then Oliver is quoted thus:] "I never saw the game played with stakes or poles used for bases instead of stones or sods. Never heard of a game of Rounders. One Old Cat, Two Old Cat, Three Old Cat have seen played, but never have taken part in it myself." To my question as to what name this base game that he played was called, he said he remembered distinctly that it was known only as BASE BALL. He further stated that he never saw men play ball until he had been in New York a few years . . . [He moved to New York from Baltimore in 1835.]

What we have here is a game called *baseball* that might or might not have sides, had no pitcher or thrower, and was played only by children. This is the sort of game that had been played by English boys and girls for well over a century before. Yet upon coming to New York in the late 1830s, Oliver notes that he saw *men* playing ball. We know today that these men might well have been Wheaton's Gothams.

Ball games of varying sorts had been played in Philadelphia long before the Olympics: The University of Pennsylvania had banned ball play near windows in 1784 (it is interesting how the earliest mentions of ball play in America tend to come in the form of prohibitions). There is a provocative mention of young men playing ball in Philadelphia in 1829, a few years before the formation of the Olympic Ball Club. In "A Word Fitly Spoken," published in *The American Sunday School Magazine* of January 1830, the anonymous writer observes:

> There is, in the city of *Philadelphia,* an asylum for children who are presented to the guardians or overseers of the poor, as objects of public charity. Without stopping to admire and approve the humane and wise provision which keeps them from much evil example and influence, and gives them that instruction which is profitable for all things, even in this world,—our present object is, to state a case of much interest, which recently occurred.
>
> Early on a Sabbath afternoon during the summer [of 1829], the matron of this asylum was pained to find a company of eighteen men, (rope-makers,) at a game of ball, in an enclosure near the building, and in view of the children. Knowing the power of such an example, she went to them—requested them to desist a moment, till they should hear what she had to say. . . . She then civilly requested them to leave their sport for a while, and go with her to the asylum, assuring them that what they would see, would be new to them, and perhaps interesting. After a short consultation, they determined to follow her; and leaving their hats and coats behind, they all followed her to the house.

Chastened to see how faithfully the children observed the Sabbath, the eighteen ball players—"one of them was considerably advanced, (supposed forty-five or fifty-five years old,) and the youngest was about seventeen"—went back to the field, "took their hats and coats in the most orderly manner, and returned home."

A reasonable guess is that they left the orphan asylum, which still stands at North 18th and Race streets, went to the Delaware River, and caught the horse ferry to Camden, there to play ball in peace. At least that is how Philadelphia's story of organized town ball begins:

with some young men taking the ferry across the Delaware to play ball at an open field off Market Street in Camden, New Jersey. The first occasion we know of for certain was the Fourth of July, 1831, as town ball derived its name from the communal ball play attached to rural holidays and feast days, when men and boys from the country would all come into the town. On the Olympics' first day of play, according to Peverelly, "there were but four players, and the game was 'Cat Ball,' or what is called in some parts of New England, 'Two Old Cat.' The players, who were then over twenty-five years old, told some of their younger friends of the pleasure and advantage they found in resuming their boyish sports, and invited them to join and make up a number large enough for a game of Town Ball."

These Olympics did not return to play in Philadelphia, perhaps because of its blue laws, until 1857, and did not convert from town ball to base ball until three years after that, but they adopted a constitution in the early 1830s (another one, published in 1838, survives in printed form), established by-laws for the conduct of their members and, in a distinct advance from the game that John Oliver played in Baltimore in 1825, they permitted no members younger than twenty-one years of age.

When, in 1883, the Olympic club observed its fiftieth anniversary, some of the original members attended the banquet. The *Police Gazette* noted that these stalwarts of 1833 had "played baseball when it was in its extreme infancy, in the good old days when the players had to make their own bats and balls, and the runner was put out by hitting him with the ball. In those days five stakes were driven into the ground, and the batsman had to make a circuit of these stakes before a run could be scored." In 1904, Chadwick, about to become embroiled in his argument with Spalding, reminded his readers that the Olympics' "old game of 'town ball' was simply an American edition of the English game of rounders . . . in vogue in the New England states as early as 1830."

Recapping the confusing claims: Philadelphia's version of town ball employed four bases plus a striker's point, resembled the New England game of round ball, and like the New York game could be stripped down to a scrub game of cat ball when not enough players were present to play the preferred game. The Philadelphia game was regarded as baseball of an infant sort, yet it was simply rounders, which in England was another name for baseball. Dizzying.

MEANWHILE IN ALL OF New England but Connecticut, where an ancient version of cricket called *wicket* held sway into the 1850s, the game of choice was round ball. Also known as the Massachusetts game, it bore similarities to the Philadelphia game and like other early variants of baseball had cat-ball alternatives for undermanned sides.

In this New England version of baseball, played on a square with sixty-foot base paths, the striker stood at a point equidistant between the first and fourth bases. He would attempt to hit a ball thrown overhand from the midpoint of the square, a distance of thirty feet (in some recorded versions thirty-five). However, because there was no foul territory, he might deliberately tick the ball behind him or employ backhanded or slide batting techniques to deflect the ball away from the stationed defenders. A side might number seven to fourteen, but eleven was the most common contingent, and several fielders would be positioned in what modern eyes would view as foul ground, including at least two "scouts" behind the striker. Three misses and the batsman was out, but if he struck the ball he would fly around the bases (marked by four-foot stakes) until he himself was struck by a fielder's throw or elected to stop his homeward course by holding to his stake. The ball was small and light and only one's pride might be injured from being plugged or "soaked." A catch for an out had to be made on the fly, not on the first bound, as those Knickerbocker sissies continued to permit until 1865. One out, side out.

The Massachusetts game of baseball was in many ways the superior version, for both players and spectators. Because first base was so easily reached (one had only to hit the ball and then run thirty feet without being soaked), the real action came between the other bases. Smart fielding and well-rehearsed relays of long hits made seeming extra-base hits into astonishingly easy outs. Because the rules contained no provision that a runner must stay within the baselines, he might run into the outfield to elude a fielder attempting to wing the ball between his ribs. A striker might turn 180 degrees as the pitch was coming to him and whack the ball just as far behind him as he might have hit it ahead.

There is no overestimating Americans' love and fear of organization, then as now. It is certain that variants of the Massachusetts game were older than variants of the New York game. No matter, the

Knickerbockers brought in *system* before the New Englanders did. And finally—has the obvious eluded us all this time?—New York may have won out because of a skillful publicity campaign in which its game of baseball, held up as a paragon of manliness, was in fact easier for unathletic clerks to play. For common men of sedentary habits who would, if they had their wish, be leisured gentlemen, such as the Knickerbockers, it was more important to comport themselves well than to play well. Did the New York game surmount all challenges because it allowed more chances to exhibit skill and nerve? In sport as in war, perhaps, the first casualty is truth.

Henry Sargent, who wrote frequently to the Mills Commission, emerges from the Doubleday miasma as a great voice for America's primeval baseball game. From one of his letters:

> Four Old Cat and Three Old Cat were as well known to Massachusetts boys as round ball. I knew both games in 1862 and Mr. Stoddard [of the Upton Excelsiors] tells me that his father knew them and played them between 1800 and 1820. They bore about the same relation to round ball that "scrub" does to baseball now. The boys got together when there was leisure for any game and if there were enough to make up a game—even if they were 2 or 3 short of the regulation 14 on a side—they played round-ball. If there were not more than a dozen all told, they contented themselves with four old cat, or with three old cat if there were still less players. . . . The main thing to be remembered is that 4 + 3 old cat seem to be co-eval with Massachusetts round-ball + were considered a modification of round ball for a less number of players than the regular game required. . . .

In another such letter Sargent added:

> If there is real interest in the beginning of baseball, you can learn more of its predecessor round-ball by a day or two spent in Grafton and Upton [Massachusetts] than in any other way. The game attained its extreme development of skill in this locality, and several of the players, who were celebrated 50 years ago [i.e., 1855], are living still. I do not know what part, if any, round-ball had in the birth of base-ball. From the arrangement of the bases it would seem that there was some

> connection. The square of round-ball was turned to make the baseball diamond, and home was made the batter's stand.

And, finally, Sargent declared to the Mills Commission, with evident irritation:

> I have stated this to you before. I repeat it now, because I find that every one who remembers round-ball at all, agrees with me. So if round-ball is the English rounders, and the difference between Mr. Chadwick and Mr. Spaulding [sic] is whether base-ball sprung from rounders or from four old cat, there is no difference between them. They are talking about the same thing, only they do not know it.

While Philadelphia, New York, and New England played their distinctive regional variants, in Connecticut an odd game called *wicket* or *wicket ball* reigned unchallenged by baseball of any sort. It resembled what Britons thought of as "country cricket," a game that had been utterly supplanted by the standardized modern game. Wicket was unknown in metropolitan New York until 1880, when a group of Connecticut watchmakers who had been transplanted to work in a Brooklyn factory staged a game there. Earlier, the game had gone wherever Connecticut emigrants settled: to the Western Reserve of Ohio and Michigan, or with the Congregational missionaries to Hawaii. Wicket was played along a seventy-five-foot alley of hard ground, rolled, skinned of grass, with the wicket bowler having to skip the ball along the ground, touching down at least once in his own thirty-seven-and-a-half-foot portion; it bears mentioning that this figure represented baseball's 1857 pitching distance of forty-five reduced by one-sixth, its probable original distance and the one recommended for inexperienced players.

The bowler would skim the ball toward a low wicket some five feet in length but only inches off the ground. The batsman held a long curved club with an enormous gnarled bulb at its curved end. The bare wicket alley, unlike the manicured grassy pitch of cricket, may survive in baseball as the mysterious strip of dirt between the pitcher's mound and home plate that is sometimes used even today in unwitting reference to a game older than baseball.

Little recalled or understood today, wicket was the diversion of choice for young Nutmeggers until nearly 1860. Indeed, the first printed reference to wicket in America came in 1725, even before any written mention of American cricket except in diary form. George Washington was documented as playing the game at Valley Forge, Pennsylvania, on May 4, 1778. Revolutionary War soldier George Ewing wrote in a letter: "This day His Excellency [i.e., Washington] dined with G[eneral] Nox [Knox] and after dinner did us the honor to play at Wicket with us."

One of wicket's hot spots was Hartford, on the campus of Washington College, today known as Trinity College, where it may well have been played by Louis Fenn Wadsworth, Class of 1844, who had left so cold a trail for Mills that almost seventy years later Cartwright's biographer could not pick it up. Before the advent of digitized newspapers, this mysterious fellow had eluded me, too, as well as several genealogical experts I had enlisted to find him in the 1980s. Even Wadsworth family histories and historians offered no clue. We knew he had played first base with the Gothams and the Knickerbockers from the early 1850s to 1862, and was generally recorded in the press as L. F. Wadsworth, but where did he live after that, when he disappeared from the New York City directories? (You may recall that Thomas Tassie of the Atlantic Club of Brooklyn stated that Mr. Wadsworth was "a gentleman and a scholar, who held an important position in the Custom House.")

BY 2004, I WAS as stuck as Mills had been when his 1908 search of the Custom House records turned up nothing, and I had fairly well given up. Then, the search tools of the Internet, particularly a horde of newly digitized ancient newspapers, pried the past open a bit wider and, little by little, the story began to unfold.

Wadsworth had indeed been attached to the Custom House, not in 1845 but a few years later: As an attorney and active supporter of the Unionist Whig political party, he won a patronage position though he was never a federal employee. He had been born in Litchfield County, Connecticut, to Amos and Amanda Wadsworth on May 6, 1825. Upon graduation from Washington College in 1844, he wavered between the study of law and a military career, applying to West Point in October

1845 but failing to gain admission. Then he went to Michigan, where his well-to-do father had bought land in the great Western Reserve boom of the late 1830s. He returned east to embark on a legal career in Manhattan in 1848. A tempestuous character, he commenced his ball playing days with the Gothams, with whom he achieved prominence as the top first baseman of his time, then moved to the Knickerbockers on April 1, 1854, perhaps for "emoluments," as recompense was euphemistically known then, as his skilled play would increase the Knickerbockers' chances of victory. One of the veteran Knicks, in recalling some of the old players for the New York *Sun* in 1887, said:

> I had almost forgotten the most important man on the team and that is Lew Wadsworth. He was the life of the club. Part of his club suit consisted of a white shirt on the back of which was stamped a black devil. It makes me laugh still when I recall how he used to go after a ball. His hands were very large and when he went for a ball they looked like the tongs of an oyster rake. He got there all the same and but few balls passed him.

Even though at that time only the Knicks, Eagles, and Gothams were organized as baseball clubs, it was clear that activity was bubbling in Brooklyn and in Manhattan for the 1855 campaign.

Wadsworth went on to resign from the Knickerbockers three times, once in each of the succeeding three years, finally returning to the Gothams. Although the newspapers sang his praises when he was an active player, he was little recalled thereafter. But he certainly should have been, whether or not he brought a diagram to the Knickerbocker playing field in the early 1850s, for he is the man responsible for baseball being played to nine innings and with nine men.

In an 1856 Knickerbocker meeting, Wadsworth, along with Doc Adams, backed a motion to permit nonmembers to take part in Knickerbocker intramural games at the Elysian Fields if fewer than eighteen Knicks were present (nine men to the side had become the de facto standard for match play by this point, though it still was not mandated by the rules of the game). Wadsworth and his allies among the Knickerbockers thought it more important to preserve the quality of the game than to exclude those who were not club members. Duncan F. Curry countermoved that if fourteen Knickerbockers were available, the game should admit no outsiders and be played short-handed, as had been their practice since 1845.

The Curry forces, or "Old Fogies" (which included James Whyte Davis), prevailed, 13–11. The Knicks, thus resolved among themselves upon an acceptable standard of seven men to the side, then settled upon a seven-inning game to replace the old custom of playing to twenty-one runs, which had recently produced a highly unsatisfactory 12–12 tie game, called on account of darkness. Because this matter of seven versus nine had been one of the most heated and divisive votes in club history, member William F. Ladd suggested that a committee be formed to cooperate with other clubs to decide upon the proper number of players for a match, leaving each club to decide for itself what was acceptable for intramural games. This motion carried unanimously, and Wadsworth moved that the chairman of the gathering, Alexander Drummond, appoint the committee. He appointed Curry and Ladd; Ladd declined, and Adams took his place, thus placing one seven-inning advocate (Curry) alongside a nine-inning advocate (Adams), as the Knicks pointed toward their next meeting, at Smith's Hotel on 462 Broome Street on December 6, 1856. The purpose of this Knickerbocker meeting was to issue a call for a convention of all the clubs. (The Eagles had come to the Knicks requesting their aid in amalgamating the two clubs' rules as far back as 1853, and they and the Gothams had agreed to conform their rules with those of the Knicks on April 1, 1854, the same date on which Wadsworth was proposed for membership in the Knicks.)

The Knicks proceeded to endorse the idea of a concord with all the other clubs on this troublesome point of how many innings should constitute a match game and other issues, such as settling the "doubtful point, as to the position of the Pitcher," and debating the merits of the fly out versus the bound catch. To this end, the Knickerbockers established a three-man commission to enlist the attendance of metropolitan area clubs at a convention. The three were Wadsworth, Adams, and William Henry Grenelle.

Wadsworth was also named the Knickerbocker representative on the "Committee to Draft a Code of Laws on the Game of Base Ball, to be Submitted to the Convention." Also on this committee, as it turned out, was to be Thomas Tassie of the Atlantics.

Prior to the convention of February 25, 1857, which later came to be termed the first National Association meetings, Section 26 of the rules was adopted by the Committee, on the recommendation of the Knickerbockers, making the game "seven innings." In the convention, however, on Wadsworth's motion, the assembled delegates modified the Knickerbockers' recommendation to "nine innings." Clearly, by enlisting the support of other clubs, Wadsworth was bucking the Knickerbocker majority.

Ten days later, on March 7, the Knicks held their regular club meeting. They voted to adopt the bylaws of the convention but to accept the new playing rules only for matches with other clubs. On March 14, the rules were formally adopted, upon which the dyspeptic Daniel S. Stansbury moved that the Knicks play no more matches with other clubs. His motion was tabled. Wadsworth moved to alter the Knickerbocker rules and bylaws to incorporate all the new changes from the convention. His motion carried, and the Old Fogy or exclusionary clique of the Knicks, as originally headed by Curry, was finished, and in a way so was the original Knickerbocker Base Ball Club.

One may understand from this account why Henry Chadwick sometimes said that the New York game of baseball dates not from 1840 or 1845 but 1857.

Wadsworth's victory was Pyrrhic as far as his own future in the club was concerned. The man the Knickerbockers had brought in as a ringer, and through inducements had become perhaps the game's first professional player, failed to appear for a game against the Eagles on June 8, 1857, though he had been named to play. Six days later, he resigned for the third and final time; by the following month he was again manning first base with his accustomed panache, but for the Gothams. When a New York all-star team was selected to play against the best of Brooklyn in the Fashion Race Course games of 1858, Wadsworth was named to play first base.

Louis (sometimes spelled Lewis) F. Wadsworth left New York in 1862 for Rockaway in Morris County, New Jersey, with his new wife, the wealthy widow Maria Isabel Meschutt Fisher, and two children from her first marriage, the younger of whom, Marianne, took his name. He later became a judge in Union County, head of the local Democratic organization, and a member of the board of education. Widowed in 1883, he took to drink and lost a fortune estimated at $300,000 (perhaps $8 million in today's terms). After some years of selling Sunday newspapers on the streets of Plainfield as his sole source of income, in 1898 he committed himself to the poorhouse. While Mills was searching for his baffling Mr. Wadsworth, his possible trump card to Doubleday, no one connected Louis F. Wadsworth, long-term inmate of the Plainfield Industrial Home, with baseball's invention. Wadsworth died on March 28, 1908, eight days after publication of the *Spalding Guide* containing Mills' final decision and five days after Mills acknowledged giving up his search for him.

In Wadsworth's belated obituary in the *Hartford Daily Times,* it was written that "He had no family of his own, and it is hardly likely that any of his brothers and sisters can be located. He rarely mentioned them and as no letters ever came to him, the attendants at the home surmised that he preferred not to let them know where he was."

3

THE CRADLE OF BASEBALL

Thanks to Pittsfield, Massachusetts, the general public today knows what only a handful of scholars had suspected: that baseball was played in America long before 1839, the year it was said to have sprung full-blown from the mind of young Abner Doubleday in Cooperstown. From the astonishingly preserved minutes of a Pittsfield town meeting in 1791, we know that in this locality a game called *baseball,* if played too close to a newly built meeting house, violated the law, at a time when the United States of America was a teenager and the Constitution a mere toddler.

While prowling the Internet late one night in 2003, I came upon a mention of the now celebrated bylaw in a book entitled *The History of Pittsfield, (Berkshire County,) Massachusetts, From the Year 1734 to the Year 1800.* Because the book was published in 1869 under the authority of the town, I had no doubts about the authenticity of the reference. The next morning, I called folks at the Pittsfield City Hall to see if they retained minute books all the way back to the eighteenth century, and was informed that indeed they did. I later shared my find with baseball author and former pitcher Jim Bouton, a Berkshires resident, who in turn passed it on to Mayor James Ruberto. The rest became history, now a part of the standard encyclopedic entries for baseball.

Still a puzzle, however, is what the Pittsfield game of those days looked like, or what its rules may have been—no eighteenth-century game account survives or is likely to have existed. Despite the bylaw's explicit prohibition of "baseball," can we recognize in this early game any of the elements visible when the Red Sox meet the Yankees?

We may reasonably assume that the Pittsfield game was different from the other ball games proscribed in the ordinance: "For the Preservation of the Windows in the New Meeting House . . . no Person or Inhabitant of said town, shall be permitted to play at any game called wicket, cricket, base ball, bat ball, football, cat, fives or any game or games with a ball, within the distance of eighty yards from said Meeting House." Several of these other games are cousins of baseball, as we have seen. Fives was a form of handball, football was the hands-off variety that is still the world's favorite sport, cat and wicket were described in the previous chapter, batball is an enduring conundrum, and cricket is of course England's national game and, until the Civil War, very nearly America's as well.

Because the old game of baseball may have developed, or at least flourished, in the Berkshires and the Housatonic Valley, this region might not unreasonably be termed baseball's Garden of Eden, a term that Pittsfield's civic boosters have been quick to adopt; for many this coinage has come to signify, in shorthand, that the national pastime was invented here. It was not. If pressed to create a date for baseball's taking root in America, I'd have to say *about 1735*, and it is because of old-timer Henry Sargent's message to the Mills Commission stating that his contemporary George H. Stoddard, an 1850s roundball player with the Upton Excelsiors whose grandfather and great-grandfather had both played the game, believed that roundball surely dated back to just after the Revolution and was not a novelty then. It had been played, Stoddard said, "as long ago as Upton became a little village." Upton was settled in 1735.

Admittedly, we are not likely to find hard evidence for that date as good as that which now resides in the Berkshire Athenaeum in support of 1791. However, we can only suppose that if baseball was banned in Pittsfield in 1791, it was not a nuisance devised in that year, that it had been played for some time before, and not only in this western Massachusetts city. The Berkshires may have been a remote region in 1791, but not immune to influence. In fact, baseball appears to have sprung up everywhere, like dandelions, and we cannot now expect to identify with certainty which of these hardy flowers was truly the first.

No ingenious lad like Abner Doubleday or inventive clerk like Alexander Cartwright created the game. Although Cooperstown is the legendary home of baseball, the Baseball Hall of Fame will not relocate to Pittsfield, and its officials no longer make special claims for Doubleday or 1839. Its status as a culture shrine will remain untarnished, for by now it has a history of its own. As Stephen Jay Gould explained not only of the Mills Commission's search for a baseball father but also Cooperstown's hold on our hearts, "Too few people are comfortable with evolutionary modes of explanation in any form. I do not know why we tend to think so fuzzily in this area, but one reason must reside in our social and psychic attraction to creation myths in preference to evolutionary stories—for creation myths . . . identify heroes and sacred places, while evolutionary stories provide no palpable, particular thing as a symbol for reverence, worship, or patriotism."

A better reason for neither Cooperstown nor Pittsfield to celebrate the spontaneous birth of baseball in its backyard is that bat-and-ball games go back to the banks of the Nile nearly 4,500 years ago in the game *seker-hemat*, or "batting the ball." In a wall relief at the shrine of Hathor, the goddess of love and joy, in Hatshepsut's temple at Deir-el-Bahari, Thutmose III is seen holding a ball in one hand and a stick in the other. The hieroglyph reads: "Striking the ball for Hathor who is foremost in Thebes." Another inscription above the king's attending priests reads: "Catching it for him by the servants of the gods." The date is c. 1460 B.C.E., but bat and ball games were played in Egypt a millennium before.

All the same, Pittsfield is a fine place to honor the spirit of baseball, the one that infuses children with the desire to play the game and grownups to watch it and recall their youth. This spirit animated young players of the Massachusetts game of roundball and was certainly the game played in Pittsfield, though it was not included among the prohibited games by that name. So why did the Pittsfield legislators of 1791 ban the game as *baseball* rather than *roundball*? My speculation is this: The border between New York and Massachusetts had long been in dispute, and had been settled only four years earlier (the New York and Connecticut border dispute wore on until 1857). The lines that were finally drawn on a map made no matter to boys playing a game of ball long familiar under a localized name; they were going to call their game whatever previous generations had called it.

AS MENTIONED EARLIER, BASEBALL was the name of a game played in southeastern England in the eighteenth century and no doubt earlier, though without a bat. In the west of England, a similar if somewhat later game, played with a bat, was known as *rounders.* Baseball's first appearance in print by its name occurs in a children's book, John Newbery's *A Little Pretty Pocket-Book*, published in England in 1744, which offers a woodcut showing boys playing baseball and a rhymed description of the game.

BASE-BALL.
The *Ball* once struck off,
    Away flies the *Boy*
To the next destin'd Post,
    And then Home with Joy.

MORAL
Thus *Britons*, for Lucre,
    Fly over the Main,
But, with Pleasure transported,
    Return back again.

That baseball is an odyssey in which a protagonist braves the perils between bases before ultimately coming home, like Ulysses, is today a familiar trope; it is delightful to note it in this first printed mention of the game. Newbery's charming alphabet book was published in pirated editions in America, too, perhaps as early as 1762 and certainly by 1787, by Isaiah Thomas. (In the American edition the word "Britons" in the second stanza is replaced by "seamen.") The bases in the depicted game are wooden posts, not sandbags, though either may be understood as safe havens from being put out, but there is no bat. So this game of baseball may be thought of as fives (handball) with bases.

(In New York City's asphalt playgrounds this game survives as *slapball* or *punchball*; the writer played both during junior high school in 1960.)

In America's straitlaced founding period, mentions of ball play came generally in the form of prohibitions or complaints. On Christmas Day in 1621, Governor Bradford was infuriated to find some men of Plymouth Plantation, who had begged off work to observe their faith, instead "frolicking in ye street, at play openly; some at pitching ye barr, some at stoole ball and shuch-like sport." In 1656, the Dutch prohibited playing ball on Sundays in New Amsterdam. In 1724, Boston diarist Samuel Sewall was sorely disappointed that his lodger "Sam. Hirst got up betimes in the morning, and took Ben Swett with him and went into the [Boston] Common to play at Wicket. Went before any body was up, left the door open; Sam came not to prayer; at which I was most displeased."

Colleges, too, were getting into the act. Anticipating Pittsfield, Dartmouth prohibited ball play near windows in 1780—wicket was the students' game of choice—and the University of Pennsylvania followed suit in 1784. Princeton student John Rhea Smith had noted in his diary for 1786, "A fine day; play baste ball in the campus, but am beaten for I miss both catching and striking the Ball." Smith used "baste" as a corruption of "base" in two separate contexts: "baste ball" and "prisoners' baste," a game of tag. This in my view renders the Princeton diary the first textual reference to a game we should regard as baseball, if not one precisely so named. Princeton, which had banned ball play against the president's house in 1761 ("under the Penalty of Five Shillings for every offence"), prohibited bat-and-ball play in 1787.

Clearly bat-and-ball games were being played everywhere, but the game called baseball in westernmost Massachusetts and round ball in the rest of the state had another incarnation in Pennsylvania and points west, where it was known first as *bullet playing* (a bullet being in this context a small ball, not a projectile from a firearm) and later as *town ball*, as described in the preceding chapter. All these games required a batsman to notch a tally by running around four bases (sometimes the striker's point could be considered a fifth, in which case it was not home base, the completion of the circuit) without being put out by a thrown ball. And all these games could be reduced to cat if there were not sufficient players to permit the four-base version, which over time sampled features from town ball, round ball, and baseball.

Each of these games varied minutely from the others, but each may be brought into the baseball family because each exhibited the essence of the game, as previously posited: a bat, a ball that is pitched or thrown to the bat, two sides alternating innings, multiple safe havens, and a 360 degree circuit that scores a run. One might object that none of these games employed the key New York innovations of foul territory and throwing the ball to the base rather than at the runner, but to such objections I would respond that the key distinguishing feature of baseball is evident in its very name: *the base*—just as the essential, defining characteristic of football, handball, racquetball, and basketball is evident in *their* names.

In 1834, another children's book provided clues as to the state of baseball in America. *The Book of Sports* by Robin Carver copied the rules for rounders that had been published in England in 1828 in *The Boy's Own Book* and added a woodcut of boys "Playing Ball" on Boston Common. Carver explained, "This game is known under a variety of names. It is sometimes called 'round ball.' But I believe that 'base' or 'goal ball' are the names generally adopted in our country." In debunking the Doubleday tale of 1839, the New York Public Library's Robert Henderson made much of another little pirated book, *The Boy's and Girl's Book of Sports* (1835). Like the Carver book, it points to round ball, the Massachusetts game, which indeed had its roots in such English forebear games as rounders. The New York game, as it came to be played in the 1830s and '40s, was another cauldron of chowder.

IN 2001, NEW YORK University librarian George Thompson hit the front page of the *New York Times* with his discovery of a newspaper reference to a game called baseball in New York City long before its presumed invention by the Knickerbockers. The *National Advocate* of April 25, 1823, contained this unsigned notice:

> I was last Saturday much pleased in witnessing a company of active young men playing the manly and athletic game of "base ball" at the Retreat in Broadway (Jones') [on the west side of Broadway between what now is Washington Place and Eighth Street]. I am informed they are an organized association, and that a very interesting game will be played on Saturday next at the above place, to commence at half past 3 o'clock, P.M.

> Any person fond of witnessing this game may avail himself of seeing it played with consummate skill and wonderful dexterity. . . . It is surprising, and to be regretted that the young men of our city do not engage more in this manual sport; it is innocent amusement, and healthy exercise, attended with but little expense, and has no demoralizing tendency.

We know nothing directly of what this game looked like or how it was played, but young men who took part in it knew they needed to make excuses for playing the game of their boyhood: it was "manly and athletic," it was a "manual" sport rather than a leisurely pastime, it was "healthy"—a significant virtue after the yellow fever epidemic of the prior summer—and it was without "demoralizing tendency," by which the unnamed writer was certainly referencing the customary concatenation of blood sport, gambling, inebriation, and wenching. From William R. Wheaton's recollections of the Gotham Club rules for the game in 1837, scholars today believe that foul territory and the abandonment of soaking were later innovations that could not have been on display in this 1823 intramural contest of an organized association, the outcome of which went unreported if indeed the game was played. Henry Chadwick endorsed the notion that a polygonal layout for baseball (four bases plus home, with varying distances between the bases but the shortest being to first base) was in vogue in New York City in the 1830s. Whether such a playing field was used at Jones' Retreat or not, we may surmise that this New York baseball game of 1823 was not very different from the one played in Pittsfield in 1791, or even in Upton in 1735. This 1823 game was baseball, and although it was played in New York, was not yet the New York game.

What to make of Jones, his retreat, and the rediscovered baseball match? At some point in mid-1822 the former William Neilson property was leased by veteran innkeeper William Jones, just in time for the sudden flush of well-to-do New Yorkers fleeing that summer's yellow fever epidemic at the foot of Manhattan Island. The fever eased with cold weather and did not return in the spring. Perhaps trying a novel idea to sustain a flagging business, Jones staged his baseball game on Saturday April 19, 1823, as mentioned in the *Advocate* of six days following. In that report, it was announced that another such contest was to take place at the Retreat on Saturday, April 26. No further word of the game is to be found. By May 14, Jones gave up his lease and retreated to a more modest porterhouse, which became his home as well as his saloon. The Neilson family presumably regained control of its property at this point.

Jones may have been financially ruined in his experiment to use baseball as a draw to sell other things, such as refreshments—"ice cream, cake, punch, lemonade, &c. &c."—and maybe to link with omnibus service (the Common Council did evaluate a proposal during this fever-panic period for a line from Trinity Church to Art Street, known today as Eighth Street). However, the plan of the Jones' Retreat—interurban transit plus food and drink—would become the model for baseball's magnates later in the century.

Charles H. Haswell, in his *Memoirs of an Octogenarian in New York, 1816 to 1860*, wrote that Columbia College students in 1816,

> alike to the students of other colleges, did not entertain or practise gymnastics as an element of college education. Of those of Columbia I write advisedly—they were not members of a boat club, base-ball, or foot-ball team. On Saturday afternoons, in the fall of the year, a few students would meet in the "hollow" on the Battery, and play an irregular game of football, generally without teams or "sides," as they were then termed; a mere desultory engagement.
>
> As this "hollow" was the locale of base-ball, "marbles," etc., and as it has long since been obliterated, and in its existence was the favorite resort of schoolboys and all others living in the lower part of the city, it is worthy of record. Thus: it was very nearly the entire area bounded by Whitehall and State Streets, the sea wall line, and a line about two hundred feet to the west; it was of an uniform grade, fully five feet below that of the street, it was nearly as uniform in depth, and as regular in its boundary as a dish.

And so we have casual, disorganized baseball play by collegians in 1816. (Columbia was then located on Church Street between Barclay and Murray.) But New York baseball, under another name, has been dated to 1805 by my indefatigable friend Thompson, who spotted this in the *New York Daily Advertiser* of April 13, 1805:

> Yesterday afternoon a contest at the game of Bace took place on "the Gymnasium," near Tyler's between the gentlemen of two different

> clubs for a supper and trimmings. One of these clubs has taken the very classical appellation of Gymnastics, and the other the no less classical one of The Sons of Diagoras, (not confined however to the number there) but with great submission to the taste of the gentlemen we think a plain modern English name would have sounded quite as well as either.
>
> Great skill and activity it is said was displayed on both sides, but after a severe and well maintained contest, Victory which at times had fluttered a little from one to the other, settled down on the heads of the Gymnastics, who beat The Sons of Diagoras 41 to 34.

The game is interesting in several respects: it was subject to a wager, it was played to a concluding score that resembles the scores of baseball games played more than half a century hence; it was played by two organized, named clubs. These details incline one to judge the game these young men played as being different from the game of tag also known as base/baste, or prisoners' base. Of further interest is that the playing grounds were near to Tyler's, a pleasure garden, the city's early playgrounds for diversions of all types, including physical sport (its site today would be located near the southwest corner of Spring and Hudson streets). Lush botanical plantings, leafy bowers, and shaded walks characterized some pleasure gardens, but these establishments were selling pleasure, not horticulture. (It is these pleasure gardens that gave the name to, for example, Madison Square Garden or Boston Garden.)

We know from other records that young men played baseball in the park south of City Hall in 1827 (the cornerstone for this landmark building was placed in 1803), but whether this was the grounds referred to in 1805 as the gymnasium we cannot know. The evidence for New York City's first grown ballplayers being Columbia College students is certainly inferential, but might one day yield to further research.

HENRY CHADWICK WAS MORE nearly correct than Albert Spalding to say that baseball—as a rounders-like game of bat and ball and bases that manifested itself in variant styles in New England, Philadelphia, and New York—came over from England. "When a schoolboy in

England nearly sixty years ago, I used to play the boys' game of ball called 'rounders.' It was a mere field exercise, requiring no skill in either pitching, batting, or fielding, the principal excitement of the game being the privilege it gave the fielders of throwing the ball at the base runners. . . ." However, Albert Spalding was more right than Chadwick in saying that the game all America knew as baseball in 1905 owed little if anything to rounders. Despite all the American and English bombast as to which was the superior country, people, and game, big-brother cricket shaped the fledgling baseball mightily, on the playing field and off.

Cricket had been played in New York at least since a match on the Commons on April 29, 1751. The *New-York Post-Boy* reported that the game was played for "a considerable Wager," with eleven players on each side, and "according to the London Method: and those who got most Notches in two Hands, to be the Winners." The New Yorkers defeated their English rivals by a total score of 167–80. Another notable New York cricket match, at the field beside "the Jews' Burying Ground" between "Americans" and "Englishmen," was advertised in the city's *Royal Gazette* on August 19, 1780; the city was at that time occupied by the British, as it had been since 1776. Cricket remained the most popular ball game among Americans long after the British went home; by any measure organized club baseball, despite its upward trajectory, remained in a distant second place until after the Civil War.

The ethos of sport in New York City into which baseball intruded in the mid-1830s—horse racing, yachting, tenpins, pedestrianism, boxing, and canine and cock fighting—arose from the materialism, personal solitude, and risk-seeking of the city's bachelor culture. Rural youths with slim prospects flocked to the city after 1825, when the completion of the Erie Canal made New York the nation's economic capital. Many hard-working, lonely men, apart from their families, succumbed to the snares of the city in political halls, gambling dens, saloons, and brothels (all of which paralleled the traditionally more genteel encouragement of vice in the city's pleasure gardens). In Knickerbocker days, before De Witt Clinton poured the waters of Lake Erie into New York harbor, before railroads and stock speculation and wildcat currency led to an aristocracy of cash rather than one of class, the city's sportsmen had been devotees of rod and reel and turf. Afterward these sportsmen were increasingly supplanted by sporting men who embraced the underside of urban life. Sportsmen and sporting men alike loved to gamble, so in this they were united and from this union a national pastime would grow, not as the purely amateur intramural game of the white-collar Knickerbockers, but as the professionalized competition between blue-collar clubs for bragging rights and gambling spoils.

Visible recreation by grown men had been a dubious notion in the 1820s, which rendered the baseball players at Jones' Retreat in 1823 brave indeed. Respectable men wishing to exert themselves could join fire companies and target (archery and rifle) companies, which invariably contained barrooms or were flanked by them, and boys could "run with the machine," that is, accompany the fire laddies on their missions of rescue. Lonely gentlemen could decently consort with young ladies at affairs such as the annual "Bachelors Ball," highlight of the social season, held every February 14 (Valentine's Day) at the City Hotel on Broadway. The hotel occupied the whole block between Thames and Cedar streets. Beginning around 1827, it came to be managed by the Young Bachelors Association, whose name was later echoed in the Jolly Young Bachelors Base Ball Club, the original name of the famed Excelsiors of Brooklyn.

Apart from the ballroom, the engine company, and the target company (these archery or rifle militia adjuncts bore such colorful if perplexing names as the Washington Market Chowder Club, Bony Fusileers, and Ham Guard Warriors, and they bear further study concerning early ball play), physical exercise taken for its own sake by those no longer in short pants brought scorn from puritanical souls and derision from men of business, who had long ago abandoned boyish things. City life was about amassing enough money to set up in business or return to country life enriched. Long hours spent in counting rooms left little time for fresh air, let alone sport. A writer for London's *New Monthly Magazine* observed in 1829:

> There are several things in the first impression of New York which ought to be mentioned: amongst these, the dull complexion and expressionless physiognomy of the common people. Whether their sallow hue and the languor of their looks, so strikingly different from the fresh and ruddy animation of the English, are the effects of a local climate, and of influences peculiar to the situation of the city, I shall not under-

take to determine; but unquestionably both the figure and countenance of the Americans improve as you proceed into the interior.

The group who would become Knickerbockers (prior to 1845 the aggregation was nameless) was composed of flaccid professional men when they began to gather for exercise at New York City's Madison Square in 1842. Before it was formally opened as a park five years later, the onetime military arsenal and parade grounds had been named a public place and had been home to the ball fields of the Knickerbockers (north end) and the New York Base Ball Club (south end). Abram C. Dayton recalled that Madison Square "was surrounded by insurmountable brick walls which were the terror of the comparatively few juvenile offenders against the law of this city." An ordinance of May 8, 1839 (still in force in 1845), forbade anyone of any age from playing ball anywhere in public spaces; players from both the Knickerbocker and New York clubs joined the juvenile offenders as scofflaws. African-American youths from Greenwich Village ("Darktown," in the parlance of the day) played at the Madison Square Park, too. On October 24, 1840, the editor of the *Colored American* spoke out on the subject:

> We wish to call attention to the practice of the lads of our City, who, in great numbers, are resorting to the suburbs of the city, as high as 25th or 30th street, for the purpose of ball playing. And we wish the parents of our people to look well to their boys, some of who[m], we are informed by a friend, as well as by the *Journal of Commerce*, have been seen in those sections of the City, on the Sabbath, playing ball.

Baseball players of all ages and hues were exhilarated by the crack of the bat and the sting of the ball and, to use Walt Whitman's description, the "snap, go, fling" of the American game. Less manly than either its English or New England counterparts—the ball was pitched to the bat gently, to provide the fielders with opportunities; an out could be recorded by catching a fly ball on a bounce—it was, all the same, lightning fast compared to cricket's languor or roundball's requirement of a hundred runs for victory. Baseball could be played, if not in a New York minute, then in less than two hours.

By 1845, the ur-Knickerbockers had seen their playing grounds, first at Madison Square and then at Murray Hill, give way to the needs of the railroad. Charles A. Peverelly (an officer of the Young Bachelors Association) described their situation with mock-epic grandeur:

> At a preliminary meeting, it was suggested that as it was apparent they would soon be driven from Murray Hill, some suitable place should be obtained in New Jersey, where their stay could be permanent; accordingly, a day or two afterwards, enough to make a game assembled at Barclay street ferry, crossed over, marched up the road, prospecting for ground on each side, until they reached the Elysian Fields, where they "settled." Thus it occurred that a party of gentlemen formed an organization, combining together health, recreation, and social enjoyment, which was the nucleus of the now great American game of Base Ball so popular in all parts of the United States, than which there is none more manly or more health-giving.

The Knickerbocker party of course did not wander about northern New Jersey looking for a place to play. They had been preceded by other clubs, both baseball and cricket, in selecting the Elysian Fields; the New York Ball Club, for one, celebrated its second anniversary in Hoboken with an intramural game in the fall of 1845 in which many nominal Knickerbockers and Gothams played. A landscaped retreat of picnic grounds and scenic vistas, the Hoboken proto-theme park was designed by its proprietors not only to relieve New Yorkers of city air and city care, but also to give new urbanites a place reminiscent of the idealized farms that had sent so many of them to the metropolis. The "prospecting" Knicks knew to come to the Elysian Fields because in this, as in so many other things, they were not the first.

At auction in 1784, the year after the British evacuation of New York, John Stevens purchased a confiscated Tory property that would become the city of Hoboken and the core of the Elysian Fields. At the turn of the nineteenth century, he further acquired "The Dueling Ground," adjacent to the village of Weehawken, where Aaron Burr shot Alexander Hamilton in 1804. A newspaper reported in 1802 that "Hoboken, the fashionable place of resort for gentlemen, has lately been used by some of 'the lower classes of society' to settle their disputes 'with the fist.' Immense crowds gather there to witness bouts between these 'sons of Mendoza.' "

To promote his real estate speculations, Stevens asserted that Hoboken was "free from the danger of Yellow fever." Among his future embellishments of the site were a race track, ball fields, a miniature railway, a predecessor of the Ferris wheel, a merry-go-round, a tenpin alley, wax figures, a camera obscura, and a flying machine or, as Stevens called it, a whirligig. Landscape historian William A. Mann notes, "In 1824, presaging future ballpark owners' entreaties to municipalities, New Jersey resident Stevens petitioned the City of New York for 'the capital requisite for . . . making the requisite improvements' to his site, since there were, in his words, 'immense, incalculable advantages' to the city to be derived from his park. The investment, he argued, would be minor" compared to the healthful benefits to the spindly legged, sickly citizens of the great metropolis.

The heavenly paradise that had been the Elysian Fields, or at least had given them their name, had already begun to decline in public favor before the Knickerbockers left the grind and grit of New York for their new playgrounds. In 1844, New York lawyer George Templeton Strong lamented in his diary, "Hoboken's a good deal cut up and built up, but pleasant still; pity it's haunted by such a gang as frequents it; its groves are sacred to Venus and I saw scarce anyone there but snobs and their strumpets. Walked on in momentary expectation of stumbling on some couple engaged in . . . 'the commission of gross vulgarity.' "

As the lure of employment and relative leisure herded country boys into crowded, pestilential cities, resplendent in vices undreamt of in distant counties, an outdoor movement was born. Advocates of exercise ferried to Hoboken or rode uptown to one of several resorts: Cato's, at about 65th Street; Hazard House, located in Yorkville, on the crown of Yorkville Hill at 82nd Street; and the Red House, at roughly 105th Street and Second Avenue and of particular interest because its enclosed field hosted cricket matches and later baseball games. From the *Anglo American* of May 2, 1846: "On the NW side, outside the inclosure [sic], the ground is so much elevated along the whole line, that there is convenience for thousands of Spectators to have a full view of the play, much better than if they were within the inclosed space, thus giving increased satisfaction to all parties." In the 1830s, Third Avenue was developed as the "Macadamized Road," and the great trotters of the day would race between Hazard House and the Red House.

All the same, visiting Englishmen like W. E. Baxter wrote contemptuously of American sporting habits: "to roll balls in a ten pin alley by gas-light or to drive a fast trotting horse in a light wagon along a very bad and dusty road, seems the Alpha and Omega of sport in the United States." Ralph Waldo Emerson wrote despairingly of the "invalid habits of this country."

This was about to change.

ON SEPTEMBER 23, 1845, the Knickerbocker Base Ball Club organized, approving a constitution, bylaws, and playing rules. It is this level of organization that won for them the title of pioneer baseball club, for it is clear that in the years after 1845 "first" meant something other than first to play the game. It might have been a shorthand for "senior among those extant," or it might have meant first "serious" approach to playing the game. As Henry Chadwick wrote in 1867:

> [Delabere Pritchett] Blaine, an English writer, says: "There are few of us, of either sex, but have engaged in base ball since our majority." Think of American ladies playing base ball! Yet the English "rounders" contained all the elements of our National game. All that it needed was systematizing and an authoritative code of rules. This it did not obtain until after 1840—and not completely until 1845.

W. H. Van Cott, a member of the Gothams, wrote in a letter to the *New York Tribune* in 1854: "There have been a large number of friendly, but spirited trials of skill, between the Clubs, during the last season, which have showed that the game has been thoroughly systematized and that the players have attained a high degree of skill in the game."

What explains the era's fascination with rules, bylaws, and system? Hadn't baseball been played for eons to general approbation, without much in the way of law and order? The answer lies outside the playing fields and in the general culture, with America's simultaneous envy of and revulsion for England and its ways, particularly its social stratification. We might reject primogeniture and aristocracy, preferring to denominate class by cash. But then there was the stately game of cricket, reliant upon law and permitting commoners to play with gentry.

Americans ultimately would reject cricket, but only after taking from it all the things of value to their own nascent national game.

Instances of patriotically driven theft abounded outside the playing fields, too. The model of Francis Cabot Lowell and his mill system, instituted in Waltham, Massachusetts, in 1814, is exemplary. On a visit to England in 1810, two years after the repeal of Thomas Jefferson's Embargo Act of 1807, Lowell studied the textile industry of Lancashire. Unable to buy drawings or a model of an English-made power loom, he memorized the plans he saw—in other words, stole them—and in a period in which patents, trademarks, and copyrights meant nothing across national borders, created an American icon. Lowell's factory, duplicated in other locales, including the city that after his death would bear his name, fully integrated the production of cotton goods under one roof, from raw material to finished product. In the years after British impressment of American seamen had driven Jefferson to the embargo of trade with the mother country, Lowell's mill was seen not only as an industrial success but also a fine specimen of patriotism. In the years following the embargo, the agrarian Jefferson came to see Hamilton's point that America needed industry it could call its own.

Also driving the rage for order was the evolution of the legal system away from English common law to statutory law, with American rather than Continental precedents. In common-law practice for half a century after independence, a judge was permitted to review a contract for fairness: if the "just price" of an asset in trade was not reflected in the contract, he had the authority to modify the price or abrogate the contract. By the 1830s, however, contracts had become limited to the terms of the agreement and nothing more. The written word trumped the custom, a development seen throughout America as a sign of progress.

By the 1830s, this pattern came into baseball as well. Young men who gathered to play baseball just for the fun of it were beneath notice, lacking the ceremony or social utility of fire companies, political clubs, benevolent societies, even the rowdy target companies, who at least bore an ostensible relationship to the local militia. Of the New York Ball Club that thrashed the Knickerbockers 23–1 on June 19, 1846, in what has come down to us as baseball's first match game, Peverelly had this to say: "It appears that this was not an organized club, but merely a party of gentlemen who played together frequently, and styled themselves the New York Club." With this setup, Chadwick could write in 1860, without exactly lying, "we shall not be far wrong if we award to the [Knickerbockers] the honor of being the pioneer of the present game of Base Ball."

The New York Club was in fact the progenitor of the Knickerbocker, and of the Gotham Club of the late 1840s as well; in the earlier period the names New York, Washington, and Gotham were more or less synonyms for the same group of men. If the Knickerbockers, who could not defeat the New Yorks in their match game, were subsequently dismissive of them, calling them "cricketers" or "disorganized," it may have been because the process by which they became two clubs may not have been an amicable subdivision but rather a secession of sorts. As Wheaton observed, "The new game quickly became very popular with New Yorkers [c. 1845], and the numbers of the club soon swelled beyond the fastidious notions of some of us, and we decided to withdraw and found a new organization, which we called the Knickerbocker. . . ."

It is perhaps worth providing here what has been alluded to earlier, that is, the original Knickerbocker rules of September 23, 1845, that have garnered for the club such high honors, despite the ample evidence that these were not the club's innovations.

1. *Members must strictly observe the time agreed upon for exercise, and be punctual in their attendance.*
   This was a big issue for the Knickerbockers, for it was a considerable annoyance to ferry across to Hoboken only to find an insufficient number of members to play. Frequently baseball games were played with six or seven to the side, if cricket players on the adjoining fields could not be enlisted to fill out the Knick ranks.

2. *When assembled for exercise, the President, or in his absence the Vice President, shall appoint an Umpire, who shall keep the game in a book provided for that purpose, and note all violations of the By-Laws and Rules during the time of exercise.*
   The Knickerbocker game books referenced here survive to this day. Those of other, earlier clubs do not. When the Knickerbocker Base Ball Club disbanded in 1882, the records were

entrusted to venerable member James Whyte Davis, who in his last days entrusted them to Henry Chadwick. Upon Chadwick's death in 1908, the books passed to Albert Spalding. Six years after Spalding's death the books were deposited in the New York Public Library, where they reside today. Regarding umpires, only one per game was deemed sufficient for decades to come, and the umpire had the authority to fine players on the spot for swearing, for disputing with him, or for flagrant disregard of the rules.

3. *The presiding officer shall designate two members as Captains, who shall retire and make the match to be played, observing at the same time that the players put opposite to each other should be as nearly equal as possible; the choice of sides to be then tossed for, and the* first in hand *to be decided in like manner.*
"First in hand" translates, in modern parlance, to "first up." In 1845, there was no custom as to which team batted in the top of an inning, home or visitor; the order was determined by chance or mutual agreement. In fact, the terms of card play served on the baseball field as well, where a "hand" could be "lost," or put out, at bat or on the base paths, and a man who reached base and came home registered an "ace," not a run.

4. *The bases shall be from "home" to second base, forty-two paces; from first to third base, forty-two paces, equidistant.*
As discussed in the preceding chapter, ninety feet between the bases was not specified until 1857, and the distance of a pace, often assumed to be three feet, was more likely two and a half feet.

5. *No stump match shall be played on a regular day of exercise.*
This may refer to such truncated games as cat ball, or it may, as my departed friend Fred Ivor-Campbell has written, mean a challenge game from outsiders: "The Knickerbockers played only one 'stump match' in their first six seasons," he wrote, "and even after they did begin to play outsiders more regularly, they played far fewer of such games than other leading clubs." What was paramount for the Knickerbockers was their regular noncompetitive exercise; match games were fine in their place, but always secondary.

6. *If there should not be a sufficient number of members of the Club present at the time agreed upon to commence exercise, gentlemen not members may be chosen in to make up the match,* which shall not be broken up *to take in members that may afterwards appear; but, in all cases, members shall have the preference, when present, at the making of a match.*
As written and later interpreted, the rights of club members to form the competing teams, even if undermanned, trumped the potential for higher quality play with a full complement of men to the side. This became a controversial rule by 1856 as some Knicks held that fourteen was sufficient for play while others insisted that eighteen was necessary, and that non-Knicks should be welcomed to fill out the teams to nine apiece. As previously described, the pro-fourteen faction won out, precipitating resignations and bad feelings when the pro-eighteen faction, led by Louis Fenn Wadsworth, prevailed at the National Association convention of 1857.

7. *If members appear after the game is commenced they may be chosen in if mutually agreed upon.*
Remember, these rules were designed to govern intramural play; the Knicks were not formed in order to engage in *match play*—competition with other clubs—and did so with reluctance.

8. *The game to consist of twenty-one counts, or aces; but at the conclusion an equal number of hands must be played.*
Note that there is no specified number of hands, or innings. Theoretically, the game of 1845 could be completed in one full inning. Nine innings did not become the rule until 1857. Ivor-Campbell's brilliant take on this seemingly innocuous rule 8 was "What undercut the Knickerbockers' game and led to its transformation into the game we play today is not the content of the rule but the fact that it was there at all. For the first time in the known written record of baseball-like games, ballplayers were told how to conclude their play, how to determine a winner and loser." When he wrote that in 2007, no other baseball rules from before 1854 except for the Knickerbocker rules were known to have survived, though it is implausible to think that

those rules sprang up ex nihilo. Larry McCray, an expert on early bat and ball games, rightly observes that a game with no provision for an ending would hold no appeal for gamblers. His observation is substantiated by the Chinese proverb: "If you must play, decide upon three things at the start: the rules of the game, the stakes, and the quitting time."

9. *The ball must be pitched, and not thrown, for the bat.*
The early baseball pitch was like today's softball pitch, only even more restricted: no wrist snap, arm perpendicular to the ground at release, and below the waist. Furthermore, the pitcher was urged to pitch the ball "for the bat." He was not regarded as an adversary to the batter, but merely as a server; the batter's true opponents were the fielders.

10. *A ball knocked out [of] the field, or outside the range of the first or third base, is foul.*
This stricture may well have included home runs! The early Knick grounds at the Elysian Fields faced the North (Hudson) River, and batters who hit the ball into the water were not hailed as heroes—the club generally had only one baseball, and that was handmade, of course. However, the more likely reason for incorporating the concept of foul ground into their rules was the Knickerbockers' chronic inability to muster a full complement of men for their appointed days of play. As Doc Adams recalled, "Our players were not very enthusiastic at first, and did not always turn out well on practice days. . . . I frequently went to Hoboken to find only two or three members present. . . . During the summer months many of our members were out of town, thus leaving a very short playing season."

Cholera had killed 3,513 in the summer of 1832, representing one death for every sixty-five inhabitants at a time when the city's population was some 230,000 (of whom fully a third fled the city that summer); an equivalent mortality in today's New York of 8 million would be more than 123,000. The popular superstition was that cholera returned every twelve years, and one might well imagine the dread overhanging New York in the mid-1840s. In fact, 5,071 more died in the epidemic of 1849, although the city's increased population brought the mortality rate down to one in eighty-nine inhabitants.

In these years there were many testaments to baseball's hygienic properties ("Let us go forth awhile, and get better air in our lungs. Let us leave our close rooms . . . the game of ball is glorious," Walt Whitman wrote in the *Brooklyn Eagle* of July 3, 1846). Might the generalized dread of cholera and its cycle of return, rather than the supposed claim of industry upon the former playgrounds of Manhattan, have been the impetus to ballplayers' flight to Hoboken in the mid-1840s?

11. *Three balls being struck at and missed and the last one caught, is a hand-out; if not caught is considered fair, and the striker bound to run.*

The responsibility of the catcher to hold the third strike is, amazingly, one of baseball's oldest rules to survive intact. (Some readers will recall Mickey Owen of the 1941 Brooklyn Dodgers.) Only swinging strikes counted. Called strikes did not enter the game until 1858 and called balls were an innovation of 1863.

12. *If a ball be struck, or tipped, and caught, either flying or on the first bound, it is a hand out.*

Almost from the beginning, skilled Knick players preferred the "fly rule" for match play; the one-bound catch was too easy (scorned by cricketers, who were the natural rivals and models for baseball players) and not "manly," especially on long drives to the outfield. While the fly rule became an option for the two captains of a match game, it was not universally adopted until 1865.

13. *A player running the bases shall be out, if the ball is in the hands of an adversary on the base, or the runner is touched with it before he makes his base; it being understood, however, that in no instance is a ball to be thrown at him.*

This rule forms the key distinction between the Knickerbocker game and other forms of base ball in which a base runner could be retired if a fielder hit him with the ball. This in turn permitted baseballs to be wound tighter around a harder core, like a cricket ball, and further permitted hits and throws for greater distance. By creating in effect a force play at all bases, with no need for a plug or tag, this rule restricted evasive maneuvers by the runners and moved baseball toward the serene formalism of cricket. In 1848 the rule was amended declaring that only at first base was the batter-runner out if the ball was held before he reached it. Perhaps tag plays had been thought too similar to the undignified plugging of earlier games. By the 1860s the emphasis of the new game would begin its long tectonic drift from a fielding/baserunning contest to a pitcher/batter conflict.

14. *A player running who shall prevent an adversary from catching or getting the ball before making his base, is a hand out.*
The interference rule, substantially unchanged today.

15. *Three hands out, all out.*
This rule is regarded as the essential point of the game of baseball as it is played today, though like the other rules recorded as of September 23, 1845, it is not a Knickerbocker innovation. In cricket, an entire side had to be put out for a change of innings. In round ball, the rule was "one out, all out."

16. *Players must take their strike in regular turn.*
Reasonable on its face. However, if the batter hit into a third out of an inning that was recorded by tagging one of the runners, the first batter of the following inning would be the one next in the batting order after the man put out. Thus, for example, if the last out were recorded in a force-out at home plate when the bases were full, the first batter in the club's next inning would be the man who had occupied second base and had been heading for third.

17. *All disputes and differences relative to the game, to be decided by the Umpire, from which there is no appeal.*
A rule observed largely in the breach, ever since umpire Eugene Plunkett fined Ebenezer R. Dupignac six cents "for saying s—t."

18. *No ace or base can be made on a foul strike.*
"Foul strike" must here be read as a "foul hit," as fouls did not count as strikes until the first decade of the twentieth century.

19. *A runner cannot be put out in making one base, when a balk is made by the pitcher.*
    The range of offenses that could merit a balk call in 1845 was huge, because of the severe restrictions on pitcher delivery. See Rule 9, for example.

20. *But one base allowed when a ball bounds out of the field when struck.*
    You are aware, surely, of the ground-rule double? Think of this as the ground-rule single. For years I had thought the intent of this rule was to keep the ball out of the river, which the Knickerbocker outfield adjoined, owing to the expense and difficulty of ball manufacture. Today, I am inclined to think that this rule reflects the wish that the hallmark of the New York game should be fielding, not running or batting or throwing.

The Knickerbockers played their first recorded game under their new rules on October 6, 1845. In this intrasquad game, seven Knickerbockers won 11–8 over seven of their fellows in three innings; the umpire was Wheaton, who had reduced the rules of the Gotham Club to writing in 1837. Clearly, nine men to the side and nine innings were not part of the 1845 rules, and the twenty-one aces (runs) feature could be ignored if so desired. Although they commenced formal play in brisk weather, the Knickerbockers managed to squeeze in fourteen games before shutting down to await April 1846 and the opening of a new season.

William H. Tucker, who in some unknown measure assisted Wheaton in laying down the Knickerbocker rules, played in ten of the fourteen contests, including the one on October 6, in which he scored three of the losing squad's eight runs. Like Wheaton and other Knickerbockers, he had been a player with the New York Ball Club and maintained a tie to them, indeed playing in two formal matches of the New Yorks with the Brooklyn Union Star Club on October 21 and 24 of 1845, a month after he had helped to form the Knicks. In a casual aside in his 1998 history of American cricket, Tom Melville pointed to an even earlier contest between these two clubs, on October 11, reported in the *New York Morning News*. Research more than a decade later has revealed a somewhat fuller account in the obscure and short-lived newspaper the *True Sun*:

> The Base Ball match between eight Brooklyn players, and eight players of New York, came off on Friday on the grounds of the Union Star Cricket Club. The Yorkers were singularly unfortunate in scoring but one run in their three innings. Brooklyn scored 22 and of course came off winners.
>
> After this game had been decided, a match at single wicket cricket came off between two members of the Union Star Club—Foster and Boyd. Foster scored 11 the first and 1 the second innings. Boyd came off victor by scoring 16 the first innings.

The Union Star players were cricketers, but so were many of the "Yorkers." Even though enough men were on hand to play regulation cricket (admittedly the sun may have been low), the selection for an ensuing game was one that pitted two skilled players against each other with a mutual complement in the field of five or fewer. The order, the science, and the character-building aspects of cricket made it forever England's national game, and today much of the world's, but it was the single wicket version, with its alacrity, its suitability to smaller sides, its wager-inspiring man-to-man quality, that made it attractive to baseball players and sporting men.

A further appeal of single wicket cricket for the unathletic and in some cases superannuated baseball players of the 1840s was that, unlike cricket or round ball, it embraced the concept of foul territory. The first rule of single wicket, as mandated by the Marylebone Club of London and reported in the *Anglo American* of July 22, 1843: "When there shall be less than five players on a side, bounds shall be placed twenty-two yards each in a line from the off and leg stump." Rule 2 commences: "The ball must be hit before the bounds to entitle the striker to a run. . . ." The remaining eight rules do not address this boundary. A response to inadequate numbers to patrol the field of the traditional game, this concept of foul territory went back long before 1843, as the laws of single wicket were a part of each cricket code from the first in 1744 (which survive only on a linen handkerchief at the Marylebone Cricket Club), until, in 1947, the provisions were dropped, for nary a man alive had played the game. We know that the 1744 rules were utilized for the great match in New York of April 29, 1751, for it was reported to have been played by the "London Method."

Major Rowland Francis Bowen, in his admirably quirky 1970 history of cricket, speculates about a possible eighteenth-century link between single wicket, rounders, and baseball. In single wicket, a batsman had to "get there and back" to score a run, traversing twice the ground required to score a run in the double-wicket game.

> Even now, in the ordinary game, one often sees batsmen running very wide and in single wicket, a somewhat circular, or oval, course can well have been followed instead of a dash and a sharp turn with the possibility of slipping. It is easy to imagine a development which would involve the batsman in running even wider, deliberately, round various objects such as stools, pickets (wickets)—or bases. Once that had occurred, "rounders" has arrived and, therefore, baseball.

As late as 1858, after the National Association of Base Ball Players had established rules to govern the play of baseball for the many clubs that had sprung up in the previous two years, Henry Chadwick proposed a radical change. He advocated narrowing the foul lines to form right angles to the pitcher, in other words, the side boundaries of single wicket.

In sum, both single wicket and the Knickerbocker game of ball adopted the notion of foul ground in deference to and/or expectation of limited available players. Further, the expectation of limited players by the Knickerbockers was often realized, not only in Adams' observation that baseball's demise was a near thing ("until 1850 . . . base ball had a desperate struggle for existence"), but also in the reality that, with the ever present threat of cholera's spread in warm weather, all Knicks who could do so fled the city in the dog days.

IF SINGLE WICKET SUPPLIES a possible missing link in baseball's evolution, another may be found closer to home. Until Randall Brown's notice of the Wheaton interview in a San Francisco newspaper in 1887, little had been known about either the New York Club or its earlier incarnation as the Gothams. Yet another mystery has remained ever since a first clue was revealed in the 1970s: the origin, laws, and playing rules of the Eagle Ball Club. An eight-page pamphlet entitled *By-laws and Rules of the Eagle Ball Club* (New York: Douglass & Colt, 1852) proclaims on its title page a founding date: Organized, 1840.

This claim is repeated in Eagle booklets of 1854 and 1858, even after they had reorganized as the Eagle *Base* Ball Club and had commenced match play against such clubs as the Knickerbocker and the Gotham at the Elysian Fields, which they took as their home grounds, if indeed they had not been there all along, before the Knickerbocker, New York, and Magnolia clubs. The latter two editions of the Eagle bylaws reflect the rules of baseball as they had been consolidated among the three clubs in response to a November 19, 1853, Eagle request to the Knickerbockers to clarify some finer points of their game. Clearly the Eagles had been playing ball, but it was a game in some respects different from the Knickerbocker model. And yet, in an account of a game between the clubs in 1856, a reporter for *Spirit of the Times* wrote: "The Eagle and the Knickerbocker, *old antagonists* [emphasis mine], played at Hoboken on Thursday. . . ."

Despite the Eagles' 1853 overture to the Knickerbockers requesting consolidation of the playing rules, the club's 1852 booklet provided rules and bylaws remarkably similar to those of the Knickerbockers, verbatim in many cases. The 1854 and 1858 editions, however, include along with the Knickerbocker-aligned rules a scaled diagram of the "Eagle Ball Club Bases," perhaps, as I had long suspected, *as they used to be.* Because we still know little to nothing about the Eagle Club's history prior to its joining the baseball fraternity in 1854, this diagram, I thought, might possess a unique archaeological quality, leaving us to infer from it, as much as from the glyph of Thutmose playing *seker-hemat*, what game was depicted and how it was played.

The implausible playing field, if taken literally, is a true diamond, that is, a lozenge shape with two acute angles and two obtuse ones, not just a rotated square. To the argument that this merely represents artistic license I could point out that all three Eagle booklets are printed in conventional portrait view, which easily would have accommodated the depiction of a playing field with equidistant sides, but the club and the printer for the 1854 and 1858 editions elected to depict the Eagle field in oblong or landscape view, the only page thus reoriented. Moreover, the Eagles thoughtfully provided a scale in which it may be seen that 1.625 inches precisely equals 42 paces, the latter a measure familiar from the earliest Knickerbocker rules as the distance between home plate and second base. The Knick rules also specify 42 paces as the distance between first and third bases, but this is not so in the Eagle diagram.

As it has turned out, however, the lozenge-shaped field with its 153-foot base paths was confirmed as a chimera only recently, by a heretofore impossible reading of the remarkable 1852 rules. The only Eagle booklet of that year known to scholars had been stolen from the New York Public Library more than thirty-five years ago, so no one could say what the club's preconsolidation playing rules were, that is, until another copy was revealed to reside (during the writing of this chapter!) in the Chicago History Museum. These rules specified base paths of forty-two paces equidistant between all bases.

Peculiar playing field or not, a schoolchild might wonder why there would be a common distance in two sets of rules independently arrived at, and why that distance should be forty-two paces rather than some other number. Is forty-two intended as a magic-number multiple (as in, twenty-one is lucky because it is the product of three and seven, so forty two must be doubly fortunate)? And that child might further ask, what was meant by a pace, anyhow?

It turns out that a square with sides of forty-two paces at the classic two-and-a-half-foot measure, producing 105 feet or thirty-five yards, is a quarter acre, very nearly on the button. An American or English-statute square of a full acre is almost 4,900 square yards, with equal sides of 70 yards, which equals 84 paces. In other words, this dimension would have been exceedingly familiar in America's antebellum period. Cricket, too, was played on a field with agrarian dimensions and so these vestiges of the country survived in the city *in its ball games*, both cricket and baseball.

As I argued in the previous chapter, the classical pace of two and a half feet was a more likely measure than the modern one of three feet, for the unathletic Knickerbockers, playing with a light, soft baseball that could not be hit or thrown very far, were unlikely to have commenced play in 1845 with baselines of nearly ninety feet.

For decades historian Ivor-Campbell and I had affably disputed the length of the pace. My belief had until very recently been that the Knicks intended the pace to be an imprecise measure (one that may be understood as roughly three feet, as Fred believed, or roughly two and a half feet, as I believed, depending upon who was doing the pacing), and that if they intended it to be a precise measure, then it would have been two and a half rather than three feet. Anecdotally, Fred was about six feet tall and had said that his comfortable walking stride was closer to three feet than to two and a half. At five feet ten inches, I politely disagreed and pointed out that the average male height c. 1845 would have been about five feet six inches.

Crucially, perhaps, Ivor-Campbell believed that a reference to "42 paces or yards" in a December 1856 number of *Spirit of the Times* that presented a diagram of the still new game of baseball à la New York served to equate the two measures. I believed the opposite: that the editors of that paper, in their attempt to describe the burgeoning game of baseball to those desirous of learning its intricacies, would not have supplied both measures (paces and yards) unless those were understood to signify *different* distances, for by 1856 the Knickerbockers and other major clubs may have been using forty-two yards while lesser clubs may have stayed with the less demanding forty-two paces.

Maybe the Putnam, Excelsior, Atlantic, Eckford, Empire, Mutual, and other clubs began play on fields that were nonstandard, or maybe they played by somewhat different rules. As these teams came to Hoboken to claim playing grounds and days for play in the early to mid-1850s, or established their own fields in Brooklyn or Harlem, a baseball version of the Tower of Babel may have begun to rise up. I suspect that it *did*, and that the multiple variations in styles of play, rules, and playing-field dimensions were what prompted the Eagles to request in 1853 that the Knickerbockers assist them in regularizing the new pastime. The Eagle rules at that time, for example, specified no way to end the game. There was no equivalent to Knickerbocker rule eight, which called for the winning team to amass twenty-one aces. It is likely, in my view, that the Knickerbockers added the twenty-one ace provision to their 1845 set of rules which otherwise they and the Eagles shared. It is also unlikely that the Eagles would have copied the Knickerbocker rules, deleted the twenty-one ace rule, then called for clarification and consolidation.

The Knickerbockers kept a game book to record their play, but the Eagles did, too; indeed, they mandated it as their fifth rule: "It shall be the duty of the Umpire to keep the game in a book prepared for that purpose . . ." Like the book of the Gothams, which survived at least into the 1850s, the Eagles' record is gone. However, if they predated the Knickerbockers in their organization, might they, like the New Yorks and Gothams, have shared a common founding after

1837? This is the year Wheaton wrote the rules that, he said fifty years later, were only barely changed for the Knickerbockers' use: "After the Gotham club had been in existence a few months it was found necessary to reduce the rules of the new game to writing. This work fell to my hands, and the code I then formulated is substantially that in use to-day."

Of the Eagles' twenty-one rules of 1852 (the Knicks had twenty), most are identical with those of their "pioneer" colleagues. When the Knickerbockers convened at Smith's Hotel, at that time located at 35 Howard Street, on April 1, 1854, for their annual meeting, "the committee on rules presented the following as having been arranged to govern the three clubs, viz. the Knickerbocker, Gotham, and Eagle." Newly consolidated rule one specified for the first time, if fuzzily, the pitching distance: "1. The bases shall be 'Home' to second base, forty-two paces; and from first to third base, forty-two paces, equidistant; and from Home to pitcher not less than fifteen paces." Newly consolidated rule two read: "The game to consist of twenty-one counts, or aces, but at the conclusion an equal number of hands must be played."

However, on the day after this meeting, a report in the weekly *Mercury* read: "There are now in this city three baseball clubs, namely the Gothams, the New Yorks and the Knickerbockers. Recently these clubs have adopted the same code of laws for playing, and they will doubtless have many friendly matches . . ." Did the paper's editor—pioneer baseball writer William Cauldwell, who was active before Chadwick—show his Freudian slip by equating the New Yorks with the Eagles?

At this same meeting, former Gotham Louis Fenn Wadsworth was proposed for membership in the Knickerbockers. Had he brought a diagram to the Elysian Fields in the fall of 1853, when the Knicks and Gothams played a match? Or would he do so in 1854, perhaps at his first practice as a Knickerbocker? Despite the impression today that the New York game was formed by 1845, there was still plenty of adjustment, as we have seen.

The stories of the Eagles, the New Yorks, and the Gothams were, respectively, unrecorded, misrepresented, and lost to history. Such powerfully influential figures as Wheaton, Wadsworth, and Adams went unrecognized in their lifetimes and became mysteries to future generations, while Cartwright was elevated from obscurity to symbolize the birth of the New York game. The structural as well as the social model that cricket supplied for New York's early baseball clubs was similarly downplayed. And there was another vexing baseball club prior to 1845, the Magnolia, that was completely written out of the history. One must ask, Why?

4
THE CAULDRON OF BASEBALL

While the Knickerbockers, Gothams, and Eagles fiddled with the rules and competed among themselves—often tepidly on the field and spiritedly off it in matters of courtliness, politeness, and banquets—baseball had already begun to move away from cricket notions of gentlemanly deportment. Long played by local rules, baseball was a rough and tumble game for boys, a holiday ritual for young men of the country flocking to town on July 4 or Election Day. In general, it was a fairly riotous affair marked by stinging throws to the ribs, taunts for poor performance, handsome prizes to the victors, and side bets galore. Compared to rural baseball, the chivalric courtliness that characterized early matches at Hoboken—a phony medievalism born of Walter Scott's *Ivanhoe*—seemed mere pomp and mummery. Emerson termed such displays "virtue gone to seed."

In short, most of American baseball in midcentury resembled cricket as it had existed in England more than a hundred years before, when it was just starting to make its way into the cities, when spectators were courted because gambling was at the core of the game's appeal. What made the sport popular, with players and public alike, were its medieval traces of martial risk, manly vigor, cathartic drama, and local bragging rights for the victors and their tribe. With countless variants of play and no nationally accepted rules, cricket in the 1730s could not yet lay claim to being the game for all England.

The scenario was similar for baseball during the sport's rise, but the story that has come down to us has been one of pristine amateurs cavorting on green fields for good fun and mild exercise in furtherance of "Uncle Samuel's sport," as Knickerbocker James Whyte Davis termed it in the 1850s. This prelapsarian state of baseball had its locus on the Elysian Fields of Hoboken, with the "fall"—induced by professionalism and gambling—attributed to the later entry of rowdy Brooklyn clubs and league play. But a national pastime could not emerge so gently from a rocking cradle. It would have to be forged in the heat of an urban sporting culture.

The Magnolia Ball Club of New York, and perhaps other clubs which have left no record, included shoulder hitters and fire laddies, Bowery Boys and ward heelers, Nativists and anti-Masons, brothel owners and saloonkeepers, sporting men and subterraneans, men who played the game not to rise above their social caste but to affirm it. Baseball was *their* game, too, as much as it belonged to Whiggish Knickerbockers or moralists like Henry Chadwick, who attempted to make baseball into an idealized cricket, covering up the roughhewn way in which both games had actually grown.

Play, as the province of children, is little documented; the same is true of adult exercise. When toys are added—implements such as bat and ball, or records such as notching scores on a stick or scribbling in club books—then play rises to the more formal level of a game. When spectators enter upon the scene, the urge to gamble may appear, leading to refinements of rules, introduction of statistics, and press accounts of the results. At this point the game has become a sport, and, when removed from the local scene to an urban center, it enlarges to become a spectacle. Until this last stage, when documentation tends to become ample, records fail to capture the passions of the age, and the modern historian is left to conjecture, from scraps of data, what the game was like when it was new. It is said in folklore circles that when a custom is too old for its origins to be remembered, a story is often devised to rationalize what would otherwise be baffling. Such has been the case with baseball.

I suggest that three essential ingredients facilitate the growth of any localized game to national sport. *First, gambling.* Adults must care about the outcome, and their willingness to place a wager is a reasonable measure of their interest. As a game matures, investors and civic boosters may pool their interests in order to absorb a greater risk, placing their bets on the protracted success of a club or a ball grounds. *Second, statistics.* Whether merely game scores or primitive box scores, these numerical attachments to prose accounts accord a mantle of importance to the matches, an importance like that of trade or transport or government; in addition, quantifying the game's constituent parts further fuels the first mover of sport, gambling. *Third, publicity.* Regular press coverage is a necessary development to convey the enthusiasm exhibited at a single contest, however it may have been fueled, to those only reading about it afterward, often at great distance from the event.

Before baseball came to dominate the sporting scene in the last quarter of the nineteenth century, these three elements had previously advanced the popularity of other sports: the turf, the ring, sculling, cricket, and the pit (blood sports such as ratting, baiting, cockfighting, and dog fighting). Whether the crowd drawn by the activity was low or genteel, the ingredients and the progression were similar. American sporting papers, beginning in the 1820s, paved the way for each sport to mature by providing records and prognostications related to events of interest to the sporting set and, underlying it all, the basis of a potential wager.

New York was all about money, and to engage in twice-weekly pastoral recreation was, for the Hoboken travelers especially, a declaration by the participants that they had money enough to buy leisure. To play ball irregularly, spontaneously, without proprietary grounds or press notices, was left to workingmen who simply liked the game for its spirit of camaraderie, enhanced by chowder and grog (upscale political chowders might be accompanied by claret). "Chowder was the national soup," wrote Herbert Asbury, "and in those times chowder was to be more eaten than drunk, for it was not the anaemic liquid which now sloshes so despairingly in restaurant bowls, but a thick and substantial mixture, compounded of eels, fish, clams, lobster, chicken, duck, and all kinds of tempting ingredients. No social function was complete without a great dish of chowder."

As the New York game rose, eventually to surpass variant games of baseball and cricket, both long established in America, the issues of inclusion and exclusion that have perplexed the nation since its beginning cropped up in baseball as well. Would workingmen be welcome in addition to gentlemen? What about professional players? Immigrants? African Americans? Women? Would the values of baseball come to symbolize America, as those of cricket had for England and the Empire?

Professionalism emerged in the 1850s as *revolving* (moving from one club to another for no obvious reason, from which an observer might infer proffered benefits). By 1870 pay-for-play was the fork in the road to baseball's future. Immigrants, especially the Irish, had expressed their determination to be American by playing baseball from the 1840s on; before long they would come to dominate league play. African Americans organized ball clubs in the North by 1859 and likely played bat and ball games much earlier, even in the time of slavery. Women formed a baseball club at Vassar College in 1866 and in the years that followed provided a rich alternative on-field history through novelty nines, barnstorming clubs, and active amateur play. They were prized as spectators at early matches because it was thought they lent tone and decorum to a game that otherwise might produce, in heated moments, unseemly verbal and physical displays.

In medieval matches between squadrons representative of larger armies, shires, or even nations, the chivalric stake was not money but honor. This explains not only the long resistance of baseball to the onset of professionals but also the affiliation of the earliest ball clubs with firehouses, political parties, and professions. The famous New York Mutuals arose from the Mutual Hook and Ladder Company #1 and later, by throwing games, became synonymous with the corruption associated with one of the club's officers, Boss Tweed. A baseball club formed by doctors was called the Aesculapians. Literature gave us the Pequods of New London, Connecticut; the Hiawathas of Kittanning, Pennsylvania; and the Mohicans of Hightstown, Maryland. The Knickerbockers and Excelsiors were Whiggish; the Atlantics were Democrats. Social factionalism and the passions of politics, with a real or perceived relation to a "prince"—the head of city, state, party, or ward—bound members to their clubs and to one another.

For a club thus aligned with a greater entity or cause, selecting a first nine to represent them in a match against a rival nine—in other words, the very concept of team sports—likewise had its roots in the dim past. In the Roman circus, chariot teams wore colors representing the aspirations of different social classes. "In the wars of the fifteenth century," wrote Johan Huizinga in *The Waning of the Middle Ages,* "and even later, the custom of two captains or two equal groups to appoint meetings for a fight, in sight of the two armies, was still kept up. The Combat of the Thirty has remained the celebrated type of these fights. It was fought in 1351 at Plöermel, in Brittany, between the French of Beaumanoir and a company of thirty men, English, German, and Bretons, under a certain Bamborough."

ALL OF THESE CROSSCURRENTS, from notions of sublimated risk to courtly engagement, from the "scourge" of gambling to conflicts of race, class, ethnicity, and political leanings, were present at the Elysian Fields of the 1840s. It is sometimes stated that early baseball provided a cultural bridge between artisanal and bourgeois cultures. Not so, and the Magnolia Ball Club provides the proof.

In 2007, rummaging through the classified advertisement section of the *New York Herald* of November 2, 1843, looking for who knows what, I was astonished to find a notice for a baseball club unrecorded in the annals of the game. Moreover, the notice made clear that this city-based club played its games across the Hudson River at the Elysian Fields, almost two full years before the formation of the "pioneer" Knickerbockers and their lease of playing grounds at Hoboken. This half-inch notice in the *Herald* has yielded clues to a much larger story about how the early game was in fact shaped, not only by young bachelors looking for a game to rival cricket, but also by the working class, the sporting culture, the sensationalist or *flash* news weeklies—named for perhaps the seamiest of such papers, *The Flash*—intended for sporting men, and the teeming political factions of New York City in the 1840s. The diminutive ad in the *Herald,* which also ran in the *Sun,* read in full:

> **NEW YORK MAGNOLIA BALL CLUB**-Vive la Knickerbocker.- A meeting of the members of the above club will take place this (Thursday) afternoon, 2nd instant, at the Elysian Fields, Hoboken.

It is earnestly requested that every member will be present, willing and eager to do his duty. Play will commence precisely at one o'clock. Chowder at 4 o'clock.
JOHN McKIBBIN, Jr., President.
JOSEPH CARLISLE, Vice President
ANDREW LESTER, Sec.
n2 1t*m

The coding at the bottom signaled that the ad was to appear one time only (1t), with that occasion being game day, November 2 (n2). While this may strike modern eyes as a late month for a baseball game, the baseball season of this era typically ran to the very end of November, in part because August, with its fevers and contagions, was regarded as unsuitable for exertion. The mention of "chowder" signaled the almost sacramental union of those assembled, partaking of food from a single pot. The chowder was a fixture of political rallies, too; the city's first target company, arising from the butcher stalls at the westside Washington Market, was named the Washington Market Chowder Club; its early founding is confirmed by the survival of a silver member's badge bearing the date 1818 (which recently sold for nearly $50,000 at auction).

Of the named officers, the Irish-born president, twenty-nine-year-old John McKibbin Jr., was a U.S. inspector, a patronage position perhaps obtained through the good offices of his father, who in an aldermanic stroke of fortune in 1835 had been named the city's first superintendent of pavements. Seven years after calling the Magnolia Ball Club to muster and chowder, the younger McKibbin was a resident of Sing Sing, convicted of bigamy.

The vice president and actual leader of the club, Joseph Carlisle, was the twenty-six-year-old proprietor of the Magnolia Lunch and Saloon at 74 Chambers Street, corner of Broadway, offering "the best of Wines, Liquors, Segars, and every other requisite." Why was this Northern eatery named for a flower symbolic of the South? Perhaps to signal to the sporting crowd that this was a full-service house of the sort pleasing to Southerners in New York on business, and to the gamblers who left New Orleans for the riverboats after the Crescent City banned their trade in 1835.

That this establishment was not merely an eating house but also one of assignation may be further divined from an even more direct notice that ran in the July 30, 1842, issue of the *Whip*, a prominent flash paper.

> MAGNOLIA LUNCH
> CORNER OF BROADWAY AND CHAMBER [sic] STREET
> This establishment, since it has fallen into the hands of the undersigned, has been entirely refitted in the most costly and elegant manner. Splendid oil cloths have been laid upon the floors; the Bar is stored with liquors of the most extravagant kinds. The saloon where ladies and gentlemen can enjoy a choice supper in the most private manner, has been enlarged, and the whole newly furnished. The new entrance for gentlemen accompanied by ladies is kept strictly from the intrusion of others, and the following delicacies of the market will be kept constantly on hand: Woodcock, Plover, Snipe, Quail, Lobster, soft-shell Crabs, Beef Steaks, Mutton Chops, Veal Cutlets, and other rarities as well as the substantials of all hours at moderate prices. Servants expressly to carry refreshments to private residences.
> CHICKERING & CARLISLE

Flash papers—with titles like the *Rake*, the *Sporting Whip*, *Venus's Miscellany*, and, eponymously, the *Flash*, covered the ring, the turf, aquatics, pedestrianism, badger baiting, and dog fights . . . all the sports designed for betting. Importantly for our understanding of baseball in the context of the time, these papers did not cover the pre-1845 game because there was as yet no money to be made from it. Sports formed only a sideline for the publishers of these ragged weeklies, whose common practice was outwardly to denounce vice while surreptitiously propagating it, providing names, addresses, specialties, and prices of brothels and their residents. The life stories of celebrity courtesans or *sports* seemed to hold a special fascination (a best-selling *Police Gazette* booklet as late as the 1880s was *The Female Sports of New York by One of Them*). The *Sunday Flash*, for instance, ran an eighteen-part series called "Lives of the Nymphs," with each part a biographical portrait of a prominent New York prostitute. Titillation was the selling principle, but as limited-circulation weeklies, the flash papers stood little chance of turning a profit from subscriptions or newsboy sales; their principal business, ultimately revealed through libel suits and ensuing transcripts of the court proceedings, was the extortion of prominent or wealthy citizens caught in public with women of questionable virtue: Their choice was to pay the editors or find themselves the talk of the town.

In the rampant sporting culture of the day, Carlisle was an up-and-comer who went on to run, in addition to the Magnolia Lunch, the Fountain at 167 Walker Street near the Bowery, the Ivy Green in Hoboken, and an unnamed sporting house at 89 Centre Street opposite the Tombs, the city's Egyptianate prison, where all the while he double-dipped as a jailer. The Magnolia Ball Club secretary, Andrew Lester, was a twenty-seven-year-old billiard-room proprietor and Tammany Democrat, linked with Isaiah Rynders' Empire Club, the pugilistic arm of the party (which also gave its name to a baseball club in 1854), enforcing discipline on the rank and file and striking fear into undecided voters.

All three Magnolia officers had impeccable working-class, sporting, ruffian, and political associations of the sort that historians have until now presumed to emerge only with the unruly Brooklyn clubs of the mid-1850s, notably the Atlantics. Indeed, the Magnolia was precisely the sort of poison for which the fastidious Knickerbocker Base Ball Club was created as an antidote two years later.

THE NEW YORK BALL Club settled into its Elysian Fields site at about the same time as the Magnolia. It has enjoyed enduring fame as the loosely organized club that pounded the Knickerbockers in that club's first match game, 23–1. Because the New Yorks and the Magnolias both relocated from New York to Hoboken in November 1843, we may reasonably suppose that they played a highly similar game of ball. Yet there had been no mention of the Magnolias in print beyond the classified advertisement pointing to their brief day in the sun amid the leafy bowers of Hoboken. Did the less than savory backgrounds of the Magnolia officers contribute to the club's near disappearance from the historical record?

Parsing the Magnolia Ball Club ad of November 2, 1843, one wonders why it would contain the curious phrase *Vive la Knickerbocker.* These were Irishmen, after all, not Dutch patroons, and they had little claim to the eighteenth century gentility of Diedrich Knickerbocker's New York. The phrase stimulates a whirl of speculation. Certainly the Magnolia motto is not a reference to the Knickerbocker Base Ball Club, whose formation was two years in the offing. Nor is it likely that at this late date it was a fervid bouquet tossed to Washington Irving, whose *History of New York* (1809) had been published long before.

Might *Vive la Knickerbocker* have been a nod to firebrand labor leader and land-reform proponent Mike Walsh, founder in early 1843 of the *Knickerbocker*, one of the many flash papers launched early in the decade? But Walsh's *Knickerbocker* seems to have been produced to only a single number, and no copy has survived. Even if the Magnolias were not lifting glasses or sitting down to chowder in honor of Walsh's *Knickerbocker*, their sympathies were surely with him, and his with them and their ballplaying efforts, as we shall see. In that same year he had regrouped to create another weekly called *The Subterranean*, which had a longer life and an ardent audience of underworld denizens: *subterraneans* or *subs*, as they dubbed themselves. Walsh was the enemy of the powerful, an idol of the masses, a declared pal of both Carlisle and Lester of the Magnolia, a regular patron at the Magnolia Lunch, and a puff reviewer of its culinary fare. Additionally, his *Subterranean* provided the perfect demographic audience for Carlisle's regular ads.

Walsh and the flash press provided plausible linkages with the character of the Magnolia Ball Club, but still I was left with no convincing explanation for what was meant by *Vive la Knickerbocker*. As soon as I saw the Magnolia Ball Club ad in the *Herald* I recalled that some months earlier, historian David Block had pointed me to a puzzling image, one he thought might be suitable to illustrate a scholarly journal article on town ball. Offered as Lot 1600 in a Leland's auction of December 2002, the item was described as a

> . . . signed copper plate engraving of the quality of paper money. The card itself is a heavy stock with a silver mirror finish. This invitation to the '1st Annual Ball of the Magnolia Ball Club' measures 5 x 3.25 [inches]. The image is magnificent. It shows the plantation like Magnolia Club with its main building and a yacht flying the 'M' flag. Half the image is a richly detailed state-of-the-art baseball game in progress. The players are wearing long pants, there are wickets instead of bases, the catcher stands steps behind the batter with no equipment (pre-mask and shin guards) and catches the ball on one bounce. The engraving is signed 'Eng. By W. Fairthorne.' Fairthorne worked in New York City

starting in 1839 until the time of his death in 1853, thereby, dating the piece from that 1839–53 time period. Finally, Magnolia is an area in southern New Jersey and the site of many stately plantations not unlike the one illustrated here.

In a *eureka* moment, I realized that I knew for certain what that plantationlike building was. It was the Colonnade at the Elysian Fields, also known as the Colonnade Hotel or McCarty's Hotel, whose proprietor provided the Knickerbockers and other clubs with many a lavish dinner, either after their exertions on the ball field or in a season-ending banquet. Built in the early 1830s, this structure survived into the 1890s. The body of water in the image is the North River.

Moving on to William Fairthorne, the auction description was correct as far as it went, but did not touch upon the fellow's brushes with the law for counterfeiting or his management of the Lafayette Gentlemen's and Ladies' Oyster Saloon at 38 Division Street, east of the Bowery and the infamous Five Points slum. By 1838, William Fairthorne, whose very name may have been a work of art or artifice, adopted as a pseudonym in honor of the notable English engraver of that name (1616–1691), had settled in with wife Hannah at his New York City home at 68 Nassau Street, with a workplace at 350 Houston Street. On February 17, 1839, the *New York Spectator* offered this police report: "A Mr. Fairthorne, an engraver, was arrested some days ago, and yesterday examined, as a suspected accomplice of Conner, the counterfeiter, forger, and alterer of bank notes. The examination resulted so strongly in his favor, that he was held to bail only in the sum of $500. . . ." Recalling that in those days "a dollar a day was very good pay," the *Spectator* was ladling out the irony generously. Now, in addition to the questionable virtues of Messrs. McKibbin, Carlisle, and Lester, we add a forger to the Magnolia mix. Was he also a member of the ball club? His verisimilitude as an engraver might make one think so; he was, as far as may be claimed at this writing, the first man ever to have depicted men playing baseball . . . and if we may judge by the textual record of the early game, he appears to have got things largely right. (Of course the vignette could not display all the features of the game, and thus does not address plugging, or foul ground.)

The auction-house description erred further in calling the Magnolia card an invitation. It was in fact, as further digging in the *Herald* revealed, a ticket providing admission to a ball that would be held on Friday evening February 9, 1844. It cost a dollar and, given its enamel-coated card stock and its commissioned rather than stock imagery, was likely intended to be saved as a memento of the event. The baseball scene on the card reveals three bases with stakes (not wickets), eight men in the field, a pitcher with an underarm delivery, possibly base-stealing, and a top-hatted waiter bearing a tray of refreshments from the Colonnade. Some of the members of the "in" side are arrayed behind a long table; others are seated upon it. The pitcher delivers the ball. A runner heads from first to second base. This is, from all appearances, the original Knickerbocker game, and that of the New York Base Ball Club, and that of the Gothams of the 1830s (shortstop was a position not manned until 1849–50), as discussed earlier.

This ticket is the first depiction of men playing baseball in America, and it may also be, depending upon one's taxonomic convictions, the first baseball card. It is also the earliest visual artifact of the New York game of baseball. But the greater significance of the card is the new understanding that its underlying story affords of how baseball really began in New York, what spin the workingman's culture of that day may have imparted to baseball's growth, and why the story may have been kept under wraps all these years.

Mike Walsh's best friend in the Red Rover fire company was Dave Broderick, a granite-cutter by trade who in 1840 opened a saloon on the corner of Commerce and Barrow streets that soon became the resort of such well known brawlers as Yankee Sullivan and John Morrissey. Once Walsh, also a saloon regular, commenced publishing the *Subterranean*, Broderick renamed his establishment for the weekly and its foursquare support of workingmen. Broderick had an easygoing manner that enabled him to move among the contending political and pugilistic factions, standing at the bar of the original Ivy Green at Elm Street when it was the favorite den of Rynders and his Tammany-affiliated Empire Club, or at the Comet on Mott Street when it was the headquarters of pugilist Tom Hyer and his Whig-supported Knickerbocker Club (yes, this name that we associate with a baseball club was first used by a bunch of street ruffians who, for complex reasons, supported the party of Henry Clay and Daniel Webster). It was a short walk from these saloons to either of the rival clubhouses, as the two flanked the old Park Theatre. As Edward van Every wrote, "the flagstones of Park Row were often thumped mercilessly with the brawny carcasses of the combatants."

As the largest social club in the land, the 20,000-strong Knickerbocker Club must have been the intended honoree of the phrase in the Magnolias' ad of November 2, 1843, *Vive la Knickerbocker.* This Knickerbocker Club, until now invisible to baseball's historians, was a band of upwardly mobile young Whigs that held rallies, sang songs, and backed the Whig ticket in expectation of victory and its spoils. This militant bunch had arisen from a pacific literary and political tradition, born at the Shakespeare Tavern at Fulton and Nassau streets in the 1820s. There De Witt Clinton dreamed up his plan for the Erie Canal, mixing with literary types from Fitz-Greene Halleck to James K. Paulding to Willis Gaylord Clark, editor of the *Knickerbocker Magazine.* Erected many years before the Revolution, the Shakespeare Tavern endured to 1836, when its last proprietor, James C. Stoneall, oversaw its demolition and relocated his clientele to a new place of his own.

On October 16, 1844, as reported in the *New York News,* a sailor named Daniel O'Connor was invited into the Knickerbocker Club for a friendly drink. "After drinking, some of the Club began singing a coon song in which O'Connor declined joining. By doing this he gave offence and a quarrel ensued, and O'Connor was set upon, overpowered by numbers, thrown down, trampled upon, and had his leg broken; and was afterwards thrown out upon the sidewalk; and left to crawl toward the stoop of the [Park] Theatre, where he was found and carried to the Hospital."

In those superheated days, antiblack sentiment was no more virulent than anti-Irish: The establishment lumped the two together as a permanent underclass. Even Henry David Thoreau wrote in his journal, "The question is whether you can bear freedom. At present the vast majority of men, whether black or white, require the discipline of labor which enslaves them for their good. If the Irishman did not shovel all day, he would get drunk and quarrel." Such was the climate when baseball arose to relieve equally the cares of both aristos and proles.

If Mike Walsh was not actually a member of the mongrel Magnolia Ball Club—it cannot be confirmed—he ought to have been. In the *Subterranean* of October 25, 1845, the day the press reported on the Brooklyn and New York clubs' second match game, he wrote: "Three different parties of whole-souled fellows are going to express their gratitude to Heaven for its manifold blessings, to-morrow [a Sunday], by playing ball and eating chowder. They could not have selected a more appropriate and sensible method of doing it, as a man is never on so good terms with his God and fellow men, as when he is enjoying himself in a healthy and rational manner." These games and chowders went unreported.

With proponents of red-blooded ball play such as this, in a raucous and violent era such as this, and with the prospect of the wrong sort of people (the Magnolias) creating a national pastime, fastidious chroniclers of the game elected to start baseball's Book of Genesis with the Knickerbocker Base Ball Club. One may only wonder whether it rankled these baseball progenitors to share their game as well as their name with a bunch of ruffians.

As it turns out, the men of the Knickerbocker Base Ball Club, including their most famous member, were not always gentlemen, either. The *New York Morning Express* of September 6, 1848, reported an "Outrageous Assault":

> INTERESTING AFFAIR.—Yesterday afternoon a scene occurred at the Lower Police Court, in consequence of constable Barber having been deputed to arrest four individuals of genteel appearance, and not altogether unknown in the City as William J. Moorehead of No. 182 Broadway, Alexander Cartwright, Jr., John M. Crowell, and a person named — Brown, on a charge of having been concerned in the commission of a violent assault and battery on James H. Hutchings, at the Franklin House. It appears from the complaint of Hutchings, that the implicated parties accused him of having uttered some remarks reflecting upon the character of a young lady, and after threatening to do him great violence unless he apologized for what he had said, Cartwright seized him by the throat, shook him very violently and kicked him in the presence of Moorehead, who aided and abetted Cartwright in his assault, and that Crowell subsequently, in the presence of Brown also, beat him and bit one of his fingers in a savage manner. Justice Timpson, after hearing the case, held the parties to keep the peace.

Nor was the Knicks' sylvan setting in Hoboken immune from violence. On May 26, 1851, the Elysian Fields was the scene of what the *Brooklyn Eagle* described as

> . . . one of the most earnest and angry promiscuous fights that has ever occurred in this country. The Germans of this city, with their families, assembled in large numbers in Hoboken, for the celebration of their Maifest. Scarcely two hours had elapsed when they were set upon by a party of [Irish] rascals called "Short Boys."
>
> At first the Germans were disposed to avoid a conflict, but finding it impossible to do so, they sallied out against them, and drove them to the Elysian Fields. The Short Boys took refuge in a house kept by one McCarthy, which was attacked by the Germans, and [were] greatly injured. McCarthy, in defense of himself and his house, shot two of the Germans with a double barreled gun, killing them, it is said.

Hotel proprietor "McCarthy" was the previously mentioned McCarty, and his "house" was the Colonnade, depicted in the Magnolia illustration. McCarty shot either one or two Germans, depending upon the paper one read. New York's *Journal of Commerce* blamed the whole affray on inebriated Germans who, upon being denied liquor by said McCarty, commenced to riot, injuring him, his wife, and their lame child, in addition to wrecking his hotel. The Hoboken police, preponderantly Irish, went so far as to deputize the Short Boys to arrest the Germans. Less than a year later, hotelier Michael McCarty took his own life.

On the very day of the riot, the Knickerbockers had come to the Elysian Fields to play ball, as was their custom on Monday, one of two appointed days of play each week. Their game book entry ends abruptly, however, with the Blacks leading the Whites 14–2 after four completed innings, in a seven-on-seven intramural game. The bottom of the scoresheet bears this terse notation: "Broke up by the Dutch [German] Fight."

Thus did violence begin to intrude upon the Elysian Fields. But baseball's early home was soon to be replaced by Central Park for fresh air and fashionable strolls; for more robust entertainment, New Yorkers would soon begin to watch baseball in enclosed ballparks in Brooklyn and circuses in Manhattan amphitheaters, for example Franconi's Hippodrome and Barnum's Madison Square Garden.

Popular culture—entertainment high and low—rises from the bottom if it is to gather the strength needed to endure. It does not start at the top of the social ladder and then descend. Despite its time-honored history as a country sport adopted by genteel fellows who loved fair play and fine manners, baseball flowered because of the rich soil from which it emerged. Gambling was not the impediment to the game's flowering but instead the vital fertilizer. Baseball was "our cricket," indeed, but not in the serene and stately ways that Henry Chadwick had more or less invented for his American audience.

THAT EARLY CRICKET, LIKE all public sport, was driven by gambling is evident in this condemnation of the game from the *British Champion* of September 8, 1743. It is offered at some length for its striking implications for baseball and America a century later:

> All Diversions, all Exercises, have certain bounds as to Expence, and when they exceed this, it is an Evil in itself, and justly liable to Censure. Upon what Reasons are all the Laws against Gaming founded? Are not these the chief, that they break in upon Business, expose People to great Dangers, and cherish a Spirit of Covetousness, in a way directly opposite to Industry? The most wholesome Exercise, and the most innocent Diversion may change its Nature entirely, if People, for the Sake of gratifying their Humour, keep unfit Company.
>
> I have been led into these Reflections, which are certainly just in themselves, by some odd Stories I have heard of Cricket Matches, which I own, however, to be so strange and so incredible, that if I had not received them from Eye-Witnesses, I could never have yielded to them any Belief.
>
> Is it not a very wild Thing to be as serious in making such a Match as in the most material Occurrences in Life? Would it not be extremely odd to see Lords and Gentlemen, Clergymen and Lawyers, associating themselves with Butchers and Cobblers in Persuit [sic] of these Diversions? Or can there be anything more absurd, than making such Matches for the sake of profit, which is to be shared amongst People so remote in their Quality and Circumstances?
>
> Cricket is certainly a very innocent, and wholesome Exercise; yet, it may be abused, if either great or little People make it their Business. It is grossly abused, when it is made the Subject of publick Advertisements, to draw together great Crowds of People, who ought all of them to be somewhere else. . . .

> The Diversion of Cricket . . . draws Numbers of people from their Employments, to the Ruin of their Families. It brings together Crowds of Apprentices and Servants, whose Time is not their own. It propagates a Spirit of Idleness, at a Juncture, when, with the utmost Industry, our Debts, Taxes, and Decay of Trade, will scarce allow us to get Bread. It is a most notorious Breach of the Laws, as it gives the most open Encouragement to Gaming; the Advertisements most impudently reciting that great Sums are laid; so that some People are so little ashamed of breaking the Laws they had a Hand in making, that they give publick Notice of it.*
>
> **The Advertisements are publish'd, it is supposed, by the Alehouse- or Ground-keepers, for their own Profit.*

The mania for gambling in mid-eighteenth century England permeated all strata of society, with huge public wagers placed on walking contests, competitions in absurdity of costume, and skill in identifying Latin quotations. Yet cosmopolitan gambling may have been the safety valve for tensions that in other times had led to violence. Gambling was regarded as an honorable, secondary level of risk—akin to the designation of "teams" to wage battle instead of entire armies, as in the fourteenth century's Combat of the Thirty.

By the 1870s, wagermania had retreated to its earlier prime arenas, principally sports and horseracing. Cricket re-emerged as the sport most amenable to wagers, and newspapers began to post odds and betting tips. Thus they were as vital to gambling as the creation of national rules for its play had been, in the 1730s, to ensure gambling practices free from dispute. As Anthony Bateman observed:

> The result was to begin to standardise the way the sport was played and, although not the prime intention, ensure that it could be disseminated and practiced uniformly on a national basis. Once this process of dissemination had begun to occur, and once cricket became the object of literary attention in the context of a widely expanding national print culture, the way was clear for it to be redefined in the interests of nationalism.

Might cricket's inadvertent path to becoming England's national game, with rules codified to enable efficient wagering, have been the same low road by which baseball became our national pastime? Despite condemnations from the pulpit, gambling was as American as apple pie and baseball. "Those who live in the midst of democratic fluctuations have always before their eyes the image of chance," Tocqueville wrote, "and they end by liking all undertakings in which chance plays a part."

Until the 1840s, baseball, even when played by grown men, was merely a game. Helping to smooth its entrance into the sporting culture was the rule that a game would be played to a conclusion of at least twenty-one aces in equal innings; although the term *notch* or *run* had been the standard for a scoring event in cricket, baseball looked instead to the card table and the domino circle for its counter: the ace. A simple box score, the game's first, accompanied the *New York Herald* account of the Brooklyn–New York contest of October 21, 1845. As I wrote in *The Hidden Game of Baseball* more than twenty-five years ago:

> The infant game became quantified in part to ape the custom of its big brother, cricket; yet the larger explanation is that the numbers served to legitimize men's concern with a boys' pastime. The pioneers of baseball reporting—William Cauldwell of the *Sunday Mercury*, William Porter of *Spirit of the Times*, the unknown ink-stained wretch at the *Herald*, and later Father Chadwick—may indeed have reflected that if they did not cloak the game in the "importance" of statistics, it might not seem worthwhile for adults to read about, let alone play.

Not visible to me at that time was the spur that gambling provided not only to the formation of standardized rules but also to the development of statistical measures. In the evolution of baseball and its bevy of associated numbers, no figure was more important than Henry Chadwick. In 1856, by which time he had been a cricket reporter for a decade or so, his eyes were opened to the possibilities in the American game:

> . . . on returning from the early close of a cricket match on Fox Hill, I chanced to go through the Elysian Fields during the progress of a contest between the noted Eagle and Gotham Clubs. The game was being sharply played on both sides, and I watched it with deeper interest than any previous ball match between clubs that I had seen. It was

> not long before I was struck with the idea that base ball was just the game for a national sport for Americans . . . as much so as cricket is for England. At the time I refer to . . . I began to invent a method of giving detailed reports of leading contests at base ball, and, seeing that every thing connected with the game, almost, was new, its rules crude and hastily prepared, with no systematized plan of recording the details of a game, and, in fact, no fixed method of either playing or scoring it, as soon as I became earnestly interested in the subject I began to submit amendments to the rules of the game to the consideration of the fraternity, generally in the form of suggestions through the press, my first improvement introduced being an innovation on the simple method of scoring then in vogue. Step by step, little by little, either directly or indirectly, did I succeed in assisting to change the game from the almost simple field exercise it was some twenty years ago up to the manly, scientific game of ball it is now.

Thus did Chadwick's cricket background shape his method of scoring a baseball game, the format of his early box scores, and the copious if primitive statistics that appeared in his year-end summaries in the *New York Clipper* and *Beadle's Dime Base-Ball Player.* While it may fairly be said that his influence on baseball's statistical record is enormous, his impact on the development of its rules and reporting was less than he liked to state. And clearly he was oblivious to the fact that while he was submitting innovations for "the consideration of the fraternity," he was helping to enhance the game for the gambling faction against which he would rail for decades thereafter. (It was said that Chadwick hoped to clean up baseball as his knighted half brother Edwin, through the Metropolitan Commission of Sewers, had cleaned up London.)

No ball club from the 1840s owed anything to Chadwick's innovations; although he had reported on cricket for a variety of papers since 1843, including the *Long Island Star* and *Spirit of the Times,* he was a journalist for hire in that decade and appears to have earned more of his daily bread as an instructor in music and a composer/arranger of sheet-music quadrilles and schottisches. He did not commence to report regularly on baseball until 1858, when the *Clipper* hired him to replace William H. Bray, the paper's first reporter of field sports.

Chadwick was baseball's greatest booster, but he was not its first.

That honor would go to William Cauldwell, who stated to the Mills Commission in 1905:

> I may say that I can speak as a New York boy from away back and in all my experiences I had no knowledge of the prominence of a ball game called "rounders." I played ball in my native city from the time I was (to use an old time phrase) "knee high to a mosquito" dating back to a period when Fourteenth Street was considered out of town, and I can speak from what I know. The game of ball in early days was very simple in its make-up. Anybody could play it; but of course some would play it better than others. . . .

Like Chadwick, Cauldwell was born in 1824. He would have played ball in lower Manhattan, for he went to primary school at the High School for Males, at No. 36 Crosby near Broome Street. In 1833, this building was transformed into a hospital to aid in the cholera epidemic, no doubt impelling his mother to send him south to Louisiana for his continuing education. He returned north a decade later and in 1848 moved to Morrisania, at that time in Westchester County but today a part of the Bronx, where a few years later he played ball with the newly formed Union Club. As editor of the weekly *Sunday Mercury*, Cauldwell made mention of baseball on May 1, 1853, and later that year devoted space to the Knickerbocker-Gotham match of July. David J. McAuslan, who wrote about baseball for the *Brooklyn Times* in the era of Cauldwell and Chadwick, emphasized for the Mills Commission that Chadwick was not the first baseball reporter. There were, he declared,

> many other reporters ahead of him, notably the State Senator William Cauldwell, the owner of the old *Sunday Mercury*, that did more for the advancement for the progress [sic] of the game in its infancy than any publication ever printed. Chadwick saw his opportunity, stuck to his reporting, made money out of it and forced him [sic] through his writings in the *Clipper* and the Brooklyn *Eagle* to be the sole authority on the game. He was no ways backward in doing so, at the same time he was not liked by other reporters, who were confined to half a dozen lines by the morning papers. I then reported base ball for the *Brooklyn Times* and had many tilt[s] with the father of the game.

As Chadwick was not the first to cover baseball, neither was the *New York Clipper.* Although it carried a report of the Knickerbocker-Gotham game in July 1853, its first year of operation, it was not the first paper to do so. The *Clipper* was never all about baseball, or even primarily so. More than any other publication, it may be said to have transformed a boys' game into the national pastime. But there were other sporting papers that preceded it.

Founded in 1831 by the aptly named William Trotter Porter, the *Spirit of the Times* was a high-toned weekly of horse literature and southwestern wit. Porter pitched his paper to "gentlemen of standing, wealth and intelligence, the very Corinthian columns of the community," rather than the crowd attracted by sensationalistic sheets like the *Flash* or the *Police Gazette* (of which outlaw Jesse James was a noteworthy subscriber).

Spirit of the Times began to cover cricket in 1837 (a match between elevens from Schenectady and Albany). Not until July 9, 1853, however, did it give notice to a baseball match, the one played between the Knickerbocker and Gotham clubs on July 5—the same one noted in the fledgling *Clipper* one week later. Over the next few years, however, the *Spirit* would cover baseball much more assiduously than the *Clipper.* For a long time after it launched, the *Clipper* was seen as a cousin of the flash weeklies rather than as a competitor to *Spirit of the Times.* But it was the editor and founder of the *Clipper,* Frank Queen, who realized early on that what people wanted was the likenesses of their darlings. The age of heroes in baseball was nigh.

5
WAR IN HEAVEN

In the decade or so before the Knicks, Eagles, and Gothams conformed their rules in 1854, almost all baseball games were intramural affairs. Which team won was of little concern; the aim was vigorous if inconclusive play. For its urban devotees with pale faces and narrow chests, baseball at the Elysian Fields was a return to the rustic game of earlier days, now promoted as a field exercise, a sort of gymnastics.

Who were the best players? These must have been evident to the participants yet did not really matter, any more than the final score of the game, except that they should be allocated evenly between the squads on a given day to provide competitive balance. Baseball was not yet a game for spectators, let alone gamblers. Within the confines of Hoboken's paradise, Knickerbocker pioneers scored runs and made outs that may be retrieved today from their Game Books, but to what purpose? Counting them up we learn, for example, that Alex Cartwright, in his 121 games from 1845 to 1848, scored 448 runs while registering 354 outs. But not one of these came against an opposing club (he did not play in the contest of June 19, 1846, the supposed first match game).

The Knickerbockers may have had baseball's age of legend all to themselves, as the traditional story goes, but they produced no heroes on the field. Only when victory became the reason for the game, more than limb stretching and camaraderie, would the quality of play advance. Who was the best player of the 1840s? Maybe it was Doc Adams, as his abilities permitted his continued play in Knickerbocker matches up until 1859, when he was forty-four.

Occasionally, in the 1850s, the best player of one club might be induced to switch his allegiance to another, for no evident reason and thus presumably for tangible inducement. But the point of encouraging such revolving was to enlarge a club's prestige, not its gate receipts, as there were none, until the mid-1860s. Early baseball reformers fulminated against "revolving" because in the amateur era it implied the sin that dare not speak its name—*professionalism*. Not until the 1870s would that epithet become synonymous with precise execution and peak achievement. Indeed, the best players of the '50s may be inferred at least in part from those who revolved, notably, Louis F. Wadsworth and Joseph C. Pinckney, or were lured over from cricket clubs, such as Harry Wright. These three were also among those named to play in the Great Base Ball Match of 1858, a best-of-three series of games at the Fashion Race Course between select nines representing the rival cities of New York and Brooklyn (the latter did not become a part of greater New York City until 1898).

As the intensity of competition and partisan allegiance picked up, gamblers flocked to the no longer childish, unstructured pastime. In 1854, rules had been made uniform among the three main clubs (Knickerbocker, Eagle, and Gotham); over time they would continue to be altered to make the game more manly, first with the addition of called strikes (1858), then called balls (1863), and then the fly game (1865). The addition of a ball-strike count transformed the role of pitcher from the game's least important player, whose servile deliveries had been designed to provide fielding opportunities, to eventually its dominant figure. No longer could a finicky batter reduce a pitcher to exhaustion and drain the drama of interest; no longer could a fielder back away from a hard-hit drive and blithely secure the out on one bound. The rising emphasis on skilled play prompted clubs to secure the services of superior players, sometimes ringers of lesser social status than could have been imagined by the nose-in-the-air Knickerbockers of 1845. Combined with the advent of enclosed ballparks, paid admissions, and sharing of gate receipts, this trend produced, inevitably, the rampant if covert professionalism of the 1860s.

The rules changes may not have been spurred by the interests of gamblers, but by reducing randomness and encouraging strategy, they surely helped them. The best players and clubs, as well as their supporters, would be rewarded. Spectating may not be all about gambling, but it *is* about shared risk. When we cheer for our favorites or implore them to do better we are summoning powers from our heroes to attach to ourselves. If they lose, so do we. If they win, the glory is ours too, for our mystical support inspired them. A baseball game contains aspects of pageant and theater, but unlike a religious rite or staged drama with their ordained outcomes, it is a real-life struggle in which uncertainty is continuously present. It is this proximity to risk that thrills whether one has a betting interest or not.

Yet of those attending a ball game in the mid-1850s, a good many would have a pecuniary interest in its outcome. Bookmakers openly prowled the sidelines, pasteboards in hand, adjusting the odds inning by inning and taking bets. Players routinely wagered on their own games, even during them. Many observers, like the aging veterans of the Elysian Fields, believed their so recently rationalized game might—were it to become just another vehicle for bettors—be on its way to hell, where it would join the brutal sports patronized by the degraded, that is, the canine ring, the cockfighting pit, the ratting circle. The heyday of open blood sports in New York was probably the 1840s, but Frederick Van Wyck's visit to Tommy Norris' livery stable in 1870 confirmed that the old diversions died hard, and continued to stir passions:

> When you start with a dog fight as a curtain raiser, continue with a cock fight, then rat baiting, then a prize fight, then a battle of billy goats, and then a boxing match, between two ladies, with nothing but trunks on . . . I think you have a night's entertainment that has enough spice . . . to fill the most rapacious needs. . . . The later performances I am afraid I shall have to skip. Your imagination can run riot, as far as you can let it!

Late in life, Henry Chadwick wrote in a letter to the editor of the *New York Tribune*, "I am thankful to say of the great National field games of England and America, the grand old game of cricket and the comparatively new game of baseball, there is not a brutal feature connected with either of them, and yet both develop the highest qualities of true manhood, courage, endurance, pluck, nerve, honorable competition, and the chivalry of sport." Yet it had been in some measure the very brutality of early baseball, when brave men donned neither glove nor mask and wore their bruises, shiners, and shinplasters as badges of honor, which attracted devotees and left the lemonade drinkers aghast.

There was no denying that the sometimes corrupt game of baseball as played in the 1860s was incomparably superior to the pure one played so recently in Eden. Without gambling and the level of interest it aroused among spectators, and the spur that it provided to professional play, baseball could not produce culture heroes and might never have risen to its status of national pastime. That laurel could be granted not by the men who played the game, but only by those who watched it.

If, today, the golden age of baseball might accurately be identified with whenever one happened to be twelve years old, for Chadwick it was forever distant and fixed, at the Elysian Fields of the late 1850s. In August 1898, the *New York Tribune* published a flattering story naming him "Father of Base Ball." After reading the notice, Doc Adams, eighty-four years old and four months from death, sent him a complimentary letter, perhaps with tongue planted firmly in cheek. Chadwick replied:

> That title of "Father of Base Ball" is out of place. Ball, like Topsy, "never had no fader"; it growed up. Still I feel proud to know that I have helped to build up a national game of ball, and have so fought against all abuses which had crept into the sport in the past, as to ensure its worthiness of the title of the most honest sport in which professional exemplars take part, as it is now.

A teetotaling, cold-showering Christian, Chadwick claimed that he had the brainstorm to make baseball into America's game back in 1856. At that time a thirty-two-year-old freelance writer and musician struggling to make a living, he had been reporting on cricket for more than a decade when he experienced an epiphany on his way home from a cricket match at the Elysian Fields. There is a Joan of Arc quality to this realization, and it might well have been a later construct, for it was not given voice until more than a decade later. Baseball, with its myriad localized variants, had as yet shown little promise of becoming a standardized national game. But Chadwick may have realized that if he would elevate the game, so might it lift him from the composer of dreary quadrilles to a national figure. Indeed, in later years he pegged 1857, the year of the first convention of New York and Brooklyn ball clubs, as the year of the game's true origin, because before then each club (besides the Eagle and Gotham) played by its own rules; the Knickerbocker model had not yet been adopted wholesale.

For the likely source of Chadwick's inspiration, whenever it may be dated, we need not look far afield. His half brother, Edwin, twenty-four years his senior, had by that time become famous in England as a social reformer and sanitation pioneer; ultimately, he would be knighted. Henry would emulate Edwin in his attempts to engineer policy, reform abuses, and serve the common weal. To clean up baseball as his brother had London, Henry would have to sanitize the history of cricket, raising it to the level of purity he wished to obtain for baseball. English cricket, as we have seen, was a game built up by gambling and by no means uneasy with it. The Marylebone Club laws of cricket, which governed play in England and North America, even contained a final section with guidelines for betting.

THAT THE NEW YORK game was the "national pastime" was declared hopefully in the *Sunday Mercury* of December 5, 1856, by "A Base-ball Lover" from Williamsburg, presumably from the Putnam Club. *Spirit of the Times* published that club's rules one day later, just as the Knickerbockers were meeting to issue a call for convening the "various base ball clubs of this city and vicinity." Doc Adams, William H. Grenelle, and Louis F. Wadsworth were appointed a committee to pursue this end, and on January 21 fourteen of the sixteen invited clubs gathered to vote on the Knickerbocker proposals.

The *Spirit* declared early in January: "We understand the object of this convention is to promote additional interest in base ball playing, by the getting up of grand matches, on a scale not heretofore attempted." That proved to be the outcome, but it was not the Knicks' intent. Recognizing that the game was growing, and wishing to exert their Nestorian influence on how it would grow, they submitted for the convention's consideration an entirely redrafted code of rules. One of these addressed a growing problem: "No person engaged in a match, either as umpire, referee or player, shall be either directly or indirectly interested in any bet upon the game."

Many of the proposed revisions were adopted by the convention's rules committee, but on all three key changes the Knicks tried to enact, they were foiled: number of innings (they wished seven, the convention voted for nine), minimum number of players to constitute a side (again they had wished seven), and the institution of the manly fly game, which went down to defeat because the newer clubs were concerned that the players might hurt their hands.

Baseball in New England continued largely as it had for a century, its practitioners barely perceiving the threat that an organized New York game would soon become. On the day that the *Spirit* published the Putnam Club rules and the Knicks decided to call a convention, correspondent "Bob Lively" wrote to the *Spirit*'s editor:

> I find, on reading an extract from the rules of the game, taken from the bye-laws, rules, &c., of the Putnam Club, and published in the *Spirit* of Dec. 6th, some matters so different as to the manner in which I myself learned and played the game from youth to manhood, that I have thought, perhaps, a statement of my experience as to the Yankee method of playing "Base," or "Round" ball, as we used to call it, may not prove uninteresting.
>
> The ball we used was, I should think, of the size and weight described by the Putnam Club rules, made of yarn, tightly wound round a lump of cork or India rubber, and covered with smooth calf-skin in quarters (as we quarter an orange), the seams closed snugly, and not raised, lest they should blister the hand of the thrower and the catcher; the bat round, varying from 3 to 3½ feet in length; a portion of a stout rake or pitchfork handle was most in demand; and wielded generally in one hand by the muscular young players at the country schools, who rivalled each other in the hearty cracks they gave the ball.
>
> There were from six to eight players upon each side, the latter number being considered a full complement.
>
> The two best players upon each side—first and second mates, as

they were called, by common consent—were catcher and thrower. These retained their positions in the game, unless they chose to call some other player, upon their own side, to change places with them . . .

The ball was *thrown*, not pitched or tossed, as a gentleman who has seen "Base" played in New York tells me it is; it was *thrown*, and with a vigor, too, that made it whistle through the air, and stop with a solid *smack* in the catcher's hands, which he generally held directly in front of his face. I have frequently heard the catcher tell the thrower, and have made the same request myself when catching, to throw as swift as he wished, and aim for my face. One of these swiftly-delivered balls, when stopped by a skillful batsman, is sure to give the outmost scout employment, and the striker time to go his rounds in safety, and score one tally as he reaches home.

The finest exhibition of skill in Base Ball playing is, I think, to witness the ball passed swiftly from "thrower" to "catcher," who being experts, seldom allow it to fall to the ground, and scarcely move their feet from the position they occupy. The "pitching" or "tossing" of a ball towards the batsman is never practiced (in New England), except by the most juvenile players; and he who would occupy the post of honor as "catcher," must be able to catch expertly a swiftly delivered ball, or he will be admonished of his inexpertness by a request from some player to "butter his fingers."

The core appeal of old-fashioned baseball or round ball was its genial backwoods sadism, epitomized in the practice of plugging a runner to put him out between the bases, and stinging the hands or battering the countenance of the catcher; these translated to courage. The New England game of round ball was the sort of game that most of the country regarded as real baseball, the game that more closely resembled the one played off the Eastern seaboard. In Connecticut and its onetime Western Reserve (Ohio, Michigan, Indiana, Illinois, Iowa), wicket flourished as well as a rough-hewn form of baseball. In Philadelphia and Cincinnati, town ball clubs organized. These clubs elected officers, codified rules, specified uniforms, and held regular days of intramural play as well as selected matches with outside clubs.

In Massachusetts, it was said that until 1854 baseball was played in largely scrub fashion—that is, with however many men were available—but such round ball clubs as the Excelsior of Upton and the

Union of Medway were playing organized ball before the Knickerbockers arrived at Hoboken. The Olympic, Elm Tree, Bay State, and other New England clubs conducted matches by mutually agreed rules at the same time that New York's clubs were starting to regularize their own. Chadwick wrote to the editor of New York's *Sun* in 1905, when he was under attack for his rounders theory of the game's origin:

> It happens that the only attractive feature of the rounders game is this very point of "shying" the ball at the runners, which so tickled Dick Pearce [in the early 1850s]. In fact, it was not until the '50s that the rounders point of play in question was eliminated from the rules of the game, [excepting the Knickerbocker variant] as played at Hoboken from 1845 to 1857.

The prissy New York game made little headway in New England until after 1857. Advocates of New York baseball tried to convince anyone who would listen that their game was more manly, yet what they meant by that adjective was *more gentlemanly* and *seemly*—a matter of decorum and bearing, not courage. A second baseman of the Gotham Base Ball Club of New York, Edward G. Saltzman, relocated his jewelry trade to Boston and with some other likeminded individuals organized the Tri-Mountain Club to play baseball by New York rules. They struggled to find clubs that would play against them (the Eons of Portland, Maine, were the first), for most other clubs continued to play happily enough by their own regulations. These included the Massapoag, Rough and Ready, American, Union, and Holliston—the clubs that on May 13, 1858, extended an invitation to all the clubs of Massachusetts to meet at Dedham to adopt a uniform code of rules. Although the Massachusetts players remained convinced of the superiority of their game, they sensed that they were losing ground as reports of the New York game dominated the sporting weeklies.

The New Englanders were too late. Their game and all other regional variants would slip into the shadows because New York was becoming, with each passing year it seemed, more important than Boston, Philadelphia, Baltimore, or New Orleans. However, a larger factor in the game's rise and the relegation of other ball games to the backwoods and back pages was its courtliness, its businesslike rules, its constrained behaviors, and its organizational accoutrements, especially after the convention of 1857. These points made the New Yorkers' game more like cricket, as orderly if not yet as manly, and thus worthy, for the class conscious, of modeling a nation. For advocates of the still puny New York game, played by a handful of nines, it did not matter that more than a thousand American cricket clubs were active in the 1850s. It did not matter that the Massachusetts game more accurately reflected American reality, who we were in the 1850s. The genteel New York game represented who we wished to become.

The New York area clubs, now numbering twenty-two, met again in March of 1858 and declared a permanent national organization. The *Clipper*, however, was unconvinced. The unnamed writer, probably Bray rather than Chadwick, huffed that the organization's new constitution

> proposes to call the organization the "National Association of Base Ball Players," a misnomer, in our opinion, for the convention appears to be rather sectional and selfish in its proceedings, than otherwise, there having been no invitations sent to Clubs in other States. . . . National indeed! Why the association is a mere local organization, bearing no *State* existence even—to say nothing of a *National* one. The truth of the matter is—that a few individuals have wormed their way into this convention, who have been, and are endeavouring to mould men and things to suit their own views. If the real lovers of the beautiful and health-provoking game of base ball wish to see the sport diffuse itself over the country—as Cricket is fast doing—they must cut loose from those parties who wish to arrogate to themselves the right to act for, and dictate to all who participate in the game. These few dictators wish to ape the New York Yacht Club in their feelings of exclusiveness—we presume. Let the discontented, therefore, come out from among this party, and organize an association which shall be National—not only in name—but in reality. Let invitations be extended to base ball players everywhere to compete with them, and endeavor to make the game what it should be—a truly National one.

In fact, while the Knickerbockers and other New York baseballists were busy puffing their game as the national pastime, the federal government had already acknowledged the rural game as the national standard, in its Indian Peace Medal of 1857. This medal, a carryover from the colonial practice of the British, French, and Spanish empires, was presented by a government agent to the chief of a tribe that the government considered to be friendly, or that it desired to become so. The American Peace Medals changed design many times. Early ones depicted George Washington shaking hands with a Native American against the backdrop of a tranquil farmstead on the obverse, and the heraldic eagle from the Great Seal of the United States on the reverse. After Jefferson, each administration's medal had for its obverse a bust of the new president (except for William Henry Harrison, who died after barely three weeks in office) and a common reverse, a pair of hands shaking each other with crossed tomahawk and peace pipe above and the legend PEACE AND PROSPERITY in surround.

For President James Buchanan in 1857, a new reverse to the medal was commissioned from engraver Joseph Willson, who created an emblematic design featuring an Indian chief in full headdress manning a plow, a farm and a church in the distance, a simple home with a woman standing in the doorway—*and a baseball game being played in the foreground.* This domesticated vignette was ringed by a bow, arrows in a quiver, a squaw, a peace pipe, and a grisly depiction of one brave scalping another. The message of the medal's border was one of primitive violence without the calming hand of civilization; that of the vignette, the possible taming of the wild through American ways in religion, tilling the soil . . . and adoption of its favorite game. All that was lacking was a steaming apple pie. Although Willson died in the year that this medal was issued, his design for the reverse was reused for the Indian Peace Medal issued in the Lincoln years. No matter what some gentlemen were saying in New York, the frontier game of baseball, in all its variety, was already perceived as the national game at the time the New York game mounted its challenge.

WHETHER ONE VIEWED THE Knickerbockers and their allies at the conventions of 1857–58 as kindly shepherds or as would-be dictators of the developing game, the locus of change had already begun to shift from Hoboken, where the early New York clubs played, to Brooklyn, where workingmen created clubs to rival them, notably the Eckford and the Atlantic. The great baseball rivalry between the municipalities began long before the Giants and Dodgers were formed.

The Eckfords of Greenpoint and the Atlantics of Williamsburgh, both Brooklyn suburbs at the time, organized in 1855. The Eckfords played among themselves in their first year and through much of their second, itching to test their mettle in a match. In late 1856, Frank Pidgeon, captain and pitcher of the Eckfords, described the scene:

> A year ago last August a small number of young men of that part of the city [Brooklyn] known as "The Island" [Greenpoint, what the Dutch had called Groen Hoek, was then also known as Manhattan Island] were accustomed to meet for the purpose of enjoying the game. Being shipwrights and mechanics, we could not make it convenient to practice more than once a week; and we labored under the impression that want of practice and our having so few players from whom to select a nine would make it almost impossible for us to win a match even if we engaged in one. However, we were willing to do the best we could if some club would give us an invitation to play. But, alas, no such invitation came, and we began to doubt seriously if we were worth taking notice of.
>
> Still, we had some merry times among ourselves; we would forget business and everything else on Tuesday afternoons, go out on the green fields, don our ball suits, and go at it with a rush. At such times we were boys again. Such sport as this brightens a man up, and improves him, both in mind and body. After longing for a match, yet so dreading (not a defeat—we were sure of that) a regular Waterloo, we finally, through sheer desperation, expressed a wish to play the winners in a match between the Baltic and Union Clubs of Morrisania.

The Unions won, graciously acceded to a game with the Eckfords, and shockingly lost to them, 22–8. Pidgeon summed up: "About seven o'clock that evening, nine peacocks might have been seen on their way home, with tail-feathers spread. Our friends were astonished, as well as ourselves, and all felt rejoiced at the result."

Not only the founder of one of baseball's fabled clubs, Pidgeon was a pioneer shipbuilder whose colleague in the Brooklyn yards and great friend was George Steers, the man who built the racing yacht *America*, for which the America's Cup is named. Pidgeon went round Cape Horn to California in 1849 to make his mark in the Gold Rush, and came back overland across the Isthmus of Panama. He was an engineer, a painter, a musician, an entrepreneur, and an inventor with several patents. For the last twenty years of his life he lived in Saugerties, New York, my longtime hometown, where today no one knows his name, no matter that his remains are marked with a prominent headstone in the village cemetery.

Despite his advanced years at the time he organized the Eckfords—he had passed his thirtieth birthday—Pidgeon played several positions. He was a competent second baseman, shortstop, and left fielder, but he won his fame as a pitcher, not of the speedy variety that emerged in the 1860s, but as the paragon of headwork, changing speeds and arcs while pitching fairly to the bat, as was the mandate back then.

New candidates for membership flocked to the Eckford Club after its defeat of the Unions—workingmen of lesser social standing than its founding shipwrights and engineers. The Atlantic Club recruited aggressively, building its ranks from workingmen of all sorts, so long as they could play ball; they would dominate the game in the ensuing decade. Brooklyn's Excelsior Club had organized somewhat earlier, first as the Jolly Young Bachelors Base Ball Club, but had been slow to engage in test matches, viewing themselves somewhat snootily as the Knickerbockers of their city. The Excelsiors' only match games were with the Putnams, the other formidable early Brooklyn club, which like the Excelsiors played no other.

Baseball's expulsion from Eden may conveniently be dated as July 20, 1858. On that day the first of the three "picked" games at the Fashion Race Course on Long Island, not far from where the modern New York Mets play, was played between the best of New York and Brooklyn. (The death of the founder of the *Spirit of the Times*, William T. Porter, was reported in that morning's press.) Among the firsts in baseball history that the opening Fashion Course game might claim were: first all-star contest, first paid admission, and first baseball game played in an enclosed park, although the first enclosed park designed specifically for baseball would come four years later. In the third (rubber) game of the series, umpire Doc Adams called three men out on strikes, the first time the new rule was applied. Yet the Fashion Race Course Games represented the old weaknesses as well as innovation; in the first contest, in which New York prevailed, 22–18, of the twenty-seven Brooklynites put out, thirteen were on balls caught on a first bound, while the New Yorks lost fourteen batters on similar catches.

A harbinger of baseball's fall from grace could be found alongside the report of the first Fashion Course game on the same page of the weekly *Clipper* of July 24. In the far right column was the report of a July 16 game between the Sylvan and Niagara clubs of Brooklyn, with the former winning by a score of 39–31. Playing third base for the Niagara was Jim Creighton, who only one year later would assault the foundation of the amateur game.

Although it is frequently written that the admission charge for the first Fashion Course game was fifty cents, in fact it was ten cents to watch the game, with optional transportation and livery costs making up the rest, to a higher level at thirty cents and another at fifty. In the announcement of this "Grand Base Ball Demonstration," the new National Association resolved

> . . . to play a grand match on the Fashion Race Course, it being a neutral ground, and sufficiently large. No intoxicating liquors or gambling will be allowed. A nominal charge of 10 cents and fee of 20 cents for 1 horse and 40 for two horse vehicles to be collected. Surplus funds will be equally divided by New York and Brooklyn clubs and by them presented to the widows and orphans funds of the Fire Departments of the two cities.

After expenses, this surplus turned out to be $35.55 for each city's charities. While the attendance was estimated to be as high as 10,000, the actual figure was reported some days later by the *New York Atlas:* "Some idea of the immense assemblage may be formed from the fact that no less than seven thousand eight hundred persons paid the admission fee (10 cents) at the entrance to the Course." While some of these were pedestrians, most came in by rail to the station adjoining the Fashion Course, the former property of Samuel Willets (Mets fans going to the ball game today get off the elevated subway at Willets Point). Milk carts, beer wagons, express wagons, and stages were commandeered for the trip to the Fashion Course; some baseball clubs chartered omnibuses to transport their partisans, while other groups traveled in their own outfits, pulled by six to fourteen horses.

The selection of the players was a delicate matter. "It is needless to say that rivalry ran high for the honor of contending in this match," noted the *Clipper*, "and that in the preparatory matches played, the various players showed off in their best style, to be considered, if possible, available men for the occasion. To this end, and to aid the [selection] committee, opposition nines were organized to play the selected nine, which resulted in various changes. . . ." Brooklyn's best players were thought to be Pidgeon and Johnny Grum of the Eckfords, Joe Leggett of the Excelsiors, and the O'Brien brothers (Matty and Pete) of the Atlantics. Of these all but Leggett were named to play in each of the eventual three games (New York won the first, Brooklyn the second, and New York the deciding game). All the others moved from one position to another, game by game.

Chosen from Brooklyn's finest for the first contest were two men each from the Eckford, Excelsior, and Putnam clubs, with three from the Atlantic. For the second, only one Putnam member was named to play, and no Excelsior—not even John Holder, who had hit the only home run in game one; the squad for game two featured five from the Atlantics. The final match roster was composed entirely of Eckfords and Atlantics, three and six respectively. This derogation particularly stung the Excelsiors, as we shall see from their subsequent actions. Of the New Yorks, Marion E. "Joe" Gelston of the Eagles, Charles DeBost of the Knickerbockers, and Joe Pinckney of the Unions were the only men to play in all three contests. (In 1859, Gelston would depart for California and join the San Francisco Base Ball Club, which played by New York rules and would be renamed the Eagle, perhaps in his honor.) Louis F. Wadsworth, now back with the Gotham, his original club, having left the Knickerbocker "through some misunderstanding," according to *Porter's Spirit*, played first base in the two contests New York won. Knickerbockers James Whyte Davis and Harry Wright played in one game each.

"Before the [first] game began," Robert H. Schaefer wrote in "The Great Base Ball Match," his fine article on the Fashion Course games, "the feeling was all in favor of Brooklyn. This was reflected by the gambling fraternity; the *New York Clipper* reported that at the start of the game the odds were 100 to 75 in favor of Brooklyn."

A highlight of that game was supplied by Brooklyn's second baseman, Holder, of the Excelsior Club, when he hit the only home run. Chadwick, describing the game in a reminiscent piece from 1873, recalled: "In the first game, in one of the innings, John Holder, just before going to the bat, bet $75 that he would make a home run, and hitting a ball to centre field he actually did score the coveted run and won his bet." However, Chadwick revised the story later in a way that is more plausible, as Holder is unlikely to have wagered such a sum on his own; $75 in 1858 would be nearly $2,000 today:

> Two Brooklyn cranks had made a wager of $100 a side on John Holden's [sic] making a home run. One was an Atlantic rooter, the other an Excelsior fan. In this game I noticed that when Holden went to bat he was very particular in selecting his bat. It appears that the man who had bet on him went to him and told him that he would give him $25 of his bet if he made the hit; so Jack was very anxious. . . . Jack, after waiting for a good ball, got one to suit him, and sent it flying over Harry Wright's head at right center, and made the round of the bases before the ball was returned, thus winning the $25.

For the second game, played on August 17, Brooklyn moved pitcher Matty O'Brien to third base. Frank Pidgeon, the shortstop in game one, became the pitcher, with Dickey Pearce of the Atlantics taking over at short. Brooklyn won easily, 29–8. New York's pitcher Tom Van Cott, who had thrown 198 pitches in game one, came back to toss 270 in a losing cause. Pidgeon threw 290. Called strikes were enacted for this year, but not called "wides," what we today term "balls."

For the third and deciding game, played on September 10, Brooklyn was the heavy favorite, based on their easy triumph in the second game. Yet New York won handily, 29–18, with the Eagles' Gelston hitting a leadoff home run that was followed by six more runs before the side was retired. Of Pidgeon's eventual 436 pitches (!), 87 came in this first inning alone.

The success of the Great Base Ball Match may have persuaded William F. Cammeyer, proprietor of the Union Skating Grounds, to plant grass in the spring of 1862 and charge admission (the same ten cents as for the Fashion Course match) to baseball games. Soon other enclosed grounds began to spring up in Brooklyn, New Jersey, Pennsylvania, and Ohio (but not New York).

On the field, the Brooklyn men had not dishonored themselves, but they had not won the match, in which they were favored from the outset, and by stacking the lineup in the final game with six Atlantics and three Eckfords, the selection committee had bred bad blood. It was made clear to the Excelsiors in particular that they were not in the same league with their rivals. Next year the National Association would ban professionalism. ("No person who receives compensation for his services as a player shall be competent to play in any match.") The Excelsiors would skirt the rules of the game, however, by adding four outstanding players from the Star club of Brooklyn: George H. Flanley, the Brainard brothers Henry and Asa, and Jim Creighton.

Frank Pidgeon, the man who authored the National Association's antiprofessional provision of 1859, was a pure amateur who played baseball for the love of it; he earned his living by other paths. He spoke out against some clubs' practice of recruiting young players with no visible means of support and then paying them expense money so that they could travel to play ball. "I suppose that you will admit," Pidgeon wrote to the editor of *Spirit of the Times* in 1858, "that a man who does not pay his obligations, and has in his power to do so, is a knave and not fit to be trusted in a game of ball or anything else; and if he has not the money, his time would better [be] spent in earning the same than playing ball—business first, pleasure afterwards."

His statement prompted the *Clipper,* which at this point remained a strong supporter of cricket, to ask whether outlawing professionals had "something of an aristocratic odor," revealing "a rather uncharitable disposition toward poor players." Cricket had accommodated professionals long ago: Each year since 1819 had been marked by a match between Gentlemen (amateur) and Players (professionals), although to make the match competitive the Gentlemen might be permitted more men than the Players' eleven.

Porter's Spirit chimed in: "If from any circumstances, personal or pecuniary, a lover of the sport cannot afford a day to travel from his home to play . . . and his brother members of the club are able and willing to remunerate him for his time and expenses, why should they not be permitted to do so? It is a good democratic rule, and tends to level the artificial distinctions between wealth and poverty."

Pidgeon responded:

> How would you like to see those you depended upon to uphold the name and fame of the club bought up like cattle, or if not bought, would you like to see the bribe repeatedly offered to them, to desert

their colors. These things have occurred, and it was thought best to nip them in the bud. . . . This rule was used to protect ourselves against the influence of money, and give "honest poverty" a fair chance, and in a struggle for supremacy between clubs to let skill, courage, and endurance decide who shall be the victors.

The contest between cricket and baseball for the hearts and minds of Americans was about to be heightened. After a £750 guarantee was secured, a dozen professional cricketers, composed equally of All-England Eleven players and those of the United All-England Eleven, signed on for cricket's first overseas tour in October 1859. Five matches were played, all against sides of twenty-two, with two in Canada (Montreal and Hamilton) and three in the U.S. (Hoboken, Philadelphia, and Rochester). The English won each time. Additionally, three exhibition games were staged. Attempts to pit the English tourists in a baseball match against the best of New York and Brooklyn came to naught because a sufficient fee could not be secured. In any event, an animated contributor to the *Tribune* wrote:

It would be no more honor for the English Eleven to beat the best nine that could be selected, playing the New York game, than it would be to beat at cricket the best Eleven they could pick from any ordinary school in England. If they want to find foes worthy of their steel, let them challenge the "Excelsior" Club, at Upton, Massachusetts, now the Champion Club of New England, and which Club could probably beat, with the greatest ease, the best New York nine, and give them three to one. The Englishmen may be assured that to whip any nine playing the New York baby game will never be recognized as a national triumph.

The English tour was an artistic and financial success: The cricketers cleared £90 above the guarantee. If the Civil War had not broken out eighteen months later, two or three follow-up tours might have been arranged in the following five or six years. As it was, the enthusiasm for cricket faded in the war years, and English support of the Confederacy through uninterrupted cotton purchases surely did not help. By the time an English team returned to America in 1868, American cricket was on its way to becoming the sport of British expatriates and urban patricians.

IN ONE OF THE cricket exhibitions of 1859, a match of eleven Englishmen against sixteen Americans, a young devotee of both cricket and baseball, Brooklyn's Jim Creighton, clean bowled five wickets in six successive balls. English cricketer John Lillywhite, upon seeing Creighton pitch a baseball, instantly saw the obstacle—though no umpire would likely detect it—that overmatched American batsmen faced: "Why, that man is not bowling, he is throwing underhand. It is the best disguised underhand throwing I ever saw, and might readily be taken for a fair delivery." The key to Creighton's success in baseball was an imperceptible though certainly illegal wrist snap, added to a swooping underhand delivery.

In the playing rules, the specifications for pitching a baseball had been unchanged since the Knickerbockers' ninth rule of 1845: "The ball must be pitched, and not thrown, for the bat"; a further explanation was added in 1858, that the ball must not be "jerked." This meant that the ball had to be delivered underhand, in the stiff-armed, stiff-wristed manner borrowed from cricket's early days. Early pitchers had taken two steps in delivering the ball, and would follow it halfway to home plate until 1858, when the pitcher's line was established at forty-five feet. Until the pitcher's box came in five years later, pitchers would still throw from a running start. Creighton, however, did not move from his original position, taking only a step with his left foot and keeping his right in place.

Creighton was a revolutionary not only for bending the rules on and off the field. He was the game's first hero and, I believe, the most important player not inducted into the Baseball Hall of Fame.

Born to James and Jane Creighton on April 15, 1841, in Manhattan, Jim grew up in Brooklyn. By the age of sixteen, his abilities in cricket and baseball were evident. He and some neighborhood youths started a junior baseball club which they called Young America. It played a handful of games in 1857 before disbanding. Jim then joined the fledgling Niagaras of Brooklyn, for whom he played at second or third base; at shortstop was George Flanley, another accomplished young player, while the regular pitcher was John A. Shields.

On July 19, 1859, the Niagaras challenged the Star Club, then the crack junior team. In the fifth inning of the game, with the Niagaras trailing badly, Shields was replaced in the box by Creighton. Pete

O'Brien, captain of the Atlantics, witnessed this game, and "when Creighton got to work," he observed, "something new was seen in base ball—a low, swift delivery, the ball rising from the ground past the shoulder to the catcher. The Stars soon saw that they would not be able to cope with such pitching. Their captain, after consulting other base ball players present, sent in his wildest pitcher. They, by these tactics, were enabled to win the game, which resulted in the breaking up of the Niagara Club, and Creighton and Flanley at once joined the Stars. The next year he with Flanley joined the Excelsior Club."

According to the sporting press, Creighton was a high-principled, unassuming youth whose gentlemanly manner and temperate habits were ideal attributes for the amateur age of baseball; all the same, he became baseball's first professional through under-the-table emoluments from the Excelsiors, who, not forgetting their snub in games two and three of the Fashion Course game, were hungry to surpass the Atlantics.

The Excelsiors' payment to one or more of the former Star players (including the Brainard brothers) was widely rumored. The *Troy Daily Whig* of July 3, 1860, offered that "the Excelsior Club of Brooklyn, who have pretty well reduced base ball to a science, and who pay their pitcher $500 a year, are making a crusade through the provinces for the purposes of winning laurels, or losing them, with the different clubs on their way."

The Excelsior tour, staged in emulation of that by English cricketers in the prior season, was the first by any baseball club, with stops in Albany, Troy, Buffalo (including a brief foray into Canada), Rochester, Newburgh, Philadelphia, Washington, and Baltimore. Creighton pitched all of the games as the Excelsiors went 18–2–1 on the season. That "1" was an umpire-declared draw against the Atlantics on August 23. The clubs had split their previous two meetings that season, so this game would settle the match and, for the press, the mythical national championship. With the Excelsiors leading 8–6 in the fifth inning Atlantic errors put runners on and the score seemed about to blow wide open. The *Clipper* described what happened next:

> These successive errors in fielding did not improve the temper of either the Atlantics or their very questionable friends [gamblers], and the rowdy spirit of the crowd again began to display itself more forcibly. . . .

> And so insulting were the epithets bestowed on the Excelsiors, that Leggett [Excelsior captain and catcher] decided to withdraw his forces from the field, and we certainly think he acted wisely in so doing, and we only regret that he was not supported in his course by the Atlantic nine.

The umpire declared a draw, all bets were off, and the Atlantics were thus permitted, with a record for the season of 12–2–2 and no loss of a home-and-home series, to retain the as yet mythical championship they had won in 1859. The two clubs would never meet again.

After the disgusted Excelsiors reverted to an intramural campaign for 1861, Creighton went through the 1862 season as not only the game's peerless pitcher but also its top batsman, being retired only four times. At the same time that Creighton was extending the frontier in baseball he was also a prominent member of the cricketing fraternity. Several other Excelsiors were good enough at cricket to play for established clubs: John Whiting, A. T. Pearsall, John Holder, and Asa Brainard, later to become famous as Creighton's successor with the Excelsiors and as the pitcher for the undefeated Cincinnati Red Stockings of 1869. Creighton performed for the American Cricket Club in both 1861 and 1862, joined by Brainard in both years.

In 1861, Brainard and Creighton jumped the gentlemanly Excelsiors for the working-class Atlantics, no doubt lured once again by covert lucre. After three weeks, without having played a game in the hated rivals' uniforms, the pair sheepishly returned to the Excelsior fold.

On October 14, 1862, in a match against the tough Unions of Morrisania, Creighton played in the field while Brainard pitched the first five innings. In four trips to the plate, Creighton hit four doubles. In the sixth he came in to pitch, and then in the next inning, calamity. John Chapman later wrote:

> I was present at the game between the Excelsiors and the Unions of Morrisania at which Jim Creighton injured himself. He did it in hitting out a home run. When he had crossed the [plate] he turned to George Flanley and said, "I must have snapped my belt," and George said, "I guess not." It turned out that he had suffered a fatal injury. Nothing could be done for him, and baseball met with a severe loss. He had wonderful speed, and, with it, splendid command. He was fairly unhittable.

Creighton had swung so mighty a blow—in the manner of the day, with hands separated on the bat, little or no turn of the wrists, and incredible torque applied by the twisting motion of the upper body—that, reportedly, he ruptured his bladder. (Later review of the circumstances, aided by modern medical understanding, pointed to a ruptured inguinal hernia.) After four days of hemorrhaging and agony at his home, Jim Creighton passed away on October 18, at the age of twenty-one years and six months, having given his all to baseball in a final epic blast that Roy Hobbs might have envied. His brief obituary notice in the *New York Times* of October 22 stated that he "died in his residence in Henry-street on Saturday, the result of internal injuries sustained while playing in a match on Tuesday last [October 14]."

Is that the way it really happened? Creighton's last run home instantly ascended to the realm of myth, giving baseball its martyred saint. Obsequies included such syrupy statements as "He was very modest, and never severe in his criticisms of the play of others. He did not care to talk about his own playing, was gentlemanly in his deportment, and very correct in his habits, and to sum up all, was a model player in our National Games [meaning baseball *and* cricket]. His death was a loss not only to his club but to the whole base ball community, which needed such as he as a standard of honorable play and ability." Rule-breaking and revolving or *sub rosa* professionalism were now dismissed as an icon was made.

Creighton's Excelsior teammates mourned him at their black-draped clubhouse at 133 Clinton Street and subscribed toward a fine monument over his remains—a granite obelisk with a baseball motif, including bats, balls, and a scorebook—in Brooklyn's Green-Wood Cemetery. The Excelsiors were not at all sure that it was a good thing for baseball to take the blame for Creighton's death; this might not promote the healthful properties of the new game. What if his injury had been sustained a day or two earlier, say, at a cricket match?

According to a contemporary account, at the National Association convention of 1862 the Excelsior president, Dr. Joseph B. Jones, "briefly made allusion to the death of Creighton, and paid high tribute to his memory; in doing which he availed himself of the opportunity to correct a mis-statement that has found its way into print in reference to his death being caused by injuries sustained in a baseball match. This, he said, was not so; the injury he received in a cricket match." An October 25 *Clipper* article suggested that Creighton actually suffered his fatal injury in a cricket match played on October 7, which leaves one to puzzle over how he played in the baseball game seven days later.

The battle for the nation's sporting allegiance was at a crucial point. Cricket had been the favored sport until only recently, when the Excelsior tour and Creighton's exploits had created a mania for baseball and had elevated it into parity. Now, with Creighton gone and the Excelsiors falling back into the pack, might the British import be restored to primacy? These fears may have been running through the minds of some in the baseball community, already concerned with the new game's incipient professionalism, and thus may have moved them to propagandize for baseball's spotlessness, as well as Creighton's.

Creighton had carried the game to new heights; in death he would prove even more useful. His death, coming as it did, in action, and at a time when the nation was preoccupied with the destruction of a generation, became emblematic of the losses of the Civil War. At the end of all the carnage, the lamented pitcher even became a symbol of national reconciliation.

On July 5, 1866, the Nationals of Washington visited the Excelsiors, reciprocating the favor of a visit to the capital six years earlier. The Brooklyn team gave them a warm reception, capped by a visit to Creighton's monument. According to the *New York Times* report, "a silent tear was dropped to the memory of the lamented James Creighton, whose beautiful monument is a prominent feature of the city of the dead." Two years later, a team in Norfolk, Virginia, took the name Creightons. And, in 1872, another Creighton club was formed in Washington, D.C. Oddly, on this team named in homage to the fallen hero, whose appetite for money had given rise to professionalism and had spurred gambling, was a young player named Albert Nichols. In 1877, he would be one of four Louisville players expelled from baseball for game-fixing.

In death, Creighton's real accomplishments rapidly took on an accretion of myth, much as his death itself may have. Baseball, today universally recognized as a vibrant anachronism, was not always a backward-looking game in which the plays and players of yore set unsurpassable standards of excellence. In the 1850s and '60s, organized baseball was new, and strictly a go-ahead business, in the watchword of the day. Creighton's death implanted the game with nostalgia, which remains a key to its enduring appeal. More than twenty years after his death, veteran observers might say without fear of challenge that Keefe and Radbourn were fine pitchers, sure, but they "warn't no Creighton."

BASEBALL IN THE REMAINING years of the Civil War was at low ebb, with several clubs disbanding for want of players; those that did continue curtailed their schedule of match games harshly. In this fallow period, the fly game was finally enacted, as was the innovation of the called strike; the New York game's plaintive claim of manliness was now coming into view. The Massachusetts game would not recover its vigor after the war. Cricket had become marginalized. The New York game, more than any other, was the one played by the soldiers in the camps (particularly in the fall and the spring; summer months were for fighting). All seemed propitious for the New York game's return to former levels of popularity after the war.

The Eckfords were unbeaten in ten match games in the lean year of 1863; their top players included Al Reach and Jimmy Wood along with up-and-comers Tom Devyr and Ed Duffy. Wood would go on to captain the fledgling White Stocking club in Chicago in 1870. Reach would become a professional (if he was not one already) by revolving to the Philadelphia Athletics in 1865, when Devyr and Duffy, having jumped from the Eckfords to the New York Mutuals, would be joined in infamy with new teammate Bill Wansley.

On September 27, 1865, gambler Kane McLoughlin paid $100 collectively to the three players to *heave*, in the favored term of the period, a game the following day to the Eckfords. "The Mutuals, fresh from two well-earned victories at Kingston—for a silver ball—and Poughkeepsie," according to the *New York Times*, "presented an excellent nine in good trim for action, yesterday" in a game played at the Elysian Fields of Hoboken. However, in the fifth inning the Mutuals amazingly allowed eleven runs to score through "over-pitched balls, wild throws, passed balls, and failures to stop them in the field. . . ." Wansley, the catcher, made so little attempt to hide his skullduggery (six passed balls, no hits in five at bats) that rumblings about something being rotten in Hoboken were aired in the press immediately. Confronted by the Mutuals president, Wansley confessed and implicated his partners in slime; all three were banned from play. Wansley and

Duffy were reinstated at the end of 1870, while the youngster Devyr was cleared to play after sitting out only one season. His sincere confession persuaded the Mutual club to leniency:

> Gentlemen—As words can make no apology for the injury done your Club or the disgrace brought on myself by my connection with this affair, the briefer I am with this statement the better; but in order that I may put myself in the true light (which, God knows, is bad enough) I have concluded to write you a full and true account of all I know about it.
>
> Between eleven and twelve o'clock on the morning of the match, I was going toward the ferry, ready to go over to the ground, when I met Wansley, Duffy and another man in a wagon. Bill [Wansley] pulled up and asked me where I was going. I told him I was getting down toward the ferry, and that I was going over to the ground in about an hour. He says, "Do you want to make three hundred dollars?" I says "I would like to do anything for that." He says "You can make it easy." I asked how? He says, "We are going to 'heave' this game, and will give you three hundred dollars if you like to stand in with us; you need not do any of the work, I'll do all that myself and get the blame. Let them blame, I can stand it all. We can lose this game without doing the club any harm, and win the home and home game. Now, you ain't got a cent, neither has Duffy. You can make this money without any one being a bit the wiser of it. You needn't do anything toward [heaving] it, I will do that myself." I said, "Bill, if you don't want me to help you why do you let me into it?" He says, "I want to give you a chance to make some money, and make [S. D.] O'Donnell sure that it can be done." Well, to make a long story short, not having a cent, I agreed. We went over to O'Donnell's house, received a hundred dollars, of which I got thirty, which was all I did receive since or before it. This is the whole substance of it.
>
> I do not write this to vindicate myself more than the rest, nor to make you believe I am any less guilty than any of the others; on the contrary, as I entered into this affair, and received my share of the gains, it is but fair that I should stand my share of the censure and punishment which the publicity of this thing will bring upon us. I simply write it to let you see how my connection with this unhappy affair was brought about. For what! for thirty dollars, which I could do nothing with but lose playing faro; and now, I have 30 hundred worth

of disgrace, all to myself, never to lose, and without one envious eye to wish one cent's worth. One word about Duffy, and I will close. I saw him last night. He says that Bill came to him the day before the match and asked him if he would go in with him in "heaving" the game; he says he refused unless I was into it. Bill says "all right, leave him to me, I can talk to him"; which he did, and with the result already too well known. I have now fulfilled a duty which devolved on me to place before you the facts of the case. I am sorry I had anything to do with it; but my sorrow, like this statement, comes too late to help me any. I close this by wishing the club a more prosperous and luckier season next year than they have this, and hope they will get no more such ungrateful players as Wansley, Duffy, and

Your humble servant,
THOS. H. DEVYR.

The Civil War had brought the New York game to this low ebb, yet even as it emerged triumphant over cricket and the New England game, it would have farther to fall. African Americans had played baseball near Madison Square in the 1840s and by 1859, they had formed three clubs in the Brooklyn area: the Unknown of Weeksville, the Henson of Jamaica, and the Monitor of Brooklyn; these would be followed by the Uniques and the Union, both of Williamsburgh. In Rochester, in 1859, Frederick Douglass Jr., son of the great abolitionist orator, played baseball with the integrated Charter Oak Juniors. A somewhat later all-black club in Albany was the Bachelors; the Excelsior, the Pythian, and L'Overture formed in Philadelphia. When young Douglass moved to Washington, he helped to form another baseball club, the Alerts.

In July 1867, the Pythians agreed to take on two Washington clubs, the Alerts and the Mutuals, in home-and-home series. The white Athletics offered their grounds for the Philadelphia matches and were broadly supportive of the Pythians. "Fred. Douglass Sees a Colored Game," reported the *Clipper* on July 13:

The announcement that the Pythian, of Philadelphia, would play the Alert, of Washington, D. C. (both colored organizations) on the 15th inst., attracted quite a concourse of spectators on the grounds of the Athletic. The game progressed finely until the beginning of the fifth

> innings, when a heavy shower of rain set in, compelling the umpire, Mr. E. H. Hayhurst, of the Athletic, to call the game. The score stood at the end of the fourth innings: Alert 21, Pythian 16. Mr. Frederick Douglass was present and viewed the game from the reporters' stand. His son is a member of the Alert.

The 1867 season was a triumph, as African-American clubs proliferated and on October 25 the Uniques and Monitors, both Brooklyn clubs, met in a contest for the "championship of colored clubs." The Pythians felt confident that their club could gain official recognition from the Pennsylvania State Association of Base Ball Players, a subsidiary of the National Association, at a convention in Harrisburg in the middle of October. The Athletics agreed to sponsor their application. As Pythian secretary Jacob White Jr. later reported:

> Whilst the Committee on Credentials were making up their report, the delegates clustered together in small groups to discuss what action should be taken. Sec. Domer stated although he, Mr. Hayhurst, and the President were in favor of our acceptance, still the majority of the delegates were opposed to it, and they would advise me to withdraw my application, as they thought it were better for us to withdraw than to have it on record that we were black balled.

Instructed to "fight if there was a chance," White finally relented, as "there seemed no chance for any thing but being black balled." The Pythian Club then tried to gain admission to the National Association at the annual meeting held in Philadelphia at the Chestnut Street Theater on December 11 and 12. *The Ball Players' Chronicle* commented that the report of the Nominating Committee, through its acting chairman, Mr. James Whyte Davis of the Knickerbockers, recommended the exclusion of African-American clubs from representation in the Association:

> It is not presumed by your committee that any club who have applied are composed of persons of color, or any portion of them; and the recommendations of your committee in this report are based upon this view, and they unanimously report against the admission of any club which may be composed of one or more colored persons.

/S/Wm. H. Bell, M.D., Jas. Whyte Davis, Wm. E. Sinn; Philadelphia, Dec. 11, 1867.

In seeking to keep out of the convention the discussion of any subject having a political bearing, the game's color line had been drawn. The committee further proclaimed, "If colored clubs were admitted there would be in all probability some division of feeling, whereas, by excluding them no injury could result to anyone."

The 1870 New York State Base Ball Association meetings added a final insult: The rules for admission of new clubs were amended so as to bar clubs composed of gentlemen of color, which prompted the *Clipper* to write, "we would suggest that the colored clubs of New York and Philadelphia at once take measures to organize a National Association of their own." At this meeting the applications for reinstatement of game fixers Duffy and Wansley were approved.

6
A NATIONAL PASTIME

After the Civil War, the gentlemanly game seemed an anachronism, a bittersweet vestige of a bygone day. The Elysian Fields had ceased to be a fashionable destination. The pioneers of the game were widely dispersed, many of them to pursue their fortunes in the Golden West. Cartwright settled in Hawaii and Wheaton in the San Francisco Bay area; Adams left his medical practice in New York to pursue banking and elective office in Connecticut; Wadsworth married fortunately, moved to New Jersey, and became a judge (at first a justice of the peace). Abner Doubleday went west, too: By decade's end, the army stationed him in San Francisco, where with three business partners he proposed and received a franchise for what became the city's first cable car line. Even Abner Graves left Cooperstown for California, then to Crawford County, Iowa, ultimately settling in Denver. Henry Chadwick stayed in Brooklyn, becoming ever more influential.

In July 1866, the Red House Grounds in Harlem, no longer home to trotting horses, cricket players, or baseballists, was made over into the Red House Hospital, specializing in the treatment of cholera, which had returned that summer with one last flourish; now that it was understood as a water-borne disease rather than an airborne "miasma," improvements in sanitation would eventually conquer the disease. With no first-class ball fields in Manhattan, and Hoboken increasingly home to old-line amateurs playing before diminished crowds, the hotbed of metropolitan area baseball shifted to Brooklyn.

The professionals were taking hold of the game. In 1859, at Frank Pidgeon's instigation, the National Association of Base Ball Players (NABBP) passed a rule forbidding the participation of paid players in any matches, but it was instantly evaded by Jim Creighton and others (clearly this had been viewed as a problem before 1859; as with the broken-window bylaw banning baseball in Pittsfield in 1791, there was no reason to institute a formal prohibition against an offense as yet unseen). Many other professional players followed who, if not compensated directly, were given featherbed jobs at high salaries in the businesses associated with club officials. Although this trend was slowed by the outbreak of war, it was plainly irreversible. In 1862, entrepreneur William Cammeyer reconfigured his Union Skating Grounds in Williamsburgh for baseball use, charged ten cents admission, and eventually gave a portion of the proceeds to the first-rank clubs he invited to play there. In 1865, Al Reach, second baseman of Brooklyn's Eckford Club, jumped to the Philadelphia Athletics for a salary openly if variously declared (some said $25 a week, others $1,000 per annum). In 1866, the NABBP reworded its stricture against professionalism, but once again to no practical effect.

The Civil War had depleted baseball rosters everywhere. Member clubs in the Association dwindled from fifty-nine in 1860 to thirty-four by 1865. In the December following war's end, the ranks swelled to ninety-one. Many of the established clubs returned to the field after having suspended match play, and a number of new clubs formed in New Jersey and Pennsylvania. But the National Association game remained an exceedingly provincial affair, confined to New York and the Middle Atlantic states. Despite the incursion of New York rules into Boston in 1857, and the steady decline of the Massachusetts game, only one New England team (the Bowdoin of Boston) had yet been represented at an NABBP convention by the end of the war. New England had been slow to warm to New York's game. The New York game as the national pastime? Chess was more widespread and better organized. The First American Chess Congress of 1857 had included four members from California on its "Committee of Cooperation," including the ever inventive William R. Wheaton, now of San Francisco. Oddly, because of the gold fever that had drawn him and so many others to California, the New York game was taking root in the Far West while the old-fashioned ball games, loosely described as town ball, maintained their venerable hold on the heartland.

In December 1866, 202 clubs attended the NABBP convention, and a good many clubs came from the "outskirts," including Kansas, Missouri, Kentucky, Tennessee, Iowa, and Oregon. By the next year, Illinois was sending more than twice as many delegates as New York. Indeed, in that 1867 convention four Western states (as all states west of the Allegheny were then termed)—Illinois, Wisconsin, Indiana, and Ohio—accounted for 145 clubs, far more than had represented the entire country only two years before. The New York game was at last poised to become what it had prematurely been dubbed a decade earlier: a truly national pastime.

Some have attributed the spread of the city game to returning soldiers sharing their wartime exposure to the new rules; Albert Spalding wrote that as a boy of thirteen he had learned the game in precisely this way in Rockford, Illinois, from a disabled veteran. Surely, lulls in battle did introduce the New York rules to some, but there is a more plausible explanation for the rapid infiltration of Gotham-style baseball after the war. The businessmen and civic leaders who organized ball clubs to play by the new rules meant to signal that their remote burg, indeed their entire region, was set to become a vital force in the nation so recently unified at so great a cost. *Union* would become a preferred name, with profound sentiment, for new clubs throughout the land, even in Richmond, Virginia, in 1867.

In that year, the Brooklyn Excelsiors, slipping from the elite ranks, nonetheless had the distinction of, yet again, as they had with Creighton, supplying baseball with a pitching innovation just outside the rules, which still demanded that a ball be pitched underhand with a straight elbow, neither thrown nor jerked. William Arthur "Candy" Cummings, graduating from the junior Excelsiors to take Asa Brainard's position in the pitcher's box, debuted a curveball that he had been working on since 1863, when he observed the curved flight of the clam shells he winged across Brooklyn's Gowanus Creek. While there has been some dispute over which game might have marked the debut of his innovation, or whether the entire story is bunk, Cummings himself reported that he tried his curveball in a game against Harvard that could only have taken place on October 7, 1867. "I began to watch the flight of the ball through the air, and distinctly saw it curve. A surge of joy flooded over me that I shall never forget. . . . The secret was mine. There was trouble, though, for I could not make it curve when I wanted to." He lost the game 18–6.

AFTER THE BROOKLYN EXCELSIOR tour of 1860, the outbreak of war had quashed any thought of new junkets. Then, in baseball's boom year of 1867 the Washington Nationals, a club that had formed prior to the war, announced that it would take a trip unlike any thus far attempted. A notice published in the *Clipper* read:

> The famous Washington club will start upon their proposed Western trip on the 10th [of July], visiting and playing friendly games with the leading clubs of Columbus, Cincinnati, Louisville, Indianapolis, St. Louis, and Chicago, reaching the latter place on the 24th. . . .

The Washington club was in fact not yet famous, but wished to become so. It had played only five match games in 1865, when it had welcomed clubs from Philadelphia and Brooklyn to play on the lot behind newly installed President Andrew Johnson's White House. Arthur Pue Gorman, who would become a U.S. senator from Maryland and, in 1905, a member of the Mills Commission, was president of the National club as well as its dashing shortstop. In 1866, though, he relinquished his position on the nine as the Nationals imported several stronger players from Philadelphia and Brooklyn as well as from Rochester. Although that aggregation won ten games against five defeats, they were by no means a club to rank alongside the Atlantics, Athletics, Mutuals, or the 1866 champion Unions of Morrisania. Those Unions were led by handsome young George Wright, the coming hero of the age, whose older brother Harry had played with the Knickerbockers in the 1850s and had lately reverted to the role of a cricket professional, in Cincinnati.

In 1867, the Nationals strengthened themselves with additional recruits, giving each a patronage government job, and somehow persuaded George Wright to join them too. Although the players were nominal amateurs, there can be no doubt of their uniformly professional status. The club president listed George Wright's place of employment as 238 Pennsylvania Avenue, at that time an open field and even today a parking lot. During the three weeks of their Western tour, the Nationals made a show of maintaining their amateur status by refusing payments of any kind, even declining reimbursement for travel expenses; these, of course, were covered by their employers, who had graciously permitted them to abandon the desks at which they had seldom been seen anyway. The aim of the National club directors in going out on tour was not pecuniary gain but social éclat and pride of place: The Western farmers had been getting a bit chesty about their brand of baseball and, it was thought back East, needed a slap of reality at the hands of an experienced ball club. Recording the tour at the Nationals' invitation was Henry Chadwick, who had been invited along as official scorer with the understanding that he would also issue detailed reports of the club's conquests in his new weekly, *The Ball Players' Chronicle.*

The Nationals prepared for their trip with easy triumphs over local cupcakes: They opened their season with a 91–8 pasting of a club from the Department of the Interior on June 3, followed by four victories over the capital's Jefferson, Olympic, Continental, and Union clubs. The first game of the Western tour took place on July 13 in Columbus, Ohio, against the Capital club of that city; the outcome was a 90–10 shellacking mercifully halted after seven innings. Their next game figured to be more competitive, as they journeyed to Cincinnati to play the Red Stockings on the 15th, in a battle of two unbeaten nines.

Harry Wright had left New York for the Queen City of the West in March 1865 to serve as the professional instructor and bowler of its Union Cricket Club. It may have seemed to him that as there was no real money to be made from baseball, and the distant cricket club was offering him $1,200 annual salary, he might as well return to the trade of his father, Sam, the cricket professional of the celebrated St. George club. Brother George may have thought the very same way, for he, too, returned to the cricket fold that year, as the resident professional of the Philadelphia Cricket Club, though he continued to play baseball with the Olympics on Wednesdays.

By the summer of 1866, the Cincinnati Base Ball Club formed, and Harry Wright was enticed into being its pitcher. To devote his full attention to the new national game for 1867, the baseball club's directors, many of them holding office in common with the cricket club, offered him the same salary he was already receiving to switch sports. The other players were local amateurs, including some doing double duty as cricketers, and they did not take the field until the end of September, playing only four games before cold set in.

Leading up to their match with the Nationals, the 1867 edition of the Cincinnati Base Ball Club—already popularly named "Red Stockings" for the innovation of hiking their pants, better to display their manly calves in carmine hose, while all other players still wore long trousers—had drubbed the Buckeye of Cincinnati (82–40), the Holt of Newport, Kentucky (by scores of 53–33 and 93–22), the Louisvilles (60–24), and the Live Oak of Cincinnati (56–18). (A low-scoring game in these days was one of forty combined runs or less; the prevalence of errors in the barehanded era, plus the continuing restrictions on the pitcher's delivery, made for high scores indeed.) But Harry's expected pleasure in playing against his brother's club soon was dashed: After initially holding their own against the Nationals, tied at 6–6 into the fourth inning, the Reds ultimately were humiliated by a count of 53–10. Although this would be their only loss of the year, it came against their only opponent from outside the tristate area, and so a lesson was there to be drawn. At the end of the season, the Red Stocking directors instructed Harry to follow the Nationals' model and begin recruiting professionals from distant places.

After crushing the Red Stockings, then the Buckeyes, the Nationals departed Cincinnati for Indianapolis, Louisville, and St. Louis, racking up ever more lopsided victories. In successive contests in mid-July they scored 106 and 113 runs. Chicago would be the final stop on the tour, with much anticipated games against that city's best, the Excelsiors and Atlantics, named in emulation of Brooklyn's finest clubs. The Forest Citys of Rockford had already played the Excelsiors twice that year, losing narrowly each time, and accordingly were invited to Chicago to play what amounted to a warm-up game against the Nationals on the 25th. Rockford was led by novice pitcher Albert Spalding, not yet seventeen years of age, who, in his own words,

> experienced a severe case of stage fright when I found myself in the pitcher's box, facing such renowned players as George Wright, [Frank]

Norton, [Harry] Berthrong, [George] Fox, and others of the visiting team. It was the first big game before a large audience in which I had ever participated. The great reputations of the Eastern players and the extraordinary one-sided scores by which they had defeated clubs in Columbus, Cincinnati, Louisville, Indianapolis and St. Louis, caused me to shudder at the contemplation of punishment my pitching was about to receive. A great lump arose in my throat, and my heart beat so like a trip-hammer that I imagined it could be heard by everyone on the grounds.

I knew, also, that every player on the Rockford nine had an idea that their kid pitcher would surely become rattled and go to pieces as soon as the strong batters of the Nationals had opportunity to fall upon his delivery. . . .

In the first innings, the Rockfords made two runs and the Nationals three, which in those days was called good ball playing. In the second innings, five runs by the Nationals and eight by the Rockfords gave the latter a lead by ten to eight. In the third, the Nationals drew a blank and Rockford made five runs, thus putting Rockford to the good by a score of fifteen to eight for the Nationals. The fourth and fifth yielded three runs to the Nationals and one to the Rockfords. In the sixth inning the Nationals made seven runs and the Rockfords eight, which made the score at the end of the sixth inning, Nationals, 18; Rockford, 24.

While the Forest Citys had by this time gotten pretty well settled and their stage-fright had disappeared, yet none of us even then had the remotest idea that we were destined to win the game over such a famous antagonist. The thought or suggestion of such a thing at that stage would probably have thrown us into another mental spasm.

At this psychological moment, Col. Frank Jones, President of the National Club, rushed up to George Wright, who was about to take his position at the bat, and said, in a louder voice possibly than he intended:

"Do you know, George, that this is the seventh innings and we are six runs behind? You must discard your heavy bat and take a lighter one; for to lose this game would be to make our whole trip a failure." Col. Jones' excited manner plainly indicated his anxiety.

This incident inspired the Rockfords with confidence and determination, and for the first time we began to realize that victory was not only possible, but probable, and the playing of our whole team from that time forward was brilliant.

Rockford and Spalding held their six-run lead, emerging victorious by a score of 29–23. There had been upsets before in baseball's brief history, but never one on this scale. Immediately it was alleged that the Nationals had tanked the game so as to narrow the odds for their coming contests against the Excelsiors and Atlantics. When the Nationals won those games by respective scores of 49–4 and 78–17 to close out their tour, the cries of fraud regarding the Rockford contest only grew louder. No one could have known that several of the Forest City lads would one day become nationally prominent players—particularly Spalding and infielder Ross Barnes.

Albert Goodwill Spalding, born September 2, 1850, on a farm in Byron, Illinois, was sent by his widowed mother to boarding school in nearby Rockford in 1863, where with a number of school companions, including Barnes, he went on to organize the junior Pioneer Base Ball Club. By 1865, the city also had two adult clubs, the Mercantile and the new Forest City, so when the Pioneers defeated the Mercantiles, 26–2, Forest City invited both Spalding and Barnes to join them. Except for a brief interlude after his victory over the Nationals in 1867, when he accepted a strangely high-paying job as a grocery clerk in Chicago so that he could pitch for the Excelsiors, Spalding stayed with the Rockford nine through the 1870 season. In the fall, he and Barnes accepted offers from Harry Wright, now with Boston along with his brother George, to play ball for the newly formed Red Stockings of Boston.

After the success of the Nationals' expedition, touring became a craze in 1868, with the perceived benefits being not only civic boosterism but also, perhaps too high-mindedly, national reconciliation. Sympathy for the ravaged South had been evidenced in October 1867 in the border city of Cincinnati, where the Red Stockings and Buckeyes played a benefit game for yellow-fever sufferers in Galveston and New Orleans, raising $500 despite a low attendance attributable to inclement weather. In January, the Brooklyn Atlantics announced a two-week tour of the South for March. Their plan was to play in New Orleans, Mobile, Savannah, and Charleston, then return home with their characters burnished and coffers filled. By the time March rolled around, however, storm season had set in, and, besides, the Southern clubs had extended no revenue guarantees, so the tour was canceled. The Philadelphia Athletics toured, too, losing to Niagara of Buffalo in an upset but defeating the Cincinnati Red Stockings. The Reds, though strengthened by the addition of several new hands and finishing with a strong mark of 36–7 in match games, were still unable to defeat the top professional clubs of New York, Brooklyn, and Philadelphia.

Writing about club tours, the ubiquitous Chadwick, editor of *De Witt's Base-Ball Guide for 1869*, asked:

> Could some prominent Southern club—the Monticellos of the University of Virginia, or the Louisville Clubs, for instance,—be induced to visit New York, we feel confident that the result would be greatly beneficial in removing some portion of the existing sectional prejudices which are among the greatest obstacles to true reconstruction.

In this perhaps naive era of hoped-for healing and good feeling, baseball was viewed as a balm, the one American institution about which all could agree. The Mutual Club of Washington, D.C.—the "colored Mutes" for whom Frederick Douglass' son Charles was both player and corresponding secretary—embarked upon an August 1869 tour. The *Utica Express* advised its readers that: "The colored gentlemen composing the Mutual Base Ball Club, and hailing from Washington, took a farewell promenade on Pennsylvania avenue the other day, and stretched their sable pinions for a Northern flight." (Casually comparing the Mutuals to blackbirds was in those days not thought racist in the least.) The tourists played against clubs in underground-railroad centers such as Lockport and Rochester in addition to Niagara Falls, Canajoharie, and Troy.

The colored Mutuals as well as the colored Alerts also played games that year against the Washington Olympics, a top-ranked white club whose co-founder and president was Abraham G. Mills, he of the Special Commission of 1905–07. When the Olympics met the Alerts, the *Brooklyn Eagle*'s Washington correspondent (uncredited but surely St. Clair McKelway, granduncle of the longtime *New Yorker* writer of the same name) opined:

> Perhaps there could not be a more striking illustration of the social change of the last eight years. Until now when a question of color has arisen, it has been based solely on a claim of equal civil and political rights for the negro. Some of the Radicals have argued that the extension of all the privileges of citizenship to the black man did not involve

> recognition of his social equality; that the former were wholly distinct from the latter. To-day, however, the social question fairly comes up. It is not a political or civil right or a privilege of citizenship that a colored base ball club shall be permitted to challenge a white base ball club, and that the challenge shall be accepted. It is purely a voluntary matter, having nothing to do with any law of Congress or amendment to the Constitution. The peaceful way in which this new war of races is carried on is significant. How long is it since such a game as that proposed to be played to-day would have provoked a riot? The Washington of to-day is not the Washington of the earlier time.

The Olympics of Philadelphia, a pioneering club dating back to 1833, also played an interracial contest in 1869, against the Pythians, who were led by African-American infielder and club president Octavius V. Catto; only two years earlier, the Pythians had been barred from joining the Pennsylvania State Association of Base Ball Players. In a further feint toward baseball comity before Jim Crow set in, a friendly contest was held in 1870 between two Boston clubs, one white and one black, both named Resolute, the winner to earn the exclusive right to use the name (the latter club won).

THAT SAME *DE WITT'S BASE-BALL GUIDE FOR 1869* proclaimed the coming end of covert professionalism. The National Association of Base Ball Players (NABBP) had given up the struggle and recognized two classes of player, basically to spare a purely amateur club the embarrassment of being whipped badly by another set of professed amateurs who actually were, at least in part, hired guns. As editor Chadwick wrote, "clubs can now openly advertise for professional players, and the latter as openly solicit employment as such."

It is often written that the Cincinnati Red Stockings of 1869 were the first professional club, which we have seen not to be so. Those inclined to nuanced definition will declare the Reds the first *openly* professional club, which is not quite true either, as any of the several clubs paying their players after 1868 no longer had to hide the fact. But the NABBP recognition of a professional class certainly enabled Harry Wright, armed by the Red Stockings' directors with an enlarged war chest, to recruit on a Steinbrennerian scale not seen before. For the

1868 club, Harry Wright had added local first baseman Charlie Gould and plucked Asa Brainard from the Washington Nationals, with whom the veteran pitcher had concluded the 1867 season. He had also signed New Yorkers John Van Buskirk Hatfield and Fred Waterman, and brought in catcher Doug Allison from Philadelphia. For 1869, he embraced the Nationals' model of total professionalism. In short order Harry Wright turned away all the club's local lads except for Gould; relinquished the revolver Hatfield back to the Mutuals, his former club; and signed Cal McVey from Indianapolis. He also reached terms with Charlie Sweasy, Andy Leonard, and Dick Hurley from the local Buckeyes, the first two having come to Cincinnati by way of their former club, the Irvingtons of New Jersey, the last named by way of Columbia College in New York. Harry's great coup was to secure the always available services of peripatetic brother George, who after playing with the Nationals in 1867 had returned to a former affiliation, the Unions of Morrisania, for 1868. Thus were the 1869 Red Stockings set to become the most accomplished club in the land and, at $9,300 in salaries alone, the most profligate. Here are the fabled figures offered to the starting nine and utility player:

Asa Brainard, pitcher, $1,100

Doug Allison, catcher, $800

Charlie Gould, first base, $800

Charlie Sweasy, second base, $800

Fred Waterman, third base, $1,000

George Wright, shortstop, $1,400

Andy Leonard, left field, $800

Harry Wright, center field/manager, $1,200

Cal McVey, right field, $800

Dick Hurley, substitute, $600

For a laborer at this time, "a dollar a day was very good pay," as in the old song about the Erie railroad, while a white-collar worker might have been expected to earn twice that. In that framework, the Red

Stocking salaries, based on a six-month term, may be seen as handsome indeed, but unlike ballplayer paychecks today, still less than ten times the average man's salary.

The hundreds of nonplaying members of the Red Stocking club knew that with so many Hessians from back East they would be "rooting for laundry" in 1869. (This term famously coined by comedian Jerry Seinfeld in the mid-1990s echoed an observation offered by Pliny the Younger in the context of chariot races in 109 C.E.: "If indeed it were the swiftness of the horses, or the skill of the men that attracted them, there might be some pretense for it [the passion of the crowd]. But it is the dress they like; it is the dress that takes their fancy. And if, in the midst of the course and the contest, the different parties were to change colors their different partisans would change sides and instantly desert the very same men and horses whom just before they were eagerly following. . . . Such mighty charms, such wondrous power reside in the color of a paltry tunic!")

George A. Wiltsee, a player in the Cincinnati Red Stocking junior club, recalled in 1916:

> Professional ballplayers were under a social ban, and the amateurs were not supposed to associate with them or even recognize them off the field—the only conversation between the two classes was on the diamond, and limited to subjects of the game. When the great Eastern players who composed the majority of the Reds were imported to Cincinnati, a trick was resorted to—a trick which has been copied at many a college and by many a semi-professional or alleged amateur ball club in more modern days. All these professionals were given jobs in the business houses of the team's backers—jobs where they reported every morning, were visible to callers or doubtful skeptics, and drew small salaries, although few of them ever did a stroke of work. In this manner, the gap between amateur and professional was bridged; the Reds became, nominally, local businessmen who didn't have to play ball for a living and, slowly, month by month, the barrier between "gentlemen" and "professionals" was broken down.

Thus, Harry Wright was listed as a jeweler, Asa Brainard as an insurance salesman, Doug Allison as a granite cutter, George Wright as an engraver, Andy Leonard as a hatter, and so on.

The Cincinnati playing season of 1869 opened on April 17, with the Red Stockings defeating a picked nine of local players, 24–15. After easily winning its first game at home against an NABBP opponent, the Great Western of Cincinnati, and then mauling the Kekionga club of Fort Wayne in a home-and-home series, the club set out on its first road trip, starting at Yellow Springs, Ohio, in a game against Antioch College. From May to November of 1869 the Red Stockings traveled nearly twelve thousand miles from Boston to San Francisco and seemingly all points in between, playing at least sixty-four games and losing not a single one. Fifty-seven of these contests came against NABBP clubs and in these games they scored an average of forty-two runs. George Wright registered five hits and ten total bases per game, collecting forty-nine home runs among his 304 hits and batting .629. To the argument that the opposition was frequently soft: In the club's nineteen games against fellow professionals (the Reds won all, of course), George hit thirteen home runs and batted .587. Against Spalding's Forest City Club, the Reds won handily three times.

The Cincinnati winning streak ran into a couple of close matches, most notably a game on June 15 in which they defeated the powerful Mutuals of New York, at Cammeyer's Union Grounds in Brooklyn, by 4–2, the lowest combined score ever recorded to that time. At a time when holding an opponent to ten runs or fewer was regarded as a masterpiece of pitching and defense, this was instantly anointed the greatest game ever played. The Reds also ran into a tough match on August 26, at home against the Unions of Lansingburgh, New York, also known as the Troy Haymakers. This contest is listed in the record as a 17–17 tie, concluded after five innings, but chroniclers accord a forfeit victory to the Red Stockings. The principal backer of the Union club, bare-knuckle boxing champion, gambler, and congressman John Morrissey, was said to have bet some $60,000 on his boys, an enormous figure at the time and the equivalent of perhaps $2 million today. To protect his bets and those of his compatriots, with the Union nine even in the score, Morrissey instructed the team to get into an argument with the umpire and stomp off the field. The umpire called a forfeit, though in some accounts the game was ruled a tie, washing all bets; subsequently, the Union club issued a written apology to the Red Stockings.

In September, the Reds visited California, traveling on the nearly completed Transcontinental Railroad (it was then complete from

Omaha to San Francisco). They won five games in San Francisco from the Eagles, Pacifics, and oddly named Atlantics, played some further exhibitions against picked nines, then returned home in October after stops in Nebraska, Illinois, Indiana, and Kentucky. The Reds brought their unprecedented season to a close on November 5, defeating the Mutuals of New York in Cincinnati, this time by a comfortable margin, then topping off their campaign with a game against the best that the Queen City's other clubs could muster.

The Red Stockings took the field again in 1870, with all their regular players returning, and started the year with twenty-four consecutive victories, including a swing through the South. George Wright had been the object of an offseason bidding war between the newly formed Chicago White Stockings and the Reds, as recalled by Chicago manager Tom Foley:

> When I set out to organize a team for Chicago in 1869, a team that would beat the up-to-that-time invincible Cincinnati Reds, I threw out a line for Wright, who was then the captain and short fielder of that team. It was in 1869, after the Cincinnati Reds had beaten every team they met, that a friend asked me why I did not organize a team for Chicago that would beat the Reds. Even George Wright, then the captain of the invincible Reds, asked me that question.
>
> I said I would if he would come and captain the nine. . . . And that winter I had a duel with the Cincinnati people over Wright. I would make him an offer, and they would raise it. I would come back and they would see my raise. I finally offered him $2,500, only to see that covered, and then I got Jimmy Wood to captain and play second.

Counting their final eight victories in 1868, this brought the Reds' three-year streak against NABBP clubs to eighty-nine; factoring in all of their games, historian Lee Allen set the undefeated skein at 130, perhaps too high. "But defeat came eventually," Allen wrote, "and under heartbreaking circumstances":

> On the afternoon of June 14, 1870, before a crowd of nine thousand at the Capitoline Grounds at Brooklyn [at a new peak admission price of fifty cents a head; each member of the Atlantics took home an incredible $364], the Red Stockings were defeated by the Atlantics, 8 to 7,

in eleven innings. . . . After nine innings, the game . . . was tied, 5 to 5. The Atlantics wanted to call the game a draw, but Harry Wright's boys insisted on playing extra innings. When the Reds scored twice in the eleventh, it appeared that victory would be theirs. But the Atlantics rallied for three runs and the game. A key play occurred when an exuberant Brooklyn spectator jumped on the back of Cal McVey as he was in the act of fielding a fairly hit ball, thereby permitting a run to score. [Fan interference was discretionary with the umpire, and with an overflow crowd standing in the outfield, the umpire exercised his discretion and made no call.] President Champion announced the sad news in a telegram to Cincinnati:

> NEW YORK, JUNE 14, 1870—ATLANTICS 8; CINCINNATI 7. THE FINEST GAME EVER PLAYED. OUR BOYS DID NOBLY, BUT FORTUNE WAS AGAINST THEM. ELEVEN INNINGS PLAYED. THOUGH BEATEN, NOT DISGRACED.
>
> AARON B. CHAMPION, CINCINNATI BASE BALL CLUB.

The bubble had burst. Attendance began to decline, and although the Reds won their next fifteen games, battled to a 16–16 tie with the Forest City of Rockford, then won three more, the club's fans and especially its financial supporters grew restless. The great tour of 1869 netted the club precisely $1.39; what would be the cost of anything less than perfection? Five other defeats followed in 1870, including one to Rockford and two to the new Chicago White Stockings, created on the Red Stocking model with players recruited from Eastern clubs. On November 21, 1870, the club's new president, picture framer A. P. C. Bonte, circulated this open letter:

> According to the custom, the Executive Board reports to the members of the CINCINNATI BASE BALL CLUB its determination in reference to the base ball season of 1871. We have had communication with many of the leading base ball players throughout the country, as well as with the various members of our former nine. Upon the information thus obtained, we have arrived at the conclusion that to employ a nine for the coming season, at the enormous salaries now demanded by the professional players, would plunge our club deeply into debt at the end of the year. The experience of the past two years has taught us that a nine whose aggregate salaries

exceed six or eight thousand dollars can not, even with the strictest economy, be self-sustaining. If we should employ a nine at the high salaries now asked, the maximum sum above stated would be nearly doubled. The large liabilities thus incurred would result in bankruptcy or compel a heavy levy upon our members to make up a deficiency. We are also satisfied that payment of large salaries causes jealousy, and leads to extravagance and dissipation on the part of the players, which is injurious to them, and is also destructive of that subordination and good feeling necessary to the success of a nine.

Our members have year after year contributed liberally for the liquidation of the expenses incurred in the employment of players. We do not feel that we would be justified in calling upon them again; and, therefore, for the reasons herein stated, have resolved to hire no players for the coming season. We believe that there will be a development of the amateur talent of our club, such as has not been displayed since we employed professionals, and that we will still enjoy the pleasure of witnessing many exciting contests on our grounds. We take this opportunity of stating that our club and grounds are entirely free of debt; and, deeming it our first duty to see that they remain so, we pursue the course indicated in this circular.

For the executive board,
A. P. C. Bonte, President

The club's assets, including the stands, were sold to satisfy creditors. Harry Wright and the other Red Stocking players quickly made new employment arrangements for 1871. Not only did Cincinnati's baseball club collapse, so did the entire National Association. For 1870, the NABBP had unwisely reunited the two distinct classes—amateur and professional—into one, to the pleasure of neither. In the following year, the two concluded to dissolve the partnership.

On the rainy evening of March 17, 1871, delegates from ten professional baseball clubs met at Collier's Rooms, an upstairs saloon run by thirty-two-year-old character actor James W. Collier at the corner of Broadway and 13th Street, just across from Wallack's Theatre, where he frequently trod the boards. The clubs had come together at the invitation of the Mutuals to establish a new professional National Association, based largely upon the rules and regulations of the amateur organization from which they had just departed. Of the ten clubs present, eight plunked down the mandatory ten dollars to join: the already established Athletics (Philadelphia), Mutuals (New York), Olympics (Washington), Haymakers (Troy), White Stockings (Chicago), two Forest City clubs (Rockford and Cleveland), plus Harry Wright's newly founded Red Stockings of Boston. The Eckfords of Brooklyn and Nationals of Washington sent delegates to the meeting, but held tight to their wallets and did not join the new National Association for play in 1871. The Atlantics of Brooklyn, who might have been expected to join, did not send a delegate, deciding to retain so-called amateur status.

In the days that followed, a surprising ninth club came across with the dues: the Kekionga of Fort Wayne, uncompetitive as an amateur club in its previous seasons but now a self-declared professional nine, based on its having picked up several stranded players from the Maryland Club of Baltimore, which had run out of funds while playing in Chicago in August 1870. The star of the Marylands was pitcher Bobby Mathews, who would now pitch for the Kekiongas. Eleven days after the meeting at Collier's Rooms, the Kekionga directors dispatched the club secretary, as well as their catcher and captain in the previous year, George J. E. Mayer, to New York to acquire additional professional players. On or before April 13, Mayer felt emboldened to write to Harry Wright:

> We take pleasure in announcing to you that our Professional Club is now in condition to meet all first class clubs, and herewith invite your club to visit us, guaranteeing that all will prove most satisfactory. Our Grounds have been greatly improved this season, and we can assure you they are second to none in America. Fort Wayne is the terminus of seven Rail Roads, and numbers over twenty-five thousand inhabitants. Therefore, should [you] favor us with a visit, we advise that as early notice as possible be sent us so games can be properly advertised. Will grant in all games one-half net receipts, and expect the same in return. Make our Western Tour in June; Eastern Tour August; Southern Tour October.

Harry Wright had wasted no time sulking over the blowup of his Cincinnati club: responding to an offer from Boston, where in recent memory the New York game had been anathema, he transferred the Red Stocking modus operandi and name to Beantown, bringing with him three Reds from the 1869–70 aggregation: brother George, Charlie Gould, and Cal McVey. Newly added to the Boston roster were Dave Birdsall from the Union of Morrisania, Harry Schafer from the Philadelphia Athletics and, stunningly, Al Spalding, Ross Barnes, and Fred Cone from Rockford.

The depleted Forest City of Rockford nine would end up as the last-place entry in the new league before folding altogether, but it did introduce a new star in Adrian Constantine Anson of the ball-playing Anson family of Marshalltown, Iowa. The first white child born in that remote outpost, on April 17, 1852, Adrian Anson was the son of mayor Henry Anson, who played third base for the state champion Marshalltown Stars of 1868. Sturgis Anson (so large that he was called "the Elephant") manned center field, and his brother Adrian, a large youngster himself, played an ungainly second base. In 1865, the thirteen-year-old Adrian had been shipped off to Notre Dame at South Bend, Indiana, then more a boarding school than a college, where for two years he studied indifferently and played ball avidly, perhaps alongside the aforementioned George J. E. Mayer of Fort Wayne, who was also enrolled at Notre Dame in 1865 through 1867.

Back home at Marshalltown and playing for the Stars, Adrian and Sturgis Anson excelled in a pair of games against Rockford in September 1870. Impressed, the Forest City club offered professional contracts to both. Sturgis declined, but Adrian, who had always wanted to play baseball against the best, signed on the dotted line. In this rare survivor from the first year of professional league play—in other words, the first season of what we today call Major League Baseball—the officers of the newly organized "Forest City Base Ball Club of Rockford, Illinois" agreed to pay Anson $66.67 each month between April and October, a $400 figure that was $200 less than the low man on the Cincinnati Reds' roster of 1869. In return Anson was obliged to offer "cheerfull, prompt, and respectfull" obedience to the directors, to abstain from alcohol and profanity, and to practice at least two and a half hours a day. (A full transcription of the contract is offered in the Notes.)

For his $400 in pay over the six-month period (a century later, players would still need to look to offseason employment to make ends meet), the nineteen-year-old third baseman led all Rockford players with a batting average of .325 and led the league in doubles.

In Boston, Al Spalding would sign a contract for reportedly $2,500, though he had trouble collecting the last $800 of that after the close of the campaign. When the Philadelphia Athletics offered Anson $1,250 to play for them in 1872, he could hardly resist, though, like Spalding, his heart was in the West. He offered to stay with Rockford for less, but the bedraggled club was already at the precipice. The idea of a reserve clause that would bind a player to his team despite lack of agreement as to the next year's terms was a management inspiration still in the future.

The National Association of Professional Base Ball Players launched its inaugural season with a single game on May 4, 1871. The Forest City of Cleveland, led by Jim "Deacon" White, came to Fort Wayne to play the revamped Kekiongas, none of whom had cut much of a figure in the baseball world outside Baltimore except Mathews, who was only nineteen. Mayer had given up his position in the nine to Billy Lennon, a stronger catcher he recruited from the Mohawks of New York. In what the Fort Wayne correspondent to the *Chicago Tribune* called "the finest game on record in this country," Mathews shut out the visiting Forest Citys by 2–0 in a game in which there were no errors by Cleveland and only three by Fort Wayne, a marvel in those days of bare hands and rutted fields. Because of threatening weather, only 500 spectators witnessed this historic game. Play was finally stopped by rain after the top of the ninth inning had been concluded, depriving the Kekiongas of their completed final at bat. (It was not yet the custom for the home club, leading after eight and a half frames, to dispense with its final turn; this practice was a vestige of baseball's original purpose, field exercise.)

But Fort Wayne's opening day turned out to be very nearly its high water mark. After winning three of its next four contests, the club went 1–11; despite winning two games at home in late August, it chose to disband on a relative high note. Secretary Mayer had traveled with the team to witness a 21–0 slaughter on June 2 in Boston, with Spalding the victor, and then another shutout loss at Rockford, 4–0 at the hands of Cherokee Fisher, Spalding's successor as pitcher of the Forest Citys, on August 3. The Kekiongas were clearly down and nearly out.

Despite the loss of Schafer to Boston for 1871, the Philadelphia Athletics would retain their strongest players and win the championship of the National Association's wild first year. On September 11, the Chicago White Stockings topped the standings with a record of 17–8, trailed closely by the Athletics at 17–9 and Boston at 15–9. (If these game totals seem low, reflect on the transportation difficulties and each club's copious scheduling of well-paying exhibition games between mandated championship contests.) However, games won and lost, and the resulting percentage, did not decide the winner in this first year of the NA as it does today; it was the number of five-game series won and lost with the other clubs. On this date, Boston and Chicago had each won three and lost none, while Philadelphia had won three but lost one, to Boston. In this first year of league play, even teams that fell out of the pennant race (or the league itself, as with the Kekiongas) could point to enduring accomplishments. Troy finished in the middle of the pack at 13–15 but provided the big leagues' first Hispanic player in third baseman Esteban Bellán, as well as a Jewish slugger in Lipman Pike, who batted .377 and tied for the league lead in home runs.

The closing events of the 1871 season are unequaled before or since. The Boston Red Stockings knew that if they won their final six games, the championship would be theirs. When they lost to the White Stockings at Chicago on September 29, the door was open to both Chicago and Philadelphia. Boston defeated Troy on October 7. On the following day Mrs. O'Leary's cow kicked over the kerosene lantern (or so the story goes), the great Chicago fire broke out, and all the White Stockings' equipment was lost as the clubhouse and grounds went up in flames. Because the club was now broke, it decided to play out its schedule on the road, wearing borrowed uniforms of varying hues and styles.

The game of October 30 between the motley-garbed White Stockings and the Athletics decided the championship. Scheduled to be played at Chicago, the game now was moved to Brooklyn, a neutral site. Chicago played well, all things considered, but the Athletics emerged on top, 4–1, as Dick McBride pitched a shutout into the final frame. So needy were the Chicago players that they opted to play November exhibitions against the Mutuals and Haymakers, in poor weather and before slim crowds, just so they could eat and earn their train fare back home. Baseball in Chicago, which had been built up with such great expectations and expenditures, would now be mothballed for the next two seasons; when the club returned in 1874 it would do so with a chip on its shoulder.

Largely unnoted in the immediate aftermath of the Chicago fire of October 8 was the murder of Octavius V. Catto, leader of the Pythian Base Ball Club of Philadelphia. Educator, radical, and civic pioneer, Catto was also the founder, captain, and second baseman or shortstop of the ball club. On October 10, Election Day, after casting his ballot, a privilege newly extended to Pennsylvania's African Americans, Catto proceeded homeward. He crossed paths with Frank Kelly, a Democratic Party operative who that day had already attacked one black voter who, like others of his race, was presumed to be Republican in his sentiments. Kelly turned after passing Catto, shot him once in the back, and then, after Catto struggled to his feet and spun around to face his attacker, fatally in the heart. Kelly was subsequently acquitted at trial.

Boston regrouped to capture the flag in each of the National Association's following four years, eventually becoming so proficient that fan interest, especially in the West, began to wane. Another contributing factor to flagging enthusiasm may have been the constant accusations in the press of inebriation and hippodroming, that is, play-acting to the tune of the gamblers. The fledgling pro circuit was run not by club owners but by the players, some of whom received monthly salaries while others shared gate receipts. Fly-by-night clubs would pay their ten-dollar fee to join the league, invite the big clubs to visit for a hometown payday, then decline to incur the expense of a reciprocal visit. Other clubs played so poorly that they could not draw at home or on the road (for example, the once proud Eckfords of Brooklyn, whose record in 1872 was 3–26, or the Atlantics of 1875, who were 2–42). Chadwick observed, "we hear old players talk of base-ball having become 'played out,' and of its not being as lively as it was ten years ago."

Even a bold midseason trip to England in 1874 by the Red Stockings and the Philadelphia Athletics, reversing the direction of the celebrated English cricketers' tour of fifteen years earlier, failed to ignite passions on either side of the Atlantic. As the architect of baseball's most famous tour, that of the Cincinnati Red Stockings in 1869, Harry Wright was enlisted as business manager of the enterprise. In March, he sent Spalding, who seemed to him to have a nose for business despite no evidence of success in that line, to England to make the arrangements. From mid-July to mid-September, the Boston and Philadelphia clubs would excuse themselves from regular season competition to play both baseball and cricket in England and Ireland to the widespread bemusement of the locals.

Although the 1874 trip was a flop financially and promotionally, it afforded Spalding a valuable experience for the world tour he would lead in 1888 and 1889 when, as a sporting-goods magnate, he had the not utterly implausible idea of making baseball an international pastime. Cricket had faded into insignificance in America, and changes in its rules made it seem even more brutal than baseball. "The modern English game," reported a sporting-goods seller in New York, "with its catapult bowling, forcing the batsman to adopt either a coat of mail or to cover himself with India-rubber padding until he looked like an armadillo, or in default of this, running the risk of having his legs or arms broken, very naturally destroyed all zest in the game." Like several of the celebrated cricketers, Spalding realized that more money might be made from selling the implements of his trade than in plying it. He was the most successful pitcher in the game, compiling a win-loss record in the five years of the National Association of 204–53, yet he knew his playing career must conclude in a professional dead end.

Nor was Spalding the first baseball player to think so, having been preceded in this notion by Harry Wright and Charlie Gould, who opened a sporting-goods emporium at 18 Boylston Street in Boston in 1871. The pair would split in 1873, with the former going on in 1879 to form Wright, Howland & Mahn. Harry was followed in short order on the mercantile path by brother George, who brought in a partner named Henry Ditson to establish a long-lasting firm, and in Philadelphia by Al Reach, who briefly partnered with Albert C. Johnston in a cigar and sporting-goods store before retreating to a venture all his own and becoming wealthy. Reach and George Wright would go on to sell their businesses to Spalding, secretly, though continuing in business under their old names; each would also be named to the Mills Commission in 1905.

SPALDING'S ENTREPRENEURIAL ACUMEN WAS further sharpened by his dealings with William Ambrose Hulbert, a director of the

Chicago Club at its founding in 1870, who became its president in 1875. Born near Cooperstown, New York, in 1832, he was fond of telling people, "I'd rather be a lamppost in Chicago than a millionaire elsewhere."

An incident that occurred in 1874 provided the spark that drove Hulbert first to despair, and then to cunning. This was a time of rampant revolving, and the White Stockings were nervous that their diminutive shortstop, Davy Force, would desert them at season's end, as he had left three other clubs in the previous three autumns. In September 1874, they signed him to a renewal contract for 1875; then they learned that, because the season was still in progress, National Association rules rendered the contract invalid. Chicago signed Force to another contract in November, but the organization blundered by backdating the contract to September, thus voiding it once again. In December, the Philadelphia Athletics offered Force a contract, and he signed it. The Association Council, led by a Philadelphia official, upheld Force's deal with the Athletics.

Spalding met with a distressed Hulbert in mid-1875, when Boston was yet again running away with the pennant race. Years later, he would write of the wounded civic pride and, by modern standards, paranoia and kettle-calling that afflicted Hulbert:

> It was borne to him one day that the reason why Chicago, whose phenomenal achievements on other lines were attracting the wonder of all the world, could make no better showing on the diamond was because the East was in league against her; that certain Base Ball magnates in the Atlantic States were in control of the game; were manipulating things to the detriment of Chicago and all Western cities; that if the Chicago Club signed an exceptionally strong player he was sure to be stolen from her; that contracts had no force, because the fellows down East would and did offer players increased salaries and date new contracts back to suit their own ends.

Hulbert reminded Spalding that he had made his name as a pitcher in the 1860s through his exploits with the Forest City club of Rockford. "Spalding, you've no business playing in Boston; you're a Western boy, and you belong right here. If you'll come to Chicago, I'll accept [in fact, continue in] the Presidency of this Club, and we'll give those fellows a fight for their lives." Within a few months, Hulbert proceeded to give the Easterners, who had rustled his prize shortstop, a taste of their own medicine. He not only raided Boston for Spalding but also snatched Ross Barnes, who would bat .364 in his final season with Boston; Deacon White, who would hit for an average of .367; and Cal McVey, who would bat .355. From the hated Philadelphia Athletics Hulbert took another Western boy and perhaps the top prize, Anson.

When word leaked in the summer of 1875 that Chicago had stripped Boston of its stars for the following season, a columnist for the *Worcester Spy* wrote of Boston's loss: "Like Rachel weeping for her children, she refuses to be comforted because the famous baseball nine, the perennial champion, the city's most cherished possession, has been captured by Chicago."

Now Hulbert had real cause for worry. Because his club's contracts had been signed yet again in midseason, the Association Council could invalidate them and even, perhaps, expel Chicago for gross misconduct. Then, he came up with a truly big idea. "Spalding," he said to his eventual ally in revolution, "I have a new scheme. Let us anticipate the Eastern cusses and organize a new association before the March [1876] meeting, and then see who does the expelling."

Spalding needed little convincing. In "Interview with Al Spalding, Captain of the Centennial Chicagos," published on November 28, 1875, an unnamed reporter for the *Chicago Tribune*, almost certainly Lewis Meacham, recorded the incendiary thoughts of Spalding, and presumably Hulbert. The reporter visited the new White Stockings' pitcher at the Rockford home of William Thayer Brown, who had married Al's sister, Mary Spalding, in August. Mary's high-school classmate and close friend Lizzie Churchill, formerly Al's fiancée, had been married earlier that year, also in Rockford, to George J. E. Mayer of Fort Wayne and its former Kekionga Base Ball Club. Completing the peculiar matrimonial triangle, Al Spalding was in Rockford on a honeymoon trip of his own, having married Josie Keith of Boston only the week before.

After reviewing the prospects of each of the clubs likely to make up the National Association for 1876, and agreeing with the reporter that the best clubs were now in the West, Spalding said of his Chicago teammates:

The boys also wish it explicitly understood that their motto is like the ancient Greek, of whom it is said:

Glory he loved for glory's sake alone,
Nor would he change the simple laurel-wreath
For India's wealth or Persia's wide domain.

There will be no games sold out,—no hippodrome business,—and when the Chicago boys lose a game their friends may rest assured it was because they could not possibly win it.

The reporter added, "So far as Mr. Spalding knew, there has [sic] not been more than half-a-dozen players who have thus recklessly risked their characters as gentlemen and sold out the game. There has been positive proof of this many, but [not] further than that. . . . If the National Base-Ball Association did not take hold of it, the base-ball players had determined to push these unprincipled men to the wall, and rid themselves once and forever of men who were a disgrace to the profession." Spalding then continued:

It is the intention of the larger clubs to make some rules about contesting for the championship, so that clubs that have no earthly chance to win will not be allowed to play with first-rate clubs. . . . The leading clubs are going to do something for their own protection, and thereby root out the small fry. Unless this was done, at least twenty clubs from different cities are about to apply for admission to contest for the [1876] championship. . . . It was especially desirable to keep out all gamblers and jockeys if possible, and unless we do this . . . I have not much hope for a healthy revival of the good old-fashioned, honest base-ball. On some of the grounds, especially in Philadelphia and New York, pools are sold on the ground, and a base-ball match is an occasion for all sorts of evil practices. It is to be hoped the West will set the East an example this year. . . .

It would set quite an example, as on February 2, 1876, in a meeting at the Grand Central Hotel in New York, Hulbert, Spalding, and the Western faction of owners would leave the National Association and create a new National League of Professional Base Ball Clubs.

7

THE BIG IDEA

The low state of the National Association (NA) after the 1875 campaign could be chalked up to rampant corruption and drunkenness, as well as to radically unbalanced competition that permitted Boston to win the championship four years running. In that final year of the first professional league, Harry Wright's Red Stockings opened the season with twenty-six victories and a tie and finished with a record of 71–8 while going undefeated at home. The association's replacement by the National League would come to be characterized by William Hulbert, and after his death by Albert Spalding, as the Hairbreadth Harry rescue of a game perched at the very edge of oblivion. In truth, the advent of the league was a clandestine coup, which Hulbert orchestrated to protect his stake in the newly strengthened Chicago White Stockings. Surreptitiously and perhaps illegally, certainly violating NA regulations, he had acquired Boston's Big Four—Spalding, Barnes, McVey, and White—plus Anson of the Athletics, and he feared that the NA directors would nullify these signings, or even expel the White Stockings. Hulbert's brilliant mix of propaganda, obfuscation, and bought-off news sources would supply his cohort Spalding with a lifelong lesson in bluff, bluster, and bravado.

Emulating the practice of traveling circuses and vagabond theater troupes, which, rather than pay for newsprint advertising, employed press agents to plant manufactured stories, Hulbert found his mouthpiece, by what route we cannot reconstruct, in *Chicago Tribune* reporter Lewis Meacham. An impecunious bachelor afflicted with chronic digestive ailments (from which he would die in 1878 at age thirty-two), Meacham had previously failed in a brush factory in Vermont, a sheep farm in Colorado, and in the proofreading department of the *Chicago Times*. He had been on his latest job only three months, with no prior involvement in baseball, when on October 24, 1875, he somehow came up with a plan for the National Association's reorganization and saw it published in the *Tribune:*

> SPORTING; The Professional Base Ball Association—What It Must Do to Be Saved. The Coming Trouble for the Game and Its Remedy.
>
> A glance over the ball-field for the season now nearly closed presents a problem for 1876 of more than ordinary importance to the game as an exhibition. At the beginning of this season thirteen clubs entered for the championship; three have disbanded and three more—the Atlantics, New Havens, and St. Louis Reds—are out of the championship race by reason of not having played any return games. . . .
>
> Now this same trick is to be attempted in 1876. Already announcements are made for the following clubs for 1876, eighteen in all: Chicago [White Stockings], St. Louis [Brown Stockings], Cincinnati [Red Stockings], Louisville [Grays], Mutual [of New York, a.k.a. Green Stockings], New York [a new club yet to be formed], Hartford [Dark Blues], Boston [Red Stockings], Athletic [of Philadelphia; a.k.a. Light Blues], Philadelphia [White Stockings], Americus [of Philadelphia], New Haven [Elm Citys], Atlantic [of Brooklyn], St. Louis [Reds], Buffalo [Bisons], Cleveland [Blues], Burlington [Illinois], Washington [Nationals of D.C.].
>
> Some of these enterprises may be still-born, but others will spring up to take their places, and the Centennial year will be opened with not less than a dozen and a half professional clubs. This may be fun for the little fellows, but it will be death to the first nine clubs named, who are really the only ones in the list who have much showing of prosperity. . . .

After detailing a plan that much resembled the eventual forming principles of the National League, Meacham, channeling Hulbert, concluded:

> It may be doubted whether the Professional Association will be willing to vote the restrictions proposed, and, if they do not, it will be the plain duty of the nine clubs named to withdraw from the Association as it now stands, and form an organization of their own,—a close corporation, too.

This shot across the bow, appearing in the most important paper in the West, should have drawn Eastern attention to the plot that was brewing. Hulbert and his allies would create a cartel with a new business model: The gate-sharing cooperative nines of the NA would give way to stock companies, firmly establishing the control of labor by capital. Gambling and speculation would relocate from the playing field and grandstand to the executive boardrooms. From being an association of players, headed by a veteran player, Bob Ferguson, the new governing body would emerge as an association of clubs. Small-market clubs, like the Kekionga of Fort Wayne or the Western of Keokuk or the Elm City of New Haven, which had plagued the NA through their inability either to compete or to complete their scheduled road trips, or to draw enough fans at home to cover the expenses of visiting clubs, would be cut adrift. Minimum population for participating cities, unspecified in the five years of the NA, would now be set at 75,000 (Meacham's draft principles had set the minimum at 100,000, except for Hartford). The former registration fee of ten dollars, which had created no barrier to entry by weak clubs, would now be raised to a hundred.

Hulbert and Spalding had been working in secret since mid-1875 to desert the Association. Following the Meacham proposal, in December they held meetings in Louisville with representatives from the three other Western clubs that ultimately would join the National League (Louisville, St. Louis, and Cincinnati). As Spalding later wrote, "The Louisville meeting was held with closed doors; and although it was known throughout the base-ball world that such a meeting had been held, the proceedings and designs of the meeting were not known until the Western Committee met the representatives of the Eastern clubs at the Grand Central Hotel in New York City, Feb. 2, 1876." Even after Hulbert sent a letter of invitation on January 23 to the four club presidents of the Eastern faction—Boston, Mutual of New York, Athletic of Philadelphia, and Hartford—there was no leak.

At the New York meeting, straws were drawn as a means to select the five directors; Morgan Bulkeley, president of the Hartford entry, thus became the league's accidental president. In 1937, through writers' ignorance of the circumstances of his ascension, he was granted a plaque in the Baseball Hall of Fame, along with Ban Johnson, the American League's first president; in 1905 Spalding would appoint Bulkeley to the Mills Commission investigating the game's origins. Hulbert, however, would not enter the Hall until 1995. In his year in office, Bulkeley did nothing of note; for 1877, the other club owners put a halt to the charade and insisted that Hulbert, who had functioned as the League's president from its first day, at last assume the title.

In another *Tribune* article, on February 7, Meacham predicted that the new league's owners would end "drunken behavior" and bring back the "honest play" that had characterized the amateur era. Gambling was to be prohibited on the ground of any of the league clubs, liquor selling was to be abolished, players were to be expelled for being interested in any wager on the game, and only one club would represent a city (Philadelphia had boasted three in 1875). Hippodroming, inebriation, and gambling in a section of the grandstand known as the pool box were all undeniable problems, but they might have been confronted directly within the structure of the National Association. Instead Hulbert used these issues as his Reichstag fire, justifying the dissolution of the N.A.'s business model and thus the Association itself.

Additionally, baseball's bad odor with the public was not exclusively a matter of on-the-field mischief. Speculation in gold in 1869 and in rail stocks in 1873 had created a national economic panic, followed by chronic unemployment and a "Long Depression" that ran uninterrupted into 1879: Only the onset of centennial fever provided the illusion of brief respite and a spur to patriotism, material culture, and bold enterprise.

Players would benefit from the revolutionary new National League, Meacham suggested, for it "assures them lucrative employment as long as they are honest and work hard." Admission to league games was fixed at fifty cents, a perhaps foolhardy tariff at a time when discretionary funds were at a premium. (In an earlier day, Harry Wright had reasoned that people will gladly pay "seventy-five cents to a dollar-fifty to go to the theater, and numbers prefer base ball to theatricals. We must make the games worth witnessing, and there will be no fault found with the price. A good game is worth 50 cents; a poor one is dear at 25.") Finally, to preempt the negative response to the league from the influential Henry Chadwick that Hulbert and Spalding anticipated, Meacham was permitted to characterize him in print as an old-fashioned "dead weight on the neck of the game."

Chadwick's response in the *Clipper* did not disappoint. Heading his article "A Startling Coup d'Etat," he wrote:

> For the past year or two we have been calling the attention of professional club-managers to the importance of doing something to put a stop to the growing abuses connected with their class of the baseball fraternity, the most prominent of which is the evil of fraudulent play in the form of "hippodroming," or the "selling" or "throwing" of games for betting purposes, practiced by knavish members of the club-teams, and countenanced by still worse club officials. While all have acknowledged the existence of the evil in question, and lamented the fact, none have hitherto taken any direct steps towards reform—at least, not prior to the close of the season of 1875. Last December, however, a meeting of club managers of Western organizations was held in Louisville, the object of which was to take the initiatory steps in a movement calculated to remove the existing odium from the professionals . . . to put a stop to fraudulent play among professional players, and to punish the clubs and their officials who countenanced it; and with this primary object there was the secondary one of revising the National Association laws so that knavish players could not be engaged after having become "marked" or suspected men. . . . Now, what was there to prevent this work from being entered upon boldly, manfully, consistently and openly, at the general convention of the National Association? . . . Why, therefore, this secret meeting, with closed doors and a star-chamber method of attaining the ostensible objects in view?

Father Chadwick's feelings were bruised. How could a thoroughgoing revision of the game take place without *him*? How could a coal dealer

(Hulbert) and a mere ballplayer (Spalding) reconstruct the game he had imagined, then willed into being? Chadwick called the National League approach an "anti-American method of doing business" but it was not long before he accepted Spalding's combined apology for Meacham's attack (which Spalding may well have crafted himself) and offer to edit his new annual *Spalding Guide*, a rival to the *De Witt Guide* and *Beadle's Dime Base-Ball Player.*

Hulbert's coup d'état swept away the opposition. The Philadelphia White Stocking and New Haven Elm City clubs of 1875, feeling particularly aggrieved because their exclusion implied crookedness, called for a convention of the semiprofessional clubs for March 1, 1876. This meeting produced nothing more than another meeting, one month later, at which time a schedule of play was proposed but not enacted. Clubs like the Atlantic of Brooklyn, Quickstep of Wilmington, Active of Reading, and Allegheny of Pittsburgh had no choice but to schedule contests with each other, with local aggregations, and—hard feelings could not endure when revenue beckoned—with league clubs having an open date in their schedules.

AS IT TURNED OUT, the National League won the war but not the peace. The Mutuals of New York and the Athletics of Philadelphia had been accustomed to determining their own fortunes. Not only were they among the original National Association franchises of 1871, they had been playing ball under their own banners since the 1850s. Once both were eliminated from the 1876 pennant race, dominated by Hulbert's new powerhouse White Stockings (finishing at 52–14, they topped Hartford and St. Louis by six games), their concluding Western swing of the season portended nothing but losses at the gate. Anticipating no consequence to their action, the Mutuals and the Athletics declined to fulfill their remaining schedule; after all, in the National Association such conduct had been tolerated. The Mutuals, who did not play fourteen of their scheduled seventy games, and the Athletics, who canceled eleven contests, were by no means the only financially straitened clubs in the NL's inaugural campaign; in fact only Chicago was in the black (a state of affairs that would endure to 1880).

At the league meetings in December 1876, despite the financial implications of losing the nation's two biggest markets and having to limp along with only six entrants in the upcoming season, Hulbert expelled the two franchises. He knew that the Mutuals were a hotbed of corruption, as they had been since the 1860s, and that it was the Athletics who had stolen Davy Force from him in 1874; he would see to it that Eastern interests would not control the National League as they had the Association.

League baseball would not return to New York or Philadelphia for six years. Chastened by experience, for 1877 Hulbert instituted the practice of determining the clubs' schedules through the league rather than through club secretaries, as had long been the custom. He also hired some umpires to strengthen the public's confidence in the integrity of the game; previously, only the home club could secure an arbiter more or less agreeable to the visiting nine.

The six clubs contending for the pennant in 1877 were Chicago, Louisville, St. Louis, and Cincinnati in the West, and only Boston and Hartford in the East. Chicago was considerably weakened by Deacon White's return to Boston, Ross Barnes' illness, and Spalding's refusal to pitch any longer, which prompted his shift to first base, where his bat proved inadequate for the position. Chicago fell to the middle of the pack as Boston and Louisville emerged as the class of the league.

Then, with only fifteen games left, Hulbert met the greatest challenge of the National League's formative years. There came an allegation of game-fixing by four players of the league-leading Louisville Grays: part-timer Al Nichols and shortstop Bill Craver (who had come to Louisville from the Mutuals), left fielder George Hall (arrived from the Athletics, with whom he had led the league in home runs in the NL's inaugural season), and, most damningly, star pitcher Jim Devlin. Louisville had endured a public betting scandal in 1876 when right fielder George Bechtel's wire to Devlin was intercepted:

> Bingham House, Philadelphia, June 10, 1876. We can make $500 if you lose the game today. Tell John [Chapman, the club's manager] and let me know at once. BECHTEL.

Devlin replied:

> I want you to understand I am not that kind of man. I play ball for the interest of those who hire me. DEVLIN.

Louisville said farewell to Bechtel, but he was re-signed by the Mutuals, his club in 1872, and played two games with them before the National Association expelled him.

Philadelphia native Devlin was vulnerable to such opportunities as Bechtel presented. He had not been paid his salary for two months, he told a *Chicago Tribune* reporter in November 1876. "I wanted to get home to see the show [the Centennial Exhibition], but I can't walk fast enough to get there now, and see no other way to go." Though Devlin begged the league office for his release so he could accept an offer from St. Louis, he found himself in Louisville again for a second campaign.

Devlin's pitching vaulted Louisville to the top of the standings by August 1877, but on the ensuing Eastern trip they lost all eight of their league contests (tying one), and lost several exhibition games too. Left fielder George Hall, who on August 16 was hitting .373 as the Grays held first place, proceeded to bat .149 over the next eighteen games as the club plummeted from the top.

Maneuvering the players to believe they had been informed upon by their co-conspirators, Louisville management extracted confessions from first Hall, then Devlin. Nichols was strongly implicated but did not confess. Craver unwaveringly asserted his innocence and no substantial proof was ever brought against him, yet because he denied Louisville's management the right to read his telegrams he, like the others, was banned from the club and subsequently by the league. The *Louisville Courier-Journal* reported the confessions on November 3, 1877:

CUSSED CROOKEDNESS.
A Complete Exposé of How Four Ball Men Picked Up Stray Pennies
Hall and Devlin Bounce Themselves
Out of the League on Their Own Testimony.
Nichols and Craver Also Take Their Gruel
for Tasting of Forbidden Fruits
A SAD, SAD STORY. . . .

George Hall asserted that the plot was the brainchild of Al Nichols, who approached him to throw league games. Hall responded fastidiously, saying he would toss only exhibition contests. Then Devlin worked his way into the mix, in cahoots with a gambler named

McCloud whom Devlin had met through the newsstand operator at Earle's Hotel in New York. When the Louisville conspirators were ready to throw a game, they were to wire McCloud the message "SASH," which would tell him to place his bets. These captured telegrams broke the story wide open and Devlin and Hall confessed. (See Notes for a partial transcript of their confessions.)

Hulbert meted out justice swiftly, expelling the four for life despite no hard evidence that any had thrown a *league* game. The result was to drive Louisville out of the league; when St. Louis, which had signed Devlin and Hall for 1878, also dropped out, the National League was reduced to four clubs. Then when Hartford—which had played its home games in Brooklyn in 1877 because it couldn't draw in Connecticut—followed suit, to save the league Hulbert had to scramble to place franchises in marginal outposts Indianapolis, Milwaukee, and Providence.

In the winter of 1877–78, the distraught Devlin made his way north to Chicago to plead with Hulbert. Spalding, present in the adjoining office of the suite he shared with Hulbert, recalled the meeting:

> The situation, as he kneeled there in abject humiliation, was beyond the realm of pathos. It was a scene of heartrending tragedy. Devlin was in tears, Hulbert was in tears. . . . I heard Devlin's plea to have the stigma removed from his name. I heard him entreat, not on his own account, he acknowledged himself unworthy of consideration, but for the sake of his wife and child. I beheld the agony of humiliation depicted on his features as he confessed his guilt and begged for mercy.
>
> I saw the great bulk of Hulbert's frame tremble with the emotion he vainly sought to stifle. I saw the president's hand steal into his pocket as if seeking to conceal his intended act from the other hand. I saw him take a $50 bill and press it into the palm of the prostrate player. And then I heard him say, as he fairly writhed with the pain his own words caused him, "That's what I think of you, personally; but, damn you, Devlin, you are dishonest; you have sold a game, and I can't trust you. Now go; and let me never see your face again; for your act will not be condoned so long as I live."

Devlin also wrote to Harry Wright that winter, on February 28 [punctuation added but spelling preserved]:

Dear Sir

As I am Deprived from Playing this year I thought I woed write you see if you Coed do anything for me in the way of looking after your ground or anything in the way of work. I Don't Know what I am to do. I have tried hard to get work of any Kind. But I Canot get it. Do you Know of any way that you think I Coed get to Play again. I Can asure you Harry that I was not Treated right and if Ever I Can see you to tell you the Case you will say I am not to Blame. I am living from hand to mouth all winter. I have not got a Stich of Clothing or has my wife and child. You Don't Know how I am Situated for I Know you woed do Something for me. I am honest Harry. You need not Be afraid. The Louisville People made me what I am today, a Begger. I trust you will not Say anything to anyone about the Contents of this to any one. If you Can do me this favor by letting me take care of the ground or anything of that Kind I beg of You to do it and God will reward you if I Dont. or let me Know if you have any Ide of how I Coed get Back. I am dumb Harry. I don't Know how to go about it. So I trust you will answear this and do all you Can for me. So I will close by sending you & Geo and all the Boys my very Best wishes hoping to hear from you Soon. I am yours Trouly

James A Devlin
No 908 Atherton St
Phila Pa

No record of Wright's response, if any, survives. Devlin went on to head west, playing ball in San Francisco in 1880 and, it is said, under assumed names elsewhere. This iconic figure of baseball's barely averted demise died in 1883, at age thirty-four.

Hulbert's Pyrrhic victory was that he had largely succeeded in removing gamblers from the ballparks, although in most cities the cognoscenti still knew where one might place a bet within the friendly confines. The gamblers' section of the ballpark, during the years of the National Association, had been known as the pool box. In 1872, the *New York Ledger* editorialized: "Two or three years ago, six or eight thousand people usually attended a championship game, but since the pool-box has been introduced one will not see more than a few hundred present, and they consist chiefly of gamblers. The square, honest players should see to this matter, and next season have the pool-box removed from the ball ground." With the onset of the league, pool selling in saloons and billiard parlors, which came to be known as poolrooms and ultimately lent their name to the game originally known as pocket billiards, proved to be an even more attractive form of wagering than placing a bet directly. With pool selling the gamblers did precisely what the baseball magnates achieved: They introduced an overarching system to replace casual relationships that were fraught with risk (for example, that the loser might renege on his bet).

James McCloud, notorious in the Louisville Scandal, sold pools at 161 Bowery, where James Murphy ran a billiard parlor and Carl Haug sold imported Rhine wines. Pools had to be sold at the ballparks surreptitiously, but traffic was in the open at nearby saloons; the prevailing odds were announced in the classified advertisements of league newspapers just as the point spread would one day be displayed for football and basketball games. David Pietrusza, in *Major Leagues*, described the complicated pool system:

> Prior to a game (actually days in advance), an auction was held, with bidding on the right to bet on favorite clubs. Then bids were made on the opposing nine. If the odds were not favorable, bets could be withdrawn. The pool seller kept records of these transactions, paid the winners, tried to maintain a reputation for honesty and received a percentage of each bet.
>
> Although by 1877 "pools" were being challenged by the new English practice of "bookmaking," they were still exceedingly popular. Strait-laced Boston alone had eight such rooms, and pools on a single game in larger New York establishments could reach as high as $70,000.

Though bloodied, the National League was unbowed, surviving its rocky first five years despite not always comprising the country's top ball clubs. In 1876, some thirty professional or semi-pro clubs, some of them refugees from the exploded National Association, were scattered over the country. These included Syracuse, Lowell, Indianapolis, and Allegheny, which frequently defeated league clubs in exhibitions. (League clubs always played such exhibitions as the visitors and may have given less than their best effort to encourage return engagements.) Of the fifty professional independents in 1877, some of them linked by loose confederations, those playing NL nines inflicted a whopping seventy-three losses in fewer than two hundred games; some of these clubs, such as the Indianapolis Hoosiers or the champion Lowell Ladies' Men of the newly fashioned League Alliance, might well have been superior to the NL's second division. In succeeding years the independent Syracuse Stars and Buffalo Bisons, before they were admitted to the league, defeated each NL club ten times in a season.

A rival league entering the picture for 1877 was the International Association, a player cooperative so named because it included two Canadian entries, London and Guelph (Ontario). Its rationale for organizing was not so much to produce an alternative championship campaign to that of the league, but to preserve the integrity of contracts and to protect independents from the depredations of touring league clubs. Candy Cummings, putative inventor of the curveball, presided over the player co-op circuit while pitching for Lynn, Massachusetts.

Also in 1877, Hulbert proposed the seemingly innocent League Alliance, modeled on an A. G. Mills initiative detailed below, as a way for independent clubs to assure themselves of contract protection, principally *from* the league but also from other independents within the alliance. With an NL club facing each of its fellow contenders for the pennant only twelve times over the course of the spring and summer, there were many open dates, either on the way to play a league contest, or after its conclusion and before departing by rail for the next, when lucrative games with independent clubs could be scheduled. Because the alliance also provided that each club respect the others' blacklists, the Mills initiative spread league rule in a way that presaged Organized Baseball, the linkage of major and minor leagues. Spalding described the situation:

> The unattached clubs derived much of their revenue from exhibition games with National League teams, and it was not unusual for a League nine to visit a small city, sign up one or more of the best players of the local organization and take them away. I recall one instance where a League club visited St. Paul and took from the "Red Caps" of that city five of their finest players, practically breaking up the team! A great outcry, of course, was raised over this high-handed proceeding, and, while there was no League rule forbidding such action on the part of League clubs, it became evident to the far-sighted Hulbert that, unless this custom was stopped, it would reflect discredit

upon not only the League but the game itself. He at once set about to institute a reform in this direction. It so happened at that time that Mr. A. G. Mills, who was then living at Chicago, appeared on the field of Base Ball reform. In a published article over his signature he severely criticised the reprehensible practice above referred to of League clubs visiting cities, accepting their hospitality, and then stealing their players. In this communication, as I recall it, he outlined a plan showing how this abuse could be done away with and called upon the officials of the National League to put a stop to the pernicious custom.

Mr. Hulbert was very much impressed with the article of Mr. Mills, and, as it conformed to his own ideas on the subject, he immediately sent an invitation to the writer, asking him to call at his office. . . . Mr. Mills evidently made a good impression on Mr. Hulbert, for just after this interview I called on the latter at his office, when he said: "I have found just the man we are looking for, and he has kindly agreed to help me in shaping up a plan that will prevent League clubs from robbing any more struggling clubs of their players."

I asked the name of the newcomer to the game, and when Mr. Hulbert told me, I replied: "That name sounds familiar. Why, A. G. Mills used to be the President of the Olympic Club, of Washington, D. C., just after the war, and it must be the same A. G. Mills who tendered me an invitation to become pitcher of that team and offered me a position in the Treasury Department just after the Rockfords defeated the Nationals at Chicago, in 1867."

Precisely. And this was the same Mr. Mills who would follow Hulbert in the office of National League president and, in 1908, help Spalding to anoint Abner Doubleday as baseball's inventor.

BY 1878, THE NL had vacated New York, Philadelphia, Louisville, and St. Louis and now played a sixty-game schedule among only six cities: Milwaukee, Indianapolis, Providence, Cincinnati, Chicago, and Boston. Such was the state of the bold, new so-called National League. Its grandiose name was reminiscent of the sport's status in the years before the Civil War, when exponents of the New York game termed their organization the National Association and their puny regional variant the national pastime. At this point, the future of Organized Baseball (i.e., capitalist combines) was very much unsettled. Player cooperatives, like the clubs in the International Association, might have won out. Or independent touring clubs like the Athletics, Mutuals, and Hoosiers might have exceeded in profitability the National League model and thus extinguished it.

The public would pay to see the best competition between the best competitors. No matter how clever or morally upstanding the management, no one paid to see them deploy their tactics. The players remained the asset: then as now, they were the game. As soon as the National League's gambling and game-fixing problems seemed to be cured, revolving returned as an even larger problem than it had been in the late 1860s. Except for a handful of stars signed to multiyear contracts, every player became a free agent at season's end. Hulbert, perhaps hearkening back to the Davy Force case of 1874, which had inspired his move to acquire Boston's Big Four and then to create a new league, on September 29, 1879, authorized the practice of reserving key players for the season following. This, Hulbert thought, would assure the fans and, more important, the clubs, that the business of baseball would be characterized by continuity rather than a game of musical chairs with each new campaign.

At first the reserve clause applied only to five players per club, who by and large were pleased to be so designated, for to be reserved meant to be assured of a job. Within four years, however, the reserve clause came to apply to nearly all the players on a roster, binding them to one employer for life and providing management with a cudgel to keep player conduct and salary demands in line. As the New York Giants' John Ward would write some years later:

> The contracts of the players for 1879 contained no reference to any right of reservation by the clubs, nor was any such in contemplation at the time the contracts were signed: so that it was an *ex post facto* rule, and therefore a positive wrong in its inception. . . . In the enactment of the reserve-rule the clubs were probably influenced by three considerations: they wished to make the business of base-ball more permanent, they meant to reduce salaries, and they sought to secure a monopoly of the game.

It did not take long for the problems attendant to the reserve clause to manifest. George Wright, who had been the greatest player in the land for a decade, with the Red Stockings of Cincinnati and then Boston, in 1879 led the Providence Grays to the championship. On April 21, 1880, however, he declined the club's final contract offer, perhaps preferring to stay in Boston and mind his sporting-goods business. As a reserved player, however, he was obligated to play for Providence and no other; he elected to sit out the season (although he did inexplicably play in a game for Boston on May 29). For 1881, no longer under reserve, he signed to play with Boston.

If bucking the reserve clause could cost the league the services of one of its top drawing cards, it would not take a seer to predict troubled times ahead. George Wright had already shown himself to be strong willed and opportunistic, moving from one situation to another throughout the 1860s. By the time he settled in with the Boston Red Stockings in 1871, his days as a home-run slugger were over, yet he led Boston to six pennants in the decade, capping it off with a flag for Providence. As late as 1911, when Honus Wagner was at the pinnacle of his career, playing the same position as Wright, writer and former major leaguer Sam Crane of the *New York Journal* still called Wright "the best shortstop ever."

At the NL meetings of August 9, 1878, Hulbert had advised that for 1879 the aggregate salaries must not exceed the sum "experience showed each club was likely to earn" and encouraged debate on the topic of fixing salaries by position. This restriction had no chance of passage, for private individuals associated with the club (like sports boosters at today's colleges) would certainly seek to retain superior players with under-the-table payments. However, a salary cap of some sort would continue as a lively subject throughout the following decade . . . and indeed to the present day.

Although the league had lost money in each of its first four seasons, salaries were climbing. Unlike today, when a team's operating losses can be tolerated in hopes of finding a buyer who will enable a handsome capital gain, nineteenth-century clubs could not repeatedly run in the red. In 1874, Boston Red Stocking salaries totaled nearly $16,000 (compare to the $9,300 of the 1869 Cincinnati Reds); with gate receipts of $19,005, the club turned a profit after all expenses of $833.12 (compare again to the '69 Reds profit of $1.39). Yet Boston did not shrink from going after talent: When Charles Hammond ("Ham") Avery, famous curveballer from Yale, graduated in 1875, Harry Wright offered him a salary of $3,400, $400 more than Chicago had paid to lure Spalding away from him. Even the financially challenged Hartford franchise somehow matched Boston's offer but Avery, a Skull & Bones Society blueblood, thought professional baseball beneath him and demurred. Average players in the National League's early years might make $100 to $150 per month, but when the opportunity arose to recruit a formidable player, price seemed, then as now, no object.

In 1880 Hulbert expelled the Cincinnati franchise for selling "spirituous and malt liquors" on the grounds, which in truth violated neither his sensibilities nor league statute. With this heavy-handed action Hulbert, the former firebrand, may have sparked an insurrection of his own: a rival league, the American Association (AA) of 1882, centered in the fun-loving, hard-drinking, and now deeply resentful city of Cincinnati. The rival circuit may also have sprung into being because its organizers saw that the NL had at last begun to stabilize and stop bleeding money. The AA soon became known as not Alcoholics Anonymous but the Beer-and-Whisky League, and by charging only twenty-five cents admission while occupying some of the very population centers the league had abandoned, it gave the NL a good run for its money for a decade.

Hulbert was not around to observe the new circuit's debut. On April 10, 1882, at the age of forty-nine, baseball's great architect died of a heart attack. Spalding took the reins of the Chicago White Stockings from their fallen leader; three decades later he would write, "I ask all living professional Base Ball players to join me in raising our hats to the memory of William A. Hulbert, the man who saved the game!"

Arthur Soden, managing partner of the Boston club and the man sometimes credited with the idea for the reserve clause, was named to succeed Hulbert as league president on an interim basis. In an election held the following year, he would be replaced by A. G. Mills, with Spalding continuing to serve as the league's Cardinal Richelieu. Mills would preside over the National League for only two years, but these proved to be momentous ones as debates intensified over the reserve clause, threatened salary restrictions, and, with the coming of additional professional circuits, intensified contract jumping.

The formation of the American Association in 1882 and its expansion for 1883 from six clubs to eight, including one in New York, gave notice to the National League that it could no longer manage solely the development of the professional game. That was the bad news; on the other hand, with the decade-long economic depression over, it began to seem that baseball might become a profitable spectator sport after all. A Northwestern League of professional clubs announced itself for 1883, featuring clubs in Quincy, Springfield, and Peoria, all of Illinois; Saginaw, Bay City, and Grand Rapids, Michigan; Toledo, Ohio; and that original National Association haunt, Fort Wayne, Indiana.

Trying to prevent contract jumping from one league with the reserve clause to another that was without it, new president Mills arranged for a Harmony Conference among the National League, American Association, and Northwestern League at the Hotel Victoria on West 27th Street in New York on February 17, 1883. He had already seen three Troy players—Buck Ewing, Mickey Welch, and Pete Gillespie—jump from their disbanded NL club, which even in disarray still held their reserves, to the Cincinnati club in the AA, which would not enforce the senior circuit's claim of contract violation. When the three leagues signed the Tripartite Agreement (later renamed the National Agreement), the effects were to expand each club's reserve to eleven men, which at that time meant very nearly the entire roster; to establish minimum salaries for players thus reserved ($1,000 for the NL and AA as major leagues, $750 for the NWL as an avowedly minor league); and to respect each other's contracts.

In a sidelight to the Harmony Conference, the American Association compelled its Cincinnati franchise to yield its three above-named Trojan horses to the new Gotham club, which the National League was poised to launch in New York. Additionally, third baseman Jerry Denny and pitcher Hoss Radbourn, both of whom had left Providence for the St. Louis Browns (AA), were returned to their former NL club. The crusty Radbourn would, for one miraculous season with the Providence Grays in 1884, channel his celebrated ill temper productively to yield a record fifty-nine victories—but in the winter of 1882–83, when he tried to bolt to the Browns, though already a formidable pitcher, he was famous mostly for a home run he had hit on August 17 to provide the only run of an eighteen-inning game with Detroit.

In the many other high-handed actions of the Harmony Conference, players' contractual rights were ruled subordinate to the interests of the three participating leagues, and were by and large disregarded. Some players were blacklisted by one league for following the directives of another; others were forgiven for the very same offenses. There was an Alice in Wonderland tea-party air to the rulings. Labor now answered to capital in baseball, but did not like it.

To THIS POINT IN their brief history, the major leagues had continued to feature some veterans of the National Association and earlier, such as Spalding, the Wright brothers, Bobby Mathews, and Adrian Anson. Like the Wrights of Boston and Philadelphia's Al Reach, Spalding turned his focus from the field to his nascent sporting-goods business, established in 1876, his last full season as a pitcher (his record was 47–12); by the following year, he had shifted to first base and in 1878 he played only once, a game at second base in September in which he booted four of seven chances. Harry Wright played one NL game in 1876 and another in 1877, closing the books at age forty-two on a playing career that had commenced with the Knickerbockers in the 1850s. Reach hung up his spikes at age thirty-five in the final year of the National Association. Mathews, who threw a shutout for the Kekiongas in the NA's first game in 1871, seemed on his way out of baseball after a losing season with the Mutuals in 1876, only to do a Lazarus bit with three consecutive thirty-win seasons for the Philadelphia Athletics of the American Association. Anson, who came to the NA in 1871 from Marshalltown, Iowa, as "Baby," went on to become "Cap," and then finished in 1897 as "Pop," may have been the most prominent player of the era, surpassing 3,000 hits in a period when the annual schedule of games did not reach 100 until his fourteenth year of professional league play.

New stars were emerging too. Boston pitcher Tommy Bond, a twenty-two-year-old veteran in his fourth season, led the NL of 1878 with a win-loss record of 40–19, while eighteen-year-old rookie pitcher John Ward of Providence led the league in "percentage of base hits" (today termed opponents' batting average), at .233, while going 22–13. He would win eighty-six games over his next two seasons, including a perfect game in 1880. Ward could hit, too (.286 in 1879), which permitted his shift to outfield, then shortstop, in later years after his pitching arm weakened. In the offseason, this polymath attended Columbia Law School, from which he graduated in 1885; his legal training gave him a valuable perspective on the labor-management disputes that were brewing in the game he loved.

Troy had entered the revamped National League in 1879, with fellow newcomers Syracuse, Cleveland, and Buffalo restoring the struggling circuit to eight entrants as Milwaukee and Indianapolis folded. The Trojans provided out-of-town previews of the men who would light up Broadway when the franchise was hijacked to New York (the Gothams) in 1883: Roger Connor, Tim Keefe, and the aforementioned Welch and Ewing. Connor was a feared hitter whose career home run record stood until Babe Ruth surpassed it a generation later. "Smiling Mickey" Welch was a 300-game winner who went 44–11 in 1885. Ewing was the nonpareil catcher of the century, a daring base runner, and a formidable batsman; he was regarded by the cognoscenti as the best all-around player, greater even than Anson. Keefe, who in his rookie season with Troy set the all-time record for earned run average with a mark of 0.86, in limited action, also came to New York from the Collar City in 1883, but pitched his first two years with the New York Metropolitans of the AA. In 1888, having returned to the National League, he won nineteen consecutive games to set another record; in each of his first six years in New York he won no fewer than thirty-two games. John Ward of Providence joined the Gothams for good measure, giving the two 1883 New York clubs five Hall of Fame players. A potential sixth, Dan Brouthers, had also broken in with Troy in 1879 and 1880, but washed out, then returned with Buffalo to become the game's top slugger.

A native-born Trojan, on the other hand, the man who would become known as King Kelly rose from a thirteen-year-old orphan working in the textile mills of Paterson, New Jersey, to become the most idolized player of the century. (He played for a big-league club in the state of New York only briefly, twenty games at the end of his trail in 1893.) Hulbert and Spalding brought him to Chicago after an 1879 season with Cincinnati in which, at age twenty-one, he had boosted his rookie batting average of .283 to .348. Dividing his time between outfield and catcher, with stints in the infield, too, Kelly brought Chicago a pennant in each of his first three seasons and, following a two-year hiatus, two more. And then, in 1886, shockingly, after he had hit .388 for the White Stockings, his contract was sold to the Boston Red Stockings for more money than the entire Cincinnati Red Stockings payroll of 1869. As the "$10,000 Beauty," Kelly will figure again in our story when players begin to object forcibly to being bought and sold like slaves.

Under Cap Anson's gritted-teeth management, the ungovernable Kelly became a great player, prodigious drinker, and the teller of uproarious stories and subject of myriad others, several of which may even be true. A handsome jester and knave, he became the popular darling of the 1880s because, understanding that baseball was theater, he played to the crowd. From his autobiography, *Play Ball:*

> Many times have I been asked the question, "To what do you ascribe the great popularity of base ball?" This, seems to me, can be answered in just two words, "The excitement." People go to see games because they love excitement and love to be worked up. That is one reason why I believe in "kicking" [demonstrative arguing] now and then on the diamond. It may be all right for the newspapers to say that "base ball will become more popular when played without kicking." I disagree entirely with these authorities on this subject. Look at the Chicago Base Ball Club. It has been the most successful in this country. Why? One good reason because they are "chronic kickers," and people flock to see them to witness the sport. You won't find the ordinary man going out to a base ball field when it's 80° in the shade to see two clubs play ball for a couple of hours, without a word being said on either side. The people who go to ball games want good playing, with just enough kicking to make things interesting thrown in.

Baseball's sense of its own theatricality, its combined elements of sport and spectacle, was evident in the elaborate banquets of amateur days—in the posturing of its pitchers and batsmen in their intricately wrought stances, and in its costuming, from the blazing stockings of Harry Wright's Reds to the yellow silk jerseys of the Baltimore Canaries (NA, 1872–74) and the different colored fez (sans tassel) worn by each member of the 1876 White Stockings to denote his position in the field. This last-named innovation, supplied from the shelves of Spalding's sporting-goods house, made the players look from the grandstand like "a Dutch bed of tulips," the *Chicago Daily Tribune* noted. Baseball's kinship with theater and circus may have been best exemplified by the riotous garb of 1882, in which each club's players wore a jockey costume, a silk jersey differentiated according to his position in the field, with common stocking colors assigned to each team by the league:

Catcher, scarlet

First Base, scarlet and white vertical stripes

Second Base, orange and black vertical stripes

Third Base, blue and white vertical stripes

Shortstop, maroon

Left Field, white

Center Field, red and black vertical stripes

Right Field, gray

Pitcher, light blue

First Substitute, green

Second Substitute, brown

A player rebellion against the absurdity of the garments (and the unbearable warmth of the silk) brought an end to the experiment in the spring of 1882, yet it was revived for 1883. Spalding's brainstorm for his Chicago White Stockings edition of that year was tomato-red jerseys *and* knickers.

Elsewhere in the baseball world at this time a spirit of innovation extended to the colors and national origins of the players themselves, as well as their gender. The 1880s was a tumultuous age of experimentation, prosperity, novelty, tasteless exploitation, and yet, in more than one sense of the word, brotherhood.

8

UNION AND BROTHERHOOD

In baseball the years after the Civil War provided a brief flowering in which Americans of all stripes could not only enjoy playing and watching the game but even think about making it a profession. Like American business, religion, and race relations after the Civil War, baseball made room for the concepts of union and brotherhood. It was a civilizing force (recall the symbolism of the Buchanan and Lincoln administrations' Indian Peace Medal), a social leveler and, in its paradigm of bleacher democracy, an agent for healing the nation's divisions of feeling.

Ultimately the forces of Jim Crow, moral absolutism, chauvinism, speculation, materialism, and monopoly, which constituted the cast-iron base of the Gilded Age, would bring baseball to the brink of suicide in its not so gay '90s. However, in the rough-and-tumble, mercurial decade that preceded it, diversity flourished, the economy boomed, and everything seemed possible. Gambling, though suppressed at the baseball parks, became rampant in society at large, as the sudden fortunes of new tycoons eroded ordinary Americans' notions of fairness and skewed the balance between wealth and risk. It would not be long before the inflammatory words of the Civil War—slavery, rebellion, secession, shackles, treason, even union and brotherhood—would be invoked to describe the conduct of both business and baseball. Mark Twain had it right when he said, at the Delmonico's banquet of April 1889, that baseball was "the very symbol, the outward and visible expression of all the drive and push and struggle of the raging, tearing, booming nineteenth century."

The National League of 1876 had been a cartel-inspired attempt to control the supply of professional baseball and to limit its expansion. Its egalitarian predecessor, the National Association, had lost public confidence through its countenance of open pool selling on the grounds, hippodroming ball clubs, player drunkenness, and unbalanced competition. Hulbert and Spalding applied corrective measures but their straitlaced reliance upon prohibition defied human nature and inspired rebellious competitors to take to the field.

Men like Chris Von Der Ahe, a saloon proprietor from St. Louis, believed that workingmen ought to be able to see a game for a quarter rather than the fifty cents that the league charged. He also thought that patrons ought to be permitted to mix their baseball with beer and whisky, as baseball lovers in bygone days had celebrated the game with chowder and grog, and on Sundays, too. In 1882, he and likeminded speculators from the other cities formed the American Association with six clubs, two fewer than the National League of that year; these six, however, represented locales that far surpassed their rivals' eight in composite population, so the association was born as a major league no matter what the senior league called it. The originally designated association franchises were in Louisville, Cincinnati, St. Louis, Pittsburgh, Philadelphia, and Brooklyn, but the last named was replaced before the season began by the Baltimore Orioles, so weak an opponent that they soon went by the nicknames Martyrs or Lambs.

The association did not at first adopt the reserve clause nor did it accept the league's blacklist; it could have drawn a number of first-rate players from among the ten alleged drunks and troublemakers who had run afoul of NL ground rules had the Nationals not anticipated such an exodus and rescinded most of the players' suspensions. New stars emerged under the AA banner, men such as Pete Browning (the Louisville Slugger who gave the name to the bat), Charlie Comiskey (first baseman and manager of the Browns and, later, pioneer owner of the American League Chicago White Sox), Guy Hecker (who as a pitcher won fifty-two games to lead the AA in 1884, and as a batter hit .341 to lead the circuit two years later), Bid McPhee (who set many fielding records as a barehanded second baseman from 1882 to 1899, and Tony Mullane (ambidextrous pitcher who won 284 games). Although the association technically banned liquor sales at its ballparks, it stood ready to make exceptions, as it did for the beer-loving denizens of St. Louis and Cincinnati.

An expansion of the American Association to eight clubs for 1883 included the Columbus Buckeyes and the Metropolitans of New York, the latter a successful independent club since 1880 that had been invited to join in 1882 but declined, preferring to retain its lucrative exhibitions with National League clubs. For 1883, it was announced that New York, which had had no major league club since 1876, now would have two, as the National League pulled its clubs from Troy and Worcester and awarded their franchises to, respectively, New York and Philadelphia, the cities it had abandoned after its inaugural campaign of 1876. The tremendous success of the association club in Philly in 1882, which cleared a profit of $22,000, more than any club in either league, prompted the NL move away from its smallest cities. In 1883, the Philadelphia Athletics of the association drew more customers than the entire National League of only two years before. As a whole in 1883, the association outdrew the league by some 70 percent. Something was happening here, and an entrepreneur had to take notice.

That entrepreneur was Henry V. Lucas, a St. Louis magnate who believed that the reserve clause, binding a player to a single club for life, was un-American, unethical, and, besides, a dandy reason to form a third major league without it: In 1884, he and other hopeful capitalists formed the Union Association. (The AA too had commenced operation without a reserve clause but, after adopting it in the Harmony Conference peace arrangement of 1883, embraced it with all the newfound fervor of a convert.) Lucas was the union's kingpin and the majority owner of its powerhouse St. Louis club (a minority owner was beer baron Adolphus Busch), which coasted to the championship with a record of 94–19. The entire baseball pie, in 1877 not large enough to sustain six National League clubs, suddenly seemed so large that it was worth fighting over to see who might get even a tiny piece.

The baseball boom of 1884, coinciding with national economic prosperity, produced three major leagues and a dizzying array of ball clubs, thirty-three in all (some were unable to complete their schedules and were replaced by new entrants from other cities). In 1881, the last year in which the National League had faced no opposition, major league attendance was 301,236. In 1884, it exceeded 2.5 million. The NL had the superior talent; American Association clubs lost their first twenty-two exhibition contests against their rivals, and were swept in the first World Series, played in 1884 between the Providence Grays (NL) and the New York Mets (AA). But the AA had the fans.

Rival major leagues were not the only available path to playing or watching the game at a high level. The Interstate Association, a minor league formed in 1883, brought top-drawer baseball back to Brooklyn, at that point the nation's third-largest city, with the pennant-winning Grays, who in the following year would join the AA and begin the big-league lineage that culminates in today's Dodgers, whose fans have not had to dodge trolleys in Los Angeles. The 1883 Brooklyn team dressed in polka-dot stockings and played on a site in Red Hook near the Gowanus Canal, at the first of three locations prior to the construction of Ebbets Field; each of these ball fields was named Washington Park. Standing strangely within the grounds of that 1883 park was the 1696 Gowanus House, which General George Washington had used as his headquarters in the Battle of Long Island in 1776. The ball club's proprietors gave the venerable landmark a new roof and made it into a ladies' powder room. A somewhat less distant vestige of former times was echoed in this year as well by the amply publicized fiftieth anniversary celebrations of the Olympic Ball Club of Philadelphia, organized in 1833 to play the long-vanished game of town ball.

The Northwestern League, another minor circuit formed for play in 1883, was instantly deemed so significant that it was made a full participant in the National, or Tripartite, Agreement, the product of the Harmony Conference. The Toledo Blue Stockings of the Northwestern League's inaugural campaign, managed by sportswriter William H. "Billy" Voltz, were notable for their employ of Moses Fleetwood "Fleet" Walker, an African-American catcher. (On March 14, in a meeting before the NWL had played its first game, Peoria club officials moved unsuccessfully to ban blacks altogether to prevent Toledo from using him.) Walker was not the first of his race to play in integrated professional baseball; Bud Fowler, born John W. Jackson in Fort Plain, New York, near Cooperstown, pitched a game for the Live Oaks of Lynn, Massachusetts, against the Boston Red Stockings of the National League in 1878, and was said to have appeared with an integrated professional nine as early as 1873. Though Fowler never played in a major league contest, he played in the white minors off and on through 1895 and continued in independent ball until 1901.

It had long been thought that Fleet Walker and his brother Weldy, by playing with the Toledo club in 1884 when it moved up from the Northwestern League to the American Association, became the first and only African Americans to play major league ball until Jackie Robinson again broke the color barrier in 1947. That distinction was amended, however, when a 2004 study revealed that William Edward White, a student ballplayer at Brown University who was the son of a Georgia slave owner and his house servant, played one game for the Providence Grays on June 21, 1879, against visiting Cleveland. White was replacing the Grays' injured regular at that position, "Old Reliable" Joe Start, who had begun play with the Enterprise club of Brooklyn back in 1860 and would continue to play in the major leagues through 1886. The *Providence Morning Star* raved about White's major league debut and the support from his Brown teammates. "The Varsity boys lustily cheered their favorite at times, and howled with delight when he got a safe hit in the ninth inning, as they also did his magnificent steals of second in that and the fifth inning," the newspaper reported. White also scored a run and registered twelve putouts without error as Providence won, 5–3. He returned to play for Brown in 1880 and never played for Providence again.

FLEET WALKER'S STORY IS more resonant. After starring in baseball with Oberlin College's inaugural nine in 1881, he was invited to play for the strong semiprofessional White Sewing Machine club, based in Cleveland. The visiting Whites ran into a problem before a scheduled game with the Eclipse club in Louisville (the Eclipse would enter the American Association as a charter member the following spring). As the *Louisville Courier-Journal* reported on August 22, 1881, "players of the Eclipse Club objected to Walker playing on account of his color. In vain the Clevelands protested that he was their regular catcher, and that his withdrawal would weaken the nine." The White Sewing Machine manager held Walker out, but when his replacement catcher bruised his hand and refused to come out for the second inning, the crowd began to call for Walker to go behind the bat. He

> . . . was disinclined to do so, after the general ill-treatment he had received; but as the game seemed to be in danger of coming to an end, he consented, and started in the catcher's stand. As he passed before the grand stand, he was greeted with cheers, and from the crowd rose cries of "Walker, Walker!" He still hesitated, but finally threw off his coat and vest and stepped out to catch a ball or two and feel the bases.
>
> He made several brilliant throws and fine catches while the game waited. Then Johnnie Reccius and Fritz Pfeffer, of the Eclipse nine, walked off the field and went to the club house, while others objected to the playing of [Walker]. . . . The crowd was so pleased with his practice however, that it cheered him again and again and insisted that he play. The objection of the Eclipse players, however, was too much and Walker was compelled to retire. . . .

"The Clevelands acted foolishly in playing," the *Courier-Journal* concluded. "They should have declined to play unless Walker was admitted and entered suit for gate money and damages. They could have made their point because it was understood that Walker was [their] catcher, and no rules provide for the rejection of players on account of 'race, color or previous condition of servitude.' The crowd was anxious to see Walker play, and there was no social question concerned."

In 1883, Walker helped the Blue Stockings win the Northwestern League championship but again had a run-in regarding his race. After arriving in Toledo for an exhibition contest, Captain Anson announced that his Chicago White Stockings would not take the field with Walker in the lineup. Toledo manager Voltz, who had planned to give Walker the day off anyway, decided to start him in right field, daring Anson to walk away from his share of the gate after having traveled some distance. Anson gave in, grumbling that he would never again bring his club to Toledo, while also beginning to nurture a personal grudge against Walker. When Toledo moved up to the American Association in 1884, Walker played in forty-two games, batting a respectable .263, but he was released near the end of the season after suffering a broken shoulder. He would be the last black player in the major leagues until 1947, but Walker played in integrated leagues each year from 1883 through 1889, seven consecutive seasons. Although the public liked him, he continued to suffer many indignities at the hands of opponents and teammates alike.

Shortly before Walker's release in 1884, Toledo manager Charlie Morton (Voltz was gone after the 1883 season) delivered to the press the following letter he had received prior to a series with the Richmond club:

> Richmond, Virginia, September 5, 1884
> Manager, Toledo Baseball Club
>
> Dear Sir:
>
> We, the undersigned, do hereby warn you not to put up Walker, the Negro catcher, the days you play in Richmond, as we could mention the names of seventy-five determined men who have sworn to mob Walker if he comes on the ground in a suit. We hope you will listen to our words of warning so there will be no trouble, and if you do not, there certainly will be. We only write this to prevent much bloodshed, as you alone can prevent.
>
> Bill Frick, James Kendrick,
> Dynx Dunn, Bob Roseman.

Eight days later, Morton received another letter from the former Confederate capital, advising him not to use Walker in the upcoming series at Toledo scheduled for September 22 through the twenty-fourth. Walker was not used, and on the twenty-ninth he was released, perhaps so that he would not have to travel to Richmond for a season-ending series. In a later, more celebrated incident, when Chicago's National Leaguers faced the Newark club of the International League in an exhibition game in mid-1887, Anson ran into Walker again, this time with a black batterymate in left-handed pitcher George Stovey. He insisted upon their removal, and this time prevailed.

Bud Fowler also ran into racist teammates, opponents, and fans while playing in the International League. So did Frank Grant—in the Baseball Hall of Fame and by general consent the best of the nineteenth century's African-American players—as well as Stovey, pitcher

Bob Higgins, and others. It became clear that for blacks to find their place in baseball, it would have to be on the barnstorming circuit, with such celebrated clubs as the Cuban Giants, or in a league of their own: a short-lived National Colored League of 1887 presaged the successful organization of the Negro National League in 1920; it was even granted official National Agreement protection as a show of good will.

The Cuban Giants were an aggregation born in 1885 from the merger of four earlier black professional clubs: the Keystones, the Orions, the Manhattans, and the Argyles of Babylon, Long Island. Not one of the players was Cuban but, given America's friendliness toward, even obsession with, its island neighbor (and historic lust for its annexation), African-American ballplayers had been led to believe they would have an easier time playing before white audiences if they pretended to be Cubans or Spaniards . . . exotics of color rather than colored Americans. James Weldon Johnson, who was raised in Jacksonville, Florida, and learned to speak Spanish from a Cuban boyhood friend, observed that while traveling by rail in the 1890s, he was treated much better by railroad employees and fellow passengers after they heard him speak Spanish and surmised that he was not African-American but Cuban. "In such situations," he concluded, "any kind of Negro will do; provided he is not one who is an American citizen."

The light-skinned Frank Grant, described as a "Spaniard" in the *Buffalo Express* in 1887, had batted .325 for Meriden, Connecticut, in the Eastern League (the original name of the International League) the previous year. When that team folded in midseason he joined Buffalo and continued his fine play. His reward was to come in for unceasing attack. Ned Williamson, second baseman of the Chicago White Stockings, told *Sporting Life*:

> The Buffalos—I think it was the Buffalo team—had a Negro for second base. He was a few lines blacker than a raven, but he was one of the best players in the old Eastern League. The haughty Caucasians of the association were willing to permit darkies to carry water to them or guard the bat bag, but it made them sore to have the name of one in the batting list. They made a cabal against this man and incidentally introduced a new feature into the game. The players of the opposing teams made it their special business in life to "spike" this brunette Buffalo. They would tarry at second when they might have easily made third, just to toy with

> the sensitive shins of this second baseman. The poor man played in two games out of five perhaps; the rest of the time he was on crutches. To give the frequent spiking of the darkey an appearance of accident the "feet first" slide was practiced. The negro got wooden armor for his legs and went into the field with the appearance of a man wearing nail kegs for stockings. The enthusiasm of opposition players would not let them take a bluff. They filed their spikes and the first man at second generally split the wooden half cylinders. The colored man seldom lasted beyond the fifth inning, as the base-runners became more expert.

Billy Voltz, who first signed Fleet Walker to a contract with Toledo, is one of baseball's seldom-mentioned visionaries. He managed Walker through much of the 1883 championship season before turning back to the sports desk at the start of 1884. On January 17, the *Cleveland Herald*, denying a report that he was about to organize a club in St. Paul, Minnesota, said Voltz "is working in this office and has sworn off on base ball, with a vow as deep as an artesian well." This would prove to be a shallow assessment. In 1885, he would come up with the idea for the Brotherhood of Base Ball Players that, as transformed by John Ward, would culminate in the Players' League rebellion of 1890. And, in 1889, as president of the Middle States League, Voltz invited the Cuban Giants club to enter championship play as an intact franchise alongside five white clubs.

Before that 1889 season, not knowing they would be invited into league play, the Cuban Giants had announced their intention to play five games a week in three locations, including the now seedy Elysian Fields in Hoboken. In distant times, baseball's Eden had provided fertile soil for the rising New York game, had hosted the Knickerbockers and Eagles, and had been the scene of mortal mayhem against the black waiters at McCarty's Colonnade House.

A *real* Cuban had played big league ball from 1871 through 1873, the first three years of the National Association of Professional Base Ball Players: Esteban Bellán, who at age thirteen had been sent from Havana to New York with his brother to be educated at Fordham University's Rose Hill preparatory school. This rite of passage was common practice among middle-class Cuban families at the time, because the important trading relation between New York City and Spain's island colony was of long standing, going back before the birth of the United States. England's brief occupation of Havana in 1762 had opened up trade between Cuba and its North American colonies.

Bellán was one of several Cuban nationals who played baseball in American schools, from Rensselaer Polytechnic Institute in Troy to Fordham in New York City to Spring Hill College in Mobile, Alabama. He returned home to Cuba in 1873, after completing a final professional season with the New York Mutuals, and one year later his team, Club Habana, defeated Club Matanzas in the first organized baseball game ever played in his homeland. (The teams employed Chadwick's otherwise disregarded experiment of ten men to the side, including a right shortstop.) In 1878, the Professional Baseball League of Cuba was founded under Bellán's direction, and it ran without interruption until 1961.

In the winter of 1879, a group of players who would become the core of the National League's Worcester club the following year, led by manager Frank Bancroft, made a winter tour of Cuba. In addition to these tourists, Hick Carpenter and Jimmy Macullar of the 1879 Syracuse Stars became the first active major leaguers to play winter ball in the Caribbean, both playing for the Colón Club while Bellán played for Habana.

BASEBALL'S EXPANDING OPPORTUNITIES FOR new enthusiasts were not limited to ethnic and racial experimentation at home or proselytizing actions abroad (American professor Horace Wilson introduced baseball to Japan in 1872; professional baseball teams toured England in 1874). Women entered the arena, at first with a competitive approach, especially at the Seven Sisters schools of the Northeast. In 1866, Annie Glidden, a student from Vassar College of Poughkeepsie, New York, wrote home describing campus life: "They are getting up various clubs now for out-of-door exercise. . . . They have a floral society, boat clubs and base-ball clubs. I belong to one of the latter, and enjoy it highly, I can assure you." Whether she belonged to the Laurel or the Abenaki club we do not know, but by 1870 these two were joined on campus by a third, the Resolute. And Miss Glidden was confident of her abilities: "We think after we have practiced a little," she added, "we will let the Atlantic Club play a match with us."

Ultimately, women's baseball largely devolved to a novelty act with a girlie-show air, or seems to have so descended from the way it was reported in the press. In 1868, in Peterboro, New York, an upstate village some seventy-five miles from Seneca Falls where the women's suffrage movement was born, a contest between two female clubs was reported in a New York newspaper called *Day's Doings*, a sensationalist sex-story journal self-avowedly devoted to "current events of romance, police reports, important trials, and sporting news."

> The young women of Peterboro, N. Y., jealous of the popular sports enjoyed by the more muscular portion of mankind, have organized a base ball club, and have already arrived at a creditable degree of proficiency in play. There are about fifty members belonging to it, from which a playing nine has been chosen, headed by Miss Nannie Miller as captain. The nine have played several games outside the town and away from the gaze of the curious. Having thus perfected themselves, this nine lately played a public game in the town of Peterboro, as may well be supposed, before a multitude of spectators.

By the mid-1870s exhibitions of women's baseball had generally taken the form of Blondes versus Brunettes, with varying geographic modifiers applied to each. These pulchritudinous nines typically used a smaller than regulation ball made only of yarn, played the game on a fifty-foot diamond, and barnstormed their way through a legion of appreciative "bald-headed men," a code name in theatrical circles for voyeurists of a certain age who liked to sit in the first row.

The great Svengali of women's baseball exhibitions was Sylvester F. Wilson (one of many names he went by, though he was born Christian Wilson). The *Brooklyn Eagle* called him "the abductor of girls on base ball pretexts." Although he proclaimed that none of his players came from the stage and that his exhibitions were of the highest class and virtue, he had been arrested in New York for kidnapping a sixteen-year-old girl from her home in Binghamton. In the *Sporting News* of September 20, 1890, a female correspondent poked fun at the prospect of a new "Ladies' League" arising amid the proliferation of men's professional circuits:

> St. Louis, September 18.—Editor, Sporting News. In looking over a New York paper today I saw the article which I forward in this letter

to you. To me the strangest thing about it is the statement that applicants for the position in question were numerous. Only twelve of the applicants, however, were fortunate enough to fill the requirements of this enviable position. One would have scarcely expected that girls were "numerous" in an enlightened American city who were so utterly lacking in modesty, self-respect, decency and common sense as to desire such a career as this. What are our American girls coming to? The next thing I suppose we shall be having "lady" jockeys on our race tracks. "Ladies' Baseball League," indeed? In many other lines of business ladies are being introduced, and with the best of success, but surely the men are able to take care of this peculiar branch. If our National Game has not enough men to carry it without organizing this new league it had better give up the ghost at once. It seems strange, after all the talk about too many base ball organizations all summer that still another one should be organized. But then of course, this one is not meant to rank with those organizations whose combats call out the better class of people in our country. It is hardly to be expected that ladies, or men who have any self-respect will turn out to see these creatures make themselves ridiculous. Yet professional ball players who are not in favor of women's rights are you going to stand idly by and see your province thus invaded? Are you going to say nothing while the "ladies" take your places on the diamond, in the sporting world, etc.? . . . Very truly yours, M. S.

The article to which the lady referred and which she enclosed in her letter read as follows:

There is a movement on foot in New York to, at least in the minds of many people, degrade baseball by organizing a number of baseball clubs with women players, and already one club is on the road. The organizer is W. S. Franklin [a.k.a. Sylvester F. Wilson], and yesterday his office, at No. 1162 Broadway, was besieged with females of all ages, who had come in answer to the following *World* advertisement, and offered themselves as candidates for baseball honors.

Wanted—50 girls to play baseball; $5 to $15 per week and all expenses; long engagement to travel to experienced players; ladies' league of 4 to 9 clubs now organized for 1891; must be young, over 20, good looking and good figure. Call 2 to 5 p.m., on Mr. Franklin,

> at Dramatic Agency, 1162 Broadway, or 8 to 10 p.m., 158 West 50th street. Applicants outside of city must send photo which will be returned. . . .

The *Kansas City Star*, commenting on the five-year sentence meted out to Wilson in 1891, wrote, "He has been arrested more than 100 times and for various crimes, and Secretary Jenkins of the New York Society for the Prevention of Cruelty to Children says he has ruined more young girls than any man living."

An absolute craze for novelty acts characterized the baseball boom of the 1880s, and press reports were no more kind or politically correct in regard to these exhibitions than they were to those put forth by the young ladies. On September 2, 1880, two baseball teams composed of employees of Boston department stores—Jordan Marsh and R. H. White—groped their way to a 16–16 tie under dim artificial lights at Nantasket Beach, Massachusetts. The experiment was repeated on June 2, 1883, with little more to recommend it, in a game between the Northwestern League squads of Quincy, Illinois, and Fort Wayne, Indiana, at the home of the latter.

Fort Wayne was also the home of George J. E. Mayer and his wife, Lizzie. In 1888, he was on the road with two teams of Chinese players. "In their practice-work," reported the *Chicago Inter-Ocean*, "they showed that they were catching on with a wonderful celerity. When one of the men made a hit, the others all yelled at him in a most side-splitting manner." The *Brooklyn Eagle* added that "Speculation as to the relative merits of the two teams has been rife, and many a good dollar has been wagered by the Mongolians [Chinese] on their favorites. The betting last night was $4 to $3 on the Chicagos, and if the San Franciscos win there will be wailing and weeping in many Celestial laundries."

Novelty games were particularly prominent in Philadelphia; ethnic teams, "colored" male and female ball teams, Native-American nines, crippled clubs, and so on. John Lang, a white barber from Philadelphia who had "temporarily deserted lather and razor" to organize pioneer black baseball clubs such as the Orion, found his true métier in New York with his Chinese teams. In Chester, Pennsylvania, Lang also created a fetching nine of "colored girl" professional players whom he named the Dolly Vardens after the fluffily and colorfully costumed lass in Dickens' *Barnaby Rudge.* Fat men contested with lean men in "Jumbos vs. Shadows" matches, just as married vs. single games had been common in the amateur era. Of the players of the Snorkey Club of Philadelphia (named for the one-armed hero of the drama *Under the Gaslight*), one had an arm off at the shoulder, another had a paralyzed arm, the rest were minus a hand; their opponents in a game of May 23, 1883, were the Hoppers, who were all one-legged or on crutches. In a reminder to modern readers of the brutality of the industrial age in America, both sides were said to consist wholly of former employees of the Pennsylvania Railroad. In 1885, two clubs of the New York State League, Binghamton and Rochester, played on roller skates at the Pioneer Rink in the former city. In 1887, George Hancock of Chicago invented indoor baseball as a winter sport; it survives as today's softball.

This mania for invention extended off the playing fields and into the offseason. There were baseball novels, beginning with William Everett's *Changing Base* in 1868 and culminating in *Our Base Ball Club and How It Won the Championship* by Noah Brooks, with an introduction by Albert G. Spalding. There were baseball songs in sheet music form, beginning with the "Base Ball Polka" of 1858 and extending well beyond "Slide, Kelly, Slide" (1893). There were numerous baseball board games, beginning with *Parlor Baseball*, a spring-action game invented by Francis E. Sebring, former pitcher of New York's Empire Base Ball Club, in 1866.

The seeds of fantasy baseball were planted in 1885 by Thomas W. Lawson's game *Base Ball with Cards*, with its now-disquieting graphic of a bodiless, four-ball, four-armed swastika. Played by four players, two on each side, Lawson's game had as its object "to secure as many tricks, or runs as possible and by skilful [sic] combinations to destroy the value of opponent's cards." A paradigm of Monopoly expressed in miniature, it was an apt metaphorical statement for the course its inventor would ultimately pursue with phenomenal success on Wall Street. The game was a hit, and, in 1885, Lawson arranged a tournament of the National League clubs, with prizes he posted himself. Unlike today's fantasy baseball, however, in which a player contents himself with statistical stand-ins for the players on his team, the *Base Ball with Cards* tournament was played by real members of the National League teams, deploying fantasy elements. Total prizes for the tourney came to $1,600 "in gold and handsome trophies."

With baseball busting out all over, to describe it as the national pastime no longer provoked a smirk among the knowing, as it had in the 1850s. In fact baseball had become more than the mere reflection of our rising industrial and political power and our propensity for bluster and hokum: The national game was beginning to supply emblems for democracy, commerce, and community that would subtly change America forevermore. In our determinedly secular nation, a fan's affiliation with his team could exceed in vigor his attachment to his creed, his trade, his political party, all but family and country, and increasingly even these were wrapped up in baseball. The national pastime became the great repository of national ideals, the symbol of all that was good in American life: fair play (sportsmanship); the rule of law (objective arbitration of disputes through an accepted umpire); equal opportunity (each side has its innings); the brotherhood of man (bleacher harmony and on-field diversity). To some, baseball looked like a new national religion all its own.

As Harold and Dorothy Seymour wrote, "With the loss of the traditional ties known in a rural society, baseball gave to many," especially in the rising urban centers, "the feeling of belonging." Rooting for a baseball team permitted city folk, newcomers and native born, a sense of pride in community that in days of yore, when they may have lived in small towns, was commonplace.

America had pulled out of its long depression that had lasted from the panic of 1873 into mid-1879. Hours devoted to the working day were in decline; city populations were on the rise; discretionary time and income were growing; increased efficiencies had come to rail transportation, particularly for the interurban short lines. The baseball business boomed, like all of show business in the 1880s, not only in the cities but also in the sleepiest burgs. The people wanted entertainment, and now they had time to enjoy and money to purchase it.

THERE WAS THIS RUB, however: Star performers were what drew the crowds, so salaries for the best players, on the ball field or on the boards, would rise in accordance with the laws of supply and demand. Before 1879 all players were free agents at the end of their contractual obligation, which was almost never greater than twelve months, and they were free to go where the dollar beckoned. In the few years immediately following, free agency described the fortunate state of all but the five men whom a National League club reserved for the following year, and even for them one need not have shed a tear. Each was guaranteed a place and a salary no worse than that which he had just received, and could be assured of continuing employ in what was even then, compared to common labor, a well-paid and agreeable line of work.

Since the dawn of the National League, its owners had been concerned that the best players would flock to the clubs that could, by virtue of their operating profits or capital investment, provide the largest rewards. (This may sound familiar.) They also distrusted each other, for early league clubs were notorious for using exhibition dates to steal the best players of a host club. It was not long before William Hulbert, during the 1878 season, sent aloft a trial balloon about limiting salaries, in particular, fixing them by the position a man played. Slowly, it dawned upon the owners that the reserve system, put in place to deter player raids and promote franchise stability, might become a hammer with which to depress salary demands, and, in time, to secure a monopoly. The latent promise of the reserve was not lost upon everyone at the time, however: The *Sunday Mercury* response to the five-man reserve upon its initial proposal was, "the players owe it to their own self-respect to form a League of their own."

In November 1883, New York Gothams owner John B. Day proposed another function for this multi-use tool when, at a league meeting, he proposed a resolution to prohibit any team in any of the three leagues that had adopted the National Agreement that arose from the Harmony Conference from signing a player who had flouted the provisions of the reserve. A. G. Mills observed that the reserve, at first not present as a clause in the standard player contract, was designed not to protect management from players but the other way around: "Professional players have never sought the club manager; the club manager has invariably sought—and often tempted—the player. The reserve rule takes the club manager by the throat and compels him to keep his hands off his neighbor's enterprise."

The final utilization of the reserve clause, and perhaps the most galling to the players, was that it became an item of value and potential commerce for the club, so that even a club disbanding at season's end, rather than releasing its players from further obligation, might sell its player contracts, with their exclusive options for hire, to another club based on the survivability of the reserve. John Ward described it:

> As the pecuniary returns of the game increased, the value of the individual player was enhanced: the strength or weakness of one position made a difference of thousands in receipts, and this set the astute managerial mind to work. Some scheme must be devised by which these gaps might be filled. It finally dawned upon him that this continuing claim upon the player's services was much akin to a right of property. Why, then, might this not be bought and sold, as are other rights of a similar nature?

After the 1884 season, for example, the Columbus club in the American Association, despite finishing a robust second to the Mets, decided to go out of business, but not before selling its player contracts to Pittsburgh. Likewise, a club having neither wish nor intention of renewing a player's contract might sell it, and thus in effect the player himself, obligating him to play in another city to which he might not care to go. Ward's August 1887 article in *Lippincott's Magazine,* provocatively titled "Is the Base-Ball Player a Chattel?," described the tightening noose of the reserve clause in terms calling to mind John Brown and Frederick Douglass:

> There is now no escape for the player. If he attempts to elude the operation of the rule, he becomes at once a professional outlaw, and the hand of every club is against him. He may be willing to play elsewhere for less salary, he may be unable to play, or, for other reasons, may retire for a season or more, but if ever he reappears as a professional ballplayer it must be at the disposition of his former club. Like a fugitive-slave law, the reserve-rule denies him a harbor or a livelihood, and carries him back, bound and shackled, to the club from which he attempted to escape. We have, then, the curious result of a contract which on its face is for seven months being binding for life, and when the player's name is once attached thereto his professional liberty is gone forever.

The National Agreement of 1883 had also naively called for a cap on salaries of $2,000, but the provision was without teeth as owners would pay whatever they had to in order to secure talent. To wit, in

1886, Hoss Radbourn, no longer with Providence, which had closed shop and sold its assets to Boston, made the top salary in the game, $6,000. Ward of the New York Giants made $3,400, and his teammate Buck Ewing made $3,000, as did Chicago's Cap Anson (who also received a percentage of the club profits).

However, the allure of a workable salary cap lingered on, and new proposals were aired regularly. After the Union Association fizzled out after its lone season, major league players objecting to the reserve clause were left with no haven. Most of those who had jumped to the UA were welcomed back, some after being slapped with fines that almost certainly were paid by their new clubs. The National League could not afford, for example, to ban all the players of the St. Louis Unions who might now stock that city's NL franchise and provide a counterbalance to Von Der Ahe's dominant Browns of the American Association. Spalding was adamant about the need to reinstate the St. Louis Union players (Henry Chadwick opposed him). He was proved right as there was great interest in the blacklisted players all around the circuit in 1885 and, whichever city they happened to visit, the St. Louis Maroons formed an excellent drawing card. These former Unions were so frequently referred to by the press as the Black Diamonds for their contract violators and reserve jumpers that owner Lucas had black diamonds affixed to their jersey fronts.

An article signed "Veteran" in the *Sporting Life* of September 2, 1885, offered a balanced and unusually intelligent view of the bubbling cauldron, saying that salaries must be reduced yet fairly stating the players' case as well.

> Editor SPORTING LIFE: [. . .] The clubs have made money while paying more than $2,000 maximum salaries and can do it again, and they cannot consistently and should not ask players of great reputations and abilities and consequent drawing powers to so reduce their salaries as to allow the management to make all the money. The clubs are, to a certain extent, pledged to maintain good salaries, for they have continually said through the press that all they wanted or expected was to make a fair profit on their investments and to remunerate them for their labor and risk.
>
> It may be, and undoubtedly will be, claimed by some that these men who make now from $2,000 to $3,000 and $3,500 in seven months

playing ball could hardly make as much in seven years at anything else that they could do. This may be true, but it is a child's argument and it is high time it was so recognized. Ball players are employed to play ball and their services are worth just whatever the management is able to make out of them.

Every good player is a drawing card of more or less attracting power and the aggregate drawing power of a team is largely due to its individual attractiveness.

If any one was to say that an opera singer, an actor, an acrobat, a minstrel or any other showman should not be paid a large salary because he could not earn one-tenth as much at anything else, he would be held up as the laughing stock of the community. He is paid for his special qualifications and ability to make money for his employer. I claim the ball player is paid in the same way, and he should be and he and his comrades are worth to the management just what their services produce. They are not hired to shovel gravel, brake on the railroad, tend bar, or any of the many kindred employments that some people think, very erroneously, they are only fitted for, but to cater to the amusement of the patrons of their employer, and when they have done so according to their contracts and the best of their ability, they are worthy of just as much salary as the management can afford to pay them, after allowing a reasonable margin for himself for his outlay and work.

Of course, I don't mean to say that players should be asked to sign for a contingent salary, or to take the risk of the management making money, but the management can tell with reasonable certainty, at least in all old base ball cities, what their receipts will be with fairly successful playing, and can, consequently, figure just what they can afford to pay. . . .

It is claimed that the secretaries of the League and American Association have schedules of the salaries of the players in the two associations and they could be scaled down uniformly by this method, but it would be next to impossible, if not quite so, to get the clubs to abide by such a rule. Then it takes two to make a bargain, and the player, while he might be willing to play for a reduced salary, might want to choose his club and so many objections could be raised to this and probably any plan broached. But let us have the matter thoroughly ventilated and perhaps we may yet arrive at a plan that is equitable and practicable and

> which will be satisfactory to all concerned. It is a business proposition and should be settled by business methods. . . .
>
> VETERAN.

Ward's response to what he and a growing number of players saw as the owners' usurpation of their rights as American citizens was to form, with other players from the New York Giants on October 22, 1885, the Brotherhood of Professional Base Ball Players. As he described the impulse three years later, "It was not to be expected that club managers [by which he meant not field leaders but management] . . . would exhibit much consideration for the rights of players. As long as a player continued to be valuable he had little difficulty, but when, for any reason, his period of usefulness to a club had passed, he was likely to find, by sad experience, that base-ball laws were not construed for his protection; he discovered that in base-ball, as in other affairs, might often makes right, and it is not to be wondered at that he turned to combination [unionization] as a means of protection."

The Brotherhood's initial aims were simple, as Giants' pitcher Tim Keefe described them in 1890:

> On the 22nd day of October, 1885, the following preamble was drawn up and signed by the players of the New York Base Ball Club:
>
> We, the undersigned, professional base ball players, recognizing the importance of united effort and impressed with its necessity in our behalf, do form ourselves this day into an organization to be known as the "Brotherhood of Professional Base Ball Players." The objects we seek to accomplish are:
>
> To protect and benefit ourselves collectively and individually.
> To promote a high standard of professional conduct.
> To foster and encourage the interests of the game of Base Ball.
>
> John M. Ward, J. J. Gerhardt, William Ewing, Roger Connor, Daniel Richardson, Michael Welch, Michael C. Dorgan, Jas. H. O'Rourke, T. J. Keefe.
>
> John M. Ward was chosen president of the new organization, committees were formed, the work of the different committees, after a short period, was finished, and the foundation of the substantial and

famous organization known as the "Brotherhood of Professional Base Ball Players" was laid.

In the year 1886 President Ward and the New York Chapter began to organize chapters in the different cities where National League clubs were located.

Ward's protective association owed much to an idea broached previously that summer by the aforementioned Billy Voltz. This notion was reported in the *Cincinnati Enquirer* and picked up by other papers on June 24, 1885. Past and future sportswriter Voltz, at that time the manager of minor league Chattanooga, was the originator of the Protective Union of Base Ball Players. His plan called for an assessment of $5 per month upon 200 players, whose approval he had arranged. Their dues would thus build up a fund during the season of $1,000 a month, or $6,000 that might benefit indigent subscribers during the winter. John Ward borrowed and extended this idea in October 1885. Although the date of this news report was June 24, the direct impetus for Ward to act on the idea may have come when Voltz reported, on October 17, that the conference of the two major leagues at the Fifth Avenue Hotel was about to enforce a $3,000 salary cap and would repeal the eleven-man reserve in order to extend the onerous clause to all players (it turned out that the reserve limit was upped only to twelve at this meeting, which with the typical fourteen-man rosters of that day was nearly universal anyway).

For 1886, the salary provision went the way of previous such attempts, as Fred Dunlap soon was signed for $7,000, King Kelly for $5,000, and Amos Alonzo Stagg, star pitcher at Yale, reportedly could have signed for as much as he wanted with any of six franchises. Stagg refused the offers because of the character of the professional game: "the professionals . . . were a hard-bitten lot, about whom grouped hangers-on, men and women, who were worse," he wrote. "There was a bar in every ball park, and the whole tone of the game was smelly." Most clubs were making substantial profits, which made their fixation on the salary cap truly puzzling. Detroit visited New York for a three-game set commencing on Memorial Day and drew 7,000 on the holiday, which fell on a Sunday, followed by a record 20,709 paid attendance the next day. Chicago announced an 1886 profit of $62,000. New York may have made even more—John Ward thought so—but owner John B. Day said he made only $50,000. Boston made $65,000, corroborated by the club's surviving account books. Among National League clubs in 1886, Washington definitely lost money, and perhaps St. Louis and Kansas City, too.

In the American Association, every club finished in the black except the Mets, and their deficit was accountable to the inaccessibility of their lavish new Staten Island ballpark. During the summer, spectators were able to look at New York harbor from the St. George grandstand and see the Statue of Liberty being assembled. In right field, owner Erastus Wiman installed a stage set for a spectacle titled *The Fall of Babylon*. Its cast included ballet dancers, elephants, camels, and other beasts who paraded across the field while the ball clubs practiced in the western part of the park near the grandstand. This park provided what may be the game's all-time oddest ground rule: A hit that pierced the walls of *Babylon* produced a double. A newspaper report of a game included this other singular feature: "Two trusty warriors stood upon the walls of Babylon and held their polished shields so that the reflection of the sun would strike the Baltimore batters full in the eyes."

The players' dispute was with the National League to a far greater extent than with the liberal owners of the American Association. Von Der Ahe, in particular, had no love for the league, and he seethed when Chicago's underhanded tactics denied his Browns a rightful victory in the 1885 World Series. Before the final game both sides had agreed that the controversial game two would be declared no contest; originally it had been forfeited to Chicago when the Browns left the field in the sixth inning of a 5–4 game in a dispute with the legendarily crooked umpire Dave Sullivan (who nonetheless officiated a few big-league games after this). Thus with the series tied at two wins apiece—game one had ended in a legitimate tie—the Browns won game seven handily, 13–4, to win the World Series . . . or so they thought. Only after the conclusion of this game did Cap Anson insist that game two should now revert to a forfeit, so that the series would end in a draw, at three wins apiece after the series-opening tie. The long-standing rivalry between St. Louis and Chicago may have originated in their competition for the nation's commerce via river or rail, but, in baseball, the ill feeling between supporters of the Cubs and Cardinals started with this dispute.

Von Der Ahe was so eager to avenge himself that, when the two clubs reconvened for the 1886 World Series, he declared that he would take no profit for himself and that as far as his interests were concerned, the series proceeds would go to the players on a winner-take-all basis. This was the first World Series ever to be played this way, and the last. Chicago's Spalding proposed a nine-game series with four games to be played in each city (no games in neutral sites such as Cincinnati and Pittsburgh, as had been the case in 1885, unless the series went to a deciding ninth game). Chicago shut out St. Louis in game one, St. Louis returned the favor in game two. The teams split the next two games. St. Louis won game five as Chicago, with a sore-armed pitching staff of John Clarkson and Jim McCormick, was forced to go with position players Ned Williamson and Jimmy Ryan in the box. Game six was settled in the tenth inning by what has come to be known as "Welch's $15,000 slide," as the winning run scored by Browns' outfielder Curt Welch assured his teammates nearly that much in shared winnings.

In truth, there was no slide, as Chicago catcher King Kelly had called for a pitchout to catch Welch napping off third, but Clarkson threw it over his head and Welch scored easily, trotting across the plate rather than sliding as in legend. Von Der Ahe offered to play another game in Chicago, as an exhibition, but Spalding replied:

> Friend Von Der Ahe: We must decline with our compliments. We know when we have had enough. Yours truly, A. G. Spalding. P. S. Anson joins me in the above message.

In the offseason prior to the 1887 campaign, Kelly would be sold to Boston for the amazing figure of $10,000, and Spalding would rid the club of two other formidable players who, like Kelly, had upset him with their dedication to drink and inattentive play—outfielders George Gore and Abner Dalrymple. Kelly increased his salary as a consequence of the deal but he was not able to secure any of the purchase price, let alone half, as Fred Dunlap was able to do when he was sold, in the ensuing offseason, from Detroit to Pittsburgh. Clarkson would join Kelly as a teammate in 1888, for the same sum as his former Chicago teammate, providing Boston with its famous $20,000 Battery. Von Der Ahe would take notice of these peculiar market conditions and before the start of the 1888 season he would sell to

Brooklyn pitcher Bob Caruthers for $8,250, along with pitcher Dave Foutz and catcher Doc Bushong for $5,500. After three successive AA pennants, a denuded St. Louis club somehow won one more before handing the pennant as well as its key players to Brooklyn.

Players were being treated as chattel, Ward wrote: "Instead of an institution for good, [professional baseball] has become one for evil; instead of a measure of protection, it has been used as a handle for the manipulation of a traffic in players, a sort of speculation in live stock, by which they are bought, sold, and transferred like so many sheep."

Ward was a hero to many and still in his prime, in his late twenties, even though his professional career had commenced a decade earlier as a pitcher. He won his last game in the pitcher's box with the New York Giants in 1884. Afterward taking the field mostly at shortstop, Ward led the Giants to the world championship in both 1888 and 1889, hitting .379 and .417 respectively in postseason play. In the pivotal sixth game of the 1889 World Series, when New York trailed Brooklyn's Bridegrooms three games to two, Ward came up with his team down 2–1 in the bottom of the ninth, with no men on base and two outs. He singled, stole second, stole third, and scored the tying run on an infield dribbler. With two outs in the eleventh inning he drove in the winning run with another hit. Long before Reggie Jackson, *he* was New York's Mr. October.

Yet, Johnny Ward was not universally beloved. Some players thought him imperious, flaunting his schooling that had culminated in a law degree from Columbia in 1885. In February 1887, there was talk of the New York Giants selling him to Kansas City, where he refused to play, saying he would retire if sold. The Giants seemed then to be on paper the class of the league, especially after raiding the Mets of Keefe and Dude Esterbook in 1885, but still they were not champions. In that year, an umpire had said of the club, "New York is a fine team but it lacks vim for some reason. There is something lacking but I don't know what. It may be jealousy as the team is made up of 'star' players, who might be compared to a theatrical troupe of stars. If not firmly handled, New York will not finish first." In July 1887, Ward yielded his captaincy to Ewing after some players complained to management that he was too strict.

By October, however, his imperious ways were deemed simply adorable by his new bride, stage actress Helen Dauvray (born Helen

Gibson in San Francisco in 1859). Her summer-long interest in the game of baseball had been fanned to such a flame that she commissioned a silver loving cup (the Dauvray Cup) as a prize for the world champion club, along with ornate medals for the champion players. The *New York Times* reported, "All through the earlier part of the Summer she was a regular attendant at the Polo Grounds, and always aggressively and enthusiastically championed the home team. Her tiny hands beat each other rapturously at every victory of the Giants and her dark eyes were bedewed at every defeat. But the thousands of spectators who observed Miss Dauvray's emotions little suspected that one of the Giants had any precedence over the others so far as her affections were concerned." The *Times* announcement of the couple's intent to marry spoke to the relative renown of players of the stage and those of the field: "Miss Dauvray's history is too familiar for detail, but the man she is to marry is not so well known, although he has made a reputation on the diamond."

Also during that busy summer of 1887, the Brotherhood of Base Ball Players organized formally at Earle's Hotel in New York on August 29. It arranged for a meeting with National League owners on November 18 and, while agreeing to the reasonableness of player suspensions for disciplinary infractions, the brotherhood wrested what looked like important concessions: the league agreed that if it violated a written rule it would comply in a reasonable time with a player's request for release; the league killed the much hated fifty-cent-deductible fee levied against players for road expenses; and it agreed that a player could not be sold without his consent. It seemed bridegroom Ward would not be shipped out of town after all.

He continued to rail against injustice, though not always in tune with the concerns of ordinary people. Few fans found endearing his letter to the newspapers in which he justified his public demand for a $5,000 salary by leaking the New York club's profit figures of $80,000 in 1886 and $110,000 in 1887. But he was a star, righteous and prideful, and a formidable match for Albert G. Spalding in the all-out war to come.

The Olympics of Philadelphia organized to play town ball, absorbing other clubs in the period from 1831 to 1833. Until 1860 they played their own antique game, mostly across the river in Camden, New Jersey. They built this clubhouse in Philadelphia in 1860. (Author Collection)

Choice refreshments are served on the spacious lawn of the Elysian Fields of Hoboken. The Colonnade Hotel, where so many banquets were held for pioneer baseball players, is out of view at the upper right. Engraved by James Smillie, c. 1835. (Author Collection)

This engraved ticket to an 1844 soirée is the earliest known image of grown men playing baseball. It depicts the Magnolia Ball Club—"a workingman's aggregation"—in action at the Elysian Fields of Hoboken. The Colonnade Hotel is at right. (Corey R. Shanus Collection)

This 1845 daguerreotype features six members of the Knickerbocker Base Ball Club, five of whom had claims to baseball paternity (excluding only Anthony). *Top, left to right:* William R. Wheaton, Alexander J. Cartwright, Henry T. Anthony. *Bottom, left to right:* Duncan F. Curry, Daniel L. Adams, William H. Tucker. (Corey R. Shanus Collection)

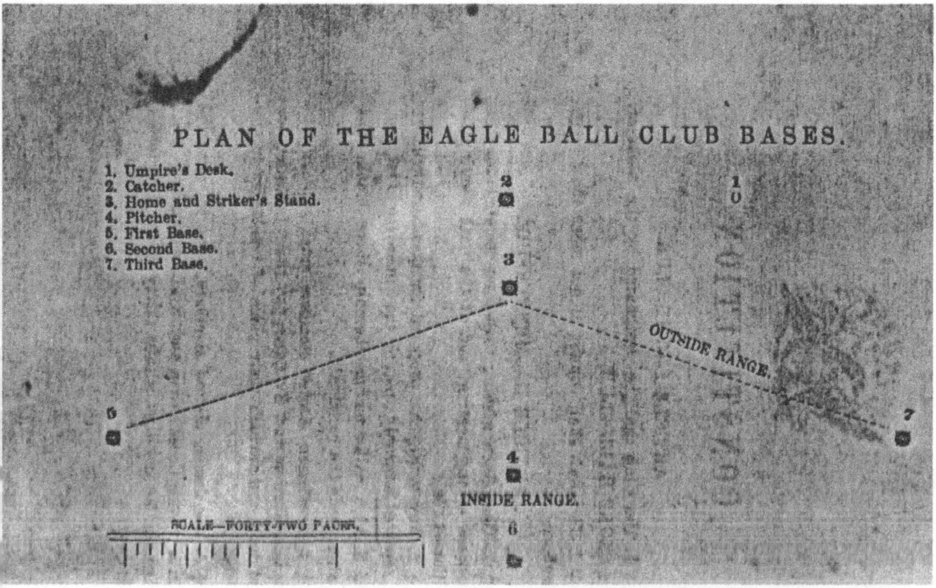

This strange diagram, purportedly to scale, was a feature of the Eagle Ball Club constitution as printed in three editions in the 1850s. Its 153-foot base paths proved a false lead, as the rediscovered Eagle rules revealed that its base paths were the same as those of the Knickerbockers. (Author Collection)

The Gotham Inn at 298 Bowery, also known as the Gotham Saloon, was built in the 1770s. It became the clubhouse for the venerable Gotham Base Ball Club and the site of several annual conventions of the National Association of Base Ball Players. (Author Collection)

The Eagle Ball Club of New York was organized in 1840, according to the title page of its long-lost bylaws and rules from 1852. Did they play a game of baseball similar to that played by the Knickerbocker, Gotham, and Magnolia clubs? Their printed rules would indicate so, but with a key difference. (New York Public Library)

This Indian Peace Medal design, used during the terms of Presidents James Buchanan and Abraham Lincoln, opposed the plow, the homestead, and baseball to the bow, the arrow, and scalping. U.S. Mint, AR small Indian peace medal, 1857. (ANS 1925.173.17. Courtesy of the American Numismatic Society)

Before the Civil War, when cricket and baseball vied for the title of national pastime, many athletes played both games. Here is the St. George Cricket Club at the Elysian Fields of Hoboken in 1861, featuring fourteen-year-old George Wright—son of the club's professional, Sam—who was destined to become baseball's first star of the post–Civil War era. (Author Collection)

Jim Creighton, nonpareil pitcher of the Brooklyn Excelsiors, was the game's first hero for his on-field exploits and early death, at age twenty-one in 1862. He was also an emblematic figure as perhaps the game's first covert professional and sly flouter of the rules for a fair delivery. (New York Public Library)

The Cincinnati Red Stockings were unbeaten in 1869 and extended their streak to June 14, 1870, when they were defeated by the Brooklyn Atlantics in a classic extra-inning contest. Photograph by Mathew Brady. (New York Public Library)

William Hulbert was a coal dealer who took a stake in the Chicago White Stockings in 1871. Five years later he unveiled a new idea: a National League of stock companies, in which labor would be subordinate to capital. (National Baseball Hall of Fame Library, Cooperstown, NY)

The 1876 Vassar College Resolute nine followed earlier women's baseball clubs, including the Laurels and the Abenakis of 1866. Women's baseball went from recreation to burlesque sideshow in the 1880s and 1890s. (National Baseball Hall of Fame Library, Cooperstown, NY)

Helena Petrovna Blavatsky and Henry Steel Olcott created the Theosophical Society in 1875. After their departure from America in 1878 they handed the reins to Abner Doubleday. (Author Collection)

Although research has revealed that Fleet Walker may no longer be termed the first African American to play major league baseball, he remains a compelling figure. From 1883 to 1889 he played on integrated teams at the highest levels of professional baseball. Here he is shown with the Toledo club of 1883. (National Baseball Hall of Fame Library, Cooperstown, NY)

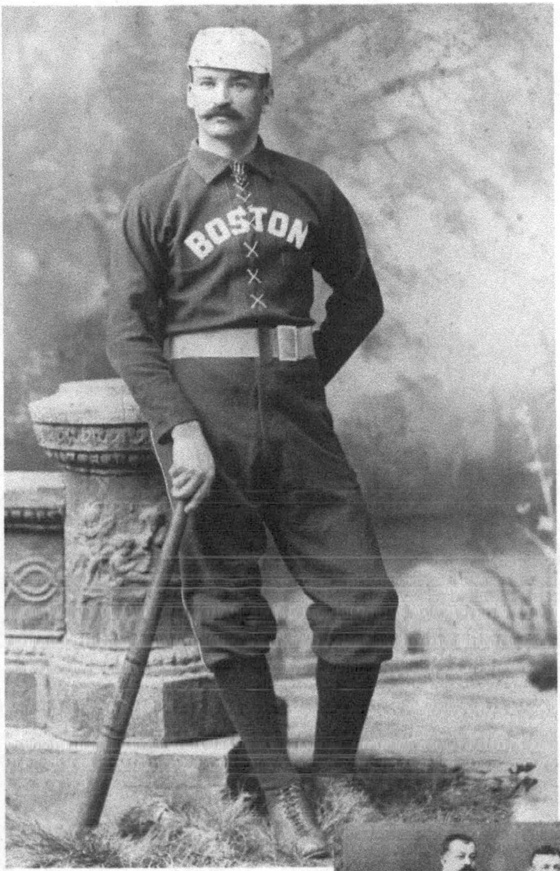

Michael J. "King" Kelly, the most popular player in the game. In 1887, in a shocking transaction, Chicago sold him to Boston, and he was termed the "$10,000 Beauty." (Library of Congress)

Integrated professional teams were commonplace in the Reconstruction period until the International League drew the color line in 1887. The Buffalo club of that year featured African-American second baseman Frank Grant (bottom row, second from right). (Author Collection)

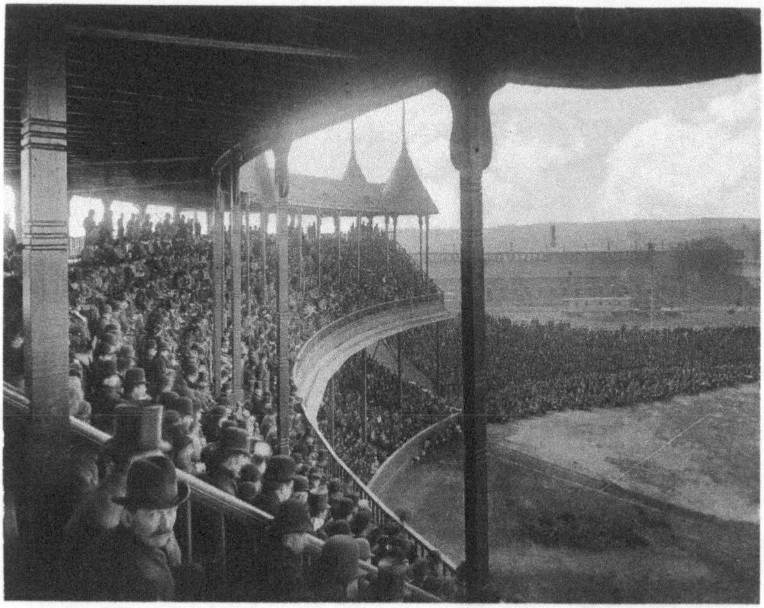

Baseball boomed in the 1880s, as attested by the sea of bowler hats in the grandstand of Boston's turreted South End Grounds. (National Baseball Hall of Fame Library, Cooperstown, NY)

The 1888 NL champion New York Giants featured Brotherhood leaders and future Hall of Famers John M. Ward and Tim Keefe. Other notables pictured here who were destined for Cooperstown are Roger Connor, Buck Ewing, Jim O'Rourke, and Mickey Welch. (National Baseball Hall of Fame Library, Cooperstown, NY)

Adrian Constantine Anson was not the most popular baseball player of the nineteenth century but he was its greatest, with a career that stretched from 1871 to 1897. He was depicted on many of the trading cards issued in the period, including this one from the 1888 Goodwin Champions set. (Library of Congress)

Britons were largely immune to the charms of baseball in 1874, when the Boston Red Stockings and Philadelphia Athletics staged a summer tour. Spalding's 1888–89 world tour was more of a success, at least in terms of promotion. But the junket lost money, including most of Cap Anson's investment. (Robert Edward Auctions)

This is what National League baseball looked like in the nation's capital in 1888. The right field and the infield of the park, known as the Swampoodle Grounds after the rail-yard district (note the B&O car behind the left-field fence), are now part of Union Station. (Library of Congress)

John M. Ward was a star pitcher, center fielder, and shortstop, but he is most notable for his leadership of the Brotherhood rebellion of 1889–90, which culminated in the Players' League, a failed utopian experiment. (New York Public Library)

Albert Spalding bought an automobile for his new wife, high school sweetheart Lizzie Churchill, the better to tour visitors around the Theosophical Society grounds at Point Loma, California. Here Lizzie takes her husband for a ride. (San Diego Historical Society)

The Raja Yoga Academy at Point Loma, California, c. 1910. How this idyllic colony came to provide so much intrigue, real and imagined, remains a wonder of the age. Was the Abner Doubleday brainstorm sprung here? (Library of Congress)

Abner Graves, the flamboyant figure whose recollection of events from sixty-five years prior, when he was five years old and Abner Doubleday twenty, was the sole source for baseball's incredibly hardy myth of creation. (National Baseball Hall of Fame Library, Cooperstown, NY)

One of many men called "the Father of Baseball" prior to Doubleday, Henry Chadwick was a great innovator, writer, and relentless promoter of America's national game. His insistence that baseball derived from the English game of rounders irked Albert Spalding and led to the formation of the Special Base Ball Commission, also known as the Mills Commission. (Author Collection)

Abraham G. Mills was baseball's "fixer"—the go-to guy whenever the game's executives needed help. The most celebrated service he rendered to baseball was to anoint, somewhat skeptically, Abner Doubleday as the game's inventor. (New York Public Library)

Mathew Brady photographed the "Hero of Fort Sumter" in the year of his triumph, 1861. Major Abner Doubleday was destined for even greater triumphs posthumously. (Library of Congress)

Albert Goodwill Spalding did not invent baseball but he helped to invent its inventor. He sat for this portrait by Pach Brothers in 1910, the year of his failed candidacy for U.S. senator from California. (Library of Congress)

9

SPORTING GOODS AND HIGHER THOUGHT

With his brother, J. Walter Spalding, Albert had established the sporting-goods business of Spalding & Brother in the spring of 1876. A surviving ledger page from that first year reveals that the brothers contributed $3,000 in working capital in addition to a loan of $800 from their mother, Harriet Irene Spalding. She lived with her daughter Mary Spalding Brown and her son-in-law in Rockford, while also spending considerable time in Chicago with her sons. Despite the small scale of the startup, the sizable diameter of Al Spalding's baseball circle permitted the fledgling firm to turn a first-year profit of $1,118.53, or a 29 percent return on investment. Harriet recalled this time in her reminiscences, privately published in 1910 when she was eighty-nine:

> The first two years after they started in business, Albert played ball in the summer time. I recall an order for shirts that the Indianapolis Club sent in. Walter had the knit shirts all right, but the great difficulty was to get the name "INDIANAPOLIS" put across the front of each shirt. He

> could find somebody who would cut the letters out of red broadcloth, but no one to sew them on. Walter was telling Albert about it at home, and I said, "Bring them down and I will sew on the letters." They had to be ready in three days. There were eleven shirts to be lettered, each letter felled with fine sewing silk. Walter marked where they were to go and I remember when I got to the last shirt it was almost dark. I took it to Josie's, Albert's wife, who was sick in bed, and asked her how it looked. She said, "Oh, Mother, you have got the N's wrong side up!" Fortunately they were only basted.
>
> The first two years of their business life were so promising Albert and Walter determined to purchase a factory in Michigan [near the timber from which Spalding model baseball bats were crafted], and at this time Mary's husband [William Thayer Brown] joined the firm and took charge of the manufacturing department, and for the next five years I spent my time with Mary in Hastings, Mich., with frequent visits to Albert in Chicago, where I greatly enjoyed their little son, Keith.

After Albert Spalding and Josie Keith married in 1875 they spent the winter in Rockford with mother Harriet and family before moving to Chicago, where he would continue to confer with Hulbert on the new league as well as to work on his plan for the sporting-goods business. Ever since the 1874 baseball tour of England, in which Harry Wright had permitted him to take an active part, Spalding was seeing his interests in baseball and business converge. With his stake in the Chicago White Stockings and the inauguration of his sporting-goods business, playing the game no longer gripped him as it once had. Although he was only twenty-eight and could have been expected to play a few years longer, he was intent on becoming a magnate. In 1878, the sporting-goods firm changed its name from Spalding & Brother to Spalding & Brothers to reflect the contribution of brother-in-law William Thayer Brown.

At this time, Albert's former sweetheart in Rockford, Lizzie Churchill, may have begun to suspect she had chosen the wrong baseball player when she married George J. E. Mayer in 1875. After losing a considerable sum backing the Kekionga club, he had followed in his father's footsteps, forming a jewelry partnership with Frank Voirol in three successive locations on East Main Street in Fort Wayne. In each, he made a modest home for himself and his new wife above the store.

("The house of Messrs. Geo. J. E. Mayer and F. Voirol, opposite the Fort Wayne and First National Banks, Main street, is among the most reliable and extensive in Indiana, and justly noted for the pure quality of their goods.") But for Mayer the entrepreneurial bent that had launched the Kekionga club to fleeting national fame could not be satisfied by selling trinkets and baubles to the hometown set. On April 25, 1876, a squib in the *Fort Wayne Daily News* reported without evident irony that "George J. E. Mayer is making preparations for the manufacture of his automatic coffin."

Lizzie's uncle, William D. Page, was the founding editor of that newspaper and, in the 1860s in Rockford, had been Al Spalding's boyhood friend. He would remain close, even joining him in residence at Point Loma, California, in later years. Moreover, Lizzie's grandmother, Frances Durand Page, also lived in the Page household, as did her own sister, Sarah Churchill, orphaned in Rockford not long after Lizzie's wedding there in 1875. Although leaving her childhood home, Lizzie settled into an extended family to which her allegiance increased as her husband's attentions shifted mercurially from one venture to another.

Dissolving the partnership with Voirol, George Mayer started a new jewelry business with Henry C. Graffe in the old hotel building known as the Mayer House, which his father had renamed for himself when he purchased it in 1850. Then, abandoning that activity, George opened a jewelry store in Oshkosh, Wisconsin. When it went bankrupt in 1884, he returned to Fort Wayne, where he would manage his father's former hotel, now owned by Charles H. Nix. When the Mayer House burned to the ground in 1885, Nix sent him to Lake Geneva, Wisconsin, to manage another of his hotels, this one called the Pishcotauqua, but George's increasingly weary wife remained in Fort Wayne.

Indeed, by the time Lizzie Churchill Mayer gave birth in 1878 to a son christened George Mayer Jr., her husband's economic vagaries may already have begun to weigh on her. Visiting her high school friend the former Mary Spalding, in Chicago, she could not help but observe the success of Mary's husband in the sporting-goods business in which he had just been made partner with Lizzie's one-time fiancé, Albert. We cannot know whether she saw Al Spalding during these visits, but such an encounter would have been entirely natural and expected.

Al Spalding's success as a semiprofessional baseball player in Rockford had been instant, but friends and family advised him to prepare for the future, to learn more about business and less about baseball. His early forays into the business world, however, were chastening to say the least. A position as bookkeeper with a grocer in Chicago in September 1867, though largely a deadhead job designed to secure his pitching talents, nonetheless came to an early end when the firm went bankrupt. Returning to Rockford, he hooked on simultaneously as a cashier in a newspaper office and a bookkeeper with an insurance company; both of these businesses also went bust during his tenure. The company to which Spalding next affixed his fortunes likewise failed. Even after he secured a fine salary to pitch with Harry Wright's Red Stockings in 1871, he sought offseason employment with first a Boston insurance company and then, in 1872, a New York newspaper; both of these soon collapsed. Apart from baseball, where it seemed he could do no wrong, this future captain of industry had lent a hand to seven successive flops.

Encouraged when Harry Wright deputized him to make arrangements for the 1874 baseball tour of England, and seeing both Harry and his brother George prosper with their separate sporting-goods enterprises in Boston, Spalding began to think that his business future might better be pursued *within* baseball. Earlier attempts to monetize the game had come first through owning the field and charging admission, then by owning the clubs and leasing the services of star players who would serve as the attraction. Men like the Wrights and Spalding and Reach next thought to capitalize upon the game by selling its implements of play, creating baseball equipment manufactories that one day might monopolize a disaggregated but nationally vibrant marketplace. Finally, those in club management thought they might insulate themselves from competition by controlling the raw material—by owning the players outright as if they too were sporting goods, the exponents of play if not exactly its implements. And, to a handful of visionaries all along the way, the thought occurred that controlling the game's past might also help to determine its future.

In 1876, Spalding would not only become right-hand man to Hulbert in the front office while leading the White Stockings on the field, but he would also establish a sporting-goods business at 118 Randolph Street. Cutting this double-edged swath, he replaced Chicago's 1875 manager, Jimmy Wood, not only between the white lines but also in the sporting-goods line, fatally weakening his store at 58 State Street and in effect driving him out of town. The Hulbert model of securing the core while eliminating weaker competitors at the fringes was one that Spalding would use to expand his business, gaining the license to supply the National League, using that exclusive perch to promote his wares, then driving out or buying out his competitors, first Wood, then in turn Harry Wright and his partner Louis Mahn, George Wright and his partner Henry Ditson, and Al Reach.

Jimmy Wood had been the star second baseman and manager of Chicago's first White Stockings club back in 1870 but, some years later, when he developed an abscess on his thigh which he foolishly lanced with a pocket knife, the resulting infection cost him the leg and his playing career; still, he continued to manage the club through the 1875 season. Turning his back on big-league baseball and Chicago following his dismissal, he took managerial jobs in the Southern minor leagues, moved to Florida, and worked in the state's burgeoning citrus industry. Circuitously Wood reattached himself to big-time baseball when his daughter wed orange grower and future Pittsburgh Pirates owner William Chase Temple, who would go on to play a singular and largely unnoted role in the Spalding saga for years to come.

AGAINST THE BACKDROP OF the rip-roaring fortune-hunting of the period, and his own lessons from Hulbert, Spalding adopted the motto that "Everything is possible to him who dares." This watchword for the Gilded Age, perhaps better termed the age of brass, is said to have been perched on Spalding's desk at 118 Randolph in 1876, yet it does not appear in print until an 1879 novel by Walter Besant and James Rice, *The Seamy Side.* In this popular book the authors offered readers a six-point guide to "How a Young Man May Prosper":

> The first moral is that everything is possible to him who dares.
>
> The second, that the world at large, and especially the genial and confiding manager of your bank, is ready to meet you half way in taking you at your own estimate.
>
> The third, that in this world you only have to help yourself. Piles of money are lying about; the man who makes his own pile is invariably

succeeded by a fool who asks for nothing but a certain originality of audacity in the adventurer who deprives him of his share.

The fourth, that the proverb *ex nihilo nihil fit* only applies to natural philosophy, the properties of matter, and so forth. It has nothing whatever to do with credit. The man who wants most gets most. It is the bold pauper who becomes rich, if he begins early. . . .

The fifth, that smartness still lingers . . . and still commands success.

There is a sixth which we reserve for the sequel. It is left for the readers of the Higher Thought, as Paul Rondelet [a character in the novel] says, to find out for themselves.

Higher Thought was a doctrine originating at about this time that stressed the potential of psychic efforts to control physical events. The six facetiously offered morals in *The Seamy Side* epitomize the mixture of materialism and spiritualism that swept both England and America in the Gilded Age. "This day and generation has no use," offered another wag, "for any young person who is not smart enough to live without actual contact with work."

Albert Spalding did not wait for social sanction to make his "manly friendship" for Lizzie Churchill Mayer something more. In the evident collapse of the Mayer marriage in the 1880s, he saw his opportunity, and he dared to take it. A hapless George J. E. Mayer, his Fort Wayne career up in flames by mid-1885, tried his luck in Chicago, ultimately landing a position as a desk clerk at the Deming European Hotel and subsequently as manager of the Cosmopolitan Hotel. Lizzie returned home with her "interesting little son," George Jr., "an irresistible young gentleman of seven years, who can spin on his toes or his heels as occasion requires, with perfect impunity," according to the *Fort Wayne Sunday Gazette*. Lizzie took comfort there amid the Page clan, her maternal family relations. On her visits to Chicago, she could save on hotel expenses by staying with high-school friend Mary Spalding Brown, whose Greenwood Avenue household included her husband, children, and mother. Albert, with wife Josie and son Keith, lived only three blocks away, on Woodlawn.

Like Albert, younger sister Mary had been born in Byron, Illinois, and was a formidable, independent thinker throughout her long life. An active member of the Daughters of the American Revolution almost since its inception, Mary nonetheless would resign in 1930 over the organization's refusal to advocate reducing armaments and its blacklist against speakers with radical ideas. In her Chicago years, before moving to New Jersey with her family in 1900, she was vice president of the Women's Club, a director of the Home for the Friendless, and served on the board of the Cook County Hospital Nurses' Training School. Her friend Lizzie would ultimately call upon all of Mary's warmth, social concern, spirituality, and maternal instincts.

Mary, more than anyone, may have influenced Lizzie Mayer's turn toward a spiritual approach to life. It may not be too much to suppose that she even encouraged Lizzie, estranged from her husband, to resume her schoolgirl romance with Albert. By Lizzie's own account, no later than 1889, at which time both she and Albert were married to others, she had joined the Theosophical Society. This would prove to be a momentous decision for Lizzie, for the Spaldings, and for baseball history, as we shall see. To understand why that is so, we will need to know something about the Theosophical Society.

Lizzie pursued an independent livelihood as a vocal instructor at the Fort Wayne Conservatory of Music. In 1889 she and George Jr. were living in a boardinghouse when a branch of the Theosophical Society was established in Fort Wayne. The Society, founded in New York on September 8, 1875, by Russian émigré Helena Petrovna Blavatsky and Americans Henry Steel Olcott and William Quan Judge, began as something of a "miracle club," for the study and elucidation of "occultism, the Cabala, &c." By 1888, however, its goals were stated as simply these three:

1. to form a nucleus of the universal brotherhood of humanity, without distinction of race, creed, caste, or color;
2. to promote the study of Aryan and other Eastern literature, religions and sciences (later restated as comparative religion, philosophy, and science); and
3. to investigate unexplained laws of nature and of the psychical (or latent) powers of man.

In its first aim, Theosophy reminded one of Masonic and other fraternal orders; in its second, it echoed some tenets of American Transcendentalism; and in its third aim, Theosophist doctrine seemed not so different from Higher Thought. Yet taken altogether, Theosophy appealed to many who had been skeptical of earlier movements.

Although in its thirteenth year, the Theosophical Society remained small in 1888, with only six hundred enrolled members nationwide, and only sixty attendees at its national convention that year; however, it was hinted that thousands more were secretly affiliated through its more than twenty branches from coast to coast. Blavatsky and Olcott had left New York in December 1878 for travel to India and Ceylon before settling in London, never to return to America. In their absence, the embryo society had been placed in the hands of Abner Doubleday—yes, *that* Abner Doubleday—and, absent direction from the founders, lay more or less dormant for some years.

While a first American branch of the New York headquarters was established in Rochester in 1882, and a second in St. Louis the following year, the Theosophical Society struggled to attract members. However, it never had difficulty attracting a skeptical press that sometimes mocked its tenets of reincarnation and karma and other times saw in it a dangerous new "popery" and threat to American values. The extent of the society's influence was invariably overstated, but this suited the Theosophists, who were struggling to attain an American foothold. In a letter read before attendees at the 1888 convention in Chicago, Blavatsky wrote in part:

> I am confident that, when the real nature of Theosophy is understood, the prejudice against it, now so unfortunately prevalent, will die out. Theosophists are of necessity the friends of all movements in the world, whether intellectual or simply practical, for the amelioration of the condition of mankind. We are the friends of all those who fight against drunkenness, against cruelty to animals, against injustice to women, against corruption in society or in government, although we do not meddle in politics.

These last words were meant to address the prevalent suspicion that, supposedly like the Freemasons, Theosophists were a secret society opposed to organized religion, hoping to convert the masses through spiritual flimflam. (At its beginning the Theosophical Society was indeed marked by secret grips, passwords, and rites reminiscent of Masonic practices.) More troubling to those inclined to see conspiratorial plots in Theosophy were its philosophical underpinnings in Tibetan Buddhism. While widely respected today, this religion was regarded by Orientalists of the nineteenth century as *Lamaism*, a faith radically apart from mainstream Buddhism and one that was dominated by magic or even black magic. Blavatsky fed this flame with her sleight of hand tricks and her "precipitated" letters from venerable Tibetan masters (the "Himalayan Brotherhood"), written documents that would mysteriously appear in her possession following a question arising from a session with skeptics.

WHEN LIZZIE MAYER, SEPARATED but evidently not divorced from her husband, sailed for Liverpool with son George on the steamer *Etruria* on July 19, 1890, she was perhaps a member of the Fort Wayne branch of the Theosophical Society. In London, she studied with William Shakespeare, the celebrated vocal instructor at the Royal Academy of Music, and with Madame Blavatsky at Theosophical Society headquarters at 19 Avenue Road. In 1921, she would recollect those days:

> What most deeply impressed me when I met Helena Petrovna Blavatsky in 1889 [this date is in error, as Mrs. Mayer entered her first passport application in 1890] was her deep insight into human nature, her marvelous wisdom, her sincerity, her generosity. I became a member of the original Theosophical Society in the same year, and have ever since been an active worker in it.

Lizzie returned stateside on October 8, 1890, on the steamship *City of New York*. However, after resuming her duties at the Fort Wayne Conservatory of Music, she abruptly tendered her resignation on November 15. A little more than two weeks later she left for Chicago, where she boarded the Limited to New York and again sailed for Europe. Once more she was accompanied by her son but this time also by her younger sister, Sarah ("Sadie") Churchill. What could explain this abrupt flight from Fort Wayne?

Mrs. Mayer had come back home not only a Theosophist but also pregnant, having conceived sometime in September but not recognizing that fact until her return the following month. For propriety's sake she could not remain in her family's hometown while her delicate condition became ever more visible. If she were to give birth, it would have to be elsewhere.

Arriving in New York on October 8 aboard the same ship with Lizzie and George Jr. was the baby's unwitting father, Al Spalding, accompanied by wife, Josie, and son Keith. Both the Mayer and Spalding parties had had first-class cabins on the *City of New York* and it is likely that George and Keith, both thirteen years old, kept each other's company.

The events that followed, heretofore untold, indicate that the romantic affair may have been an open secret among the Spalding clan, even tolerated by Albert's wife, Josie. Somehow, the near-penniless Lizzie managed to take a house with a servant at 12 Bloomsbury Place in Brighton for herself, Sarah, and young George, who became so proficient in football (soccer) at school that he was named captain of the team. In the United Kingdom census of 1891, taken on April 5, Mrs. Mayer listed herself as widowed and "living on her own means." On June 14, five weeks after the death of Madame Blavatsky on May 8, she gave birth in Brighton to a son listed in the national birth index as "Male Brown." One may understand her wish for privacy, even secrecy, in the naming of a child born out of wedlock whose father was wed to another, but by giving him the surname "Brown," the same as that of Mary Spalding Brown, she supplied a clue to the boy's parentage as well as his future.

Upon her return to America in August 1892, Lizzie, who now preferred to go by the more dignified Elizabeth C. Mayer, deposited her year-old son with Mary and William Thayer Brown in Chicago. They raised the foundling as Spalding Brown, taking him along to Massachusetts and then New Jersey when Spalding Company business compelled them to move east. The so-called widow Mrs. Mayer, looking to distance herself further from her inconveniently living husband, persuaded her older son to shed his first name of George and replace it with Durand, the maiden name of his great-grandmother, Frances Durand Page. A few years later, Durand Mayer would move legally to change his name to Durand Churchill, thus adding his mother's maiden name and removing nominal evidence that he had ever had a father. Although she continued to call herself Mrs. Mayer as she transformed her Theosophical calling into a career, she would continue to aver, even in the 1900 United States census, that she was widowed.

The widow Mayer stayed in New York upon her return and provided vocal instruction in the Lotus Circle, or Sunday School, of the Theosophical Society outpost in Harlem (known as the "H. P. B." branch for founder Helena Petrovna Blavatsky), with performances at the main "Aryan" branch at 144 Madison Avenue. In the years to come, she would become a key player in the movement and its touring crusades, carrying the message to distant places.

Husband George Mayer, however, would continue to prove an embarrassingly hardy corpse; this was, after all, the man who in 1876 had thought it worthwhile to invent an automatic coffin. This was the man who had played ball with Anson at Notre Dame, who had played catcher in games against the famous Cincinnati Red Stockings of 1869. This was the man who had built the Kekionga into one of the charter clubs in professional baseball's first league. True, he had returned to Fort Wayne a failure in the ensuing decade, and his "interesting little son" was not exactly a chip off the old block . . . but despite his "widow's" efforts, George J. E. Mayer was not so easily buried. He continued to dabble in baseball, pitting his two Chinese nines in a series of games at Spalding's National League ballpark in 1888; he even returned to Fort Wayne to umpire a game in mid-1891, less than a month after his wife had given birth to another man's son. In 1899 he and a partner devised a chess and checkerboard newspaper premium designed to provide revenue to the clients of their advertising agency. In 1901, he ran his own newspaper, the *Truth Teller*, in St. Louis. Though said by his wife to be deceased, he continued to live vigorously in the open.

George J. E. Mayer was an inventive man, a creative thinker, and for all his business failures and personal failings, something of a visionary. He had a speculative bent as well as a practical one, and thus was well fitted for the age of brass. So was Elizabeth Churchill Mayer, so fierce and pragmatic in the pursuit of a vision that one is left to wonder, in her revived romance with Al Spalding, who seduced whom. Yet she presented herself publicly as a spiritual woman, capable of such idealized pronouncements as this tribute to Madame Blavatsky, in whose presence she spent but a few hours but whose legacy she would wear the rest of her life:

> Words fail to express the gratitude I feel to Mme. Blavatsky. Only her peers can estimate the greatness of her character, her wisdom, her self-sacrifice, her devotion to Truth and the Cause of Humanity; and she was without peer in the nineteenth century. As Foundress of the present Theosophical Movement, and its first Teacher, she proclaimed again the Truths of the ancient Wisdom-Religion. Through its teachings—the Divinity of Man, the Freedom of the Soul, Universal Brotherhood, Karma, Reincarnation,—she gave a new meaning to life and opened the way for a new understanding of its problems; she brought new hope to the world and has made Humanity her debtor.

BEYOND SUCH FLUFF, THE real Mme. Blavatsky is more difficult to assess. Born Helena Petrovna Hahn on August 12, 1831, in Ekaterinoslav, Russia (today Dnepropetrovsk in Ukraine), she was married off at age sixteen to General Nikifor Vassilyevich Blavatsky, age forty (though Blavatsky later said, for unknown reasons, that he was seventy-three at the time they wed). She traveled broadly in Europe, the Middle East, India, Kashmir, and perhaps Tibet; she was said to have survived a shipwreck, penetrated the Sphinx, lost a fortune, and made another. In 1853, she journeyed to Canada and the United States but was soon recalled to Russia. From Paris in the ensuing decade she departed for America once more, this time at the instruction of her Tibetan master. A report of her life, the product of an interview in the offices of the *New York Daily Graphic* (November 13, 1874), produced all these supposed facts, many of which she contested in a personally marked copy of a reprint in the November 19 *Spiritual Scientist*, published in Boston. "These lies are circulated by American reporters," she wrote in a jagged hand, "with which this land of canards and unwarranted exaggeration so fully abounds. H. P. Blavatsky."

America certainly seemed an unlikely place to plant the seeds of a new religion based on a revival of the lost mysteries of antiquity. But H. P. B. had her orders, so she came. There may have been another, more mundane reason as well: She wished to become an American citizen. On September 22, 1874, she made her application, and on July 8, 1878, by the decree of Judge Larremore in the special term of the Court of Common Pleas, she became the first subject of the tsar to renounce her allegiance and become an American. In her naturalization papers she declared herself the widow of N. V. Blavatsky, neatly ignoring her recent (1875) marriage and divorce from Michael C. Betanelly, a Philadelphia import-export dealer of Georgian descent. Also ignored was the fact that her first husband was, like George J. E. Mayer, contrarily alive.

To what end did Blavatsky wish to be an American citizen? In July she said, "I must say that I feel proud of the title. You ask why I have renounced my allegiance to my country? I answer because I love liberty. There is but little liberty in Russia to-day. Here it is the reverse. . . . This is, indeed, a great country, but then you have one great drawback. The people are so shrewd, and there is much corruption. But with all this, I prefer it and its freedom to all other countries." Five months later, as she hastened to leave New York for India with Olcott, she offered a reporter for the *New York Daily Graphic* this expanded explanation:

> I am glad to get away from your country. You have liberty, but that is all, and of that you have too much, too much! Do you wonder I am anxious to leave it when you know how I was received and the treatment I have met? They said I was a spiritualist, a heathen, a believer in all manner of impossible things; that I was an adventuress and had neither title nor family; that I was a felon and a forger; that I had been married seven times and had murdered six of my husbands; that I was a free lover and had never been married; that I was the mistress of Pio Nono [Pope Pius IX], and that I came here a fugitive from justice. Think of it all! . . . Ah, you have liberty. I had none. I could not be protected by Russian consuls and so I will be protected by American consuls. . . . Now I shall have the protection of my citizenship both here and abroad.

In her first year in America, Blavatsky had nimbly offered an equivocal defense of spiritualist hucksters, notably the Eddy brothers of Chittenden, Vermont, who in 1873 caused something of a nationwide sensation with their séances, including such spectral effects as disembodied voices, levitation, telepathy, and myriad phantoms produced on command. It was at the Eddy property that she met Henry Steel Olcott, a journalist more skeptical of the brothers' manifestations, who would join her and William Quan Judge in founding the Theosophical Society.

In New York, H. P. B.'s drawing room at 302 West 47th Street became an occult salon, with visitors constantly traipsing in and out.

It was dubbed "the Lamasery" by journalists for its numerous Asiatic curios mixed in with Western oddities, including "a large stuffed baboon, decked out with a collar, white cravat," and, Olcott wrote, a "pair of my spectacles, carrying under one arm the manuscript of a lecture on 'Descent of Species' and dubbed Professor Fiske." Blavatsky meant not to signal her opposition to Darwin's theory of evolution—Theosophy, too, was an evolutionary view of man—but rather to mock his emphasis on physical change unguided by a divine hand, and without parallel spiritual development. Evolutionist Alfred Russel Wallace, a defender of spiritualism as well as a cotheorist with Darwin of natural selection, was more to her liking.

It was in her New York lamasery that in 1877 H. P. B. completed *Isis Unveiled*, the massive two-volume cornerstone of Theosophy, a system of speculation founded in the correspondence between divine nature and the natural world: "As above, so below." In this book and in her numerous periodical writings, Madame Blavatsky provided a "skeleton key to mysterious gates," as she had originally titled this book. With *The Secret Doctrine* a decade later, an equally weighty and no less impenetrable tome, she added a dizzying theory of human evolution through root races. Here's a taste:

1. There are seven rounds in every *manvantara*; this one is the Fourth, and we are in the Fifth Root-Race, at present.
2. Each Root-Race has seven sub-races.
3. Each sub-race has, in its turn, seven ramifications, which may be called Branch or "Family" races.
4. The little tribes, shoots, and offshoots of the last-named are countless and depend on Karmic action . . .

The reader will be spared further direct quotation.

ON SEPTEMBER 25, 1843, Lieutenant Abner Doubleday, a dream-filled young man of twenty-four based at Fort Johnson, North Carolina, sent three dollars to James Munroe, editor of *The Dial*, the flagship journal of the Transcendentalist movement, the movement advocated by Ralph Waldo Emerson and Henry David Thoreau, among others, that argued that intuition rather than authority might lead one to the divine. Almost two years later, stationed at Fort Preble, Maine, he would pen a fawning letter to Emerson himself in which he revealed his spiritual agony, his doubts about both pursuing a military career and the justness of a potential war with Mexico, and his yearning to embrace the mystical life. In this never before published missive, we may see who Abner Doubleday was at heart, beyond the military exploits to come. We may also understand something of why Blavatsky and Olcott, after their flight from New York in the last days of 1878, left the Theosophical Society in his hands, and why, almost thirty years later, their successors thought to exhume him to play a legendary role in baseball.

Fort Preble, Portland, Maine
August 16th 1845. In the morning

Dear Sir

I like to paint the locale, so you may fancy me sitting on my piazza holding a conversation with nature. The atmosphere is delightfully clear and transparent and a gentle breeze is coquetting with the flag, sporting amid the vine leaves and gently waving the long matted grass. The sun glistens from the bayonet of the sentinel lazily walking under the gateway; and is reflected from the two field pieces in front of the quarters. The massive cannon and the pyramid of heavy balls seem to add to the repose of the scene. The masons are engaged in the construction of their new batteries, but notwithstanding the regular clink of their hammers and the occasional rumbling of those earth carts, you can hear the chirp of the insects in the grass, the buzzing of flies in the window panes and occasionally the far off singing of birds. How beautiful is the city in the distance, with its white and brick buildings interspersed with green trees, as if the whole had grown up together and the one was struggling to exclude the other. Over the rich green of the near meadow land I watch the blue water cover[e]d with white sails below, and the blue sky with its white clouds above. Ah, do look at that butterfly! Is it not gorgeous? Stop him; what business has he to be rustling by in such an unceremonious manner.

But hark! My reverie is broken by the sharp tones of my housekeeper. She "*will* have the stove taken down" but why should she be so vociferous about it.

Evening

A sudden indisposition prevented me from continuing my letter this morning, but now I will resume it. But why do I write to you at all—you who are away up there on that platform breathing a purer air than any to which I have attained? What right have I to occupy your time; already too much occupied by the impertinence and frivolity of others? I often feel the need of expression but I should hardly dare to offer my small casket of pearls in exchange for your treasures. But still I have felt a strong desire to thank you for existing. Your essays came to me when all things seemed dark and confused. My mathematical education at West Point led me to believe I could subordinate all thought to mathematical forms of reasoning. I failed to demonstrate Christianity by external evidences and I found in consequence the results I had obtained were at war with my innate sense of right. In short I was living through the French Revolution. Far up the horizon loomed this dread form of doubt and distrust; beyond its uncertain figure lay the dim land of frozen wastes and sepulchral silence. At this time your essays fell into my hands. They gave me a gleam of light which is still broadening and deepening. I have obtained a placid contentment of which I never dream but still my moods are often sad. I feel a strong desire for sympathy which I cannot obtain. Every where I am surrounded by dead men. They look upon me as a visionary who dares to set up his individual judgment against the opinions of the so called great men. Not having seen what the latest review says, they are not prepared to give an opinion on the subject of transcendentalism, but at present they are content to hold it as words and fury signifying nothing. Therefore must I be silent. I may not cast pearls before swine. Yet the other night I met a beautiful spirit, through whom the Divine nature shone with a strange lustre. This young girl apparently neglected by others, seemed both to contain and enlarge me. Doubts too frequently assail me. Doubts concerning my profession. It seems clear as a general principle that the armed body should *act,* not deliberate, but when I think I may be employed to oppress instead of to defend, the case does not seem so clear. Yet War is already declared. It is more than probable that a few months will see my regiment stationed along the Nueces. The Government which has educated, fed, and clothed me calls for my services. Those services must and shall be given to the best of my abilities. It is no time now to deliberate.

Do not think I mean to repine. I accept every event as a lesson, the good of which must be obtained, and this is indeed a consolation for every misfortune. I sometimes think that I lean too much upon you, but I shall strive to rely wholly upon the spontaneous element. It will put you to but little inconvenience to read this. I am too well aware of the value of your time and your many occupations to expect you will send me an answer. Could you not manage to deliver some lectures here. My quarters are situated opposite the city, a distance of about a mile and a half. Our barge usually goes twice a day. It is unnecessary to say that I should feel honored to have you spend any length of time with me. I have ample room; my quarters being large for a bachelor. I should be glad to see you, though your presence would be a continual accusation.

Very respectfully
Your obedt srvt
A. Doubleday
Lieut. 1st. Reg. Arty.

P.S. I have not yet obtained clear ideas concerning the relation which exists between the *me* and the *not me*, yet is this a foundation thought. I hope however to live through this also.

To knowing fans of the national pastime Doubleday is merely a joke, the man who did not invent baseball but instead was invented by it. All the same, he was not a cardboard cutout, and his breathless letter to Emerson is but a single step onto a well-documented spiritual path. After leaving the army in 1873, he translated alchemical works from French and studied Sanskrit; the bookish lad who "early imbibed a taste for reading," who was "fond of poetry and art and much interested in mathematical studies," was father to the man.

Doubleday joined the Theosophical Society in 1878 and stopped by the lamasery with sufficient regularity that Blavatsky referred to him familiarly in her diary. He had visited her in the evening of July 8, no doubt to congratulate her on receiving her naturalization papers that day. He visited her as well on December 14, the day that her steamer trunks were sent off to Bombay. On January 17, 1879, Olcott, writing from London, made him president of the society. "In making choice of my substitute I cast about for a man of unblemished character, of ripe age, of energy, and moral courage and quick intelligence and found him in you. . . ."

Although his interim presidency was distinguished largely by inaction and bureaucratic tussles with India and Ceylon (today's Sri Lanka), Doubleday remained a member of the society nonetheless and oddly defended Madame Blavatsky's character in *The Religio-Philosophical Journal* of April 28, 1888:

> I have read the attack made by Wm. Emmette Coleman on Madame Blavatsky, and as he is a man who deals largely in personalities, I cannot say that I am surprised at his averments. I saw a good deal of Madame B. when she was in New York. Attracted by the marvelous erudition displayed in "Isis Unveiled," and by the novel explanations given in the work in regard to the psychical and spiritual phenomena, I hastened to make her acquaintance. . . .
>
> It is quite true that Madame Blavatsky is an exceptional person. I have heard her at times express herself in language which was not [at] all conventional and much more forcible than polite. I can also relieve Mr. Coleman's anxiety about her moral condition by assuring him that she actually did smoke cigarettes.
>
> With regard to her marriage in Philadelphia, it was explained to me in this way: I was told that a Russian proposed to her, and as she saw that he was impelled by some of the dark denizens on the other side of the line to commit suicide in case he was refused, she consented to the ceremony, but made it a condition that she was never to see him again. She felt herself forced to do this, as in the first flush of her youth and beauty, two young men had committed suicide for the same reason, and she did not desire to have a third shade haunting her. The groom attempted to pursue her, but finding she would have nothing to do with him, obtained a divorce for desertion and married again. . . .
>
> A. Doubleday, F. T. S.
> [Fellow of the *Theosophical Society*]

At his death, Doubleday willed his notebooks (perhaps as many as seventy) and correspondence to the Theosophical Society, which continues to monitor access closely.

Baseball had a Theosophist in the midst of its ranks, although it wasn't Doubleday: William Chase Temple, father-in-law of one-legged baseball man Jimmy Wood. Before becoming president of the Pittsburgh Pirates club in 1891, the restless Temple had worked, among many other jobs, four years as president and general manager of the Metropolitan Electrical Service Company in New York City. During his last year in New York Temple enlisted as a member of the Theosophical Society and quickly became a prominent player. In July 1889 he—along with society heavy hitters William Quan Judge and Henry T. Patterson—was designated a trustee for the first year of the newly incorporated national Theosophical Society in New York City. Moving to Pittsburgh later that year, he became president of that city's branch lodge. In 1893, the press coverage of the World's Congress of Theosophy held in conjunction with the Columbian Exposition named him among the Society's "most distinguished expounders" in attendance, including Annie Besant, Claude E. Wright, and Bertram Keightley from England.

Temple sold his stock in the Pittsburgh ball club in 1893 but, as a parting gift to the National League, by then a twelve-team circuit with no rival against which to play a World Series—the American Association having folded its operation after 1891—he donated a silver cup (called the Temple Cup) to reward the winner of a postseason playoff between the top two finishers in the National League. This cup was awarded to the New York Giants in 1894, the Cleveland Spiders in 1895, and the Baltimore Orioles in 1896 and 1897, at which point it was retired. At the Theosophical Convention of 1897, held in New York, he made a speech to address a rift within the society. In the spring of 1902, Temple was called back to baseball to break a deadlock between warring owners and serve as National League president, at Spalding's special invitation. After seriously considering the offer for twenty-four hours, he was persuaded by his business associates to turn it down.

Temple's business success continued, with interests in steel, iron, machinery, coal, plate glass, telephone, and railroad enterprises. Yet in 1905, not yet forty-three years of age, he declared his exit from the business world. He retired and relocated to the serene Theosophist compound at Point Loma, California, where he remained for three years as a neighbor of the Spaldings and other wealthy notables who had been converted to the cause. The three years of his tenure at this westernmost part of continental America coincided with the period of the Mills Commission investigation into the origin of baseball.

10
THE GOSPEL OF BASEBALL

Despite looming storm clouds of labor unrest, baseball in the late 1880s had boomed at every level of play, in every city and hamlet. The national pastime was a binding force, one thing that everyone seemed to enjoy. Thrilling pennant races culminated in annual World Series that millions of fans followed in the ever-expanding sports pages. (The term was first applied not in 1903, as many believe, but in 1884, the year of the first postseason battle between league champions.) As attendance in both the National League and the American Association grew at a healthy rate, player salaries and transaction prices increased too.

Big-league owners feinted in the direction of a salary cap at each year's winter meeting, but invariably went on to ignore it. So when, in the fall of 1888, Indianapolis owner John T. Brush proposed a "classification plan" to limit salaries for 1889, the players might have paid no attention. Mildly worrisome, however, was the timing of the announcement of Brush's plan, while the leader of the players' union or Brotherhood, John Ward, was on a steamship in the Pacific Ocean, as a member of Albert Spalding's entourage promoting America's game to the world.

Spalding had announced on March 20, 1888, that he would lead a troupe of baseballists—his Chicago White Stockings, plus a glittering aggregation of other major leaguers to be called the All-Americas—on a trip originally slated only for Australia. (Over time, the trip itinerary expanded until it became clear that the tourists would indeed circumnavigate the globe.) Two weeks later, unruffled by the antebellum values it might indicate to foreign observers, he announced the sale to Boston, for $10,000, of his ace pitcher, John Clarkson. This followed the previous year's sale of Kelly to the same club for the same amount. Clarkson was not a live wire like his batterymate, but he was wired strangely: emotional, hypersensitive, his own worst enemy, it seemed. Cap Anson once said of Clarkson, "Scold him, find fault with him and he could not pitch at all. Praise him, and he was unbeatable." The winner of fifty-three games with Chicago in 1885, he would win forty-nine with Boston, so there was no doubting his fortitude, yet he ended his years at age forty-seven in a variety of sanitariums and asylums, depressed, alcoholic, and disoriented. As *Sporting Life* noted at the time of his death, "He seemed to have no memory at all for things of today, but talked clearly and lucidly of matters connected with the past."

By the 1880s, Clarkson's heyday, baseball was supplying national heroes like King Kelly (who backed out of the tour at the last minute), Cap Anson, Buck Ewing, and John Ward, whose likenesses were distributed on baseball cards packed in with cigarettes. Boys badgered men coming out of tobacconist shops for the pictures in their cigarette packs, or took up smoking early to acquire the cards. (Once it became clear who the real customers for the cards were, candy and gum manufacturers got into the act, including cards with *their* products; by 1920 or so baseball cards ceased to be packed with cigarettes.)

Baseball had become not only an entertaining spectacle at the ballpark or a sport on which one might bet in saloons and pool halls, it had now spun off artifacts of popular culture and, through legends made larger with each retelling, this former boys' game began to populate an American pantheon. The structure of the game, the multiple ethnicity of its players, the spirit of fair play, the strict observance of the rules. These made it our game, a model institution as cricket was for

England. Novels and short stories in the general-interest monthlies proliferated; the dime novel format, which had propelled baseball via the Beadle and De Witt guides since the 1860s, now gave rise to Frank Merriwell and other Apollos of the ball yard, real and fictional. Baseball songs became top sellers in sheet music and in the new recorded form of Edison cylinder rolls. Colorful baseball games with spinners and dice and player endorsements proliferated. Baseball lithographs and statuary decorated working family households. Baseball took to the boards, with vaudeville numbers, musical reviews, full-blown dramas, and a "ballad for the republic" called "Casey at the Bat."

Written by Ernest Lawrence Thayer (under the pen name "Phin," a shortening of his collegiate nickname, Phineas), the poem was first published on June 3, 1888, in the *San Francisco Examiner*, a paper owned by his Harvard classmate William Randolph Hearst. After that initial appearance it fell into the oblivion of all the freelance articles the paper bought at the going rate of five dollars apiece. That is all Thayer ever was paid for his immortal composition because: It was anonymous; as a magna cum laude Harvard man with a degree in philosophy, he didn't think much of it; and as he receded into the background, running a woolens mill in Worcester, others claimed authorship. Also muddying the waters was the haste with which municipalities vied for the honor of being identified as the real Mudville just as ballplayers from King Kelly to Dan Casey claimed to be the real Casey. The poem had almost as many fathers as baseball itself.

However, the man who made Casey a national figure was not the one who wrote the poem, nor the one on whom it was based, but the one who first recited it. On the evening of August 14, 1888, the actors in the light opera *Prince Methusalem*, about to end its run at Wallack's Theatre in New York, had invited the hometown Giants and visiting Chicago White Stockings to a special baseball evening. (The visitors had triumphed over the hometown heroes that afternoon by the score of 4–2, the same as that in the opening stanza of the poem.) De Wolf Hopper, a star of the play who liked to perform non sequitur comic bits between or even during the acts, needed something special to satisfy his distinguished guests. Into the breach leaped novelist Archibald Clavering Gunter, recently returned from San Francisco, who on the afternoon before the event handed Hopper a certain clipping from the *Examiner* that he had kept in his wallet for more than two months.

"Casey" proved an instant sensation as Hopper commenced his recitation with:

> The outlook wasn't brilliant for the Mudville nine that day;
> The score stood four to two with but one inning more to play;
> And then when Cooney died at first, and Barrows did the same,
> A sickly silence fell upon the patrons of the game.

You know the rest, don't you? In his autobiography, *Once a Clown, Always a Clown*, Hopper wrote of that evening's debut:

> I interpolated *Casey* in a scene in the second act. . . . It was, I presume, the first time the poem was recited in public. . . . On his debut *Casey* lifted this audience, composed largely of baseball players and fans, out of their seats. When I dropped my voice to B flat, below low C, at 'the multitude was awed' [the poem in fact reads: "the audience was awed"], I remember seeing Buck Ewing's gallant mustachios give a single nervous twitch. And as the house, after a moment of startled silence, grasped the anticlimactic denouement, it shouted its glee. . . . They had expected, as any one does upon hearing *Casey* for the first time, that the mighty batsman would slam the ball out of the lot, and a lesser bard would have had him do so, and thereby written merely a good sporting-page filler.

Hopper would go on to repeat his five-minute-forty-second recitation on some ten thousand occasions, each time eliciting wonder with the words "But there is no joy in Mudville—mighty Casey has struck out." In the cocksure Casey, baseball and America found an endearing and enduring hero . . . or like Rip Van Winkle, his literary partner in failure, their antihero, although few used that term then. And, as Casey got his comeuppance, so too would baseball in the last years of the century.

Even Walt Whitman was caught up in the baseball fervor of 1888 and the impending overseas tour. The good gray poet had written of the game as early as 1846: "In our sun-down perambulations, of late, through the outer parts of Brooklyn, we have observed several parties of youngsters playing 'base,' a certain game of Ball." He had followed baseball offhandedly since, reporting on contests for the *Brooklyn*

Eagle, mentioning the game in *Leaves of Grass* in 1855 ("upon the race-course, or enjoying picnics or jigs, or a good game of base-ball"). But, by the 1880s the "certain game of Ball" had become for Whitman the lone institution that could assure the great American democratic experiment.

In his last years, living in Camden, New Jersey, Whitman had a devoted admirer at his side, Horace Traubel, who invaluably recorded their conversations. Upon reading in the newspaper of April 7, 1889, that Spalding's world tourists had returned home, Whitman said to Traubel:

> "Did you see the baseball boys are home from their tour around the world? How I'd like to meet them—talk with them: maybe ask them some questions."
>
> I [i.e., Traubel] said: "Baseball is the hurrah game of the republic!" He was hilarious: "That's beautiful: the hurrah game! well—it's our game: that's the chief fact in connection with it: America's game: has the snap, go, fling, of the American atmosphere—belongs as much to our institutions, fits into them as significantly, as our constitutions, laws: is just as important in the sum total of our historic life."

For Whitman, the grand tour affirmed America's prophetic role among the world's nations, bringing immigrants together in a "transcendental Union" of manifest destiny's children. "Long ere the second centennial arrives," Whitman declared, "there will be some forty to fifty great States, among them Canada and Cuba." This prediction was indeed borne out, not in the USA's constituent parts, but in its professional baseball leagues.

If baseball were, like liberty, to be America's gift to the world, some began to feel it might be wise to make certain its origins were American. In 1888, Ward, before departing as one of Spalding's tourists, published a book that denounced Henry Chadwick's rounders theory of baseball's birth. Though he agreed with Ward on little else, Spalding too saw the benefits of wrapping baseball in the grand old flag. And the world tour provided him with the opportunity not only to spread the gospel of baseball and proselytize for American values, but also to extend the reach of his sporting-goods empire.

Untroubled by the values such a move might signify to the peoples his tourists were to visit, Spalding's White Stockings adopted as a mascot, in Philadelphia on June 7, 1888, a juvenile black actor named Clarence Duval, who had been appearing as an extra in the traveling-company light opera *Starlight*, topped by the buxom prima donna Vernona Jarbeau. Duval would travel with Anson's men for the rest of the season until jumping the club in New York in mid-August, right after the debut of "Casey at the Bat."

After playing their first game in Chicago on October 20, the White Stockings and All-Americas went west, stopping to play ball in St. Paul, Cedar Rapids, Omaha, Denver, and stops in between. In Omaha, bad-penny Duval turned up, as Anson relates:

> Clarence was a little darkey that I had met some time before while in Philadelphia, a singer and dancer of no mean ability, and a little coon whose skill in handling the baton would have put to the blush many a bandmaster of national reputation. I had togged him out in a suit of navy blue with brass buttons, at my own expense, and had engaged him as a mascot. . . . I told him that he was on the black list and that we had no use for deserters in our business. . . . [but] I finally consented that he should accompany us as far as San Francisco, and farther, provided that he behaved himself . . . To my astonishment he kept his word, remaining with us all through the trip and returning with us to Chicago. Outside of his dancing and his power of mimicry he was, however, a "no account nigger," and more than once did I wish that he had been left behind.

On November 4, following two games in Salt Lake City, the tourists played in San Francisco, with the All-Americas defeating the Chicagos 14–4 before a crowd of 10,500. On November 11, the squads played their last game until their ship, the *Alameda*, reached Auckland, New Zealand, more than a month later. (They had stopped in Honolulu, expecting to play a game but, arriving a day late, on a Sunday, the players ran afoul of the kingdom's blue laws and had to content themselves with a banquet; this was Spalding's failed opportunity to meet Alexander Cartwright.)

On November 22, while the tourists were at sea, the baseball magnates passed the Brush Classification Plan to limit salaries by performance level, on field and off; Giants owner John B. Day was reported to have called the measure the "Spalding Classification Plan," inadvertently revealing its true author. Whoever its mastermind, the plan classed players into five categories and specified a standard salary for each, with a range between $1,500 and $2,500. Not surprisingly, the Brotherhood voiced its displeasure. The next day, the Giants announced that they would sell Ward to Washington for a record $12,000. When word of these events reached the players, their ship became a hotbed of dissension, if not outright mutiny. (Four months later, back on American soil, Ward would force cancellation of the deal by refusing to play in Washington if he did not receive most of the transaction price.)

On December 15, after the stopover and exhibition at Auckland, Spalding's troupe played its first game in Australia, drawing 5,500 curious spectators in Sydney. They would spend two weeks in Melbourne, moving on to Adelaide and Brisbane before sailing to Colombo, where Blavatsky and Olcott had established a branch of the Theosophical Society in 1880. There is no evidence that in 1888–89 Spalding was as yet drawn to Theosophy, as Lizzie Churchill Mayer was. Still, he had planned to play in India, too, where the Theosophical Society founders were headed when they left America in December 1878, but was warned off landing at Calcutta because of an outbreak of disease. So, the baseball boys and their entourage, including Spalding's mother and Anson's wife, sailed across the Indian Ocean to Aden and thence to Egypt, where they played a game before the Sphinx and a handful of baffled Egyptians. A reporter traveling with the tour noted:

> The surface of the Desert was hard and firm, not unlike the snow crust of the North, and formed a by-no-means-poor ground for ball playing. Ward's forces were again "out for blood," and though Anson made a good start by the capture of two runs in the opening inning, All-America by good stiff batting piled up seven runs in the second and secured a lead which Chicago could not afterwards approach. . . . At the close of the game we returned to the Sphynx and the Pyramids and looked over the great masses of stone at our leisure. A couple of Bedouins performed the dangerous task of climbing to the apex of the big Pyramid and down again within ten minutes' time, for a ten-piastre piece, and then Ward, [Jim] Fogarty and [Jim] Manning, accompanied by attendants, undertook and accomplished the ascent.

At Naples, Spalding's wife and son joined the expedition party for the final leg of the journey. After stops at Brindisi, Florence, and Rome, the world tourists spent ten days in Paris and another ten in London. By this time, near the end of March, Ward had skipped home to settle his own ball-playing future, either in New York or Washington, and to prepare the Brotherhood for what promised to be a season of high drama.

HAVING STAGED TWENTY-EIGHT GAMES overseas since leaving home on November 1, the tourists arrived in New York City on April 6, 1889. Only a day earlier, the national news divulged that President Benjamin Harrison was exhibiting conspicuously, on a mantelpiece in the White House, a large baseball scorecard. To a visitor this demonstrated conclusively that "the Administration was all right, for it endorsed the game of baseball."

The world tour was a promotional bonanza but a financial disaster. Spalding didn't much care, as he candidly explained to sportswriter Harry Palmer, who went on to accompany and document the tour. "In undertaking such a trip I do so more for the purpose of extending my sporting goods business to that quarter of the globe and creating a market for goods there, rather than with any idea of realizing any profit from the work of the teams I take with me." The ball clubs' visit to Australia, for example, produced retail outlets for Spalding Company goods in Sydney, Melbourne, and Adelaide.

Anson, who invested $3,750 in the trip, lost about $1,500 of it, "that being my share of the losses incurred in advertising the sporting goods business of the Spaldings. . . ." But this fact went unreported for several years amid the frenzied celebration of the baseball men's epic return. Although the tour would not formally end until a game in Chicago brought it full circle on April 20, the big welcome-home event had already taken place, at New York's Delmonico banquet hall on the evening of April 8, following a game the squads played that afternoon in Brooklyn.

Delmonico's was known as the most fashionable restaurant in New York at the time. Although first established at the foot of the island on William Street in 1827, since 1876 it had been based on the south side of Twenty-sixth Street between Fifth Avenue and Broadway in the heart of the throbbing Tenderloin district. With its frescoed ceilings, silver chandeliers, flower-decked fountain, and French haute cuisine, it was the gaudiest establishment in the city and the site of some of the grandest private entertainments of the era.

The baseball banquet of 1889 may have been the most lavish in Delmonico's history. Given what was to follow, it may also be seen in retrospect as the high point of baseball in the century. The *New York Times* reported, on the morning after:

> Baseball heretofore has been regarded as an athletic game in which music and a desire to dispute the umpire have been potent factors. But that is all a mistake. Baseball is an intellectual pursuit, which is indulged in only by gentlemen of the highest mental calibre, and by those whose minds have undergone a singularly stringent training in the matter of intellectuality. This fact was established last night at a dinner given in the great banquet hall at Delmonico's to the players whose tour through various foreign lands gave the American national game a world-wide fame . . . Among the speakers calling the deepest and heartiest cheers from the lungs of the listeners were Mr. "Baby" Anson. [He] was considerably embarrassed when he rose to his feet, but was also thankful that he had been permitted to assist in teaching the world what it most needed to know, and Mr. "Johnny" Ward seemed glad of the opportunity given him to display his singularly correct knowledge of the English language.

Asked about the most impressive thing he had seen on the tour, Ward patriotically replied, "the Fire Island Light." Chauncey Depew and Albert Spalding were among the many other speechmakers, the latter saying that the coldest reception the players received on the tour was from the Sphinx, "who, with cynical eye and battered nose, looked down in disdain." Helen Dauvray Ward was in the balcony at Delmonico's hall, along with Spalding's mother and wife, when A. G. Mills gripped the podium. He declared that the game of baseball, "which quickens all the senses, stirs the blood, brings into play every muscle in the body—and usually develops the lungs of the spectators," was distinctly American in origin; that claim was vindicated by "patriotism and research." His words were met by a table-thumping, champagne-fueled, staccato response of "No rounders! No rounders!" In his estimation, Spalding's lads were not only star baseball players but also "worthy examples of American manhood and citizenship." Warming to the task, Mills concluded, before proposing several toasts:

> And who shall say that this tour of our base ball-players—bearing no diplomatic mission—unversed though they be in the arts of statecraft,—a tour devised to display in foreign lands a manly sport developed by Americans,—who shall say that it has not also been a useful contribution toward that universal peace and good-will among the nations of the earth that we as a people are ever foremost in promoting? All honor, then to Mr. Spalding and to every man in his party. They have reflected credit alike upon our National Game, our enterprise, our manhood, and our citizenship. . . .

De Wolf Hopper recited "Casey at the Bat." Digby Bell, his frequent partner in comedic turns, offered "Spalding's Ride," a parody of "Paul Revere's Ride," concluding with thanks

> To Spalding, who, freighted with ardor sublime,
> Played our national game in every clime
> From 'Frisco, globe-circling to New York Bay,
> In lands ten thousand miles away.

Teddy Roosevelt, too, was among the hundreds of celebrated attendees, but it was Mark Twain who stole the show with a rambling speech about the Sandwich Islands (as the Hawaiian Islands had been named by Captain James Cook in 1778) and the noble baseballists, concluding: "And so I drink long life to the boys who ploughed a new equator round the globe, stealing bases on their bellies!"

THE 1889 BASEBALL SEASON proved to be one of alternating light and shadow. On Memorial Day, May 30, Brooklyn drew the largest one-day crowd in baseball history to that point, as 8,462 saw the morning game against the St. Louis Browns at Washington Park and another 22,122 ringed the field for the afternoon contest. What made these totals all the more amazing was that Washington Park's grandstand had burned to the ground only eleven days earlier; the hastily erected seats could accommodate only 3,000, so the great majority of the paying customers stood. Emblematic of the tense underside of this baseball season, two weeks later, after the Louisville Colonels had lost their nineteenth consecutive game, their owner, Mordecai Davidson, threatened each of his players with a $25 fine if the next game, in Baltimore, did not yield a victory. Some of his players struck and had to be replaced by local amateurs for the next game, which, unsurprisingly, Louisville lost.

By July 4, a general strike was in the air. The Brotherhood requested a meeting at which the owners would hear player grievances. The owners refused. Spalding, questioned about the possibility of a strike and a third league for 1890, was reported to have said, "Oh, pshaw! The players won't do anything." As the rumbling mounted in September he added, with unintended irony, given his prior and future allegiances, "Will the public have confidence in . . . an oath-bound, secret organization . . . ?"

Baseball was booming in Brooklyn, where the Bridegrooms—so called because of their several newlywed players—were the rising power in the American Association. While they were poised to set a record for season attendance, the New York Giants opened the campaign as homeless vagabonds, for the city had built 111th Street through the center and right fields of their Polo Grounds in the fall of 1888. Thus, the Giants were compelled to open their regular season with a brace of games in Jersey City and then, until midsummer, to conduct their home games at the St. George Cricket Grounds on Staten Island, where the Metropolitans had played from 1886 to 1887. There they drew barely 2,000 fans per game. On July 8, they opened their new Polo Grounds uptown at 155th Street and Eighth Avenue, and commenced to attract twice their first-half traffic. While Brooklyn outdrew New York by 353,000 to 201,000, the latter defeated the former when they met in the World Series. Brooklyn seethed with a resentment that would find no balm in the next century either.

Not long after the World Series ended on October 29, Chicago's players announced that they would refuse to sign new contracts for 1890. Spalding threatened to enjoin them from playing elsewhere. On November 4 war was declared, as the Brotherhood issued a "Manifesto" that read in part:

> There was a time when the League stood for integrity and fair dealing; to-day it stands for dollars and cents. Once it looked to the elevation

> of the game and an honest exhibition of the sport; to-day its eyes are on the turnstile. . . . Players have been bought, sold, and exchanged as though they were sheep instead of American citizens. "Reservation" became with them another name for property right in the player. . . .
>
> Upon their final refusal to meet us, we began organizing for ourselves and are in shape to go ahead next year under new management and new auspices. We believe it is possible to conduct our national game upon lines which will not infringe upon individual or natural rights. We ask to be judged solely upon our work, and believing that the game can be played more fairly and its business conducted more intelligently under a plan which excludes everything arbitrary and un-American, we look forward with confidence to the support of the public and the future of the national game.

The phrasing of this vision, surely Ward's, may well have owed something to the recently formed Nationalist Club in Boston, founded in December 1888 by Edward Everett Hale, author of the once-famous story "The Man Without a Country," and utopian novelist Edward Bellamy (whose *Looking Backward* was first published in 1888). In an age of public disgust with the manipulation of government and the economy by combinations, syndicates, and trusts, the Nationalist Club of Boston was an instant sensation, rapidly spinning off 166 other branches. The movement's statement of principle was summed up as: ". . . so long as competition continues to be the ruling factor in our industrial system, the highest development of the individual cannot be reached, the loftiest aims of humanity cannot be realized. . . . Therefore those who seek the welfare of men must endeavor to suppress the system founded on the brute principle of competition, and put in its place another based on the nobler principle of association." If this Nationalist Club credo sounds not only like the wording of Ward's Brotherhood Manifesto but also like the words of Blavatsky, one may not be surprised to learn that in her *Key to Theosophy* (published in 1889), she praised both Bellamy and his Nationalist movement: She and he were utopians, and both believed that a small group of educated leaders, rather than a revolution rising from the streets, would engineer change of an orderly and evolutionary nature. They were populists of a decidedly Victorian sort.

In the week before the Delmonico banquet of April 8, William C. Temple, who in 1889 had launched the Theosophical Society branch in Pittsburgh, helped to form the New York branch of the Nationalist Club and became one of its officers. He also joined the Aryan Branch of the Theosophical Society in New York City, where he now conducted much of his business life and where he would soon cross paths with the society's musical director, Elizabeth Churchill Mayer. In the wake of the player revolt of 1890, he would become a National League owner and a lifelong ally of Albert Spalding. A sportsman and statistics enthusiast, Temple was the first to come up with the idea of the designated hitter, back in 1891. His idea was for the DH to replace the pitcher in the batting order throughout the game. James W. Spalding, Albert's brother, alternatively suggested that the pitcher's spot in the order be skipped, so that only eight men would bat. The National League actually voted on Temple's proposal in 1892, declining to adopt it by the narrow margin of 7–5.

To the Brotherhood Manifesto, Spalding replied with extensive reference to his personal history with Hulbert. Some found amusing his pomp and bluster, recalling that he himself had been a contract jumper in his day. If the players would swaddle themselves in the stirring language of liberty and bondage, he too would reach back to the rhetoric of the Civil War and wrap himself in the flag: "The refusal of the Brotherhood Committee to meet the League in conference at the close of the season proves incontestably that the imperative demand for a conference in mid-summer, to redress grievances that have never yet materialized, was a mere pretext for secession."

THE PLAYERS FORMED A new league, which they called the Players' League. While the players put some of their own money into the new venture, they also sought the backing of industrialists and easily found it. Albert L. Johnson, a former railway conductor in Cleveland who became a rail magnate in several midwest cities, headed the Cleveland club and provided the financial muscle behind the entire Players' League. Most of the National League's best players abandoned their clubs, sometimes after clever salary jockeying; Buck Ewing was said to have played both sides brilliantly if shamelessly for personal gain. Anson stayed in the old League, in part because he owned stock in the Chicago club. Ward joined the Brooklyn club in the Players' League, holding stock in it and in the New York PL club as well, presaging the syndicate trend that would afflict the game for the next two decades. Ewing, Keefe, and Connor joined the New York rebel club. Clarkson stayed with the league club in Boston but Kelly left for the city's PL entry. Spalding tried to break the strike by offering Kelly, the most influential of all players and the biggest drawing card in the land, a $10,000 bonus and a blank check for three years' salary if he would jump back to the National League. But the King declined, winning Spalding's grudging admiration by saying, "I can't go back on the boys." The carousing habits that Spalding could not abide, which had led him to sell his star to Boston in 1887, would lead to Kelly's death seven years later at the age of thirty-six.

Prior to the opening of the 1890 season, the National League's owners sued Ward for violating the reserve clause in his contract. They further sought a temporary injunction against his playing for any club other than the Giants, but Judge Denis O'Brien of the New York State Supreme Court handed the owners a stinging defeat in his denial of the injunction. After considering the reserve clause and its implied perpetual contract, which would bind the player for one year but the club for only ten days' notice of its intent to terminate, he said:

> Not only are there no terms and conditions fixed, but I do not think it is entirely clear that Ward agrees to do anything further than to accord the right to reserve him upon terms thereafter to be fixed. He does not covenant to make a contract for 1890 at the same salary, nor upon the same terms and conditions as during the season of 1889. . . . The failure of the existing contract to expressly provide the terms and conditions of the contract to be made for 1890 either renders the latter indefinite and uncertain, or we must infer that the same terms and conditions are to be incorporated in the one to be enforced, which necessarily includes the reserve clause, for no good reason can be suggested, if all the others are to be included, why this should be omitted. Upon the latter assumption the want of fairness and of mutuality, which are fatal to its enforcement in equity, are apparent, as will be seen when we consider to what extent under such circumstances each of the parties is bound.

In the Giants' parallel case against Ewing, Judge William J. Wallace also denied the request for injunctive relief, saying, "In a legal sense it [the baseball contract] is merely a contract to make a contract if the parties agree" but as a basis for damages or enforcement of specific performance it is "wholly nugatory."

As it unfolded, the 1890 baseball campaign was one of all-out war, with inflated attendance figures, contract jumping, player raiding, bribes to players and press, lawsuits, lowered ticket prices, and self-destructive head-to-head scheduling in cities with a club in each league. The pennant winners of the National League and the American Association squared off in a World Series of so little interest that after Brooklyn tied the Series with Louisville at three games apiece before an intimate gathering of 300 in the late October cold, neither club felt motivated to play a deciding game. The Boston Players' League champions, led by future Hall of Famers Kelly, Dan Brouthers, and Hoss Radbourn, were certainly the best club in baseball, but for them there would be no postseason opponent.

Although the rebel league had won all its skirmishes with the senior circuits, it lost the war at season's end when its backers, staring at the balance sheets, proved more prone to cave than the no-less-wounded financiers of the National League. Following the disastrous season, in which everyone lost money, Ward envisioned a truce between equals, with mutual respect for contracts, no conflicting playing dates, exchange of exhibition contests, league maintenance of discipline, and a postseason world championship series, but Spalding cut the brotherhood out of the negotiation, insisting that talks be conducted between the money men alone, knowing that the greenhorn Players' League owners would break ranks and fold. (Poker was the model for the conduct of American business, then as now.) Spalding reviewed the wreckage two decades later:

> It was with very great satisfaction, therefore, that in the fall of 1890, at the close of that season, I received a delegation from the management of the Players' League, bearing a flag of truce. I was not President of the National League, but, as chairman of its "War Committee," I was fully authorized to treat with those who came asking for terms. Of course, I was conversant with existing conditions in both organizations. I knew that they were on their last legs, and I was equally aware that we had troubles of our own. We had been playing two games all through—Base Ball and bluff. At this stage I put up the strongest play at the latter game I had ever presented. I informed the bearers of the

> truce that "unconditional surrender" was the only possible solution of the vexed problem. To my surprise, the terms were greedily accepted. I had supposed that they would at least ask for *something*.

Why did the Players' League die? John Ward blamed "stupidity, avarice, and treachery." According to the *Sporting News* of November 22, 1890, the Players' League was "organized on the most beautiful principles. . . . Its theories were captivating, but so were some of Sir Thomas More's, and so are some of Bellamy's . . . unfortunately they did not work."

Another utopian scheme, John Ward's marriage to Helen Dauvray, collapsed shortly before the Players' League season began and, after several trial separations and attempted reconciliations, ended in a luridly detailed divorce action commenced in September 1893 and concluded three years later. By the terms of the decree, Ward was barred from remarrying during his wife's lifetime rather than the five years then customary in New York State law; seven years later he had to go back to court to seek permission to remarry. Helen Dauvray, meanwhile, had remarried in 1896. The Dauvray Cup, retired in 1893 when Boston won it for the third time, disappeared and has not been seen since.

AFTER THE DEMISE OF the Players' League, some of the owners were granted concessions to induce their orderly liquidation. First New York, then the Pittsburgh PL clubs, were combined with their same-city NL counterparts. Then, Spalding's Chicago club bought the Chicago Players' franchise outright for $18,000 plus a contingency of some $7,000 to settle salary issues of men under contract for future years. Players were permitted to reenter the NL and AA without reprisals; Spalding reprised the strategy he had employed with the St. Louis "black diamonds" after the collapse of the Union Association in 1884. Nick Young, NL secretary, who was charged with the distribution of PL players, doled them out unevenly in the view of the AA owners, which led to disputes. These ultimately were settled by a newly created National Board of Control, under the aegis of the ever-willing A. G. Mills (who had just declined the offer of a return tour as National League president), but the AA thought the Board's decisions biased, which of course they were: The National League, flush from its triumph in wrecking the Players' League, was ready now to go after the American Association, which entered its tenth and, unknown as yet, final season.

In an informal meeting with Ward at the Manhattan Club in December 1890, Spalding asked, "Can you offer any suggestion as to the best way to clear up things?" According to a third party at their lunch, one who was unnamed in the *Sporting Life* report but may well have been Mills, Ward replied presciently, not only for baseball in the 1890s but also for the strife-ridden 1990s:

> I should say that settling up the business end of the muddle would be the most important just now. And in doing that you must be very careful how you handle the public. While apparently it is disinterested you will find that they are watching with a jealous eye to see that all the arrangements are fair and above board. The game of base ball would amount to very little when stripped of its sentimental features. As a commercial business the game would be a big failure. The patrons of the Players' League must be satisfied or you will have to depend on a new generation for the support of the game. You may replace myself or any of the players at short notice, but you can't replace the patrons of the game so quickly.

Spalding announced his retirement from the presidency of the Chicago club, handing the reins to James A. Hart, whom he had brought in from Boston to serve as his secretary. Anson, who would continue to control the club on the field until being fired in 1898, would later write of this maneuver:

> At that time I received a long letter from Mr. Spalding, in which he took particular pains to assure me Mr. Hart was a mere figurehead, who would always be subject to his advice and control, and just so long as he, Mr. Spalding, was connected with the club I should be retained by that organization. In the face of such an assurance as that, and in view of the fact that I had been associated so many years with Mr. Spalding in business, having first come to Chicago at his solicitation, I could see no reason for doubting his word, though subsequent events have shown me differently.

Only two years prior, at the Delmonico banquet, baseball had lined up alongside Lady Liberty as an American beacon to the world; now it was becoming a national embarrassment. When the American Association packed up its tent after the 1891 season, the NL absorbed four of its franchises—St. Louis, Louisville, Baltimore, and Washington—and finished the decade as a twelve-team monopoly.

The magnates' dreams of unending rivers of profit, now that all rivals were crushed, were dashed by external as well as internal factors. An economic depression, commencing in 1893 and lingering for years with low wages and high unemployment, reduced discretionary income; the 1898 war with Spain added to social as well as economic anxiety; and the league's competitive imbalance in these monopoly years of 1892 through 1899 produced first or second place finishes for only Boston, Baltimore, Cleveland, New York, and, in 1893, Pittsburgh.

The ingenious magnate John T. Brush, in 1895 still the owner of the Indianapolis club, formerly a big-league entry but now a minor-league franchise, was also owner of Cincinnati in the National League. He developed a sort of farm system by sending six of his Reds to Indianapolis and calling up players from that city to replace them. In that same year, Tammany Hall big shot Andrew Freedman, owner of the Giants, proclaimed that the pursuit of baseball's business should be a league matter, not that of twelve franchises, each with a different local challenge. He suggested the annual pooling and redistribution of players and profits, provided that the "strongest and most lucrative franchises" got the best players. Another Freedman innovation, mirrored by today's luxury boxes, was his 1895 notion that reserved seats could attract a business clientele seeking separation from the sweaty bleacher set. Freedman also fined his star pitcher, Amos Rusie, so unreasonably that he sat out an entire season and returned only when owners of other NL clubs pooled their resources to pay both his fine and the amount of his lawsuit against Freedman for back salary.

Monopoly seemed like a good idea to the National League magnates when they emerged victorious over their competitors for public favor. Unfortunately, there was no getting around the absence of a rival league for that season-ending crescendo of the prior decade, the World Series. For their first year of solitary play, 1892, the monopolists came up with the idea of a split season, engineered to create a championship match between first-half and second-half winners. On July 12, 1892, the day before the National League concluded the first half of the only split season in its first century, Alexander Joy Cartwright Jr. died in Hawaii, not yet celebrated as the inventor of this pastime seemingly hell-bent on extinction. A year later, he would be followed in death by Abner Doubleday, not yet publicly connected in any way with baseball.

In 1893, after William C. Temple's Pirates finished a strong second but had no place to go once the season ended, he came up with the idea of a postseason series matching the first-place finisher against the second, seemingly not much of an improvement, if any, over pitting the first-half and second-half winners. Temple commissioned an elaborate silver trophy for the winner, even more expensive than the Dauvray Cup, though his Pirates never qualified.

Rules experimentation also characterized the period. As the gradual removal of pitching restrictions took hold—the movement had been from stiff-wrist underhand in 1845 to bent-elbow and jerked deliveries in 1872 to sidearm throws in 1880 to full overhand in 1884—batters struggled to keep up. The Players' League in its one year of existence had hoped to entice fans with more offense by extending the pitching distance from fifty to fifty one and a half feet and introducing a lively baseball. The troubled National League of 1893 was more radical, moving the pitching distance from fifty feet to fifty-five and a half (not sixty and a half as is commonly thought; see below). This move boosted overall batting performance by degrees that make the so-called steroid era pale by comparison. In 1894, all teams averaged more than seven runs per game; pennant-winning Baltimore scored more than nine runs per game. Hugh Duffy of Boston hit for a batting average of .440, an all-time high (excepting the results of 1887, when walks counted as hits and Tip O'Neill of St. Louis thus hit an inflated .485). Ten men batted over .370; five of these were over .400; and four of those five were from the same Philadelphia Phillies outfield of Ed Delahanty, Sam Thompson, Billy Hamilton, and Tuck Turner. In 1894, the Phillies altogether, including pitchers, posted a .349 team batting average, yet finished in fourth place, eighteen games behind the leader.

In a long-misunderstood nicety, the pitching distance until 1893 was measured from the front of a pitcher's box, initiated in 1863 to replace the original pitcher's line, set forty-five feet from home in 1857. Thus, when the pitching distance was specified as fifty feet beginning in 1880, the back of the box was five and a half feet farther back. The pitching distance mandated for 1893 and still in force today was sixty feet six inches, as measured from the front of a slab with which the pitcher's back foot was required to remain in contact. (Although this slab rendered the pitcher's box obsolete, ineffective hurlers today are still said to be "driven from the box.") So, while the increase in the pitching distance of 1893 was not the incredible ten and a half feet that fans (and credulous writers) have marveled at for decades, it still produced an explosion of hitting.

This slugging style was unattractive to John Ward, who retired after leading his second-place Giants to a four-game sweep of the first-place Orioles in the initial Temple Cup Series. In a final insult, the Giants placed him on their reserve list for 1895 to ensure that he would not change his mind and attempt to play elsewhere. The Orioles were the cream of the league, winning the pennant three times in a row and, even when they finished second in 1897, taking the Temple Cup. They matched skill, daring, and inventiveness with extraordinarily dirty play, vile language, and relentless umpire baiting. But the more they scrapped, the better they played, and the more the fans admired them.

This feeling was not universal, however. In 1894, Cincinnati sportswriter Ban Johnson was named to head up the reorganized Western League (a minor circuit, under the same name but with differing organizations had gone belly-up three times in the ensuing seasons) through the influence of his friends Charlie Comiskey and John Brush. The straitlaced Johnson thought that what baseball needed to draw fans was not the constant threat of impending violence and language unsuitable for delicate ears, but instead the rule of law and the practice of decorum. By backing his umpires, he set an alternative path from the one the National League was spiraling down. In the next century, Johnson's model for the Western League would produce, when he renamed it the American League, a new rival that the National League tried to kill but could not.

In the NL, Brush tried to introduce reforms and to punish miscreants, partly from conviction and partly because he thought it made business sense. He didn't have rabbit ears for insults like Giants' owner Andrew Freedman, whom he detested, but the league attendance figures, stagnant on a per-club basis, worried him. At a league meeting in March 1898, Brush pushed through a resolution to "suppress obscene, indecent, and vulgar language on the ball field by players."

It passed unanimously, and then a shocking secret memorandum was delivered by hand to each of the twelve clubs and perhaps each league player—its obscenity made it undeliverable by ordinary mail without risk of federal prosecution—detailing precisely the language that had been complained of in the previous year. The "Special Instructions to Players" is so screamingly blue that it is not quoted verbatim; here is a considerably expurgated paragraph:

> That such brutal language as . . . "Kiss my ass, you son of a bitch!" . . . and many other revolting terms are used by a limited number of players to intimidate umpires and opposing players, and are promiscuously used upon the ball field, is vouched for by the almost unanimous assertion of those invited to speak from personal knowledge. Whether it be the language quoted above or some other indecent and infamous invention of depravity, the League is pledged to remove it from the ball field, whether it necessitates the removal of the offender for a day or all time. Any indecent or obscene word, sentence, or expression, unfit for print or the human ear, whether mentioned in these instructions or not, is contemplated under the law and within its intent and meaning, and will be dealt with without fear or favor when the fact is established by conclusive proof.

Apart from a schoolboy delight in reading this memo with its exceedingly colorful insults of yesteryear, unknown until only recently when a single copy surfaced, the memo testifies to the moral climate of the single-league era, when professional baseball was losing ground to college football for many reasons, including the hair-curling atmosphere at the park.

Ladies' Day had been a popular innovation of the 1880s, though its origins stretched back to the amateur era. In the '90s women were seen at the ballpark more frequently than they had been in the early 1870s, but the crudeness and violence of the "evolved" game was now deterring their patronage.

If women were becoming disinclined to watch professional baseball, they were still interested in playing it. Bloomer Girls clubs, named for the ridiculed but liberating harem pants invented by Amelia Jenks Bloomer in the 1850s, started up in Boston, New York, and Kansas City and barnstormed successfully for many years. A milestone event occurred on July 5, 1898, when Lizzie (Stroud) Arlington, with the blessings of Atlantic League president Ed Barrow, later famous as the general manager of the Boston Red Sox and New York Yankees, pitched an inning for Reading against Allentown. She gave up two hits but no runs in this first appearance of a woman in Organized Baseball.

Three weeks later, on July 25, 1898, Giants owner Freedman took offense at an anti-Semitic remark hurled his way by Baltimore Orioles' outfielder Ducky Holmes, who formerly played for him in New York. (Responding to typical taunts from his former teammates, Holmes shouted across the diamond, "Well, I'm —— glad I don't have to work for a *sheeny* no more.") Freedman ordered his men off the field, forfeiting the game to Baltimore despite his own players' sympathy with Holmes: Who didn't hate Freedman? Holmes was suspended, Freedman was fined. When the suspension was rescinded but the fine was left to stand, animosity increased. The incident boiled over into Freedman's extended attempt to destroy the Orioles, the Giants, the National League, and seemingly everything and everyone he knew. Amid all the intramural bloodletting of the National League from 1898 to 1899, Ban Johnson saw his opening to rename his Western League the American League, move a franchise into Chicago to challenge Spalding directly, and save baseball from itself.

In the National League ownership construct of that day, syndicates controlled the shares of several clubs at once and shuffled players between them as the need or opportunity arose. In 1899, the Robison brothers, who owned both the St. Louis and Cleveland clubs, denuded the roster of the latter (including the unparalleled pitcher Cy Young, ultimately winner of 511 major league games) for the benefit of the former, condemning the Cleveland Spiders to an all-time-worst record of 20–134. Brooklyn and Baltimore, too, were commonly owned; Ned Hanlon acted as manager of the Superbas (a.k.a. Bridegrooms and Dodgers) and as team president of the Orioles.

THIRD BASEMAN JOHN MCGRAW had been the Orioles' player-manager in 1899, and a highly skilled one at that: He batted .391 and posted an on base average (not computed when he was active) of .547, a record surpassed only twice in all of baseball history, by Ted Williams in 1941 and Barry Bonds in 2002. However, when McGraw got wind of the NL's intent to drop Baltimore in 1900 as part of a restructuring by which the League would be reduced from twelve teams to eight, he threatened to form an American League team with Ban Johnson, a most unlikely partner, and assist Johnson in mounting a major league threat. Like Freedman, McGraw was no stranger to conflict and unpredictability. Johnson's inability to secure a Baltimore ballpark in time to open the 1900 season, however (Hanlon was no longer using the Union Grounds, but he'd be damned if he'd let McGraw have them), doomed the AL franchise and did nothing for McGraw's bargaining position. In mid-February he sheepishly renewed as manager of the NL Orioles.

Only two weeks later, however, the other shoe dropped at last, as the league's rumored contraction of Baltimore, along with Cleveland, Washington, and Louisville, was announced as fact. The syndicate clubs hoped that by consolidating their interests they could cut their losses, and by reducing the league to eight teams they might heighten interest in the pennant race . . . or at the very least conclude the season with only seven also-rans rather than eleven. Louisville owner Barney Dreyfuss, who was paid a measly $10,000 to disappear, nonetheless outflanked his adversaries, borrowing money to buy a half-interest in Pittsburgh and then moving the best of his Louisville players there (including future Hall of Famers Honus Wagner and Fred Clarke), thus turning the consolidated Pirates into a dominant team. (By this time, W. C. Temple had long distanced himself from any involvement with the club.) The radically reformed NL of 1900 would remain immune to further franchise shift until 1953; through the Great Depression, two world wars, expansion from forty-five states to forty-eight, and the introduction of air travel, the National League represented eight cities, none farther south or west than St. Louis.

The Brooklyn club of 1900, because it had conjoint ownership with the contracted Baltimore, picked up the contracts of McGraw, catcher Wilbert Robinson, and rookie pitching sensation Joe McGinnity, as it had done one year earlier with shortstop Hughie Jennings and outfielders Willie Keeler and Joe Kelley. All six men today are honored with plaques in the Hall of Fame. Robinson once went seven-for-seven in a single game, but he made it to Cooperstown for a distinguished career as a player and as a manager of the Brooklyn club, known as the

Robins in all the years he was at the helm. Underhand ("submarine") pitcher McGinnity became famous as the "Iron Man," winning 246 games in his ten seasons of major league ball and 207 more in the minors afterward, pitching until he was fifty-four. Jennings was perhaps the top shortstop in the game until Amos Rusie drilled him with a beanball in 1897 that left him unconscious for four days; in the prior season he had hit .401, driving in 121 runs without hitting a home run—a record to this day. As a manager he took the Detroit Tigers to three straight pennants from 1907 to 1909. Like Jennings, Kelley probably enjoyed his best year in 1896, when he hit .364 and stole eighty-seven bases to lead the league.

When McGraw and Robinson were assigned to Brooklyn in 1900 they refused to report, citing their business investments in Baltimore, which included a shared interest in the Diamond Café, a billiards parlor where, incidentally, duckpin bowling was first seen. As punishment, they were sold to St. Louis. The pair held out until late May, when the Cardinals acceded to their demand that the reserve clause be stricken from their contracts, freeing them to play where they wished in 1901.

Chances are that when McGraw signed with St. Louis he had already reached a tacit understanding with Johnson that the two would do their utmost to make the American League a major league for 1901. McGraw wished revenge against Hanlon and the Brooklyn club that had ravaged the Orioles, and Johnson knew that to solidify his new league, he would have to raid the old, not simply take its leavings.

The great consolidation from twelve clubs to eight, which left many major league players suddenly unemployed, had emboldened Johnson. In 1900, he had renamed his Western League, well-established as a top-rank minor circuit, the American League, with designs on East Coast cities. Foremost among these was New York, where the Giants had fallen on hard times under Freedman's enigmatic ownership. The AL had to bide its time, however, as its designs on a stadium site in Gotham were foiled with even more political muscle than they had been in Baltimore. As soon as Johnson's emissaries began sniffing around a ballpark-sized lot in Manhattan, Freedman's gang saw to it that a road was cut through it.

The American League operated as a minor circuit in 1900 but, in the fall of that year, Johnson made a peace overture to the NL, asking for parity as a major league, with access to certain lucrative territories while forgoing certain others and assuring respect for NL player contracts. As Johnson expected, however, the proffered olive branch was rebuffed. NL president Nick Young wished success to Johnson's new venture, but said he considered it an outlaw league, not a major league. So Johnson went to war, abrogating the National Agreement, thus opening the door to raids on NL player contracts. Johnson also placed franchises in current NL cities Philadelphia and Boston as well as former sites Washington and Baltimore. These complemented his strong Midwestern franchises in Chicago, Cleveland, Detroit, and Milwaukee. For 1901 three of the American League's original clubs—Indianapolis, Minneapolis, and Buffalo—were dropped. Baltimore, as McGraw was secretly assured in 1901, was the stalking horse for New York, ready to be moved once a ballpark site and politically connected ownership were secured.

Relying upon the adage that "the enemy of my enemy is my friend," Johnson and McGraw set aside their evident temperamental differences: Johnson had pledged that one of the main tenets of his new major league would be respect for umpires; McGraw was the game's premier umpire baiter. As might have been predicted, they were bound to collide. As manager of the AL entry in Baltimore, the feisty McGraw and his Orioles quickly reverted to their NL ways: spitting, cussing, kicking, and even punching umpires with whom they had a difference of opinion. On August 7, Johnson felt compelled to suspend Orioles first baseman Burt Hart for belting an umpire. Two weeks later in Baltimore, Joe McGinnity, who had returned to town after his year in Brooklyn, spat in the face of umpire Tom Connolly. "Turkey" Mike Donlin, a McGraw favorite, then decked Detroit's Kid Elberfeld, and an on-field riot ensued, involving players, fans, and police. This was not the decorous league Ban Johnson had envisioned.

In the swirling sands of baseball in 1901, McGraw had detected an opening for a new supply of talent: African Americans. In preseason training at Hot Springs, Arkansas, he tried to pass off Charlie Grant, a celebrated black second baseman who had played with Chicago's Columbia Giants, as a full-blooded Cherokee, on the assumption that a Native American could be brought up to the big club despite the "gentlemen's agreement" against admitting black ballplayers. However, Chicago White Sox owner Charles Comiskey, also with spring-training facilities in Hot Springs, "outed" Grant, who had to return to the Columbia Giants. "If Muggsy [McGraw] really keeps this Indian," Comiskey is reported to have said, "I will get a Chinaman of my acquaintance and put him on third."

The 1901 Orioles finished three games over .500 but drew poorly. Johnson couldn't wait to get them to New York, but the Big Apple was not yet ripe. McGraw visited the city several times in the offseason to meet with potential investors and scope out possible ballpark sites. Unbeknownst to Johnson, however, on these visits McGraw was talking to National League people, too, including the hated Freedman, whose master plan to transform the NL into one huge syndicate of eight clubs, run centrally, had been defeated by forces led by Al Spalding. After seeing his own effort to become NL president thwarted, Spalding succeeded in electing as new NL president William C. Temple. This apotheosis lasted only twenty-four hours, however, as Temple was persuaded by his business associates to decline the offer. No one at that time, the first days of April 1902, or since made the connection that Spalding, new husband of an ardent Theosophist and in some measure one himself, had appointed as his surrogate another Theosophist to oversee the future of baseball. (Soon he would settle upon another Theosophist to preside over its past.)

Andrew Freedman, meanwhile, wished to sell his Giants to Brush and buy into an American League franchise in New York. Johnson, however, once burned in his alliance with McGraw, was twice shy about welcoming as a new owner an even more combative figure.

McGraw marked the opening of the Orioles' 1902 season by being booted out of a game in Boston. At the end of April, he protested the calls of umpire Jack Sheridan by sitting down in the batter's box until he was expelled. Johnson then handed him a five-day suspension. The AL was still at war with the NL, but McGraw seemed now to be at war with Johnson as well, and in June all hell broke loose. Severely spiked by Dick Harley in a game with Detroit on May 24, McGraw was forced to sit on the sidelines until June 28, when he marked his return by again tormenting umpire Connolly, getting tossed, and refusing to leave the field. Connolly forfeited the game to Boston.

This time, Ban Johnson had had enough. He sent McGraw a wire on June 29: "As of today, you are suspended indefinitely." John McGraw would never again wear an Orioles uniform.

Was his provocation deliberate? Was he looking to justify actions he had already planned to take? McGraw had in fact participated in secret meetings during his convalescence from the spiking, first with Frank Farrell, a racehorse owner with political connections who in 1903 would become the owner of the New York Americans, forerunner of today's Yankees, then with Fred Knowles, secretary to Freedman, who asked whether McGraw might wish to consider managing the Giants. McGraw, still under the June 29 suspension he had appeared to incite, met with the Orioles' board of directors, who owed him $7,000. He offered to forgive the amount in exchange for his unconditional release. Unwilling or unable to cough up the dough, the directors freed him to do as he pleased.

McGraw had somehow gotten wind of Johnson's intent to move into New York in 1903 without him, and that the managerial spot of the New York Americans had been offered to Clark Griffith, Comiskey's ally on the Chicago AL club since its inception in 1900. Let McGraw tell his side of the story, as he did to Fred Lieb some eighty years ago:

> Do you want to know why I left Baltimore, and the American League, in 1902? Well, I'll give you the real story. The move to shift the Orioles to New York had been contemplated for some time. In fact, I did much of the ground work, built up the contacts, scouted around for grounds, and was to get a piece of the club. Naturally, I assumed I would be manager. Then I suddenly learned that I no longer figured in Johnson's New York plans and that he was preparing to ditch me at the end of the 1902 season. So, I acted fast. If he planned to ditch me, I ditched him first, and beat him to New York by nearly a year.

If revenge is a dish best served cold, McGraw's next steps were absolutely frigid. On July 8, his four-year deal with the Giants was officially revealed. Next, he set about to wreck the team and the league he was leaving, combining with Brush, on behalf of Freedman, to buy 201 shares of Orioles stock from team president John J. Mahon for $50,000. McGraw also swapped his half-interest in the Diamond Café for Wilbert Robinson's stock in the Orioles. On July 16, the announcement went to the press that National League owners Brush and Freedman, with McGraw's clandestine assistance, now owned a majority interest in the American League Orioles and were free to send the club's players to either of the other clubs they owned, the Reds or the Giants. McGraw secured for the Giants pitchers McGinnity and Jack Cronin as well as rising stars Dan McGann and Roger Bresnahan. Brush claimed Cy Seymour, Joe Kelley, and Mike Donlin for the Reds, although Donlin was still in jail after being sentenced to six months' time for assaulting an actress and her escort. Such was the climate in baseball, which only a decade earlier had been regarded as potentially the international pastime.

On July 17, the day after this spectacular climax to the era of syndicate baseball, the Orioles, left with only five players, forfeited a game to the St. Louis Browns and their franchise to the American League, which was forced to borrow players from other teams so that Baltimore could complete its schedule. Two days later, McGraw managed his first game in New York, losing to the Phillies. On August 25, Johnson announced what McGraw had already known: his league's intention to move the Orioles to New York in 1903, with Griffith as the Americans' manager. Johnson had found two men with the necessary money and influence to push the deal through. The publicly revealed owner was Farrell, the gambler and racing-stable owner; the other, unannounced at the time, was Big Bill Devery, a former chief of police and political bagman. The pair paid $18,000 for the Baltimore franchise, selected coal dealer Joseph Gordon to act as their president, and, in time for the home opener on April 30, 1903, built a ramshackle ballpark in the Washington Heights section of Manhattan.

Meanwhile, before the 1902 season was over, Brush sold the Reds and bought the Giants from Freedman, who took the money and ran away from baseball. In January 1903, representatives of the two leagues got together and came to a peace agreement of sorts that recognized the admission of the New York American League club, soon to be dubbed in the press as the Hilltoppers or Highlanders, although the Giants family would always call them the Invaders. In October 1903, baseball would hold its first World Series since 1891. But Brush never relinquished his resentment of Johnson's move into New York, and his animosity toward the American League extended to the end of the 1904 season, when he and McGraw withheld their Giants from that year's planned World Series against the Boston Red Sox.

11
THE WHITE CITY AND THE GOLDEN WEST

Born from a struggle to the death between the National League and its rivals, big-league baseball in the 1890s was run as a monopoly with little regard for players or fans. Owners faced no competition in their own cities and, through interlocking ownerships, created covert farm clubs within their own league; it was no wonder that in this era some players declined opportunities to play in the National League, preferring the climate in the high-classification minors. Effectively cut off from its play roots of the amateur era, baseball was at real risk of demise. From a national pastime with so many adherents in the '80s that it seemed almost a secular religion, baseball took on the aspect of just another trust or cartel, of the sort most Americans hated. When the warring factions in the game came to a peace agreement in early 1903, a new era dawned, baseball again exploded in popularity, and high-toned pundits once again began to describe it as a model institution.

Big-league attendance in 1900, when the eight-team National League was the only game in town, was 1.7 million; three years later, with two eight-team major leagues, it was 4.7 million. The upward trend line for the game's popularity was evident, and Theosophist leaders took note. For us to understand how Albert Spalding, Abner Doubleday, Abner Graves, William C. Temple, and others may have become players in a plot to redefine baseball's past, and thus gain a hold on its future, we will need to understand something about the prospects and perils for the Theosophist movement in the 1890s when its survival, like that of the national pastime, hung in the balance.

What did the men who had made baseball grow in the 1840s and '50s think of the game's turn toward monopoly, rowdyism, and suicidal business practice? Few would live to see the new century and none but the venerable Chadwick continued to take an active part. Alexander Joy Cartwright Jr. died in Hawaii in 1892, with no mention of baseball in his obituary notices. Duncan F. Curry, first Knickerbocker president, died in 1894 and was laid to rest under a tombstone that grandiosely termed him "Father of Baseball"; as we have seen, taking credit for the accomplishment of others was already a well-established tradition in baseball. Knickerbocker catcher and Fashion Race Course all-star Charles DeBost passed on in 1895. Harry Wright, who had played with and managed baseball clubs for almost half a century, departed in the following year. He was mourned officially by the National League with ball games staged in several venues to raise money for a suitable burial monument. For Harry Wright Day at Rockford, Illinois, Al Spalding squeezed into his old uniform and pitched for a team of his Forest City playmates.

In 1899, as major league baseball confronted its own mortality, forefather Doc Adams died; in his last days he told an interviewer, "we pioneers never expected to see the game so universal as it has now become. . . . It is an important industry." James Whyte Davis, his Knickerbocker Base Ball Club comrade who had seemed to breathe baseball every minute of his life, also died in this last year of the century.

A few years ago, an unusual item came up for auction: a trophy presentation of a silver baseball and miniature bats that had been given to Davis in 1875 to commemorate his twenty-five years of play with the Knickerbockers. The award presentation had taken place at a banquet following baseball's first old-timers' game, played at Hoboken's Elysian Fields between the Knicks of 1850, including Adams and William H. Tucker, and those of 1860, for whom Davis pitched. The recipient's name was engraved on each of the bats, and the ball read: "Presented to James Whyte Davis on the Twenty Fifth Anniversary of his election as a member of the Knickerbocker Base Ball Club by his fellow members. 1850 Sept. 26 1875. Never 'Too Late.' " Davis had been such an ardent and energetic player that his vehement protests at being excluded from play when he showed up a few minutes after the appointed time won for him the twin nicknames of "Too Late" and "The Fiend."

Famous in his day if forgotten in ours, James Whyte Davis was born in New York on March 2, 1826, to John and Harriet Davis, both from Connecticut. Drifting away from his father's trade as shipmaster and sometime liquor merchant, James became a broker successively of fruit, produce, general merchandise, and, finally, stock certificates. Like so many early ballplayers, he belonged to a volunteer fire company, in his case the Oceana No. 36. He married Maria Harwood of Maryland, with whom he had two sons and one daughter, but she left him a widower at a young age. These are the prosaic details. Truly his life was wrapped up in baseball, as in death he would come to be.

On the twenty-seventh of August, 1855, a month shy of their ten-year anniversary, the Knickerbockers unfurled their first banner from the newly erected flagstaff over their clubhouse at the Elysian Fields. Designed by Davis, the triangular pennant, with a blue "K" in a white circle surmounting one red and one blue horizontal panel, flew over the Knickerbocker clubhouse for the last time at this 1875 celebration, "worn to ribbons by long service," reported the *Sun*. Afterward, it was draped over Davis' dresser until his death. The Knickerbocker Base Ball Club, a proud anachronism even before professional play began to dominate the game, limped along until 1882, when it returned its corporate charter to the state.

Davis entered his final years living in want in a Manhattan apartment when, on July 27, 1893, the *Sun* printed his letter to Edward B. Talcott, a principal owner of the New York Giants:

> My good friend,
>
> Referring to our lately conversation on Baseball I now comply with your request to write you a letter on the subject then proposed by me and which you so readily and kindly offered to take charge of, after my death, namely, to procure subscriptions to place a Headstone on my grave.
>
> My wish is that Baseball players be invited to subscribe Ten Cents each and no matter how small a sum is collected, it will be sufficient

to place an oak board with an inscription on my resting place, but whatever it may be, I would like it as durable as possible without any ornamentation—simply something that "he who runs may read. . . ."

All relations and immediate friends are well informed that I desire to be buried in my baseball suit, and wrapped in the original flag of the old Knickerbockers 1845, now festooned over my bureau and for the past eighteen years and interred with the least possible cost.

I suggest the following inscription in wood or in stone:

Wrapped in the Original Flag
Of the
Knickerbocker Base Ball Club of N.Y.,
Here lies the body of
James Whyte Davis,
A member for thirty years.
He was not "Too Late,"
Reaching the "Home Plate."
Born March 2, 1826.
Died ______

I should be pleased to show you my Glass case containing the trophies of my Silver Wedding with the Old Knickerbockers in 1875 and which I intend to bequeath to you, should you so desire as a mark of appreciation of the kindly act which you have undertaken to perform. Kindly acknowledge receipt of this.

And I am Yours sincerely and
thankfully,
James Whyte Davis.

Through the Talcott family, perhaps with ensuing stops along the way, Davis' trophies came to auction. The dismaying thing is that while the auction of his trophies yielded proceeds of $76,118.99, not a dime was ever collected for his headstone. Too late to find home plate, Davis lies, dressed in his Knickerbocker uniform and shrouded in his Knickerbocker flag, in an unmarked grave in Brooklyn's Green-Wood Cemetery, Section 135, Lot 30010.

Pioneer William R. Wheaton, the man who wrote the rules for the Gotham Club in 1837 that later were adopted by the Knickerbockers, had died in California a decade earlier, in 1888. Like Cartwright, he made such a name for himself through business dealings in the West that his long-distant baseball accomplishments went unnoted in an otherwise extensive obituary.

A few early Knicks lived into the twentieth century, but Louis F. Wadsworth, the man who gave us nine men, nine innings, and perhaps the diagram of the playing field, disappeared from view. A heavy drinker after the death of his wife in 1883, Wadsworth became increasingly erratic in the performance of his duties as a judge in Plainfield, New Jersey. Descending into solitude and pauperdom, in 1898 he committed himself to the local almshouse, the Plainfield Industrial Home, where according to his obituary he spent the next ten years in seclusion, without a single visitor.

> A veritable book worm, day after day, he would sit reading. The bent old man, on his trips between the home and public library, was a familiar sight. Always carrying books, and with few words for those he met, he went back and forth. In the summer he was particularly interested in following the scores of the ball games of the big leagues, and of late years the game was the one great object of interest to him. His associates came to forget him. Politicians who had sat in state conventions where he presided and where his exercise of parliamentary rules was able and astute lost him out of sight.

When A. G. Mills went looking for Wadsworth at the end of 1907, there was hardly a man alive who could help.

Lost along the way to baseball's murderous decade of the 1890s was not only a brief Eden in which men had played solely for love of the game, but also a golden age of good honest gambling, when individuals might make a wager on the outcome of a game in order to imagine themselves, for a moment, players. Replacing the simple bet—an age-old pledge honored by reputable men no matter the view from the pulpit—was a management swindle so large and so brazen that to the contemporary public it was hidden in plain sight: syndicate baseball, which by creating a rigged league made a mockery of fans' faith in the integrity of each and every game. This practice of dual ownership may be seen as a fraud more pervasive in its impact on the institution than the heaving of occasional games in the 1870s, more repugnant, even, than baseball's "original sin," the Black Sox Scandal of 1919, in which eight Chicago White Sox players conspired with gamblers to throw the World Series.

The practice of syndicate ball had begun with the combined ownership of the New York Giants and New York Mets of 1883, but these clubs at least played in separate leagues. With interlocking ownerships in the bloated National League of 1892 through 1899, a club trailing in the pennant race might transfer a star to an allied club that was closer to the top. Another franchise, situated in a large market, might pool its players with its wholly owned mate in a smaller market, moving the top talent where the greater profit beckoned, in conformance with Andrew Freedman's model. Yet another club might exert less than its best effort in a head-to-head series to benefit an affiliated club that stood higher in the standings. All of these things came to pass in the solitary big league of the 1890s, culminating in Andrew Freedman's National League Base Ball Trust, which nearly succeeded in placing all clubs and players under a single management.

The new American League, which came into being as a corrective to the brutishness of the National League, was not immune to syndicate ball, either. Charles Somers, a coal magnate from Cleveland, was the cornerstone of the junior league's finances, at one time or another taking a piece in five of its eight clubs: Cleveland, Chicago, St. Louis, Philadelphia, and Boston (which as a result was briefly called the Somersets instead of the Red Sox). When, in 1910, the American League officially renounced syndicate ball, the National League followed in short order, outlawing dual ownership yet leaving a loophole in place by which an owner in one club might continue to hold stock in another. For example, Charles P. Taft, half brother of the president of the United States, continued to own stock in both the Chicago Cubs and Philadelphia Phillies. This state of affairs endured until mid-decade, at which time a third major league sprang into being, the Federal League of 1914–15.

The monopolist practices of the 1890s and relentless "pursuit of the almighty dollar"—a saying coined by novelist Edward Bulwer Lytton, inventor of the occult energy source "vril" and inspiration to Mme. Blavatsky—had given rise to a range of utopian responses. These included the doomed Players' League of 1890, the Nationalist Clubs based on Edward Bellamy's philosophies, and an upsurge in the activity of fraternal and secret societies, not least among them the Theosophists.

THE CHICAGO WORLD'S FAIR of 1893, also known as the Columbian Exposition, marked the 400 years since the arrival of Columbus in the New World with an electrically illuminated "White City." This became a metaphor for the American way as a light to the world, even in that time of labor unrest, an unpopular influx of immigrants, and a severe economic downturn that became known as the panic of 1893. Opening on May 1, the fair ran for six months, through October, while the stock market crashed and banks and businesses failed nationwide at an alarming rate. Unemployment peaked in 1897 at 14.5 percent, a figure not surpassed until the Great Depression. Where the Centennial Exhibition of 1876 in Philadelphia had celebrated American industry and ingenuity, the Chicago Fair instead celebrated the nation's architecture, its arts, its spirit. The 264-foot-high Ferris wheel made its debut at the fair, thrilling thousands each day and, like the Gothic cathedrals of old and the concrete-and-steel skyscrapers in the Loop, bespoke the ascent of man.

The spiritual highlight of the exposition, however, was the Parliament of the World Religions, bringing together for the first time representatives of Eastern and Western traditions. When Swami Vivekananda, on September 11, 1893, stood up in his orange robe and turban and began his speech extemporaneously, "Sisters and brothers of America," the 7,000 in attendance "went into inexplicable rapture with standing ovation and clapping that lasted for more than three minutes," according to a contemporary account. He continued:

> I thank you in the name of the most ancient order of monks in the world; I thank you in the name of the mother of religions; I thank you in the name of millions and millions of Hindu people of all classes and sects . . . I fervently hope that the bell that tolled this morning in honor of this convention may be the death-knell of all fanaticism, of all persecutions with the sword or with the pen, and of all uncharitable feelings between persons wending their way to the same goal.

Vivekananda's further speeches over the seventeen-day course of the Parliament all stressed tolerance and universal brotherhood. The *New York Herald* declared, "After hearing him we feel how foolish it is to send missionaries to this learned nation."

The Theosophists held the floor at the Parliament of Religions from September 15 to 17, highlighted by speeches from Annie Besant of London, William Quan Judge of New York, and Jerome Anderson, the leading Theosophist of California. William Chase Temple, who only recently had stepped down from his presidency of the Pittsburgh Pirates, was in attendance, and was featured in the press; Mrs. Elizabeth Mayer is presumed to have attended as well. While the Theosophists were in their glory at the fair, not everyone was impressed. Vivekananda later wrote, wryly: "The Theosophists claim to possess the original divine knowledge of the universe. We are glad to learn of it, and gladder still that they mean to keep it rigorously a secret." Annie Besant he praised faintly while taking a slap at other Theosophists, saying she "meant well at least." Midway through the Parliament, the Rev. William Cook proclaimed in the *Chicago Tribune* that Theosophy was "chiefly mist and moonshine" and reminded readers that "Mme. Blavatsky has been legally proved by the London Society of Psychical Research to have acted the part of a charlatan at her headquarters in Madras, India." William Emmette Coleman had been no less harsh, in the month before the fair opened, accusing Blavatsky, by this time two years dead, of literary theft:

> *The Secret Doctrine*, published in 1888, is of a piece with *Isis*. It is permeated with plagiarisms, and is in all its parts a rehash of other books. . . . [Ignatius L.] Donnelly's *Atlantis* was largely plagiarised from. Madame Blavatsky not only borrowed from this writer the general idea of the derivation of Eastern civilisation, mythology, etc., from Atlantis; but she coolly appropriated from him a number of the alleged detailed evidences of this derivation, without crediting him therewith.

While she lived, Blavatsky was regularly charged with all sorts of outrages, to the extent that Abner Doubleday, who had succeeded her as head of the Theosophical Society in America, felt compelled to defend her honor against Coleman's charges, as previously noted. His support would not be forgotten by the Theosophists in the years to come, when the mystical war hero, who had died earlier in this year of the World's Fair, would be nominated to perform one last great service.

In her *Secret Doctrine*, Blavatsky had advocated a variant form of American exceptionalism by situating her adopted country at the apex of a grand evolutionary pyramid. She held that the mixture of racial types in the United States constituted a suitable nursery for the emergence of the coming advanced race. Eventually, she wrote, "there will be no more Americans . . . for they will have now become a new race, and many new nations." Blavatsky believed California to be a remnant of the ancient land mass of Lemuria, also known as Atlantis (why Atlantis should be found overlooking the Pacific is puzzling).

The vacuum of leadership in the American Theosophical Society by the mid-1890s was filled, to the surprise of many, by Katherine Tingley, a relative unknown who had only recently become a Theosophist—in October 1894, after some years of social work in New York City, coupled with "faith cure" and clairvoyance schemes.

Elizabeth Mayer, now that her son by George J. E. Mayer was a freshman at Massachusetts Institute of Technology under the name of Durand Mayer, settled permanently in New York City and attached herself to its Aryan Theosophical Branch. The son she bore to Albert Spalding in 1891 continued to live in Chicago as Spalding Brown. In the period after the World's Fair, she worked closely with Mrs. Tingley.

Because she was not yet a Theosophist, Mrs. Tingley did not attend the Society's functions at the Parliament of Religions in 1893, but upon her ascent to the top she recognized the useful symbolism of the White City. Of the girl born Catharine Augusta Westcott in Newbury, Massachusetts, in 1847, it was written in later years that she had dreamed of a white city she would one day build in the golden West, where she would "gather together children of all nations and teach them how to live rightly."

Starting her tenure atop a shaky throne, with challenges from the international Theosophical Society based in Adyar, India, Mrs. Tingley sensed the need to establish America as the world center of new-age philosophy. Mme. Blavatsky had left ample indication that the course of America's emerging spiritual race was westward, and that not only the Theosophical Society but all of mankind would face an epically stern challenge in 1897–98.

> We are in the very midst of the Egyptian darkness of Kali-yuga, the "Black Age," the first 5,000 years of which, its dreary first cycle, is preparing to close on the world between 1897 and 1898. Unless we suc-

> ceed in placing the T. S. [Theosophical Society] before this date on the safe side of the spiritual current, it will be swept away irretrievably into the Deep called "Failure," and the cold waves of oblivion will close over its doomed head.

Krishna's death in 3102 B.C.E. was said to have initiated the 5,000-year age of strife and discord from which the world was scheduled to emerge uncertainly in 1897–98. Perhaps the Age of Aquarius would dawn; perhaps it would not. In the Theosophical community the coming year was viewed with mixed hope and dread.

Whether feeling a need to act before the Kali Yuga came to a close, or simply sensing an opportunity to consolidate her newly won power, Katherine Tingley swung into action. She focused the Society on social activism and educating children rather than the former goals of contemplative pursuit and self-improvement. In April 1896 she announced the prospective founding of a School for the Revival of the Lost Mysteries of Antiquity (SRLMA), at a location later to be revealed as 196 acres at Point Loma, a seaside district of San Diego and the westernmost spot of the U.S. continental land mass.

In April 1897 the Theosophists gathered for their third annual meeting at New York's Madison Square Garden. W. C. Temple decried the political ambition of some to seize the reins of the Society. As Doubleday had once defended Mme. Blavatsky—no Victorian gentleman could stand by silently as a woman came under attack—Temple stood up for Mrs. Tingley, cementing his high standing in the Society and indebting Mrs. Tingley to him forever after. She and her cabinet, which included not only Temple but also her devoted aide Mrs. Mayer, embarked upon a ten-month World Theosophical Crusade to strengthen the Society trunk and add branches.

At this time Temple was still deeply engaged in business matters. Though never losing his passion for baseball, he had retreated from it, withdrawing his Temple Cup from the National League to protest the contesting clubs' secretly arranged pooling of receipts; as a result, the National League of 1898 was without a postseason championship.

At a ceremony at Point Loma in November 1897, attended by a thousand San Diegans, Mrs. Tingley placed the cornerstone of the School for the Revival of the Lost Mysteries of Antiquity. "The future of this school," she declared, "will be closely associated with the future of the great American republic. While the school will be international in character, America will be its center." After the ceremony the American flag was unfurled, then replaced by the purple and gold flag of the school. (By this time the society's leader was referred to in the press, seldom kindly, as the Purple Mother.) The *Fort Wayne News*, the newspaper still run by Mrs. Mayer's uncle, William D. Page, published a lavish account of the ceremonies, furnished "by request."

The Theosophist leaders returned triumphantly from their crusade to a rousing welcome at the February 1898 convention in New York. Amendments to the Society constitution were signed by Tingley and by her leadership group, including Mayer and Temple. But in this month the tensions regarding Cuba, which had been escalating between the U.S. and Spain ever since Jose Martí led an invasion of the island in 1895, erupted with the sinking of the battleship *Maine* in Havana harbor. With relentless jingoistic pressure from the New York press, particularly Hearst's *Journal* and Pulitzer's *World*, the mysterious explosion made inevitable a war that neither Spain nor the United States ever wanted. To Theosophists, Mme. Blavatsky's "darkness of Kali-yuga" for 1897 and 1898 appeared prophetic indeed.

In the period immediately after the Spanish-American War, Theosophists saw in Cuba an opportunity to practice the racial harmony they preached, without having to go so far as to welcome African Americans into their new compound at Point Loma, except as day laborers. In 1899, the International Brotherhood League, a department of the Theosophical Society, landed in Santiago de Cuba to provide postwar aid. Mrs. Tingley intended to start a Theosophical school there, but at first she arranged to send selected Cuban children all the way to Point Loma. She had lined up teachers for her new Raja Yoga school there, but what good were they without children? Many of those who moved to the Point Loma colony in its early period were aged or childless; Cuba could provide a stock of orphans, as well as children whose parents wished them to be educated in America. Beginning in 1899, the Cuban children came to Point Loma in small groups, but in 1901 forty came over en masse, sent by Mayor Emilio Bacardí of Santiago de Cuba by way of New Orleans. It would not be long before the majority of students at Point Loma were Cuban.

In 1900, the national membership of the Theosophical Society had been estimated at 6,000, but the census offers testimony that only ninety-five individuals lived at the Theosophical grounds, most in tents and bungalows while awaiting the construction of more substantial edifices. One of these intrepid residents was Elizabeth Mayer, director of the Isis Conservatory of Music. On June 23, 1900, some thirty-five years after they had commenced their affections, she and Albert Spalding, widowed in 1899 when Josie Keith Spalding died of appendicitis, wed at last. On the day of the Spaldings' nuptials at Point Loma, twelve Cuban children arrived to join other young "Lotus Buds" at the Raja Yoga School.

THE BRIDE AND GROOM went off to Europe on a wedding trip, which Albert combined with business: President McKinley had appointed him American commissioner to that summer's Olympic Games at Paris. The newlyweds returned to Meade Lawns at Seabright, New Jersey, the country seat where he and his first wife had lived in the summers since 1893, leaving the day-to-day management of the Chicago baseball club to James Hart. Albert and Josie's son Keith was off at The Hill School in Pottstown, Pennsylvania, until 1896, then attended Yale until 1902. To conduct his sporting-goods business comfortably, A. G. Spalding also maintained homes in Chicago and New York City. By this time bicycles, not baseball, had become the cornerstone of the Spalding sporting-goods empire; the game's decline in the 1890s contrasted with the rise of the League of American Wheelmen. Businessman Spalding turned his efforts to where the money was to be made, but his heart was still with baseball.

On May 15, 1901, Albert and Elizabeth Spalding petitioned the Orphans Court of Monmouth County, New Jersey, so that they might adopt Spalding Brown, a boy whose parents they asserted to be dead. For the legally required "Next Friend" of the child the court approved none other than William Thayer Brown, who with wife Mary Spalding Brown had raised the boy almost since his infancy. Albert and Elizabeth proposed to the court that, upon adoption, the former orphan's name be changed to the unwieldy Spalding Brown Spalding. The adoption was confirmed on July 5 and, although there is no evidence that his name was ever changed legally, the boy was thereafter known as Albert Goodwill Spalding Jr. In his will, A. G. Spalding

Sr. perpetuated the convoluted fiction that this was not his son by birth:

> I give and bequeath to my adopted son, ALBERT GOODWILL SPALDING, JR., (formerly known as Spalding Brown Spalding, and adopted by me by decree of the Monmouth County Orphans Court in the State of New Jersey July 5–1901, by which decree he was given the name of Spalding Brown Spalding, but is now more generally known as Albert Goodwill Spalding, Jr., and is hereinafter so called), the sum of One Hundred Thousand Dollars. . . .

As we have seen, Elizabeth's other son, Durand Churchill Mayer, who had begun his life as George Mayer Jr., had changed his first name to Durand after his mother's separation from his father. (I have been unable to confirm that the Mayers were ever divorced prior to Elizabeth's marriage to Spalding.) Upon the father's death in April 1902, his son wasted little time in petitioning the courts in Chicago to change his name legally to Durand Churchill, thus intending to erase any sign of his actual paternity. The *Chicago Tribune* observed, with perhaps a sly hint at cuckoldry, "Durand Churchill Mayer was well satisfied with Durand Churchill, but he wanted the court to cut out the Mayer. The saw was applied and the name was dehorned."

When the newlywed Spaldings returned to Point Loma on July 16, 1901, they were accompanied by Albert's mother, Elizabeth's son, and their newly "adopted" son. They had sold Meade Lawns and intended to make their home, for much of the year, at the Theosophical compound. There they would join several other upper-class Americans of means who found Theosophy so appealing that they would, if necessary, leave behind family and friends to build homes at Point Loma. Several were advanced in years and lived on inherited or previously earned wealth. Besides the Spaldings, influential colonists included August Neresheimer, a New York diamond broker who funded much of the enterprise; Clark Thurston, president of the American Screw Company; Lyman J. Gage, president of the First National Bank of Chicago and then U.S. Secretary of the Treasury under Presidents McKinley and Roosevelt; and Gertrude Wyckoff Van Pelt, a physician who briefly would figure in the Spalding story.

As Upton Sinclair noted in *The Profits of Religion*:

> Here in California is Madame Tingley, with a colony and a host of followers in a miniature paradise. Men work at money-lending or manufacturing sporting-goods, and when they get old and tired they make the thrilling discovery that they have souls; the theosophists cultivate these souls and they leave their money to the soul-cause, and there are law-suits and exposés in the newspapers.

Litigation misery would come to the Spaldings by and by, but in mid-1901, their situation appeared to be above and beyond reproach: Elizabeth was a valued part of the society hierarchy, the right hand to leader Tingley, and Point Loma would be her touchstone; Albert was still active in business and would travel extensively, but his amethyst-domed villa, overlooking the Pacific in ornate tribute to the Purple Mother, who lived next door, would be their permanent home.

At the end of 1901, A. G. Spalding Sr., who had reduced his baseball involvement, suddenly found himself embroiled in the fight against Freedmanism and Brushism and their proposed National League Baseball Trust. New York Giants kingpin Andrew Freedman had won over to his side three other NL owners, including Brush, but could not get a majority; the four other clubs, desperate for strong leadership, turned to Spalding and, in a rump election, named him league president. Two days later, however, responding to a suit from the Freedman-Brush faction, a court voided that election and enjoined him from serving. Old Nick Young, who had organized the meeting at which the National Association of Professional Base Ball Players had been created back in 1871, resumed his ineffectual and largely titular presidency of the National League. Spalding, however, remained the head of the four loyal clubs and continued to act as if he had been legitimately elected. In a February 1902 letter from Point Loma released to the press, he wrote that the advocates of the Baseball Trust "will be forced by public opinion to get off the baseball map for the good of the sport."

Spalding could not break the impasse. In a further communiqué of April 2, 1902, he resigned as NL president, saying that while he was personally resolved to restore honor to the game, a further prolonged dispute would not be in the best interests of the game as the playing season neared. The Freedman-Brush faction refused to recognize his letter as a resignation, as Spalding had never been properly elected, and simply filed it. Ultimately, however, all eight owners unanimously followed his guidance to offer the presidency to William C. Temple, who was once again based in Pittsburgh, where he had shifted his sporting interest to professional football: In the autumn of 1898, he had recruited stars to his Duquesne Country and Athletic Club by offering them salaries and thus became the pro game's first club owner. Temple was also an early enthusiast of the automobile, a charter member of the American Automobile Association in 1902 who regularly raced his forty-horsepower Pierce against all comers. Temple considered the National League offer, but declined.

IN THE FIRST TWO years following his mid-1900 nuptials, Albert Spalding was generally regarded as the husband of a Theosophist rather than as a committed member himself. When Cap Anson heard that Spalding had joined the Theosophist colony, he opined: "Well, I don't know what in thunder a theosophist is, but if it's something you can make money out of you can bet Al Spalding will be one. Spiritual culture at the expense of the physical, eh? That's a change for your life. When I knew Al he didn't care a tinker's malediction for the spiritual."

The unending barrage of attacks upon Mrs. Tingley, especially as regards the schooling of the Cuban children at Point Loma, made such distinctions pointless. If she and by extension Lizzie were to be attacked as Theosophists, well then, Spalding would be a Theosophist too.

In November 1902, medical doctor and Theosophist pioneer Gertrude Wyckoff Van Pelt went to Cuba and returned to New York with eleven more children for Point Loma education. They were detained at Ellis Island, at the request of the New York Society for the Prevention of Cruelty to Children (SPCC), on the ground that they would soon become public charges and a burden to the taxpayers; the Children's Society recommended to the Commissioner of Immigration that the youths be returned to Cuba. At a hearing before a Special Board of Inquiry, the Spaldings were among those questioned about what these "Lotus Buds" would really be doing at Point Loma, and were asked to address the character of Mrs. Tingley, who one year before had been roasted in the pages of Harrison Gray Otis's *Los Angeles Times*. Her colony was called a "spookery" and "roost" at which gross immoralities were conducted in the moonlight by disciples of both sexes in their night robes.

President Vernon Davis of the SPCC testified that the atmosphere at Point Loma was, by report, not suitable for children. The next day he enlisted his celebrated predecessor in the post, Commodore Elbridge Thomas Gerry, to question those who would testify in support of Mrs. Tingley and Point Loma. Gerry asked Albert Spalding, whose "adopted" child was now in school at Point Loma, "When you first met Mrs. Tingley, Mr. Spalding, did you or she arrange for the interview?" According to the *New York Journal* of November 5, a plainly furious Spalding declined to answer, walking "up and down in front of the table at which the board members sat, with his hands in his pockets, his frame shaking with a rage which he tried hard to suppress." Spalding concluded his appearance by also declining to answer Gerry when he produced a circular from a disaffected Theosophist, Jerome Anderson of San Francisco (who had been of such stature in the society that he had addressed the throng at the Parliament of Religions in 1893), and asked: "Isn't it true that a little black spaniel dog is known as the 'Purple Inspiration' . . . ? Is it not true that the children are taught that that little black spaniel contains the soul of a human being . . . ? Are not the children under Mrs. Tingley taught that shrubbery and plants marry and produce children?"

Spalding requested an opportunity to cross-examine the witnesses against Mrs. Tingley, but was told that this was a hearing, not a civil trial. Further testimony against Mrs. Tingley was adduced. An Adyar Theosophist who had succeeded in removing two of her grandchildren from the Raja Yoga School testified that

> children all sleep in tents, about twenty boys and girls in a tent, on a bunk. Every night a girl of about fourteen years old comes and ties their hands together, then fastens them about their necks. . . . All children are made to stand up when visitors come and say, "We like our Lotus Mother and are glad to be here." Children have meat only once a week; for noonday lunch they are given a cracker and an apple, the biggest boys getting two crackers. My grandchildren were there six weeks: they never saw their mother except as she marched by with a white robe on at sunrise, holding up her hand—as they are sun worshippers.

After soliciting further blackguarding of the colony at Point Loma, Commodore Gerry commented that he was sure that more such testimony could have been obtained were it not for Mrs. Tingley's "hypnotic power" over witnesses who feared occult reprisals. The SPCC ruled, on November 7, that the children were to be returned to Cuba. While Albert Spalding fumed, his wife wrote a protest letter to the editor of the *Boston Globe*. Ultimately, California conducted its own health and welfare investigations into the Point Loma colony and came away impressed; Governor Henry T. Gage weighed in at a national level and, in a move presaging the Elián González case a century later, the SPCC recommendation to the Immigration Board was overturned in Washington.

Still, the Gerry forces held such sway in New York political circles that they may have felt emboldened to seize the children if they were taken to New York City from their federal detention at Ellis Island. Recalling that "everything is possible to him who dares," Spalding hired a launch, picked up the children himself, and conveyed them to Jersey City. There they were met by Dr. Van Pelt and a dozen burly members of the local Spalding Athletic Club, who placed them in a private railcar attached to a train bound for points west. SPCC president Vernon Davis said that Spalding's action "was a neatly executed move" as now "the matter is entirely out of our hands, as we have no jurisdiction outside of this State."

When asked four months after this escapade whether he was a Theosophist, Spalding answered differently than he had before. As reported in the *Fort Wayne Daily News*, Mrs. Spalding

> induced him to lease ground inside of the community boundaries and build a pretty house overlooking the ocean. Then she induced the ex-athlete to attend meetings at the community. . . . He said when asked if he was a Theosophist: "I am, in the sense that I am in sympathy with the work done by this society, at whose head is Katherine Tingley. I am especially interested in the educational work they are doing for children. I find here at Point Loma many educated, cultured people, the equals of and perhaps superiors of any I have met anywhere. If all these things and more make me a Theosophist, I am willing to stand for it."

Spalding may by now have begun to feel besieged on all sides. In this epochal year of 1902, he had failed to secure the presidency of the National League and to save the game he loved from the monopolists who had taken his model structure of 1876 and transformed it into a menace. Although he covered his tracks by marrying his mistress and adopting his own son, his manhood was called into question when petty civil servants implied that not only had he become a hypnotized acolyte of Mrs. Tingley, but he had also given up his own son to her cult.

The following year would bring further indignity when old Father Chadwick, whom Spalding continued charitably to employ, would use the pages of the 1903 *Spalding Guide* to characterize the American national pastime as little more than "rounders, you know." Not brought to heel by early 1904, Chadwick continued along his infuriating path, equating baseball with town ball, which was, according to him, nothing more than American rounders.

The final straw may have come when the most popular magazine in the land, the *Nick Carter Detective Weekly*, introduced on February 13, 1904, a character named Irma Plavatsky, a beautiful Russian princess with a dual personality: kind when she was Irma, but deadly when possessed by the male Tibetan magician Dazaar, who could possess the body of not only Irma but also, simultaneously, seven prominent New York socialites, of the sort who might murder at his behest (or, readers might have understood, abandon all that they knew of respectable life and, zombielike, march off to Point Loma). Dazaar, the invention of pulp novelist Frederick Van Rensselaer Dey, was expelled from the Great White Lodge for taking on a female form, yet he continued to practice the Lodge's art of soul transference. This archvillain was also capable of throwing a jackknife across a street and having it land point first in a door lock, or of killing an intended victim slowly by inserting radium in his hatband. Pursuing Dazaar, Nick Carter even found in the Tibetan Himalayas a lost race of blond-haired, white-skinned Aryans who were masters of "vibrational science." Mme. Blavatsky was not so long removed from the terrestrial plane that people failed to get the joke; Nick Carter had made his dime novel debut in 1886 and had earned his own publication in the year of her death, 1891. The gender-bending Dazaar continued as one of the detective's most popular foes through nine novels until he/she committed suicide, for love of our hero, in the *New Nick Carter Weekly*, number 396, of September 30, 1904.

Spalding's life choices and beliefs, so long a source of pride, had become subject to widespread ridicule. By the time A. G. Mills, his old ally in previous campaigns of bluff, bluster, and bravado, came to visit him at Point Loma in the late summer or early fall of 1904, Spalding may well have been ready, with the aid of his wife, Mrs. Tingley, and William C. Temple, to reassert control.

12

THE RELIGION OF BASEBALL

Extending a conversation no doubt commenced face to face in his ornately Victorian parlor at Point Loma—with its Oriental carpets, sculpted archways, sentimental statuary, and soaring palm fronds—Albert Spalding wrote to A. G. Mills on October 31, 1904, inquiring about certain luminaries who had been in attendance at the Delmonico's banquet of fifteen years before. His purpose in writing was surely to obtain help from his venerable ally in forming a commission to determine the origins of baseball, an idea he had already suggested to Henry Chadwick, his eighty-year-old antagonist: "Let us appoint a commission to search everywhere that it is possible," Spalding had proposed, "and thus learn the real facts concerning the origin and development of the game. I will abide by such a commission's findings regardless."

A somewhat distracted Mills, who after seeing the Spaldings at Point Loma had embarked upon a European holiday from which he had just returned, replied six days later. Overwhelmed by the need to catch up with his correspondence, he confusedly recalled that the Delmonico's affair had occurred

> in 1888 (I believe it was) or was it '84 . . . Senator Gorman was selected to speak for the old-timers [but] . . . at the last moment he could not come . . . I do remember the circumstance that "Teddy" [Roosevelt] was there among the subscribers, and I know that he was recognized at the time among us as being interested in athletic sports and indeed as being considerable of an athlete himself. Beyond this my memory does not serve me. But if, in the light of the above, you think I can do anything further in the matter, command me.

The old chums' initial talk about the commission in late summer or early autumn may well have taken place in earshot of not only Elizabeth Churchill Mayer Spalding but also Katherine Tingley, who lived in the home next door and was a constant presence upon social occasions. As Mills would sign off to Spalding in a letter of March 1, 1905, "Hoping that you and your good wife are in the continued enjoyment of health and happiness, I am, with kind regards to you both and friendly remembrance to Mrs. Tingley, Yours very truly, A. G. Mills."

Clearly Spalding had given thought to naming the president of the United States to the Special Commission, but we do not know if he extended a formal invitation. Not much of a baseball fan, "Teddy" would have been an anomaly alongside eventual appointees Arthur Pue Gorman, a Maryland senator but onetime shortstop and club president of the Washington Nationals; sporting-goods magnates, star players, and surreptitious Spalding business partners George Wright and Al Reach; league officials Morgan Bulkeley and Nick Young; and, finally, the ubiquitous Mills. Presiding over the data gathering as secretary to the commission was James E. Sullivan, president of the Amateur Athletic Union and an American Sports Publishing (i.e., Spalding) employee.

While preparing a major speech for delivery before the Springfield, Massachusetts, YMCA on November 17, 1904, one that would be reprinted in newspapers and in the 1905 *Guide*, Spalding wrote to several veteran baseball figures regarding their earliest recollections of the game. As he elaborated to Massachusetts pioneer player John Lowell, "I have become weary of listening to my friend Chadwick's talk about base ball having been handed down from the old English game of 'Rounders,' and am trying to convince myself and others that the American game of Base Ball is purely of American origin, and I want to get all the facts I can to support that theory."

Mills, in the aforementioned letter to Spalding of March 1, 1905, also landed on Chadwick rather brutally, in words that Sullivan, upon his culling of correspondence for material that would be shared in précis form among the commission members, crossed out with vehement charcoal strokes: "Chadwick is a feeble old man now, and I am inclined to advise you not to be too hard on him. In the course of nature, he will pass away soon and then it will be time enough to wipe up the floor with his peculiar theories."

When syndicated to newspapers, Spalding's contribution to the *Guide*, based on the YMCA speech, was variously headlined: It appeared, for example, in the *Akron Beacon Journal* of Saturday, April 1, 1905, as "The Origin of the Game of Base Ball." In that form, it was read by Abner Graves, a seventy-one-year-old mining engineer who for reasons unknown had drifted east from his home in Denver, Colorado, to bed down for a few nights at Akron's Hotel Thuma. On Monday, April 3, the mysterious traveler had someone type for him a bombshell letter revealing that as a five-year-old boy in Cooperstown he had witnessed twenty-year-old Abner Doubleday scratch out in the dust the diagram of a new game called *baseball*. He sent this original letter, typed on his personal stationery, to Sullivan. He also arranged for a messenger to deliver a carbon copy to the *Beacon Journal*, which published it the very next day under the headline "Abner Doubleday Invented Base Ball: Abner Graves of Denver, Colorado, Tells How the Present National Game Had Its Origin."

Did the *Beacon Journal*'s publisher, Charles Landon Knight, whose heirs went on to build his holdings into the Knight-Ridder newspaper chain, for a time the nation's largest, hold space in reserve for a long letter he had been given reason to expect? The newspaper printed it not as a letter to the editor but instead as an article, complete with two-column headline. Although addressed to the newspaper's unnamed editor, Graves' composition was intended principally for Sullivan and Spalding. "I notice in saturdays [sic] 'Beacon Journal,'" the letter began, "a question as to 'origin' [sic] of 'base ball' from pen of A G Spalding, and requesting data on the subject be sent to

Mr J E Sullivan, 15 Warren Street, New York." Then he launched into his minutely detailed recollection, which the *Beacon Journal* published in full: "The American game of 'Base Ball' was invented by Abner Doubleday of Cooperstown, New York. . . ."

Did Graves have a family or business reason to be in Akron? The *Beacon Journal* offered that the Colorado mineralogist was "stopping at the Thuma Hotel." Stopping on the way to what? For what? Alas, these questions have yielded no answers—indeed, perhaps no one has thought even to ask them until now. The focus of alternative theories to Doubleday for the past century has been on the details of Graves' testimony, not on his motives.

Spalding's search for "an American dad" for the game (as he put it) was boosted immeasurably by the entrance onto center stage of this aged miner, gold-rush forty-niner, ardent Mason, possible Theosophist, and certain vagabond, crank, and teller of tall tales (he frequently claimed, for example, to have been a rider with the Pony Express at age eighteen in 1852; however, that organization was not founded until 1860). If there was a plot to concoct a "useful" origin of baseball, was it dreamed up by Spalding and Graves in concert? Or by some combination of the Spaldings, Tingley, Sullivan, Graves, Mills, and Knight? Was Graves' intricate recall of play and playmates more than six decades past a genuine memory, or was he somehow scripted and enlisted to do another's bidding?

Apart from the evidentiary gaps in baseball's creation of an Edenic past, there are tide-and-time trends to consider, too. America's spiritual and materialistic tracks, which had seemed parallel and irreconcilable, began to bend toward each other with the dawn of the Progressive Era. Secular perfectibility, heaven on earth, suddenly seemed possible to both utopians and capitalists. The Theosophist experiment at Point Loma was imitated in short order by a House of David colony at Benton Harbor, Michigan. In 1903, Benjamin Purnell had a vision in which he was proclaimed the Sixth Son of the House of David, with a mission to unite the Lost Tribes of Israel before Judgment Day. His colonists, who rapidly numbered more than a thousand, gave all their earthly treasure to Purnell and swore off sex, smoking, drinking, and shaving. Along with its amusement park at Benton Harbor, the group's most profitable promotional device was a bearded baseball club, the House of David, that barnstormed into the 1930s.

The House of David story came to a fiery climax in 1993 with the siege of the Branch Davidian compound in Waco, Texas.

Chicago's White City of 1893 had been followed in 1901 by a bloodstained World's Fair in Buffalo, where President McKinley was assassinated by anarchist sympathizer and crackpot Leon Czolgosz. No matter, the next festival of national optimism was already in the planning stage and was not about to be canceled, even though its time and place were shifted from Chicago in 1903 to St. Louis one year later. The 1904 Olympic Games likewise were awarded to St. Louis rather than Chicago, infuriating Windy City denizens.

The original Olympic Games, which had combined sports with religion as well as civic pride, were not so different from the nineteenth-century fairs, which had made the primordial seem less mysterious. The *Village Nègre* of indigenous peoples in "natural habitat" had been the sensation of the 1878 and 1889 Paris World's Fairs. Buffalo's Pan-American Exposition of 1901 had also included ethnological exhibits ("human zoos" was the more candid contemporary term). While trumpeting mankind's limitless future, each international gathering also displayed a fascination with ancient ways, primitive power, and lost knowledge.

The indefatigable James E. Sullivan took on yet another task in August 1904. For the Louisiana Purchase Exposition, he headed up the Department of Physical Culture and the Department of Exploitation (the fair's official name for its marketing department). Seeking to boost the cause of American athleticism while highlighting Spalding's sporting goods, he dreamed up "Anthropology Days," a two-day event matching Plains Indians, Mohawks, and Senecas against "primitives" from other parts of the globe in track and field competitions for which none of the participants was in any way prepared. The use of a starting pistol provided no assurance that all participants would start; the finish line proved equally confounding, as some contestants would stop short of the tape while others would run below it.

Events Sullivan thought more congenial to aboriginal talents, from mud flinging to tree climbing to javelin throwing, were no more successful. From a public-relations standpoint, Anthropology Days was an embarrassment, but Spalding and Mills, meeting with Katherine Tingley in the shadow of the School for the Revival of the Lost Mysteries of Antiquity in Point Loma, may have been influenced to think that for their investigations into baseball's dim past they might need to create something of a show.

In New York, Sullivan received Graves' letter of April 3, 1905, on the very next day and replied to him immediately. Although he must soon have shared its intriguing assertions with his boss, there survives no Spalding response to Graves until November 10, some seven months later. In between, however, Sullivan placed a trial-balloon article containing the Graves claims in the *Wilkes-Barre Times* (and perhaps elsewhere) on July 18, then a handful of Sunday newspapers picked up the story five days later.

It has been stated in the baseball histories that the general public was surprised to learn—and then only upon publication of the Special Commission report in the *Spalding Guide* in late March 1908—that Abner Doubleday was even possibly the inventor of the national pastime. Yet, in the August 12, 1905, issue of *Sporting Life*, one of two leading national sports weeklies, the Graves story was treated at some length in "Base Ball Origin: Spalding's Move Bearing Excellent Fruit." This special report was datelined July 25, New York, and its source was unquestionably Sullivan, as its content was virtually identical to the newspaper reports of a few days earlier. The *New Century Path*, a Theosophical weekly at this time (later a monthly), also aired the story of Doubleday's tie to baseball in its issue of August 13, but that by itself cannot prove a Theosophical Society campaign for its one-time leader to be named the game's father.

Furthermore, it is possible that as early as three months earlier, on May 2, 1905, an unnamed writer in New York's *Sun* may have meant to refer to Abner Graves in this possibly garbled concluding remark to an article titled "Archaeology of Baseball" that described the Special Commission and the dispute between Spalding and Chadwick: "One man has written to Secretary Sullivan from California [Colorado?] to say that baseball was invented in Jamestown [Cooperstown?], N.Y., and that he will come on and prove it."

SO, WHO WAS ABNER Graves? If we cannot definitively name him as a co-conspirator with Spalding and Tingley, is there any basis for connecting him with the Theosophists?

The temptation is to make much of Graves' presence in San Diego in the mid-1890s. Following a financial embarrassment and litigious denouement to his career in the cattle business in Crawford County, Iowa, he left his wife and son back in Iowa and became a real-estate huckster in Southern California; when his wife died in 1902, his son Nelson joined him out West. This was in 1895–96, not long before Mrs. Tingley and Mrs. Mayer (a "widow" and not yet the second Mrs. Spalding) commenced to shop around for a permanent home for their society. In May 1895 his presence in Pasadena was reported, "in the interest of an elevated railway whose cars are said to be able to make a speed of 200 miles an hour." In August of that year, now in San Diego, he wrote a long letter to the editor of the *Los Angeles Times* in which he gushed, "This is my first visit, and a four months' residence about equally divided between Pasadena, Los Angeles, Avalon, and San Diego, has convinced me that Southern California is the ideal place for live people to live in, and has decided me to pull up my eastern stakes and come out here to stay." However, Graves subsequently decided that consulting in the mining industry suited him better, and he became a resident of Denver, with frequent trips to the properties he tended in Utah, Nevada, and Sonora, Mexico.

The temptation is also to make much of Graves' documented devotion to fraternal orders: the Masonic cause, beginning with his time in Iowa, and his active membership in Denver's Masonic Temple as well as its El Jebel Shrine. As Theosophical activity began to pick up steam in Denver in mid-1896, the local branch leased three rooms from the Masonic Temple. When Katherine Tingley's Theosophical Crusade blew into town on March 7, 1897, the proselytizers were greeted at the Temple on Welton Street by some 5,000 curious citizens. Abner Graves may or may not have been among those there.

Graves had also been a miner in Nevada, and Albert Spalding had invested heavily in the Milford & Addison group of properties, consisting of eight full claims in the Yellow Pine District of Clark County, Nevada. Could Spalding and Graves have met in a business/investment context prior to 1905?

We may say "maybe" to all these possibilities, but we must stop short of making a personal connection between Graves and any of the likely conspirators. Often the best explanation for the otherwise inexplicable is dumb luck; Graves' tale is not likely to be entirely a fabrication. For all its implausible and self-contradictory elements, his story does offer a wealth of seemingly congruent data, too. If the conspirators' aim was to find a suitable father for baseball, one draped with heroism in the material world yet keenly attuned to the celestial realm—and, ideally, a Theosophist—they could have done no better than this gift of Abner Doubleday.

Thinking back to a summer's day when he was five years old, Abner Graves provided America with a tale of baseball's first game that no other soul with personal knowledge of the event could confirm or contradict. Graves was born in 1834, and the players in the game he recalled were at least ten to fifteen years older. As he wrote to Spalding on November 17, 1905, replying to the magnate's *faux-naïf* request for more supporting data:

> Of course it is almost impossible to get documentary proof of the invention, as there is not one chance in ten thousand that a boys drawing plan of improved ball game would have been preserved for 65 years as at that time no such interest in games existed as it does now when all items are printed and Societies and Clubs preserve everything. [*Here commences a passage that Sullivan struck from the Commission record.*] All boys old enough to play Base Ball in those days would be very old now if not dead, and this reminds me of a letter. I have a letter dated April 6th, 1905 from Mary, wife of "John C. Graves," mentioned in my printed letter saying, "Dear Cousin, I received a paper this eve from Akron, Ohio, with an article you wrote about Base Ball! [Mary and John Graves, who was "about 85," lived in nearby Cleveland.] Every one of the boys you named [Abner Doubleday, Elihu Phinney, John C. Graves, Nels. C. Brewer, Joseph Chaffee, John Starkweather, John Doubleday, Tom Bingham] are dead except John [Graves], and perhaps you do not know that John has been sick over a year with the gout, and now his mind is very weak so sometimes he does not know me." She was mistaken in saying *all* for I am aware that Nels C. Brewer whom I mentioned now lives in Cleveland, Ohio. . . . My Typewriter [referring here to his typist] thinks this a pretty long letter on one subject and I guess that is about correct, but your letter asked for as full data as possible and I have given you all the items I can in a rambling sort of way, but I think you have read enough to pick out the gist of it and

> be better satisfied than if I had been less explicit or prolix. Just in my present mood I would rather have Uncle Sam declare war on England and clean her up than have one of her citizens [referring to Chadwick no doubt] beat us out of Base Ball.

To this letter Graves appended a hand-drawn diagram—on his alternative stationery that proclaimed an occupation of Immigration Agent. It depicted "Abner Doubleday's plan of 'Base Ball,' made in Cooperstown, N.Y. 1839[,] –40 or –41." It featured positions for eleven men, including five infielders (the three basemen, a left shortstop, and a right shortstop) and four outfielders, as well as a pitcher and catcher. This would have been a plausible alignment for a New England style game of baseball.

During the next two years, Graves wrote no more on this subject to Sullivan, Spalding, or the newspapers. Upon release of the findings of the Special Commission on March 20, 1908, the *New York World* concluded that the report

> . . . settles an old controversy and is entitled to the respect of all investigators of the origin of the horse or discoverers of "missing links." Base ball is thus proved to be, like poker, a genuine American product. It did not come "out of the mysterious East," like our religions and languages, like chess and cards, peaches and sherbet. It was not played in ancient Rome, like hop-scotch and jackstraws. It is native, indigenous, all our own, and the fact is a just subject for pride.
>
> Has Doubleday a monument? He is now shown to have been illustrious in two fields. Cooperstown has acquired a second famous son whose achievements will deserve centennial commemoration. [The year 1939, the writer was aware, would mark the sesquicentennial of James Fenimore Cooper's birth as well as the centennial of baseball's; in fact the Cooper celebration was pushed back to 1940 to mark, instead of his birth, his arrival in the village in 1790.]

Cooperstown's *Freeman's Journal* reprinted the article from the *World* on its front page on March 26, under the headline "Home of Baseball: Game Originated in Cooperstown; Abner Doubleday, Afterward Major General, Its Originator—A Monument Suggested." The further ideas of a Doubleday Field and a Baseball Hall of

Fame would take shape later. But the notion of a 1939 celebration in Cooperstown was first broached with the deft observation that baseball was as American as not apple pie but poker.

With the death of all the Knickerbocker Base Ball Club members from their first decade of play—unbeknownst to the baseball world, Louis F. Wadsworth was the last to go—no one was left to gainsay the declaration by Bruce Cartwright in 1909 that his father had been the one to invent baseball. Journalists who should have known better rallied around this alternative theory in reaction to what they saw as the absurdity of the claim on behalf of Doubleday. Journalist Will Rankin wrote:

> The latest of all the fakes [regarding the theories of baseball's ancestry] was the one with the Cooperstown flavor in which one Abner Graves of Denver, Colo., declared that the late General Doubleday was "its designer and christener." He said he was a "kidlet" and was on the ground when General Doubleday turned the trick in 1839. What a pity he did not select some other year so that his air bubble could not be pricked so easily. The records of West Point, N.Y., and the War Department at Washington, D.C., were the means of exposing his fake.

Referring to his father, Bruce Cartwright Sr. wrote in 1909:

> I remember as a child he had among his personal belongings a baseball that he treasured very highly, stating that it was used by the Knickerbocker Club in their early games. This ball was used by myself and others in the first baseball club organized in Honolulu, and was finally lost or destroyed [although it "miraculously" turned up at auction in 1999]. My father also had at that time valuable data pertaining to the early history of the Knickerbocker Club. None of this, however, is available to-day. Far out in the mid-Pacific, in this little island-world of ours, it is quite natural that we should lose touch with the later progress of this noble pastime, and I can easily conceive how my father could be almost forgotten by his old-time friends in the United States.

As FURTHER DISPLAY OF the oblivion into which this contending father of baseball had fallen, George W. Smith, a prominent druggist in Honolulu who had introduced some local residents to the world tourists on November 25, 1888, wrote to his cousin Albert Spalding, whom he had greeted that day on board the *Alameda*, to inquire about Cartwright's possible innovative role in the game. Recall that when Spalding's men landed at Honolulu they did not inquire after Cartwright, that Smith evidently did not think to include him in his shipboard delegation, and that the inventor of baseball was likewise not present at that evening's royal luau. Smith's letter does not survive, but Spalding replied candidly on March 1, 1909.

My Dear Smith:

Replying to your communication of the 19th of February, in which you ask for historical facts connecting Alexander Joy Cartwright with the early beginnings of our national game, I regret that I cannot supply your friend with fuller information than is found in the records of the old Knickerbocker Club in my possession.

That Mr. Cartwright was one of the founders of that first organized base ball club, there can be no doubt. Not only does his name appear frequently in records of the social side of the organization, but at the very beginning of the club's history Mr. Cartwright was in evidence at every practice game. I have on my desk as I write this letter the old Knickerbocker Score Book of Games played in 1845, and the name of Cartwright, with more than the average number of runs to its credit appears at each succeeding game. That he was a very active spirit in guiding the counsels of the great original club, is also most apparent. Beyond this statement of fact, I find nothing in these records that would interest your friend. Further research would simply multiply the number of practice games in which he participated and the number of meetings at which his voice was heard in earnest espousal of the game's best interests. Hoping this will be quite satisfactory, and with the assurance of my appreciation of the honor to him of having been identified with that grand old organization, believe me.

Yours Most Truly,
A. G. Spalding

[P.S., handwritten] Can you not secure for me a photo and some historical data personally of Mr. Cartwright [?]

In his 1909 *Collier's* series about the origin of the game Will Irwin wrote, "I regret to say General Doubleday certainly did not invent the name 'baseball,' and in 1839 he was at West Point. However, Mr. Cartwright may have got his game from Cooperstown and not out of his head." A. G. Mills' imagined double-play invention of Doubleday to Wadsworth did not pan out, but on February 6, 1916, an uncredited writer for the *New York Times* produced a hilarious mash-up of Cartwright and Doubleday.

> Baseball before the days of the National League dates seventy-seven years back to 1839, when Abner Doubleday, at an academy at Cooperstown, N.Y., invented a game of ball on which the present game is based. Doubleday afterwards went to West Point and later became a Major General in the United States Army.
>
> The game as played at the school in Cooperstown consisted of hitting the ball and running to one base. First it was called "One Old Cat," then with two bases "Two Old Cat," and finally with three bases "Three Old Cat."
>
> Another boy at the Cooperstown school, Alexander J. Cartwright, one day evolved a rough sketch of a diamond and the boys tried it with great success. From that day to this the general plan of the diamond has changed only in a few details.
>
> It was at Mr. Cartwright's suggestion in 1845 that the first baseball club was formed.

IN THE FIRST YEARS of the new century, following a disastrous period of conflict, consolidation and, for Spalding, personal humiliation, baseball's need to look backward seemed strategically evident: without a vision of its former glory as national pastime it might go the way of other bygone or discredited amusements, such as pedestrianism or ratting. However, at some point the public ceased to focus any longer on feuding owners and brutish players, although these types did not disappear. Instead, the public was gripped by a general baseball mania. Peace between the warring National and American leagues spurred higher attendance and, by the end of the decade, the construction of capacious concrete and steel ballparks. New heroes like Christy Mathewson, Honus Wagner, Nap Lajoie, Ty Cobb, Walter Johnson, and Three Finger Brown found a public hungry for knowledge of their every action, their every thought. Baseball still attracted and countenanced plenty of gambling, but by and large fans now loved the game for its own sake: as a vehicle for expressing local pride, as a safety valve for pent-up emotions, and as a theatrical presentation more thrilling than any that might be staged before the footlights.

When the Giants and Cubs tied for the National League pennant in 1908, as a result of the Merkle Boner no-decision game of September 23, a one-game replay that amounted to a playoff had to be scheduled in New York for October 8. The Giants lost, as Brown outpitched Mathewson, but the game attracted a frenzied 250,000 fans to the Polo Grounds, which at that time could seat not even 30,000. Although most would-be spectators were turned away, some 40,000 watched the game gratis from behind home plate, atop Coogan's Bluff. The Giants played to a record 910,000 attendance in that remarkable year, a figure that would be unmatched in major league baseball until 1920.

In bad odor when the decade began, baseball would become not only a huge financial success but also a moral and cultural exemplar, a broad-based religion fitting all creeds, a secular faith of the sort Theosophists could only envy. Who needed Abner Doubleday when *Sporting Life* was unembarrassed to publish, in its issue of May 28, 1910, a page-one headline of RELIGION OF BASEBALL, followed by an interminable subhead of "Our National Sport Founded upon the Same Principles as Underlie All True Religion and All Other Essentials to Moral and Physical Welfare and to Rightful Conduct in This Life." Who needed Theosophical palaver about the brotherhood of man when in this article Edgar Taft Stevenson—a newspaper editor from Franklin, Pennsylvania—could write:

> Would it not be a great thing if some preacher . . . could have a church made up of members with the qualities of religion and character demanded by a good game of base ball! Would we not all of us, be somewhere near the hearts of God and free from much of earth's sorrow and strife and foolish throwing away of our powers, and foolish gossip and slander and forgetfulness, if, in the ordinary affairs of life we could be just good ball players for God Almighty, the captain of the great game we play while we abide in this existence! If we could stand quietly and wait our opportunity to strike, as do the players of this game; if

> we could simply step aside when we fail, as do the best batters, saying nothing and finding no fault, hoping for better skill next time; if we could accept the calls of duty for us to make a sacrifice play, as do the men who make base ball games the wonder of the world, knowing that in the private records of the great Captain every sacrifice is counted in the estimate He makes of what we are; if we could play the center field place, as well as the catcher's, and with as much enthusiasm, in the game of banking, or love, or farming, or housekeeping. . . . The secret of the success of base ball is that it is on the square. The game that is bought or bargained for will destroy the nine, or the league, were it once even hinted about in the homes of the people. The games that we play best in this life, those we win, are, every last one of them, if they give us any real good, won also "on the square."

Leaders of recent immigrant groups advised their peoples to learn the national pastime if they wanted to become Americans. Foreign-language newspapers devoted space to educating their readers about America's strange and wonderful game. Baseball seemed to offer a textbook on how to be an American, to be part of the team. These were precisely the outcomes envisioned by the Theosophists, particularly Mrs. Tingley and Mrs. Spalding, who thought they might attach their own narrow following to baseball's ubiquity—only now baseball had sped off to its glorious future without visible need of a creation myth. Over the ensuing years, when the nation came to be plagued by stock-market scandals, economic panics, fixed elections, and race riots, and its boys were sent off to die on foreign fields, baseball was seen as the last bastion of fair play and decency.

In fact, as we have seen, the national game had arisen from a gambling culture in the 1840s that was never free of corruption, despite the leagues' success in banning hard-liquor sales and organized betting at the ballpark. To support the notion of baseball's wholesomeness, Sunday ball remained off limits in several big-league cities. In New York, the ban was temporarily lifted on Sunday April 29, 1906, when, in a symbolic display of national unity, the Highlanders played against the Philadelphia Athletics to benefit victims of the San Francisco earthquake. But not until 1919 were Sabbath restrictions on baseball withdrawn in Gotham; Boston held out until 1929, Philadelphia until 1934.

Meanwhile, weekday betting continued unabated in all the league cities, and betting rings tried to fix the newly revived World Series as soon as it was proposed. In 1903, a gambler introduced to him by John McGraw offered Boston Red Sox catcher Lou Criger $12,000 to "lay down" in the first World Series between the American and National leagues. Criger, who was earning $4,000 a year at that point, rejected the proposal, reported the gambler, and helped his underdog Bostons defeat the Pittsburgh Pirates. In gratitude, the American League awarded Criger a lifetime pension at a time when no player received postcareer benefits.

Despite fines and bans and the inclusion of antigambling statutes in league and municipal bylaws, betting remained a constant feature of the game. In the winter of 1903, an earlier alleged fix of an exhibition city series with the rival White Sox led the Chicago Cubs to trade star righthanded pitcher Jack Taylor to the Cardinals for a then unpromising prospect, Three Finger Brown. Two years later, Philadelphia pitcher Rube Waddell was said to have received $17,000 to fabricate a tale of a sore arm resulting from a stumble over a teammate's suitcase, thus rendering himself useless for the World Series with the Giants. Attempted fixes, or successful ones, we'll never know for certain, were also alleged for the fall classics of 1914 and 1918, and for many regular-season contests through the period.

As had happened in 1884, the skyrocketing profits in baseball's two major leagues prompted the entrance of a rival, in this case the Federal League of 1914–15. As the Feds ignored the reserve clause and did their best to woo away the game's greatest stars, average player salaries escalated amid the generalized competition for services. But when the rival league collapsed and the war in Europe reduced the playing season and player salaries (and shut down the racetracks), sporting men began more brazenly to toss the occasional game. Along with the notorious first baseman Hal Chase, who not only threw games himself but also worked with gamblers to bribe other players, respectable figures were linked to game tossing: Ty Cobb, Joe Wood, Tris Speaker, and, always at one remove, John McGraw.

By and large, such allegations were kept from the public and revealed only years later. Reporters, whose travel and meal tabs often were picked up by the teams they covered, acted more like publicity agents, protecting the game, its players, and their own perks. Oblivious to the seamy side of the game, highbrow pundits and philosophers continued to marvel at baseball's democratic blessings. Baseball was "second only to death as a leveler," wrote essayist Allen Sangree for *Everybody's Magazine* in 1907, ten years before World War I would level American youth more literally. Even after the carnage, in July 1919, Morris R. Cohen, whom Bertrand Russell called "the most significant philosopher in the United States," could still write a glowing paean to the game:

> . . . when two thousand years hence some Antarctic scholar comes to describe our civilization, he will mention as our distinctive contribution to art our beautiful office buildings, and perhaps offer in support of his thesis colored plates of some of the ruins of those temples of commerce. And when he comes to speak of America's contribution to religion, will he not mention baseball? Do not be shocked, gentle or learned reader! I know full well that baseball is a boy's game, and a professional sport, and that a properly cultured, serious person always feels like apologizing for attending a baseball game instead of a Strauss concert or a lecture on the customs of the Fiji Islanders. But I still maintain that, by all the canons of our modern books on comparative religion, baseball is a religion, and the only one that is not sectarian but national. . . .
>
> Imagine what will happen to the martial spirit in Germany if baseball is introduced there—if any Social Democrat can ask any Herr von Somebody, "What's the score?" Suppose that in an exciting ninth-inning rally, when the home team ties the score, Captain Schmidt punches Captain Miller or breaks his helmet. Will the latter challenge him to a duel? He will not. Rather will he hug him frenziedly or pummel him joyfully at the next moment when the winning run comes across the home plate. And after the game, what need of further strife?

Fringe elements in Weimar Germany would gravitate not to baseball as a secular religion but instead to a virulently racist caricature of Theosophy, which now was waning in America but still a force in Europe. German folklorists with a political ax to grind found much to like in Theosophy's secret doctrine and symbology.

Morris Cohen's national religion of baseball, with its potential for quelling Germany's martial instincts, began to seem quaint long before the Nazis. Only months after his article was published in mid-1919, even before the very first pitch was thrown in what became Cincinnati's so-called upset victory over the Chicago White Sox in the 1919 World Series, rumors swirled that the fix was in. It took a year for them to be revealed as true: In September 1920, a Chicago grand jury convened to investigate charges about the 1919 World Series found that eight Chicago players, immortalized ever after as the Black Sox, had conspired with gamblers to throw the World Series to the Reds.

After inventing baseball's inventor, Spalding appeared ready to rest on his laurels, playing golf or going for leisurely oceanfront drives with his wife. Like his friend, neighbor, and fellow automobile enthusiast William Chase Temple, who had left Lomaland in October 1908 after a three-year stay, he retained an active interest in baseball. For him it was the game of his past, and he took no further active position in it. Temple, however, again was offered the National League presidency in late 1909 when incumbent president John Heydler seemed unlikely to garner the votes for reelection. This overture came to nothing and, in his last years, Temple returned to the orange groves of his native Florida, where he proceeded to organize the state's citrus industry. In 1917, the year of his death at age fifty-four, the Temple orange was named in his honor and introduced to the public.

With the baseball public willing to accept the Doubleday story, Spalding next devoted most of his time to writing *America's National Game*, the history of baseball that had fallen to him when Henry Chadwick died a month after publication of the Special Commission's "Final Decision." In this effort he benefited from the aged scribe's extraordinary library, which included the archive of the Knickerbocker Base Ball Club that James Whyte Davis had bequeathed to him. By this time thoroughly gentrified and fabulously wealthy, Spalding seemed content to tend to his legacy, which he knew the public would tie to baseball, not to his religious beliefs or even his sporting-goods empire.

Then, in 1910, boosters of Southern California real-estate interests persuaded this former pitcher, fading magnate, and reluctant Theosophist to run for the Republican nomination for the United States Senate. Spalding's onetime lapdog *Chicago Tribune*, which back in the glory days of 1875 and 1876 he and Hulbert had forcefully bent to their will to form the National League, now turned snippy. It speculated that although Republicans ruled the Golden State and Spalding's nomination would be tantamount to election, his performance in office might owe a great deal to Mrs. Tingley. The Purple Mother "dominates not alone her colony but her colonists," the newspaper opined. "To be quite plain, will Katherine Tingley's influence on A. G. Spalding, United States Senator, be the same as on Spalding, member of the theosophical colony?"

The would-be politician was only barely involved in his own campaign, preferring to devote his energies to finishing *America's National Game,* in which he was aided substantially by Point Loma neighbor and personal secretary William D. Page—his wife's uncle and longtime journalist. Spalding liked to surround himself with the old posse. He enlisted the ever ready James E. Sullivan to run his campaign and Mills, whom he had known since 1867, to write glowing endorsements and to pull strings with some Republican bigwigs. Otherwise, however, this captain of the world's sporting-goods industry made only a desultory effort to campaign and lost the nomination that had seemed his for the asking. Leaving Page to fulminate publicly about the injustice of his defeat among Republicans in the State Legislature (senators were still chosen by state legislatures, not elected by the public then), he once again retired from public life to pursue privately a range of business interests and civic causes.

After the failed California campaign, Mills returned to his work with the Otis Elevator Company, a connection he maintained until his death in 1929, while shifting his athletic interests to the amateur arena. He stayed in touch with some old-time baseball players who lived in New York, such as Davy Force and Jimmy Wood, and joined with a dozen veterans of the National League's inaugural campaign at the fiftieth anniversary banquet at the Hotel Astor on February 2, 1926. The machinations involving the Special Commission, Abner Doubleday, Abner Graves, and Cooperstown were very distant indeed, so Mills may well have been surprised when he was asked a question that evening about what evidence he had for Cooperstown as baseball's birthplace. "None at all," he answered.

SO, WHILE BASEBALL FANS were busy forgetting about the origins dispute and its surprising resolution, Cooperstown still took pride in both Abner Doubleday and his presenter, Abner Graves. The Mills Commission had given the sleepy village a gift, one that would be cherished and exploited, if haltingly, in the years to come. In 1916, National League President John K. Tener came to Cooperstown to assist in dedicating the new Delaware and Hudson Railway passenger station, adorned with paintings of local scenes and notables, including Abner Doubleday. While touring the village with Cooperstown worthies, Tener was taken to the old Phinney Lot, where village residents believed Doubleday had once worked his magic. Tener suggested that by constructing a regulation baseball field on the spot, Cooperstown might persuade major league baseball one day to establish a fruitful link with its real or imagined origin. Shortly thereafter, a game was planned for the 1919 centenary of Doubleday's birth.

Abner Graves, more dotty with each passing year, responded to the 1916 news of a possible Doubleday Field by writing a letter to the editor of Cooperstown's *Freeman's Journal*, saying that "a game should be played just like those original games were, and if such is done I wish now to enter my name as one of the players, and want to take my old position of 'left infielder (now shortstop).'" Four years earlier, the *Denver Post* had reported an interview containing his somewhat enhanced recollections (it will be instructive to recall that Graves was born in 1834).

> You know, they don't play ball like they used to. Why, I played in the very first game of ball that was ever played. And that game—well, it was some baseball, young man. . . . I was a student at Green College in Cooperstown, N.Y., at that time. Abner Doubleday, the man who invented the game, if you call it an invention, came to our school and interested us boys in his idea. . . . That was in 1840, and the boys of that college played the first game of baseball in the history of the American game . . . The bat we used was four inches wide, and the ball was fairly soft, being made of rubber and twine.

Graves went on to celebrate his ninetieth birthday on February 27, 1924. Six months later he shot his wife of fifteen years four times. A dispute had arisen earlier that day when she refused to sign over to him a bill of sale to their home. He claimed that she had tried to poison his coffee at the evening meal. "I had to do it," he said upon his arrest. "One of us had to go." In the hospital Minnie Graves, at forty-eight nearly half her husband's age, sent him a message of forgiveness. His response was reported as "I hope she dies." She did. A jury committed Graves to the state asylum in Pueblo, where he died two years later.

James E. Sullivan, as secretary of the United States Olympic Committee, faced opposite-sex problems of a nature less dire. In 1912, the hosts of the Stockholm Olympic Games had opened competition to female swimmers and divers. Sullivan, however, refused to let American women compete, presumably defending their modesty. In the following year, Ida Schnall, one of these barred American swimmers, wrote to the *New York Times*, now as a member of the New York Female Giants, a baseball club: "He objects to a mild game of ball or any kind of athletics for girls. He objects to girls wearing a comfortable bathing suit. He objects to so many things that it gives me cause to think that he must be very narrow minded and that we are in the last century." Sullivan died suddenly one year later, before he could see Miss Schnall in her next starring role, as a movie actress wearing what appeared to be a very comfortable bathing suit.

Spalding followed his loyal retainer not long after. On September 9, 1915, at his home in Point Loma, he suffered a stroke, his second within a month, and died at the age of sixty-five. His wife had not informed his mother or his sons of the first stroke. By the time she got around to sending telegrams back east, no member of the family could cross the continent in time for the cremation and funeral, presided over by Katherine Tingley. Immediately, a storm erupted over Elizabeth Spalding's conduct and the validity of the will, a conflict that would go on for more than two years. Although an onset of dementia during his last years at Lomaland appears to have been a contributing factor in Spalding's unusual last testament, there had been prior whisperings of undue influence, to the point of mind control, by Mrs. Tingley and her trusted lieutenant Mrs. Spalding.

In his last will and testament, Albert Goodwill Spalding bequeathed $100,000 to each of his three sons, after deducting various cash payments which were to be "treated as advances." Keith, his son with his first wife, netted only $35,000 after accounting for such advances; stepson Durand Churchill (born George Mayer Jr.) similarly saw his bequest reduced to $35,000; "adopted" son Albert Goodwill

Spalding Jr. came in for a net of $99,000. The remainder of the Spalding estate, valued at some $2 million, was left to his wife.

Keith had been promised by his father, in front of witnesses, that he would take control of the family business. Quickly, he moved to contest the will, attacking his stepmother and Mrs. Tingley in his filings before the court. He charged that his father had for several years not been in his right mind, that his mental and physical strength had been sapped by age, sickness, and worries resulting from the loss of half a million dollars in recent business ventures. The family fortune, he maintained, had been built up entirely while his own mother was alive, and had been diminished during his father's time at Point Loma. He was joined in the challenge by Albert Jr., who was off fighting in France on behalf of the British.

Keith charged that the funeral was suspiciously rushed, that the will was not signed or witnessed properly, and that Mrs. Tingley and his stepmother had been plotting for at least four years to alienate his father from him and seize his anticipated fortune for the Theosophical cause. He further alleged that those residing at Point Loma, particularly Mrs. Tingley, Mrs. Spalding, and Durand Churchill, who was said to have involved his own son, Durand Jr., born at the colony, had entered into a conspiracy to warp the aged millionaire's mind, that he was taught to give "blind and implicit obedience" to Mrs. Tingley and to his wife, and was "coerced" to be a member of the "inner cabinet" at Point Loma.

Mrs. Tingley was deposed in the case, made some thirteen hundred corrections to the transcript, and then refused to sign it, compelling Keith Spalding to bring additional action. For two years, the trial provided sensational claims and counterclaims. Spalding claimed his stepmother had been abrasive to his wife and to his ninety-five-year-old grandmother, who his father had always said was the real guiding force behind the Spalding business. He alleged that Mrs. Spalding "maintained with Mrs. Tingley a relationship of the most intimate and confidential character" and was utterly under her control because she had been promised, perhaps partly in exchange for financial considerations, that one day she would succeed Tingley at the helm of the Theosophical Society.

While the legal maneuverings continued, Lieutenant Albert Spalding Jr., of the Coldstream Guards, Royal Inniskilling Fusiliers, died in battle in France, on July 1, 1916, having just turned twenty-five. His will, administered by his uncle J. Walter Spalding, left the bulk of his estate to half brother Keith.

Also during the contest of the will, Durand Churchill, said to be on a personal trip, was revealed in an *Oakland Tribune* front-page scoop of April 8, 1916, to be an inmate at the Livermore Sanitarium, where he had been housed for some time as a mental incompetent. Churchill's wife, Marion, who ordinarily would have been in line to act as his guardian, raced off to Vancouver, thus permitting his mother to apply successfully for his legal guardianship. Of the couple's three children, one (Durand Jr.) continued to live in Lomaland, supervised by Elizabeth Spalding, while the other two went with their mother to Vancouver. Durand Churchill never recovered and died in an asylum twenty-one years later.

On July 13, 1917, a settlement was reached in the suit, with Keith getting five-twelfths of the roughly $2 million and the right to buy at a favorable price all of his stepmother's shares in the Spalding Company. He went on to live a long and from all appearances happy life, sport fishing with his first wife, Eudora, from their launch the *Goodwill*, and living out his eighty-three years as a rancher and patron of the arts.

Elizabeth Minott Churchill Mayer Spalding continued her active service in the Theosophical Society up until her death of stroke at age seventy in 1926. To the end, she remained a close friend and colleague of Mrs. Tingley, who never turned control of the society over to her. Ten years after Mrs. Spalding's death, the managers of her estate were sued for $130,000 for alleged malfeasance by her surviving family: Marion Churchill, wife and guardian of her institutionalized husband, and their three children, Durand Jr., Marcellus, and Albert.

Katherine Tingley died in an automobile crash in 1929, at the age of eighty-two, while on a European lecture tour. By then, she and her White City had long since been sued into near oblivion for alienation of affections, for breach of promise, for financial mismanagement. Lack of a sustainable endowment and diminishing numbers of wealthy adherents forced the society to sell off most of Lomaland's acreage and then, in 1942, to pull up stakes altogether and move, in a decimated state, to Covina, near Los Angeles. The current, exceedingly modest Theosophical Society headquarters is located nineteen miles from Covina, in Altadena. A larger rival group, the Theosophical Society in America, is based in Wheaton, Illinois. It is affiliated with the international Theosophical Society, Adyar. Some of the original Theosophist colony buildings, including the Spalding home with its amethyst dome, survive on what is today the campus of Point Loma Nazarene University.

Helena Blavatsky and Katherine Tingley had seen California as the dawn of a new age, the seedbed for all that was fresh and vital in the spiritual evolution of the race. Their vision would live on in a variety of new-age sects (remember Heaven's Gate?), many of them borrowing from Theosophical precepts, but the apogee of their movement was past. Once Point Loma failed as a residential colony amid the Depression, the cultural influence of the Theosophical movement in America withered.

DURING THE DEPRESSION RURAL New York State's economy was also in disarray, and so was that of major league baseball, most of whose clubs went into receivership at some point in the 1930s. The packaging of a patron saint and pilgrim shrine took on renewed appeal. Abner Doubleday and Cooperstown were again dragooned into service.

In 1934, the idea for a baseball hall of fame and museum came to Alexander Cleland, a New York City resident and director of Clark House, a Lower East Side settlement house established and funded by the Clark Foundation. In that same year, his millionaire employer and friend, Stephen C. Clark, bought an old, misshapen baseball from a farmer in Fly Creek who, in readying a building for destruction, found it in a trunk that was said to have belonged to Abner Graves before he departed for the Gold Rush in 1849. Upon its display on a mantle in the Village Club, the artifact was identified as the Doubleday Ball, and so it is winkingly termed today in its exhibit at the Baseball Hall of Fame.

Gathering baseball relics, documents, and literature proved difficult for Cleland. He solicited material from baseball's living legends, but the response was tepid, even after an overture to Cy Young to become the Hall of Fame's custodian and greeter. Edgar Taft Stevenson, editor of the *Titusville* (Pennsylvania) *Herald* and the same man who had penned "The Religion of Baseball" article that appeared in *Sporting Life* in 1910, offered to help. He had been a classmate of Christy Mathewson at Bucknell and volunteered to approach his widow about donating some of the great pitcher's keepsakes. (Mathewson had died in 1925 of tuberculosis, brought on by an accidental gassing in a World War I drill). This overture proved successful, and slowly memorabilia drifted in from other quarters. Cleland placed the bibliographical gathering in Stevenson's charge while pursuing the artifacts himself; thus were Cooperstown's baseball museum and library separated at birth.

Beginning in 1934, Cleland worked tirelessly to gain support for "a building on Doubleday Field where a collection of all past, present, and future historical data of the game could be shown." He enlisted the support of Ford Frick, president of the National League, Will Harridge, president of the American League, and Commissioner Kenesaw Mountain Landis. Everyone thought that a celebration of baseball's centennial would be a good thing for the game, not to mention a bonanza for Cooperstown.

The first class of Hall of Fame inductees was announced in 1936: Ty Cobb, Honus Wagner, Walter Johnson, Christy Mathewson, and Babe Ruth. The next year's class was larger, and consisted of Connie Mack, John McGraw, Nap Lajoie, Tris Speaker, George Wright, and Cy Young; Ban Johnson was included for his role in creating the American League and so was Morgan Bulkeley, in the mistaken belief that his selection as first president of the National League had been meaningful—William Hulbert would not be admitted until 1995.

The election of 1938 added plaques, to be placed in the Hall of Fame under construction at some distance from Doubleday Field, for Grover Cleveland Alexander, Henry Chadwick, and, startlingly, Alexander Cartwright. Abner Doubleday did not get a plaque then or now but Bruce Cartwright Jr. lobbied so hard, implying that his Honolulu allies would somehow spoil Cooperstown's Centennial of Baseball in 1939, that the Knickerbocker pioneer of indeterminate accomplishment won a place in the hallowed hall.

When the hall opened in a magnificent ceremony on June 12, 1939, the early inductees were joined in immortality by Lou Gehrig, Eddie Collins, Charles Comiskey, Candy Cummings, Buck Ewing, Willie Keeler, George Sisler, Hoss Radbourn, Cap Anson, and last but hardly least, Albert Spalding. If in the end no one invented our national game, and its innocent Eden is a continuing state of delusion, he, as unwittingly as Abner Doubleday invented baseball, invented its religion and its shrine.

ACKNOWLEDGMENTS

When I began my research into baseball's paternity in 1983 I could not have imagined that the subject would be of continuing mystery and fascination for so long. Indeed, while I am not likely to write on this subject again, there remain some doubtful points which, had I permitted them to delay further the publication of this book, might have left me in possession of our game's largest bundle of undigested facts. The specter of the longest book never written, Joe Gould's *The Oral History of Our Times*, was constantly before me.

So it is with both satisfaction and relief that I have come to the end of this trail, with some new answers to the question, how did baseball really begin? It is with regret, however, that along the way several of the people who helped me have gone to where they are beyond receiving my thanks. I will make no special category for the departed, as a reader picking up this book in years to come will find its ranks swelled.

The help of some individuals has been general and constant over the course of decades—as role models and great souls—and thus they merit first mention. Most have been my friends, but I have felt a kinship with even those whom I never knew personally. Alphabetically they are: Lee Allen, John Rickard Betts, Bob Carroll, Foster Rhea Dulles, Johan Huizinga, Cliff Kachline, David Neft, Pete Palmer, Frank Phelps, David Pietrusza, Larry Ritter, Mark Rucker, Harold and Dorothy Seymour, Jules Tygiel, and David Voigt. Truly, I could not have written this book without any of you.

Those whose help has been more specific to this book include early baseball experts, many of them fellow members of the Society for American Baseball Research and particularly its research committee on nineteenth-century baseball. Some have written for the scholarly publication *Base Ball: A Journal of the Early Game*, which I commenced in spring 2007. Jed Thorn has been my coeditor of that publication; as he is also my eldest son, he is first among the experts otherwise listed here alphabetically: Charles C. Alexander, Thomas L. Altherr, Gary Ashwill, David Ball, David Block, Randall Brown, James E. Brunson, Jim Charlton, David Dyte, Ed Folsom, Richard Hershberger, Beth Hise, Joanne Hulbert, John R. Husman, Fred Ivor-Campbell, Don Jensen, Larry McCray, Angus Macfarlane, Peter Mancuso, William A. Mann, Peter Morris, David Nemec, Monica Nucciarone, Kate Phinney, Bob Schaefer, Alan Schwarz, Debra Shattuck, Dean Sullivan, Bob Tholkes, George Thompson, Bob Tiemann, Craig Waff, Bill Wagner, and Paul Wendt.

Of all these, three come in for special mention: David Block, Larry McCray, and David Nemec. They graciously read the manuscript in a late stage and offered critical suggestions for improvement and clarification. If the book retains factual error and linguistic infelicity, the fault is not theirs but mine for not adopting every last bit of their counsel.

No book of research would get very far without the advice and kind cooperation of librarians and archivists. At the National Baseball Hall of Fame Library, I was aided over the years by Cliff Kachline, Jack Redding, Tom Heitz, Bill Deane, Jim Gates, Tom Shieber, Tim Wiles, and Pat Kelly. Other institutions and individuals who come in for special thanks are, alphabetically: Chicago History Museum; Cleveland Public Library, Mears Collection; Fort Wayne Public Library; Houghton Library, Harvard University (Jennifer Rathbun); Monmouth County, New Jersey, Hall of Records; New-York Historical Society; New York Public Library, Spalding Collection; Pro Football Hall of Fame (Saleem Choudhry, John Kendle, Pete Fierle); Rockford, Illinois, Public Library (John Molyneaux); Rollins University Archives (Wenxian Zhang); Society of California Pioneers (Pat Keats); Superior Court, San Diego County; Theosophical Society in

America, Wheaton, Illinois (Janet Kerschner); Theosophical Society, Pasadena (David Wietersen); University of Notre Dame Archives (Angela Kindig); Watkinson Library, Trinity College (Peter Knapp); Winter Park History and Archives Collection, Winter Park Public Library (Barbara J. White); Yale University Manuscripts and Archives.

Those who have enriched my understanding of the game at key points in the research for this book include Jim Bouton, Ken Burns, Harry Higham, Gary Mitchem, Lynn Novick, Dick Perez, Dave Smith, Greg Spira, John R. Wheaton, and Suzanne Winston. Friends in the collecting hobby and trade have been very helpful to me over the years, particularly Rob Lifson, Lew Lipset, Peter Nash, and Corey Shanus.

Besides my son mentioned above I would like to thank my family for their unflagging support and years of sweetly feigned interest: sons Isaac and Mark, daughter-in-law Jenna, grandchildren Bryce and Guinevere, life mate Erica.

I save for last, that honored place, my literary representative and my editor, for they have lasted with me when others might not, as the book flew past deadline after deadline. Andrew Blauner is not my first agent but he will be my last; there has been none better in my experience, which runs some four decades in publishing. Bob Bender is my editor at Simon & Schuster who alternated sympathetic understanding with tough love, holding fast to principle on a number of points where he was right and I was not. Thanks, Bob. I would also like to thank Johanna Li of Simon & Schuster and copy editor Barbara Hanson for their unfailing professionalism.

Last words of gratitude go to baseball itself, this great game that opened the mysteries of America to an immigrant boy and opened mysteries of its own to that boy grown old.

NOTES

INTRODUCTION

xi *Reflecting on the appeal:* Jane Austen, *Northanger Abbey* (London: Simms and M'Intyre, 1853), 61.

xi *Mrs. Morland was:* Ibid., 6.

xii *Yet before April 1937:* Robert W. Henderson, "How Baseball Began," *Bulletin of the New York Public Library* (April 1937), 291.

xii *Oh, Abner of the Doubledays:* John Kieran, "Caught Off Base," Sports of the Times column, *New York Times,* April 11, 1937.

xiii *Recent scholarship:* Particularly worthy of mention are David Block, *Baseball Before We Knew It* (Lincoln: University of Nebraska Press, 2005); "The Protoball Chronologies," managed by Larry McCray and online at http://www.retrosheet.org/Protoball/; and Thomas L. Altherr's scholarship, especially "A Place Leavel Enough to Play Ball," first published in *NINE: A Journal of Baseball History and Perspectives* 8:2 (2000), 15–49.

xiv *In* The Death of the Past: J. H. Plumb, *The Death of the Past* (London: Macmillan, 1969), 22–23.

xv *And it is because of baseball's success:* Mrs. Schuyler Van Rensselaer, *History of the City of New York in the Seventeenth Century* (New York: Macmillan, 1909), v–vii.

xv *More recently, the paleontologist:* Stephen Jay Gould, *Bully for Brontosaurus: Reflections in Natural History* (New York: Norton, 1992), 45.

xvi *In the words of psychiatrist:* George E. Vaillant, *Adaptation to Life* (Boston: Little Brown, 1977), 197.

xvi *Although Doubleday did not:* Robert Underwood Johnson, Clarence Clough Buel, eds., *Battles and Leaders of the Civil War* (New York: Century Co., 1887), 47.

xvi His apotheosis: Block, *Baseball Before We Knew It,* 42–46. Credit for breaking the story on the Theosophical underpinnings of Albert Spalding and the Mills Commission goes to Philip Block, in a chapter he contributed to his brother David's book. His key find was an article in a Theosophical Society publication, *The New Century Path,* of August 13, 1905, that demonstrated Spalding's full knowledge that Doubleday had been a Theosophist, a conflict of interest he never publicly addressed during the Mills Commission deliberations or afterward.

xvii *"Baseball," he once declared:* Albert G. Spalding, *America's National Game* (New York: American Sports Publishing, 1911), 4.

xviii *Who controls the past:* George Orwell, *Nineteen Eighty-Four* (New York: New American Library, 1977), 35.

CHAPTER ONE: ANOINTING ABNER

1 *From the nature of the case:* Letter from James E. Sullivan to A. G. Mills, October 12, 1907. A. G. Mills Papers, BA MSS 13, National Baseball Hall of Fame Library, National Baseball Hall of Fame and Museum, Cooperstown, New York.

1 *Mills had been waiting:* Letter from Mills to Sullivan, December 31, 1907, from which the fact of Sullivan's letter may be divined. Mills' letter in full: "Dear Sullivan, Receiving a letter from you, yesterday, reminded me of what you said in our talk in the subway recently, to the effect that you had heard from all the others on the Base Ball question, excepting only me. I was then waiting, and still am, for a reply to a letter I wrote in regard to the Mr. Wadsworth who presented a diagram of the game to the Knickerbocker Club; but, when your letter came yesterday, it occurred to me that if I got anything off on the subject this year I would have to hustle, and, accordingly, in the afternoon I dictated a letter which I intended as an original draft to be amended, but the star stenographer of our staff quickly presented it to me in such perfect typographical form that I fired it off as it was." A. G. Mills Papers, BA MSS 13, National Baseball Hall of Fame Library, National Baseball Hall of Fame and Museum, Cooperstown, New York.

2 *I was brought up: The Sun* (New York), March 25, 1888. "From Mendham N J comes the little note of Major Gen. Abner Doubleday dated Nov. 20, '87 and written in a neat running hand. 'You ask for some information as to how I passed my youth. . . . As I am moving to New York I am much hurried and cannot give more details at present.' "

2 *On April 12, 1861:* Abner Doubleday, *Reminiscences of Forts Sumter and Moultrie in 1860–'61* (New York: Harper & Brothers, 1876), 146.

2 *A. G. Mills (the press:* Joseph E. Chance, ed. *My Life in the Old Army,* by Abner Doubleday (Fort Worth: Texas Christian University Press, 1998), 10.

3 *None at all:* Richard J. Tofel, "The Innocuous Conspiracy of Baseball's Birth," *Wall Street Journal,* July 19, 2001.

4 *Let Spalding describe:* "When Base Ball Was Organized," *Wilkes-Barre Times,* July 18, 1905. Also appeared in *Spalding Official Base Ball Guide,* 1905, ed. Henry Chadwick (New York: American Sports Publishing), 15 ff.

4 *When professional baseball players:* A correspondent signing as "Grandmother" wrote to the London *Times* on August 11, 1874: "Sir——Some American athletes are trying to introduce to us their game of base ball, as if it were a novelty: whereas the fact is that it is an ancient English game, long ago discarded in favor of cricket. . . ."

5 *Chadwick had it largely right:* Letter from Henry Chadwick to Daniel Lucius "Doc" Adams of August 16, 1898. This letter resides unremarked within a folder of fourteen letters from the distinguished scholar Daniel Adams to his son, Daniel Lucius Adams, when the latter was a student at Yale, 1833–1835. Yale Miscellaneous Manuscripts Collection. Manuscripts and Archives, Yale University Library. Misc MSS A. Box 1, Folder 4.

5 *On November 5, 1904:* Letter from Spalding to John Lowell, November 5, 1904. Jack M. Doyle, Albert Spalding Scrapbooks, BA SCR 42, National Baseball Hall of Fame Library, National Baseball Hall of Fame and Museum, Cooperstown, New York. These files have been available to researchers since shortly after their acquisition in 1999.

6 *Later in the month:* The speech was delivered November 17, 1904. The *Association Seminar,* the monthly journal of the YMCA Training School, at Springfield, published the address in December. It later appeared in the 1905 *Spalding Guide.*

6 *Space in the* Guide: Sullivan's promise appeared in the 1908 *Spalding Guide,* ed. Henry Chadwick (New York: American Sports Publishing), 36.

7 *His raw, unedited files:* These may be viewed in the Jack M. Doyle, Albert Spalding Scrapbooks, BA SCR 42.

7 *Sullivan had urged restraint:* Letter from James E. Sullivan to A. G. Mills, October 12, 1907. A. G. Mills Papers, BA MSS 13, National Baseball Hall of Fame Library.

7 *The* Beacon Journal *article:* "Abner Doubleday Invented Base Ball," *Akron Beacon Journal,* April 4, 1905.

8 *At some point:* Letter from Spalding to Abner Graves, November 10, 1905. Jack M. Doyle, Albert Spalding Scrapbooks, BA SCR 42.

9 *Long before Spalding's response:* "Birth Place of Base Ball Was at Cooperstown," *Otsego Farmer,* April 14, 1905, 5. The Sunday papers bore a date of July 23, 1905.

11 *Mills wrote, however:* Mills' letter to Spalding, March 27, 1905. Jack M. Doyle, Albert Spalding Scrapbooks, BA SCR 42.

11 *On that memorable evening:* The precise language, reported differently in various newspapers and periodicals of the day, was subject to confirmation only recently with the location of Mills' "Master of Ceremonies" notes tucked into a program and menu from the banquet. A. G. Mills Papers, BA MSS 13.

11 *The* New York Times: "Baseball at Delmonico's: Banquet to the Ball Tossers Who Went Around the World," *New York Times,* April 9, 1889.

12 *Ward was also a sturdy:* His book was published in Philadelphia by the Athletic Publishing Company, 1888.

13 *Indeed, this circuitous document:* Sullivan to Mills, December 31, 1907. Jack M. Doyle, Albert Spalding Scrapbooks, BA SCR 42.

13 *Reading Mills' letter:* Mills to Sullivan, December 30, 1907. This letter was published in the 1908 *Spalding Guide* under the heading "Final Decision of the Special Base Ball Commission," 45–48.

17 *In this innovation:* Lowell letter to Spalding, November 12, 1904. Jack M. Doyle, Albert Spalding Scrapbooks, BA SCR 42.

17 *On the day the* Guide: Chadwick to Mills, March 20, 1908. A. G. Mills Papers, BA MSS 13. Jack M. Doyle, Albert Spalding Scrapbooks, BA SCR 42. The substance of this 1877 meeting was as well the subject of William M. Rankin's "Base Ball's Birth: Wadsworth Made Diagram of Diamond," in the *Sporting News,* April 8, 1905, 2.

18 *Duncan F. Curry:* A. G. Mills, "Final Decision of the Special Baseball Commission," December 30, 1907, in *Spalding Official Base Ball Guide,* 1908, ed. Henry Chadwick (New York: American Sports Publishing), 47. Also, Rankin had written about his interview with Curry in a letter to the Commission on January 15, 1905.

18 *Spalding replied eleven days:* Spalding to Rankin, January 26, 1905. Jack M. Doyle, Albert Spalding Scrapbooks, BA SCR 42.

19 *On February 8, Spalding:* Spalding to Rankin, February 8, 1905. Jack M. Doyle, Albert Spalding Scrapbooks, BA SCR 42.

19 *By this time scholarly research:* Principally Robert W. Henderson, "Baseball and Rounders," *Bulletin of the New York Public Library* (April 1939), 303–313, and *Ball, Bat and Bishop: The Origins of Ball Games* (New York: Rockport Press, 1947); and Harold Seymour, "How Baseball Began," *The New-York Historical Society Quarterly* (October 1956), 369–385.

19 *Reviewing the flawed work:* Harold Peterson, *The Man Who Invented Baseball* (New York: Scribners, 1973), 181.

19 *On December 20, 1907:* A. G. Mills Papers, BA MSS 13.

20 *On January 6, 1908:* Ibid.

21 *On that same day Mills:* Mills to Rankin, January 6, 1908. Jack M. Doyle, Albert Spalding Scrapbooks, BA SCR 42.

22 *Rankin, who in early 1905:* William M. Rankin, "Game's Pedigree: Alex Cartwright Was Father of Base Ball," the *Sporting News,* April 2, 1908, 2. Rankin also wrote an undated letter to Mills, presumably from January 16, 1908, as it is referenced such in Mills' reply. In this letter Rankin declared, "In the article dated Jan 15, 1905 I quoted Mr. Curry as saying, that someone had presented a plan showing a ball field (or words to that effect), but that he (Mr. Curry) could not remember who it was. *In that I was mistaken*. During the month of March 1905, while hunting up some other matters, I ran across a letter given to me by Mr. H. G. Crickmore, the noted turf authority, who was during the Summer of 1876 a sporting writer on the N.Y. World. *On the back of the letter I had written*

Mr. Alex J. Cartwright, father of baseball. The moment I saw it I remembered writing it there at the time Mr. Curry told me about it." Jack M. Doyle, Albert Spalding Scrapbooks, BA SCR 42. In his reply of January 20, 1908, Mills brushed him off thus: "The whole subject is a very interesting one, but, leaving aside all minor details about which recollections must vary, I think we are fully in accord that the game is of American origin. . . . Thanking you heartily for the trouble you have taken. . . ." A. G. Mills Papers, BA MSS 13.

22 *In the opening installment:* He even had Cartwright in 1842 "scratching with a stick in the dust, mark[ing] off the diagram of a baseball diamond." Will Irwin, "Baseball; I—Before the Professionals Came," *Collier's,* May 8, 1909, 12–13, 32–34.

23 *In fact, the game's:* In *America's National Game,* Spalding fancifully places Cartwright in the scene without evidencing that he saw him. "Alexander J. Cartwright, among many other thousands, was one of the devotees of Base Ball disappointed by reason of the failure of the steamer 'Alameda' to make schedule time. . . ."

CHAPTER TWO: FOUR FATHERS, TWO ROADS

25 *Two roads diverged:* Robert Frost, "The Road Not Taken," *Mountain Interval* (New York: Henry Holt, 1916), 9.

26 *John Ward had it right:* John Ward, *Base-Ball: How to Become a Player* (Philadelphia: Athletic Publishing Company, 1888), 21.

28 *Carried baseball to Pacific Coast:* Monica Nucciarone, *Alexander Cartwright: The Life Behind the Baseball Legend* (Lincoln: University of Nebraska Press, 2009).

28 *Hawaii resident William Castle:* William Castle, "The Introduction of Baseball," *The Friend* (March 1924), 70. For this citation I am indebted to Monica Nucciarone.

28 *He surprised me by saying:* Ibid.

28 *In 1866, Charles A. Peverelly:* Charles A. Peverelly, *The Book of American Pastimes, Containing a History of the Principal Base Ball, Cricket, Rowing, and Yachting Clubs of the United States* (New York: Published by the Author, 1866), 340.

28 *The Knickerbocker game:* This assertion is supported by a complete review of each game played by the Knickerbocker Base Ball Club of New York, 1845–1854. Albert Spalding Baseball Collections, Knickerbocker Base Ball Club of New York Game Books, b. October 6, 1845–1856, New York Public Library.

29 *Yet even this:* The prior existence of the diamond is claimed for 1837 in William R. Wheaton's interview in "How Baseball Began: A Member of the Gotham Club of Fifty Years Ago Tells About It," *San Francisco Daily Examiner,* November 27, 1887, 14. ("We laid out the ground at Madison square in the form of an accurate diamond, with home-plate and sand-bags for bases.") The diamond is evident also in Robin Carver's *Book of Sports* and other chapbook depictions of boys playing ball.

29 *Cartwright may have umpired:* Photographic reproductions of this scoresheet from the Game Books cited above are indistinct as to the umpire's name; Cartwright was certainly not among the players. Checking against the original has been impossible for decades, since some miscreant excised the sheets with a blade in the 1980s.

29 *As early as 1889:* Author unknown though suspected to be William M. Rankin, *Mercury Sporting Guide for 1889 Containing the History and Records of Baseball, schedules of games to be played by the National League, American Association, International League, Atlantic Association* (New York: Sunday Mercury Print), 1. Ink annotations are consistent with Rankin's hand. Charles W. Mears Baseball Collection, Cleveland Public Library.

29 *In 1860, in the premier:* Henry Chadwick, *Beadle's Dime Base-Ball Player: A Compendium of the Game, etc.* (New York: Irwin P. Beadle and Co., 1860), 6.

29 *All the same:* Ibid., 5.

29 *These efforts extended even to crafting:* For a thorough treatment of this subject see Monica Nucciarone, *Alexander Cartwright: The Life Behind the Baseball Legend* (Lincoln: University of Nebraska Press, 2009).

30 *The junior Adams:* His degree from Yale is reported in an untitled article in the *Connecticut Courant,* August 24, 1835, 3. His medical degree is reported in "Harvard University," *The Boston Medical and Surgical Journal,* September 26, 1838, 127. His work as an attending physician is reported in "New York Dispensary," *The New-York Spectator,* February 27, 1840, 1.

30 *I was always interested:* "Dr. D. L. Adams; Memoirs of the Father of Base Ball; He Resides in New Haven and Retains an Interest in the Game," the *Sporting News,* February 29, 1896, 3. The present writer's extensive biography of Adams appeared as "The True Father of Baseball," first in *Elysian Fields Quarterly* in Winter 1992, vol. 11, no. 1, 85–91, and then in several of the eight editions of the encyclopedia *Total Baseball* (John Thorn, Pete Palmer, et al., various publishers, 1989–2004).

32 *The game played in New York:* This 1823 match, advertised in the *National Advocate* of April 25, 1823, page 2, column 4, was first noticed in the modern period by George A. Thompson Jr., and was trumpeted in Edward Wong, "Baseball's Disputed Origin Is Traced Back, Back, Back," *New York Times,* July 8, 2001. Thompson wrote his own account, "New York Baseball, 1823," in *The National Pastime* (Cleveland: Society for American Baseball Research [21], 2001), 6–8.

32 *The New York game:* "Yesterday afternoon a contest at the game of Bace took place on 'the Gymnasium,' near Tyler's between the gentlemen of two different clubs for a supper and trimmings. . . . Great skill and activity it is said was displayed on both sides, but after a severe and well maintained contest, Victory, which had at times fluttered a little from one to the other, settled down on the heads of the Gymnastics, who beat the Sons of Diagoras 41 to 34." "Sporting Intelligence," *New-York Evening Post,* April 13, 1805, 3. This is another great find by George Thompson, from 2005, although there remains some ambiguity regarding the nature of the game—baseball or prisoners' base.

32 *It is reported:* William Wood, *Manual of Physical Exercises* (New York: Harper & Brothers, 1867), 189–190. ("Both of these clubs played in the old-fashioned way of throwing the ball and striking the runner, in order to put him out.")

32 *In fact, baseball:* Undated *Clipper* article of 1855 in Charles W. Mears Baseball Collection, Cleveland Public Library. Scrapbook Collection, Volume One: Box Scores and Articles, compiled by William Rankin, 1853–1870.

33 *I used to play shortstop:* "Dr. D. L. Adams," 3.

33 *We had a great deal of trouble:* Ibid.

34 *Here is the definition:* Noah Webster, *An American dictionary of the English language: intended to exhibit, I. The origin, affinities and primary signification of English words, as far as they have been ascertained. II. The genuine orthography and pronunciation of words, according to general usage, or to just principles of analogy. III. Accurate and discriminating definition, with numerous authorities and illustrations. To which are prefixed, an introductory dissertation on the origin, history and connection of the languages of Western Asia and of Europe, and a concise grammar of the English language* (New York: S. Converse, 1828). Also referenced is the later edition (Springfield, MA: George and Charles Merriam, 1853).

34 *In describing the rules:* Dick and Fitzgerald, *The American Boy's Book of Sports and Games: A Repository of In- and Out-door Amusements for Boys and Youth* (New York: Dick & Fitzgerald, 1864), 83.

35 *The playing rules:* "Dr. D. L. Adams," 3.

35 *At this meeting:* "Our National Sports," *New York Herald,* January 23, 1857, 8. Also, for announcement of the adjourned portion of the meeting, advertisements in the *Herald* of January 28 and February 2, 1857. The rules changes and the dispute over the number of innings are detailed in "City Intelligence," *New York Herald,* March 2, 1857, 8. These were ratified in the meeting in May.

35 *Adams recalled:* "Dr. D. L. Adams," 3.

36 *On such occasions:* Ibid.

36 *Knickerbocker comrade:* Letter from Davis to Adams of April 4, 1862. This letter resides unremarked within a folder of fourteen letters from the distinguished scholar Daniel Adams to his son, Daniel Lucius Adams, when the latter was a student at Yale, 1833–1835. Yale Miscellaneous Manuscripts Collection. Manuscripts and Archives, Yale University Library. Misc MSS A. Box 1, Folder 4.

36 *Adams indeed returned:* Davis' announcement of the veterans' contest in the *New York Clipper* is reprinted in the *St. Louis Globe-Democrat* of September 27, 1875. The box score and ages of the competitors was provided in "Rational Pastimes," *Forest and Stream,* September 30, 1875, 19. (Walter T. Avery, at sixty-two, was the oldest to play.) An extended report of the pomp, ceremony, and ball play is in "The Knickerbocker Club: Baseball in the Olden Time," *New York Clipper* of October 9, 1875, 221.

37 *Born in 1814, like Adams:* Completion of legal studies at Utica in *New-York Spectator,* July 24, 1841; Whig affiliation in *New York Tribune,* March 9, 1842, 2; biographical sketch in *Facsimile Reproduction of the California State Library Copy of J. Horace Culver's Sacramento City Directory for the Year 1851, with a History*

of Sacramento to 1851, Biographical Sketches, and Informative Appendices (Sacramento: California State Library Foundation, 2000), 157–169.

37 *Of the five others: New York City Directories,* various (Doggett, Rode, Trow).

37 *Wheaton was a solid cricketer:* "Cricketers' Chronicle," *Spirit of the Times,* July 31, 1847, 263; "Cricketers' Chronicle," *The Anglo American,* August 7, 1847, 382; "Cricketers' Chronicle," *Spirit of the Times,* September 4, 1847, 323.

37 *He umpired two: New York Herald* and *Brooklyn Eagle,* October 22 and 23, 1845; *Herald,* October 25, 1845.

37 *Wheaton umpired:* Albert Spalding Baseball Collections. Knickerbocker Base Ball Club of New York Game books b. Oct. 6, 1845–1856. New York Public Library.

37 *By the spring:* Wheaton is absent from the roster of Knickerbockers for 1846 as recorded in Knickerbocker Base Ball Club of New York, 1845–1854. Albert Spalding Baseball Collections. New York Public Library.

37 *Three months later: New York Weekly Herald,* February 10, 1849, 41, and February 24, 1849, 62. Also, *Facsimile Reproduction of the California State Library Copy of J. Horace Culver's Sacramento City Directory for the Year 1851, with a History of Sacramento to 1851, Biographical Sketches, and Informative Appendices* (Sacramento: California State Library Foundation, 2000), 157–161.

38 *It is possible:* Angus Macfarlane, "The Knickerbockers: San Francisco's First Baseball Team?" *Base Ball* 1, no. 1 (Spring 2007): 7–21.

38 *In a story titled:* "How Baseball Began," *San Francisco Daily Examiner.* Also discussed by its modern discoverer Randall Brown in "How Baseball Began," *National Pastime* (Cleveland: Society for American Baseball Research, 24 [2004]), 51–54.

39 *Gotham shortstop:* "The Old Atlantics of Fifty Years Ago," 1905 clipped article, perhaps from *Brooklyn Eagle,* otherwise undated. Albert Spalding Baseball Collections. Chadwick Scrapbooks, Volume 5. Chadwick quotes from a letter he received from Commerford. (In other words, the New York Club's grounds lay outside today's Madison Square but within the pre-1844 park; the Parade, as Madison Square was called prior to its formal dedication as a public park in 1847, was originally a twenty-acre tract bounded by Third and Seventh avenues and Twenty-third and Thirty-fourth streets.)

39 *There was a roadside resort:* Ibid. This resort was named the Madison Cottage but was also known as Thompson's for its proprietor.

39 *I remember very well:* The murky relationship between the original Gothams of 1837, the Washingtons, the New Yorks, the Knickerbockers, and the later Gothams may be summarized thus: Because they were the original organized club, the Gothams were also called, sometimes, the Washingtons (denoting that they were, like the father of our country, first). At some point in the early 1840s this club was officially renamed the New York Ball Club, retaining most but not all of its Gotham members. The New Yorks then spun off the Knickerbockers, as Wheaton relates. The Gotham, meanwhile, continued to play ball among themselves and in 1850 re-formed as the Washingtons and challenged the Knicker-

bockers to match games that are in the historical record. This club reverted to its old name of Gothams in 1852.

39 *To provide additional gloss:* *New York Herald* and *Brooklyn Eagle,* October 22 and 23, 1845; *Herald,* October 25, 1845.

40 *The first match:* Archibald Douglas Turnbull, *John Stevens: An American Record* (New York: The American Society of Mechanical Engineers, 1928), 490. For this citation I am indebted to William A. Mann, "The Elysian Fields of Hoboken, New Jersey," *Base Ball* 1:1 Spring 2007, 7–21.

40 *Peverelly, writing:* Charles A. Peverelly, *Book of American Pastimes,* 342.

40 *Wheaton concluded:* "How Baseball Began," 14.

41 *When baseball's early players:* For cricket's first organized play in New York the sources are multiple but dispositively from I. N. Phelps-Stokes, *Iconography of Manhattan Island, 1498–1909* (New York: Robert H. Dodd, 1915–1928), Vol. V. no. 4, p. 628: " . . . this day, a great Cricket match is to be played on our commons, by a Company of Londoners against a Company of New-Yorkers. *New-York Post-Boy,* 4/29/51."

42 *He also claimed:* This claim arose in 1889 but may have been asserted earlier, either by Chadwick or his supporters, who in the summer of this year began to campaign for his elevation as the "Father of Baseball." In his first article on baseball in the *New York Clipper,* on July 31, 1858, he "advocated a team of eleven men on a side, the extra two to field fouls, and called the home plate a 'wicket.' " (This comment cannot be verified from the *Clipper* as the issue is missing from the microfilm.) Preston D. Orem, *Baseball (1889) from the Newspaper Accounts* (Altadena, CA: self-published, 1967), 410–411.

42 *Writing in 1868:* Henry Chadwick, *The Game of Base Ball* (New York: George Munro, 1868), 10. Repeated in 1889; see note above. Letter from Henry Chadwick to "Joe," April (date obscure) 1907. Per photocopy in the HOF's Giamatti Center "Origins" file. "Reference will show you that I knew of base ball in the sixties when—according to 'mine enemy' [Will Rankin]—I knew nothing about any game but cricket. Although in November 1848 I played as short stop in a field adjoining the old Knickerbocker grounds at Hoboken."

42 *Sometimes he would opine:* Ibid., 9. "As usual, with every thing imported, we do not possess it long before we endeavor to improve it, and as our old American edition of base ball, in vogue in New York some twenty-five years ago, was an improvement on Rounders, so is our present National game a great step in advance of the game of base ball as played in 1840 and up to 1857."

43 *Chadwick also declared:* Additionally, a useful article by Geoffrey Mullerton Christine in the *New York World* of June 19, 1894, located in the Chadwick Scrapbooks, offers Chadwick's view that baseball was played in Philadelphia by the Olympics since 1833 (though in the form of town ball) and in New York in 1845 by both the New York and Washington clubs.

43 *References in current:* However, David Block, in an email of April 5, 2010, shared his find of an explicit early association of the term "town ball" with the Olympic Club of Philadelphia. He wrote: "It is found in a letter to the editor of the *Public*

Ledger of Philadelphia, published in the issue of May 14, 1838. The letter's writer described what he encountered during a stroll in the countryside near Camden, New Jersey. The relevant portion is as follows: 'A small distance from the woods, I beheld a party of young men, the majority of whom I afterwards distinguished to be Market street merchants; and who styled themselves the "Olympic Club," a title well answering to its name by the manner in which the party amused themselves in the recreant pleasure of town ball, and several other games.' "

43 *When the Olympics:* Peverelly, *Book of American Pastimes,* 474.

44 *Oliver's friend: Yonkers Statesman* editor John Oliver's reminiscence comes from the Mills Commission Papers under date of September 26, 1905. Jack M. Doyle, Albert Spalding Scrapbooks, BA SCR 42.

45 *In "A Word Fitly Spoken":* Anonymous, "A Word Fitly Spoken," *American Sunday School Magazine,* January 1830, 3–5. *History of the Orphan Asylum in Philadelphia; with an account of the fire, in which twenty-three orphans were burned. Written for the American S. S. Union, and revised by the Committee of Publication* (American Sunday School Union, Philadelphia: No. 146 Chestnut Street, 1831). This little volume also contains fine woodcuts, including one of the children playing ball and other sports. The connection of Philadelphia's famed Rebecca Gratz, model for the character Rebecca in Sir Walter Scott's *Ivanhoe,* to this orphanage tale is elaborated in the blog "Rebecca Gratz & 19th-Century America," at http://rebeccagratz.blogspot.com/2010/08/rebecca-gratz-baseball.html.

45 *At least that is how:* Peverelly, *Book of American Pastimes,* 472–475. Also, Horace Fogel, "Evolution of Baseball from 1833 Up to the Present Time," *Philadelphia Daily Evening Telegram,* March 22–23, 1908.

46 *On the Olympics':* Ibid., 472.

46 *The* Police Gazette: "Our National Game," *National Police Gazette,* October 20, 1883, 11.

46 *In 1904, Chadwick:* Albert Spalding Baseball Collections. Chadwick Scrapbooks, Volume 5. These sentiments were expressed in similar language in the *Spalding Guides* of 1903 and 1904.

48 *From one of his letters:* The first cited letter from Grafton's Henry Sargent to James A. Sullivan of the Mills Commission is from May 31, 1905. The second cited is from May 18, 1905, and the third is from June 25, 1905. Jack M. Doyle, Albert Spalding Scrapbooks, BA SCR 42.

49 *Wicket was unknown:* "Wicket: A Match at the Athletic Grounds," *Brooklyn Eagle,* August 26, 1880, 3; "A Queer Game Called Wicket," *New York Times,* August 28, 1880, 8. However, there is an earlier record of a wicket club forming in Brooklyn: *Brooklyn Eagle,* August 12, 1858, 3. One year earlier, a correspondent naming himself "Wicket" wrote to the editor of *Porter's Spirit of the Times* thus: "I would like to see the old game of WICKET (not Cricket) played. It is a *manly* game . . . can a club be started?"

49 *Earlier, the game had gone:* Ethel M. Damon, *Sanford Ballard Dole and His Hawaii* (Palo Alto: Pacific Books, 1957), 41. "One game they all enjoyed was

wicket, often watched by small Mary Burbank. *Aipuni,* the Hawaiians called it, or rounders, perhaps because the bat had a large rounder end. It was a forerunner of baseball, but the broad, heavy bat was held close to the ground." On May 24, 1854, the editor had written to correspondent "J. L. McL.": "What do you mean by a 'Wicket' club? We have cricket and base ball clubs here, but no 'wicket' that we are aware of." Also, in Rochester, New York: "The Express Robbery," *The National Police Gazette,* April 18, 1846, 277. Finally, wicket appears to be the game played in the earliest pictorial depiction of American bat-and-ball activity: an engraving first published in *The Massachusetts Magazine* in 1793, it was labeled: "A front View of Dartmouth College with the Chapel and Hall" by J. Dunham.

49 *Wicket was played:* George Dudley Seymour, "The Old-Time Game of Wicket and Old-Time Wicket Players," in *Papers and Addresses of the Society of Colonial Wars in the State of Connecticut, Volume II of the Proceedings of the Society* (n.p., 1909), 295.

50 *Indeed, the first printed:* "March, 15. Sam. Hirst got up betime in the morning, and took Ben Swett with him and went into the [Boston] Common to play at Wicket. Went before any body was up, left the door open; Sam came not to prayer; at which I was most displeased." *Diary of Samuel Sewall, in Collections of the Massachusetts Historical Society,* Volume VII-Fifth Series (Boston: Published by the Society, 1882), 372.

50 *George Washington was documented:* George Ewing, *The Military Journal of George Ewing (1754–1824), A Soldier of Valley Forge* (Yonkers, NY: Private Printing, 1928), 47. "[May 2d] in the afternoon playd a game at Wicket with a number of Gent of the Arty [gentlemen of the artillery]" and "This day [May 4, 1778] His Excellency dined with G Nox [General Knox] and after dinner did us the honor to play at Wicket with us."

50 *Upon graduation:* Name Index to U.S. Military Academy Cadet Application Papers, 1805–1866 in the National Archives and Records Administration (NARA), Washington, D.C., microfilm serial *M688,* microfilm rolls *1* and *159.* Register of Cadet Applicants, 1819–1867 in NARA, microfilm serial *M2037,* microfilm roll *2.* Obituary, *Hartford Courant,* April 6, 1908, 14. "Commencement," *Hartford Daily Courant,* August 2, 1844, 2. *Catalogue of the Officers and Students of Washington College, Hartford, for the Academic Year 1842–3* (Hartford: Case, Tiffany & Co., 1842). (Lists Louis Fenn Wadsworth as member of the Junior Class, residing in Litchfield, in room 11 of the college.) *Catalogue of the Officers and Graduates of Trinity College, Hartford, Connecticut, from Its Foundation in A.D. 1823* (Hartford: Case, Lockwood and Company, 1862), 33. Glenn Weaver, *The History of Trinity College, Volume One* (Hartford: Trinity College Press, 1967), 48–95. (When Wadsworth attended the school, it was known as Washington College; it did not take the name Trinity until 1845.) New York City Directories, 1848–1862, various. Obituary, *Hartford Daily Times,* April 4, 1908. Correspondence with Peter Knapp, Special Collections Librarian and College Archivist, Watkinson Library, Trinity College, February–April 2004.

51 *Then he went:* Michigan Land Grant to Amos Wadsworth, signed by President Martin Van Buren, September 5, 1838, MI1690, document no. 1098.
50 *A tempestuous character:* He resigned twice from the Knickerbocker Base Ball Club, only to rejoin the club within days. The third time he resigned it was for good. Albert Spalding Baseball Collections, Knickerbocker Base Ball Club of New York Club Books 1854–1868, New York Public Library.
51 *One of the veteran:* "Ball Players of the Past," *The Sun,* January 16, 1887, 10.
51 *In an 1856:* Albert Spalding Baseball Collections.
52 *Wadsworth was also named:* Ibid.
53 *In the convention, however:* "City Intelligence," *New York Herald,* March 2, 1857, 8.
53 *His motion carried:* Albert Spalding Baseball Collections.
53 *Louis (sometimes spelled Lewis):* "Obituary," *Hartford Daily Times,* April 4, 1908. Federal Census 1860 for Maria J. Fisher née Meschutt and her son Charles W. Fisher, 1870 and 1880 for the household of the married Wadsworths with daughter Marianne Wadsworth. Also letter from Louis F. Wadsworth as Town Superintendent of Rockaway in *Documents of the Ninety-First Legislature of the State of New Jersey and the Twenty-Third under the New Constitution* (New Brunswick, NJ: J. F. Babcock, 1867), 546.
53 *He later became a judge:* In the federal census of 1880, he is listed as a justice of the peace. As Judge Wadsworth he lost the 1886 election for mayor of Plainfield, New Jersey. "Election at Plainfield," *New York Times,* December 8, 1886, 1. "Once Rich, Dies a Pauper," *New York Times,* March 28, 1908, 5. "From Riches to the Poor Farm," *New Brunswick Times,* March 28, 1908.
53 *Widowed in 1883:* "Once Rich, Dies a Pauper," *New York Times,* March 28, 1908, 5. "From Riches to the Poor Farm," *New Brunswick Times,* March 28, 1908.
53 *After some years:* Ibid.
54 *While Mills was searching:* 1900 Federal Census, Union County, New Jersey, city of Plainfield, Supervisor's District No. 1, Enumeration District N. 130, Sheet 1. "Lewis E. Wadsworth" is listed as an inmate of the institution at West Front Street, the Industrial Home for the Poor, a new term for what had formerly been called an almshouse.
54 *In Wadsworth's belated obituary:* "Obituary," *Hartford Daily Times,* April 4, 1908. Transcript courtesy of Peter Knapp, Watkinson Library, Trinity College.

CHAPTER THREE: THE CRADLE OF BASEBALL

55 *Thanks to Pittsfield:* The author's discovery of baseball play in Pittsfield in 1791 is described in Frank Litsky, "Baseball; Now Pittsfield Stakes Claim to Baseball's Origins," *New York Times,* May 12, 2004. Also Joseph Edward Adams Smith, *The History of Pittsfield, (Berkshire County) Massachusetts, from the Year 1734 to the Year 1800* (Boston: Lee and Shepard, 1869), 446–447. Also *National Advocate,* April 25, 1823, 2.
55 *I later shared:* Litsky, "Now Pittsfield Stakes Claim."

56 *It had been played:* Jack M. Doyle, Albert Spalding Scrapbooks, BA SCR 42. Henry Sargent letter to James E. Sullivan of the Mills Commission, May 23, 1905, as follows: "Mr. Stoddard [an 1850s roundball player with the Upton Excelsiors] believes roundball was played as long ago as Upton became a little village. Upton was settled in 1735. Mr. Stoddard knows that Round Ball was played by his father in 1820, and has the tradition from his father that two generations before, i.e., directly after the revolutionary war, it was played and was not then a novelty."

57 *As Stephen Jay Gould:* Gould, *Bully for Brontosaurus*, 57.

57 *A better reason:* Robert W. Henderson, *Ball, Bat and Bishop: The Origins of Ball Games* (New York: Rockport Press, 1947), 20. Peter A. Piccione, "Batting the Ball," *College of Charleston Magazine* 7, no. 1 (Spring/Summer 2003), 36.

57 *The date is:* Piccione, ibid.: "The earliest known references to seker-hemat (transl.: batting the ball) as a fertility rite and ritual of renewal are inscribed in pyramids dating to 2400 B.C."

58 *As mentioned earlier, baseball was the name:* Block, *Baseball Before We Knew It*, 22–31.

58 *Baseball's first appearance: A Little Pretty Pocket-Book, Intended for the Instruction and Amusement of Little Master Tommy, and Pretty Miss Polly. With Two Letters from Jack the Giant-Killer; as also a Ball and Pincushion; the use of which Will Infallibly Make Tommy a Good Boy, and Polly a Good Girl* (London: John Newbery, 1744).

58 *Newbery's charming alphabet book: A Little Pretty Pocket-Book*, etc. New York, 1762; Worcester, MA, 1787.

59 *On Christmas Day:* [Governor William Bradford] *Bradford's history "Of Plimoth plantation": From the original manuscript with a Report of the Proceedings Incident to the Return of the Manuscript to Massachusetts* (Boston: Wright & Potter Printing Co., 1898), 134–135. "One ye day called the Christmas-day, ye Govr called them out to worke, (as was used), but ye most of this new-company excused them selves and said it wente against their consciences to work on ye day. So ye Govr tould them that if they made it mater of conscience, he would spare them till they were better informed. So he led away ye rest and left them; but when they came home at noone from their worke, he found them in ye streete at play, openly; some pitching ye barr, & some at stoole-ball, and schuch like sports. So he went to them, and took away their implements, and tould them that was against his conscience, that they should play & others worke. If they made ye keeping of it mater of devotion, let them kepe their houses, but ther should be no gameing or reveling in ye streets. Since which time nothing hath been attempted that way, at least openly."

59 *In 1656, the Dutch:* In October 1656, Director-General Peter Stuyvesant announced a stricter Sabbath Law in New Netherlands, including a fine of one pound Flemish for "playing ball," cricket, tennis, ninepins, dancing, drinking, etc. *Manual of the Reformed Church in America (Formerly Ref. Prot. Dutch Church), 1628–1902*, E. T. Corwin, D.D., Fourth Edition (Reformed Church in Amer-

ica, New York, 1902), Source 13, doc. hist., volume IV, pp. 13–15, and Father Jogues' papers in New York Historical Society Collection, 1857, 161–229.

59 *In 1724, Boston diarist: Diary of Samuel Sewall, in Collections of the Massachusetts Historical Society*, Volume VII, Fifth Series (Boston: Published by the Society, 1882), 372.

59 *Anticipating Pittsfield, Dartmouth:* "If any student shall play ball or use any other deversion [sic] that exposes the College or hall windows within three rods of either he shall be fined two shillings. . . ." In 1782, the protected area was extended to six rods. John King Lord, *A History of Dartmouth College 1815–1909* (Concord, NH: Rumford Press, 1913), 593. Per Thomas L. Altherr, "Chucking the Old Apple: Recent Discoveries of Pre-1840 North American Ball Games," *Base Ball* 2, no. 11 (Spring 2008), 35. Rules for the Good Government and Discipline of the School in the University of Pennsylvania (Philadelphia: Francis Bailey, 1784). Per Altherr, "A Place Leavel Enough to Play Ball."

59 *Princeton student:* John Rhea Smith, March, 22, 1786, in "Journal at Nassau Hall," Princeton Library MSS, AM 12800.

59 *Princeton, which had banned:* Howard James Savage, Harold Woodmansee Bentley, John Terence McGovern, Dean Franklin Smiley, *American College Athletics* (New York: Carnegie Foundation for the Advancement of Teaching, 1929), 14–15. George R. Wallace, *Princeton Sketches: The Story of Nassau Hall* (New York: Putnam's Sons, 1894), 77. Per Altherr, "Chucking the Old Apple," 35–36. Varnum Lansing Collins, *Princeton* (New York: Oxford University Press, 1914), 208. (The faculty admonished: "It appearing that a play at present much practised by the smaller boys among the students and by the grammar Scholars with balls and sticks in the back common of the College is in itself low and unbecoming gentlemen Students, and in as much as it is an exercise attended with great danger to the health by sudden and alternate heats and colds and as it tends by accidents almost unavoidable in that play to disfiguring and maiming those who are engaged in it for whose health and safety as well as improvement in Study as far as depends on our exertion we are accountable to their Parents & liable to be severely blamed for them: and in as much as there are many amusements both more honourable and more useful in which they are indulged Therefore the faculty think it incumbent on them to prohibit both the Students & grammar Scholars from using the play aforesaid.")

59 *Clearly bat-and-ball games:* "In General Assembly, Saturday, February 22, 1794. An act for the prevention of vice and immorality and of unlawful gaming and to restrain disorderly sports and dissipation" (Philadelphia, printed by T. Bradford, 1794). "Bullet" derives from the French *boulette,* which is a diminutive of boule, or ball, from the Old French and from the Latin *bulla*. Gambling at bullet play had been banned in Pennsylvania even earlier, by the 1779 "Act for the suppression of vice and immorality." A modern Irish game of road bowling is called, in the County Armagh term, *bullets* or *long bullets*.

60 The Book of Sports: Robin Carver, *The Book of Sports* (Boston: Lilly, Wait, Colman, and Holden, 1834), 37–40. William Clarke, *The Boy's and Girl's Book of Sports* (Providence: Cory & Daniels, 1835).

60 *In debunking:* Robert W. Henderson, "Baseball and Rounders," *Bulletin of the New York Public Library* (April 1939), 303–313.

60 *In 2001:* Edward Wong, "Baseball's Disputed Origin Is Traced Back, Back, Back," *New York Times,* July 8, 2001.

60 *The* National Advocate: *National Advocate,* April 25, 1823, 2.

61 *At some point:* "Notice, Republican General Committee," *National Advocate,* September 27, 1822, 2. "In consequence of the prevalence of the fever in the lower Wards, the stated meeting of the Republican General Committee, will be held at the *Retreat,* corner Broadway and Art-street, *(Jones')* on Thursday afternoon. . . ." That summer, Jones had placed an advertisement in the *National Advocate* of June 21, 1822.

61 *By May 14:* Card: "William Jones of the Retreat, Boadway, has removed thence to No. 27 James' street, and is now ready to entertain his friends and the public, in the general line of his business. . . ." *National Advocate,* May 19, 1823, 1.

62 *Jones may have been:* Such refreshments were sold at the Retreat from the time of its launch as a new hotel in 1821, when it was called Hyer's Retreat. ("THE RETREAT—NEW HOTEL. The subscriber begs leave to inform all those who wish to encourage him with their patronage, that the elegant house at the corner of Art street and Broadway, opposite Vauxhall, is now open for their reception. Gentlemen may be accommodated with Board by the week or month. He keeps a constant supply of Ice Cream, and parties may be accommodated with Coffee, Tea and Relishes of various descriptions. HEYER. N. B. The Retreat is opposite Vauxhall Garden. The proprietor has thought proper, with the advice of his friends, to issue a limited number of Tickets of Admission to this House, on the day of Mr. Guille's Ascension, at twenty-five cents each, to be had in refreshments, such as Ice Cream, Cake, Punch, Lemonade, &c. &c. *New-York Evening Post,* June 5, 1821.) I am indebted to George Thompson for this citation.

62 *Charles H. Haswell:* Charles Hayne Haswell, *Memoirs of an Octogenarian in New York* (New York: Harper and Brothers, 1896), 81–82.

62 *But New York baseball:* "Sporting Intelligence," *New-York Evening Post,* April 13, 1805, 3. Also, meeting announcements for the Diagoras in the *Daily Advertiser* for April 11–12, 1805.

63 *Of further interest:* Thomas M. Garrett, "A History of Pleasure Gardens in New York City, 1700–1865," unpublished doctoral dissertation, New York University, 1978, 143–157. The "Tyler's" cited in George Thompson's 1805 "bace" find went by several names: Brannon's Garden, New-York Garden, Gray's Garden, Washington Garden, Tyler's Garden, and Hogg's Garden. A pleasure resort since 1779, its site would be located today near the southwest corner of Spring and Hudson streets. It was known as Tyler's especially during the years in which it was leased by the actor Joseph Tyler, 1798–1806 (his sons managed the property in 1807–08).

63 *We know from:* "The Park, 1827," is a McSpedon & Baker lithograph published as the frontispiece to *Valentine's Manual for the Corporation of the City of New*

York (1855). In its depiction of City Hall Park there is a ball game in progress with a pitcher, batsman, a close-in catcher, two distant fielders and three spectators.

63 *When a schoolboy:* "Old Time Games," *Brooklyn Eagle,* May 11, 1888, 2.

64 *The* New-York Post-Boy: *New-York Post-Boy,* April 29, 1751.

64 *Another notable:* The location of the field was reported in *Royal Gazette,* September 6, 1780.

65 *Lonely gentlemen:* Abram C. Dayton, *Last Days of Knickerbocker Life* (New York: G. P. Putnam's Sons, 1897), 61. Also the "Young Bachelor's March," copyrighted by Firth, Hall & Pond, 1846. Its well-known composer and dance instructor, Allen Dodworth, dedicated the song to the members of the "Committee" of the "Young Bachelor's Society"; among those named was sporting writer Charles A. Peverelly.

65 *Apart from the ballroom:* Henry Collins Brown, *Valentine's Manual of Old New York,* Volume 5 (New York: Valentine's Manual Inc., 1921). "City Intelligence," *New York Herald,* December 1, 1849. "The Military Spirit in New York—The Target Companies on Thanksgiving Day," *New York Weekly Herald,* December 14, 1850, 397. Wesley Washington Pasko, "Target Companies in New York," *Old New York: A Journal Relating to the History and Antiquities of New York City,* vol. 1–2 (New York: W. W. Pasko, 1890), 294–295.

65 *A writer for:* "Letters from New York," *New Monthly Magazine* no. II, 282 (October 1829).

66 *Abram C. Dayton:* Abram C. Dayton, *Last Days of Knickerbocker Life* (New York: G. P. Putnam's Sons, 1897), 318.

66 *An ordinance: By-Laws and Ordinances of the Mayor, Aldermen, and Commonality of the City of New York.* Revised 1838–1839 (New York: William B. Townsend, 1839), 215.

66 *African-American youths:* Randall Brown, "Blood and Base Ball," *Base Ball* 3:1 (Spring 2009), 25.

66 *On October 24, 1840: The Colored American,* October 24, 1840. Per Randall Brown, ibid.

67 *Charles A. Peverelly:* Peverelly, *Book of American Pastimes,* 340.

67 *They had been preceded:* "Sporting Intelligence," *New York Herald,* November 11, 1845, 2.

67 *At auction in 1784:* William A. Mann, "The Elysian Fields of Hoboken, New Jersey," *Base Ball* 1:1 (Spring 2007), 80.

67 *A newspaper reported: New-York Gazette & General Advertiser,* October 5, 1802. Per Phelps-Stokes. Daniel Mendoza (1764–1836) was a champion English pugilist.

68 *To promote his real estate:* Mann, "Elysian Fields," 83.

68 *Landscape historian:* Ibid., 82.

68 *In 1844:* George Templeton Strong, *The Diary of George Templeton Strong* (New York: Macmillan, 1952), 236.

68 *From the* Anglo American: "Cricketers' Chronicle," *The Anglo American,* May 2, 1846, 46. I am indebted for this citation to Bill Wagner, in an email of February 15, 2009.

69 *All the same:* W. E. Baxter, *America and the Americans* (London: George Routledge and Co., 1855), 99. Per Foster Rhea Dulles, *America Learns to Play: A History of Popular Recreation, 1607–1940.*

69 *Ralph Waldo Emerson:* Ralph Waldo Emerson, *The Conduct of Life* (Boston: Houghton Mifflin, 1860), 115.

69 *As Henry Chadwick wrote:* Henry Chadwick, "The Ancient History of Base Ball," *Ball Players' Chronicle,* July 18, 1867, 4. Blaine's *Encyclopaedia of Rural Sports* (London: Longman, Orme, Brown, Green, and Longmans, 1840), 131.

69 *W. H. Van Cott:* Letter in *New York Tribune,* December 19, 1854, 5.

70 *On a visit:* John Mayfield, *The New Nation 1800–1845* (New York: Hill & Wang, 1982), 68.

70 *In the years:* Ibid.

70 *In common-law practice:* Ibid., 75–76.

70 *Of the New York Ball Club:* Peverelly, *Book of American Pastimes,* 342–343.

71 *With this setup:* Henry Chadwick, *Beadle's Dime Base-Ball Player,* 6

71 *As Wheaton observed:* "How Baseball Began: A Member of the Gotham Club of Fifty Years Ago Tells About It," *San Francisco Daily Examiner,* November 27, 1887, 14.

71 *It is perhaps:* The original rules of September 23, 1845, appear not to have existed in printed form but were reproduced in Peverelly. The first publication of these rules was in *By-laws and Rules of the Knickerbocker Base Ball Club: Adopted September 23d, 1845, Revised, April 1848* (New York: W. H. B. Smith, 1848).

72 *This may refer:* Fred Ivor-Campbell, "Knickerbocker Base Ball: The Birth and Infancy of the Modern Game," *Base Ball* 1:2 (Fall 2007), 56.

74 *Larry McCray:* Personal communication, September 1, 2009.

74 *As Doc Adams recalled:* "Dr. D. L. Adams," 3.

74 *Cholera had killed:* Regarding the constant apprehension of cholera's return at that time, "leases contained a provision for the reduction of rent in the event of the depression of business consequent on a cholera visitation." See "Epidemics in New-York," *New York Times,* February 16, 1896. Data on mortality in 1832 and 1849 from *Appendix C to the Report of the General Board of Health on the Epidemic Cholera of 1848 & 1849. Report of Dr. [John] Sutherland, Abstract of Report [Appendix C] by James Wynne, M.D.* (London: George E. Eyre and William Spottiswoode for H.M.S.O., 1852), 38–39.

76 *A rule observed:* Albert Spalding Baseball Collections. Plunkett thus fined Dupignac in a game of April 26, 1849. But the first of many Knicks to be penalized "for improper language" in the prior four seasons was John O'Brien, who was fined six-and-a-quarter cents for (a "bit") swearing in the Knicks' third intramural contest of October 1845.

77 *The Knickerbockers played:* Ibid.

77 *In a casual aside:* Tom Melville, *The Tented Field: A History of Cricket in America* (Bowling Green, OH: Bowling Green State University Popular Press, 1998), 168.

77 *Research more than: True Sun,* October 13, 1845, 2.

78 *A response to:* The first recorded single-wicket match took place in Surrey in 1726. The *London Evening Post* of August 27 carried an advertisement for a single-wicket match between players Perry (of London) and Piper (of Hampton, Middlesex). The venue was Moulsey Hurst, near Molesey in Surrey. "The oldest form of the game is probably single wicket, which consists of one batsman defending one wicket, but this has become obsolete, though it was very popular in the time when matches were played for money with only one or two, or perhaps four or five, players on a side. Matches between an unequal number of players are still sometimes arranged, but mainly in the case of local sides against touring teams, or 'colts' playing against eleven experienced cricketers." *Encyclopaedia Britannica,* 11th ed., vol. VII (1910), 437.

78 *We know that: New-York Post-Boy,* April 29, 1751.

79 *In single wicket:* Major Rowland Francis Bowen, *Cricket: A History of Its Growth and Development Throughout the World* (London: Eyre and Spottiswoode, 1970), 42.

79 *Further, the expectation:* "Dr. D. L. Adams," 3.

79 *Until Randall Brown's:* Brown, "How Baseball Began," 51–54.

79 *An eight-page pamphlet:* Irving Leitner, *Baseball: Diamond in the Rough* (New York: Abelard-Schuman, 1972), 39–42.

80 *And yet, in an account: Porter's Spirit of the Times,* September 20, 1856.

81 *In other words:* "In the statute acre, a square perch is 272.25 square feet, and the acre, therefore, is equal to 272.25 x 160=43560 square feet, = 4880 square yards." My computation comes to 4,840 yards, but the point is the same. William Laxton, *The Civil Engineer and Architect's Journal. Scientific and Railway Gazette,* vol. IX (London: William Laxton, 1846), 357. The cricket pitch of twenty-two yards is precisely equal to an "Edmund Gunter chain," as devised in 1620 and which distance, John Nyren attested in 1832, he knew to be that of the cricket pitch as far back as 1682. One acre not only is the square with sides of 84 paces but also, as traditionally understood, one chain times 10 chains (at 43,560 square feet, admittedly an approximate measure). The larger point is that playing-field measures come from agricultural ones.

82 *Crucially, perhaps: Porter's Spirit of the Times,* December 6, 1856, 229.

83 *This is the year:* "How Baseball Began," 14.

83 *When the Knickerbockers:* Peverelly, *Pastimes,* 346–347.

83 *However, on the day:* [William Caudwell] *Weekly Mercury,* April 2, 1854. *Mercury Sporting Guide for 1889 Containing the History and Records of Baseball, schedules of games to be played by the National League, American Association, International League, Atlantic Association* (New York: Sunday Mercury Print), 2.

CHAPTER FOUR: THE CAULDRON OF BASEBALL

85 *Compared to rural:* Ralph Waldo Emerson, "Manners," in *Essays,* Second Series, (Boston: Phillips, Sampson & Co., 1850), 127.

86 *The scenario:* James Whyte Davis, "Uncle Sam's Sport," or "Ball Days," his composition to the tune of "Uncle Sam's Farm," sung at a banquet of the Knickerbocker Base Ball Club for the Excelsior of Brooklyn, August 20, 1858. *The Ball Player's Chronicle,* January 9, 1868.

87 *Chowder was:* Herbert Asbury, *Ye Olde Fire Laddies* (New York: Knopf, 1930), 103.

89 *In the Roman circus:* Edmund Kerchever Chambers, *The Mediaeval Stage, Volume 1* (London: Oxford Clarendon, 1903), 20. "A number of documents deal with the choice of a *pantomimus* to represent the *prasini* or 'Greens,' [circus factions were Blues vs. Greens and Reds vs. Whites] and show that the rivalry of the theatre-factions [like ball clubs in our era] remained as fierce as it had been in the days of Bathyllus and Pylades."

89 *In the wars:* Johann Huizinga, *The Waning of the Middle Ages* (London: Edward Arnold & Co., 1924), 87.

90 *The chowder:* Richard H. Thornton: *An American Glossary: Being an Attempt to Illustrate Certain Americanisms, Etc.,* Volume I (Philadelphia: J. B. Lippincott, 1912), 173: e.g., 1836 [The Mayor] is off to Long Branch, to enjoy *otium cum dignitate,* or in other parlance eat chowder and drink claret.—Phila. Public Ledger, Aug. 2, 1838. I was duly initiated into the mysteries and merits of "a chowder. We had 'clam chowder' and 'fish chowder.'——E. C. Wines, 'A Trip to Boston,' 79, 1840. The chowder-builder and the poet must alike be born. ——'Discursive Thoughts on Chowder,' *Knickerbocker Magazine,* xvi, 26 (July)." As to the Washington Market Chowder Club, see "The Military Spirit in New York——The Target Companies on Thanksgiving Day," *New York Weekly Herald,* December 14, 1850, 397; also, *The Subterranean,* October 25, 1845, 2 ("Three different parties of whole-souled fellows are going to express their gratitude to Heaven for its manifold blessings, to-morrow, by playing ball and eating chowder." The Washington Market Chowder Club token sold as lot 2127 at the Baltimore Coin and Currency Convention, November 8–11, 2006.

90 *Why was this Northern eatery:* When Carlisle and partner Silas Chickering purchased the saloon in 1842 they advertised this fact, suggestively, in the New Orleans *Daily Picayune* of July 16. ("*New York Advertisement.* MAGNOLIA LUNCH. CHICKERING & CARLISLE beg leave to inform their New Orleans and other friends that they have purchased that old and favorite resort of Southerners, The Magnolia Lunch, on the corner of Chambers Street and Broadway, where they will be always ready to furnish them with every delicacy which the New York market affords. N.B. handsomely furnished private rooms for parties."

92 *The Magnolia Ball Club:* 1850 Federal census and *Subterranean,* December 20, 1845; classified ad for 1845 Holiday Ball of the "Original Empire Club," at Tammany Hall, Tuesday, December 30.

93 *Offered as Lot 1600:* http://www.lelands.com/bid.aspx?lot=1600&auctionid=212. Link since removed.

94 *Built in the early: Jamestown Journal,* May 28, 1834.

94 *By 1838, William Fairthorne:* New York City Directory, 1839. Federal census, 1850.

94 *On February 17, 1839:* "Police," *New-York Spectator,* October 17, 1839.

94 *The auction-house description:* Classified advertisement, February 6–9, 1844, *New York Herald.* The ad describes the actual event for which the Magnolia card provided admission. It read: "**THE FIRST ANNUAL BALL** of the New York Magnolia Ball Club will take place at National Hall, Canal st. on Friday evening, Feb. 9th, inst. The Club pledge themselves that no expense or exertions shall be spared to render this (their first) Ball worthy the patronage of their friends. The Ball Room will be splendidly decorated with the insignia of the Club. Brown's celebrated Band is engaged for the occasion. Tickets $1, to be had of the undersigned, and at the bar of National Hall. JOSEPH CARLISLE, Chairman. PETER H. GRAHAM, Secretary, f6 4t*cc." That Carlisle would be the ball's chairman comes as no surprise, but the new name appearing above, that of Peter H. Graham, may point to a fresh area of inquiry. Speeding eight years forward, we come across three notices in the *Herald* about the reorganization of the Unionist Whigs, no longer known as the Knickerbockers. Silas Chickering, Carlisle's partner in the Magnolia Lunch, is cited as a former president of the group and the two secretaries are Peter H. Graham and . . . Louis F. Wadsworth, the formidable first baseman and mysterious outcast from the Knickerbocker Base Ball Club.

95 *As Edward van Every wrote:* Edward van Every, *Sins of New York as "Exposed" by the Police Gazette* (New York: Frederick Stokes, 1930), 8; quoting from undated *Police Gazette* item.

96 *After drinking:* "Outrage," *Brooklyn Eagle,* October 19, 1844, 2. This story was picked up from the *New York News.* A "coon song" in this 1840s context was probably a good-naturedly if undeniably racist "Ethiopian delineator" melody, like "Old Zip Coon." "Ole Zip Coon he is a larned scholar (x3), Sings possum up a gum tree an coony in a holler." This song, similar to "Turkey in the Straw," was popularized by George Washington Dixon, a mulatto who ran a flash paper (*The Polyanthos*), thus predictably served a term in prison for libel, and mounted a mock campaign for president in 1844.

96 *Even Henry David Thoreau:* Bradford Torrey and Francis H. Allen, eds., *The Journal of Henry David Thoreau,* vol. 5 (Boston: Houghton Mifflin, 1906), 411.

97 *The* New York Morning Express*:* "Outrageous Assault"—that is how the story is headed in the *New York Morning Express* but it was also printed in the *New-York Daily Tribune* on the same date, September 6, 1848, 2. George Thompson posted this unusual story to the 19th Century Baseball Committee listserv of the Society for American Baseball Research (SABR) on May 3, 2009.

97 *On May 26, 1851: Brooklyn Eagle,* May 27, 1851, 2.

98 *New York's* Journal of Commerce: "Dreadful Riot and Loss of Life at Hoboken," *Liberator* (from *New York Herald*), 91. "The Hoboken Riot—Its Causes and Results," *New York Herald,* June 7, 1851. *North American and United States Gazette,* May 28, 1851. The *Tribune* reported that before the riot "beer flowed in torrents from the barrels on tap, down hundreds of thirsty throats." Another newspaper reported that "all this time the women and children were screaming with terror and running in all directions from the showers of stones that were flying."

98 *Less than a year later:* "Melancholy Accident," *Brooklyn Eagle,* March 4, 1852, 2.

98 *The bottom of the scoresheet:* Albert Spalding Baseball Collections. (Note that in the term "Dutch Fight," the Knickerbocker scorer was using the popular term for Germans [Deutsches].)

99 *It is offered: British Champion* of September 8, 1743, No. 63, per *The Gentleman's Magazine,* London, September 1743.

100 *As Anthony Bateman observed:* Anthony Bateman, " 'More Mighty than the Bat, the Pen . . .': Culture, Hegemony and the Literaturisation of Cricket," *Sport in History* 23, no. 1 (Summer 2003), 6.

101 *Those who live:* Alexis de Tocqueville, *Democracy in America,* Vol. II, Translated By Henry Reeve, ESQ. (Cambridge, MA: Sever and Francis, 1862), 190. In earlier times, play and pledge, *plezha* and *plega,* were perceived to be inextricable—and, like the dance, the ballad, and the game (all derived from *ballare,* the Greek for ball), were all regarded as sublimated sex. The Oxford English Dictionary records usages of the word "game" to mean amorous sport or lechery as early as 1230; to illustrate a perhaps more familiar instance, Shakespeare wrote, in *Troilus and Cressida* in 1606, "Set them downe For sluttish spoyles of opportunitie; and daughters of the game." In recent memory, a television advertiser touted its hair coloring product as a way for graying men to "get back in the game." Early prohibitions, especially against games involving bats or balls, tended to the extreme: in England c. 1635, Richard Allen's preaching at Ditcheat convinced a parishioner that "a maypole was an idol, and setting up of him [!] was idolatrie" and that "it was a greater sin for a man to play at Bowles on the Sabboath daie, then [*sic*] to lie with another mans wiffe on a weeke daie."

101 *As I wrote:* John Thorn and Pete Palmer, *The Hidden Game of Baseball* (New York: Doubleday, 1984), 9.

101 *In 1856:* Henry Chadwick, *Game of Base Ball,* 10.

102 *No ball club:* Henry Chadwick, "Matamoras Grand March" (Louisville and Cincinnati: W. C. Peters, 1846); "The Black Quadrilles" (Brooklyn: P. K. Weizel, 1854); "Hazel Dell" (Brooklyn: Wm Hall & Son, 1855); "The Operatic Serenaders" (New York: Firth & Pond, 1855); etc. For the composer/arranger's handwritten list of forty-five "Piano Forte Compositions and Arrangements by Henry Chadwick," see: http://www.robertedwardauctions.com/auction/2007/624.html.

103 *That honor would go:* Jack M. Doyle, Albert Spalding Scrapbooks, BA SCR 42.

103 *He would have played ball:* "A New Library Building," *New York Times,* January 21, 1878, 5.

103 *There were, he declared:* Jack M. Doyle, Albert Spalding Scrapbooks.

104 *Porter pitched his paper:* William T. Porter, *Spirit of the Times,* May 11, 1835. Two short-lived predecessors were *Annals of the Turf* (1826), published by George W. Jeffreys in North Carolina, and the *Farmer's, Mechanic's, Manufacturer's and Sportsman's Magazine,* published briefly (March 1826–February 1827) in New York. J. Betts, "Sporting Journalism in Nineteenth-Century America," *American Quarterly* 5, no. 1 (1953), 39–56. For the scruffy set, a sporting paper meant a sensationalistic sheet like the *Whip,* which, according to its editor George B. Wooldridge, was "devoted to the Sports of the Ring, the turf, and city life—such as sprees, larks, criminal conspiracy, seductions, rapes." Other scurrilous weeklies of the day included the *Flash,* the *Rake,* and the *National Police Gazette,* first published in 1845 by George Wilkes, whose path would later intersect with that of Porter. Another early 1830s competitor to Skinner and Porter was the sumptuous (and thus not surprisingly short-lived) *New York Sporting Magazine and Annals of the American and English Turf,* published by Cadwallader R. Colden with colored aquatints. Colden had written for Skinner's publication under the pseudonym "An Old Turfman." His own venture, launched in March 1833, ceased publication a year later, but it presaged the illustrated sporting papers to come. For a broader discussion of this topic, see John Thorn, "The *New York Clipper* and Sporting Weeklies of Its Time," *Base Ball* 3:1 (Spring 2009), 107–113.

CHAPTER FIVE: WAR IN HEAVEN

105 *Counting them up:* Paul Macfarlane and Leonard Gettelson, eds., *Daguerreotypes of Great Stars of Baseball* (St. Louis: Sporting News), 36. Based on Albert Spalding Baseball Collections, Knickerbocker Base Ball Club of New York Game Books, b. October 6, 1845–1856 at the New York Public Library.

107 *The heyday of open:* Frederick Van Wyck, *Recollections of an Old New Yorker* (New York: Liveright, 1932), 114.

107 *Late in life:* Henry Chadwick, "Selections from the *Mail,*" *New-York Tribune,* January 9, 1893, 5.

108 *In August 1898:* "Married for Fifty Years," *New-York Tribune,* August 14, 1898, A4.

108 *After reading the notice:* Letter from Henry Chadwick to Daniel Lucius "Doc" Adams of August 16, 1898. Yale Miscellaneous Manuscripts Collection, Manuscripts and Archives at the Yale University Library, Misc MSS A. Box 1, Folder 4.

109 *The Marylebone Club:* "Laws of Cricket, the Marylebone Club," *Anglo American,* July 22, 1843, 303.

109 *Doc Adams:* "Convention of Base Ball Clubs," *New York Herald,* January 22, 1857; "Our National Sports: The Game of Base Ball, etc.," *New York Herald,* January 23, 1857.

109 *The* Spirit *declared:* "On Dits in Sporting Circles: Convention of Base Ball Clubs," *Spirit of the Times,* January 3, 1857, 558.

110 *Many of the proposed:* "Base Ball Convention," *New York Herald,* March 2, 1857; *Porter's Spirit,* March 7, 1857, 5.

110 *On the day:* Bob Lively, Letter to Editor, *Porter's Spirit of the Times,* December 27, 1856, 276–277.

112 *Chadwick wrote to the editor:* "Baseball's Origin," *The Sun,* May 14, 1905, 8.

113 *The unnamed writer: New York Clipper,* April 3, 1858, 396.

114 *For President James Buchanan:* Joseph Willson was born at Canton, St Lawrence County, New York, in 1825. He studied portrait painting with Salathiel Ellis, followed him to New York in 1842, and began cutting cameos and die sinking. In 1848 he removed to Washington, under the patronage of the Honorable R. H. Gillet, member of Congress from St Lawrence County, New York, associated himself in business with Salathiel Ellis, and made the reverses of the Indian medals of Presidents Fillmore and Pierce. In 1851 he went to Italy to study sculpture, and remained abroad three years. He died, September 8, 1857. "Cameo Portraits," *Daily National Intelligence* (Washington, DC), October 25, 1847. Atticus, "From Italy," *New York Times,* July 3, 1854. "Studios of American Artists," *Home Journal,* January 26, 1856, 1. Also, Georgia S. Chamberlain, "Joseph Willson, American Medalist," *Numismatist,* LXVIII (November 1955), 1185–1187. Francis Paul Prucha, *Indian Peace Medals in American History* (Lincoln: University of Nebraska Press, 1976).

115 *In late 1856:* Frank Pidgeon, in January 1857, per Peverelly, *Book of American Pastimes,* 430–432.

116 *Yet the Fashion Race Course Games:* "The Great Base Ball Match," *Spirit of the Times,* July 24, 1858, 288. Spalding, *America's National Game,* 73. The bound outs included fair and foul catches.

117 *In the announcement:* "Grand Base Ball Demonstration," *Brooklyn Eagle,* July 10, 1858, 3.

117 *While the attendance: New York Atlas,* July 25, 1858. Per Robert H. Schaefer, "The Great Base Ball Match of 1858," *NINE,* 14:1 (Fall 2005), 47–66.

117 *It is needless to say:* "The Great Base Ball Match," *New York Clipper,* July 24, 1858, 110.

118 *Louis F. Wadsworth:* "X," "Base Ball Sketches No. 3," *Porter's Spirit of the Times,* November 7, 1857, 148.

118 *Before the [first] game began:* "The Great Base Ball Match of 1858."

118 *Chadwick, describing the game:* "Sporting Reminiscences," *Brooklyn Eagle,* July 16, 1873, 4.

119 *However, Chadwick revised:* In Spalding, *America's National Game,* 73–74.

120 *I suppose that:* Frank Pidgeon, Letter to the Editor, *Porter's Spirit of the Times,* March 26, 1858, 52.

120 *His statement prompted: New York Clipper,* March 19, 1859, 386.

120 Porter's Spirit *chimed in: Porter's Spirit,* March 19, 1859, 35.

120 *Pidgeon responded: Porter's Spirit,* March 26, 1859, 52.

121 *In any event:* "The Game of Base Ball with the English Cricketers," *New York Tribune,* October 18, 1859, 5.

121 *As it was:* From an Occasional Correspondent [in fact Karl Marx], "The American Question in England, *New-York Daily Tribune,* October 11, 1861, 6. "London, Sept. 18, 1861. Mrs. Beecher Stowe's letter to Lord Shaftesbury, whatever its intrinsic merit may be, has done a great deal of good, by forcing the anti-Northern organs of the London press to speak out and lay before the general public the ostensible reasons for their hostile tone against the North, and their ill-concealed sympathies with the South, which looks rather strange on the part of people affecting an utter horror of Slavery. Their first and main grievance is that the present American war is "not one for the abolition of Slavery," and that, therefore, the high-minded Britisher, used to undertake wars of his own, and interest himself in other people's wars only on the basis of "broad humanitarian principles," cannot be expected to feel any sympathy with his Northern cousins. . . . The Confederate Congress boasted that its new-fangled constitution, as distinguished from the Constitution of the Washingtons, Jeffersons, and Adams's, had recognized for the first time Slavery as a thing good in itself, a bulwark of civilization, and a divine institution. If the North professed to fight but for the Union, the South gloried in rebellion for the supremacy of Slavery. If Anti-Slavery and idealistic England felt not attracted by the profession of the North, how came it to pass that it was not violently repulsed by the cynical confessions of the South?"

122 *English cricketer:* William M. Rankin, *New York Clipper,* August 5, 1911 (citing the observation of cricketer John Lillywhite). The event Lillywhite witnessed occurred in a game between Americans and Englishmen played at Hoboken, N.J., in 1859 or 1860, when Creighton clean bowled five of the English wickets in six successive balls, "a feat which has been rarely performed by anyone else in a match of any note at all" (*New York Clipper Annual,* 1891, 34).

123 *Pete O'Brien:* Creighton posed for a photographer in the backswing of his underhand motion; the image is preserved as the front of a *carte de visite* issued after his death. Glued to the back of the card was a tattered and torn biographical note, the source of the Pete O'Brien quotation cited. Mark Rucker and I found his card in the archives of Culver Pictures in 1983.

123 *The* Troy Daily Whig: "Base Ball," *Troy Daily Whig,* July 3, 1860, 3. I am indebted to Craig Waff for this citation.

123 *The* Clipper *described:* "Third Grand Match at Base Ball: The Game Broken Up by Rowdies; A Drawn Game," *New York Clipper,* September 1, 1860, 154.

124 *After the disgusted Excelsiors:* Henry Chadwick, *Beadle's Dime Base-Ball Player: Comprising the Proceedings of the March Conventions of 1872. Together with the New Rules Adopted, a List of Prominent Professional Players, Official Record and Club Averages of 1871, and Diagram of a Base-Ball Field* (New York: Beadle and Co., 1872). In its copious averages, this edition of the guide provides "BEST

AVERAGES SINCE 1858." Only one player ever recorded a season with an average of outs per game of zero—Creighton in 1862.

124 *John Chapman:* Alfred Henry Spink, *National Game,* 128. Spink credits the Chapman quote to "a recent article in the *Boston Magazine.*"

125 *His brief obituary notice:* "Death of a Base Ball Player," *New York Times,* October 22, 1862.

125 *Obsequies included:* Creighton *carte de visite.*

125 *According to a contemporary account:* Albert Spalding Baseball Collections, Chadwick Scrapbooks, vol. 5 (*Clipper,* 1862, undated, 293).

126 *According to the* New York Times: "Out-Door Sports," *New York Times,* July 7, 1866, 8.

127 *The New York game:* "The Protoball Chronologies: Ballplaying in the Civil War Camps, a Working Chronology, managed by Larry McCray and online at http://www.retrosheet.org/Protoball/CivilWar.htm.

127 *The Mutuals, fresh:* "Out-Door Sports," *New York Times,* September 29, 1865, 8.

128 *His sincere confession:* " 'Hippodrome' Tactics in Base Ball," *New York Clipper,* November 11, 1865, 242.

129 *Fred. Douglass: New York Clipper,* July 13, 1867, per Randall Brown, "Blood and Base Ball," *Base Ball* 3:1 (Spring 2009), 34.

130 *As Pythian secretary:* Philadelphia, Dec. 18, 1867, "To the President & Members of the Pythian B. B. C." Leon Gardner Collection, American Negro Historical Society Papers, at the Historical Society of Pennsylvania.

130 The Ball Players' Chronicle: Henry Chadwick, ed. *The Ball Player's Chronicle* (December 19, 1867), 2.

131 *The 1870 New York:* Henry Chadwick, *New York Clipper,* November 19, 1870, 258. "Base-Ball Association of New York State," *Wilkes' Spirit of the Times,* November 19, 1870, 212. ("Mr. Barnum, of the Gotham Club, moved to suspend the rules for the purpose of admitting the clubs last before mentioned to full membership, which was amended, on motion of Mr. Macdiarmid, of the Star Club, so as to provide that, in case any of these clubs should be composed of gentlemen of color, then their membership in the association to be considered as forfeited. This amendment called up a smile all around, but was unanimously adopted.")

CHAPTER SIX: A NATIONAL PASTIME

134 *But the National Association: Chadwick's Base Ball Manual for 1871* (New York: American News Co., 1871).

134 *The First American Chess Congress:* William R. Wheaton, "The Pacific Chess Tournament Will Commence," *San Francisco Bulletin,* March 17, 1858.

136 *I began to watch:* W. A. Cummings, "How I Pitched the First Curve," *Baseball Magazine,* August 1908.

136 *A notice:* Marshall D. Wright, *The National Association of Base Ball Players, 1857–1870* (Jefferson, NC: McFarland, 2000), 139–140.

137 *Recording the tour:* Henry Chadwick, *Ball Players' Chronicle,* commencing July 18, 1867, 1; continues in the July 25, August 1, and August 8 issues, concluding August 15 with final player averages.

138 *Rockford was led:* Albert G. Spalding, *America's National Game,* 109–112.

140 *In January: Ball Player's Chronicle,* January 2, 1868, 4.

140 *By the time March: Ball Players' Chronicle,* March 5, 1868, 77.

141 *Writing about club tours:* Henry Chadwick, *De Witt Base Ball Guide for 1869* (New York: Robert M. De Witt), 90.

141 *The* Utica Express *advised: Utica Daily Observer,* May 5, 1870.

141 *When the Olympics: Brooklyn Eagle,* September 20, 1869, 5. I am indebted for this citation to David Dyte.

142 *In a further feint: New York Clipper,* October 8, 1870. "The game was played on the 20th inst., on the Union Grounds, Boston, Mass., and resulted in a victory for the sons of Ham, who 'fought nobly' for their cherished title, outplaying their fair-faced friends at every point of the game, especially in the field." I am indebted for this citation to Randall Brown.

143 *Here are the fabled:* Lee Allen, "Baseball's Immortal Red Stockings," *Bulletin of the Historical and Philosophical Society of Ohio* 19(1961), 191–204.

143 *This term famously:* "Letter VI, to Calvisius," *The Letters of Pliny the Consul,* Translated by W. Melmoth, Esq. (London: W. Suttaby, Crosby & Co., & Scatcherd and Letterman, 1810), 358.

144 *George A. Wiltsee:* Lee Allen, "Baseball's Immortal Red Stockings," 192, 194.

145 *The umpire called:* Ibid., 197.

146 *George Wright had been:* Al Spink, "Memories of Old White Stockings," *Auburn Citizen* (New York), November 3, 1921, 9.

146 *But defeat came:* Ibid., 200. For playing in this game of June 14, 1870, each Atlantic player took home $364, according to John Chapman in Spink's *National Game,* 8. Attendance was over 9,000 at fifty cents a head.

147 *On November 21, 1870:* Allen, "Baseball's Immortal Red Stockings," *The Bulletin,* 202–203.

148 *On the rainy evening:* "National Association of Professional Base-Ball Players," *New York Times,* March 18, 1871.

149 *On or before April 13:* Albert Spalding Baseball Collections. Harry Wright Papers, reproduced in Irving Leitner, *Baseball: Diamond in the Rough* (New York: Abelard-Schuman, 1972), 104. George J. E. Mayer is signed in print as "GEO. J.E. MAYERS."

150 *In 1865, the thirteen-year-old:* Adrian C. Anson, *A Ball Player's Career: Being the Personal Experiences and Reminiscences of Adrian C. Anson, Late Manager and Captain of the Chicago Base Ball Club* (Chicago: Era Publishing Co., 1900), 15–16.

150 *In this rare survivor:* Roger H. Van Bolt, " 'Cap' Anson's First Contract," *Annals of Iowa* 31 (April 1953), 617. The contract is held by the Illinois State Historical Association. Precise full transcription follows:

Memorandum of Agreement: made and entered into this 31st day of March A.D. 1871, by and between John P. Manny, John C. Barbour, Henry W. Price, Hosmer P. Holland and Jerome C. Roberts of the City of Rockford, Illinois, party of the first part; and Adrian C. Anson of Marshalltown, Iowa, party of the second part:

Whereas divers residents of said city of Rockford have associated themselves and contributed a common fund for the organization and maintenance of a first class base ball club, to be known and called "The Forest City Base Ball Club of Rockford Illinois";

And whereas the said party of the second part, being desirous of playing in said club; has represented to the party of the first part that he is a first class base ball player and possessed of the skill, and physically competent, to play said game as a member of a first class club;

Now therefore, this Agreement Witnesseth: That the said party of the second part, in consideration of the premises and of the promises and agreements of the party of the first part, hereinafter expressed, has, and does, covenant and agree, to and with said party of the first part, to play the game of base ball with said Forest City Base Ball Club, and in any position, he may be therein assigned by the Directors of said Club, for and during the season of A.D. 1871, to wit: from April 15th A.D. 1871, to and including October 15th A.D. 1871.

And in further consideration of the premises said party of the second part promises and agrees to keep and observe the following rules of conduct and discipline, viz:

To use his best efforts to advance the interests of said Club, by cheerfull, prompt and respectfull obedience of the Directions and requirements of the Directors thereof, or of any person by said Directors placed in authority over him, as well as the by laws of said Club;

To abstain from the use of Alcoholic Liquors: unless medically prescribed, and to conduct himself, both off and on the Ball Ground, in all things like a gentleman;

To report promptly for duty at the grounds of the Club for all games, and for practice at the hours designated there for by the officers of the Club, and upon the grounds, to abstain from profane language, scuffling and light conduct, and to discourage the same in others.

To practise at least two and a half hours per day. On each and every practise day of the Club, and at all times both in games and at practise, to use his best endeavours to perfect himself in play. Always bearing in mind that the Object in view in every game is to win.

And in further consideration of the premises said party of the second part promises and agrees that he will not make, or procure to be made for him, or in any [way] be concerned or interested in, any bet or wager upon the result of any game, or upon the playing of any member of the club, or upon anything connected with any game, in which said Forest City Club, may engage during the time of his engagement hereunder.

And in consideration of the premises, said party of the first part promise and agree to pay said party of the second part the sum of Sixty six and two third ($66 2/3) Dollars per month for each and every month of the time he may play with said Forest City Club, payable as follows; to wit: Sixty Six and two third ($66 2/3) Dollars on the 1st day of June A. D. 1871, and sixty six and two third ($66 2/3) Dollars on the first day of each and every month thereafter of the term of his employment, as aforesaid, the balance due to be fully paid on the 1st day of November A. D. 1871.

A. C. Anson [signed]
J. C. Barbour [signed]
Hosmer P. Holland [signed]

151 *In what the Fort Wayne:* "The Sporting World," *Chicago Tribune,* May 5, 1871, 4.

153 *Kelly was:* John Shiffert, *Base Ball in Philadelphia* (Jefferson, NC: McFarland, 2006), 184–187.

153 *Chadwick observed:* Henry Chadwick, *De Witt Base Ball Guide for 1874* (New York: Robert M. De Witt, 1874), 14.

154 *The modern English game:* "Bats, Balls and Mallets," *New York Times,* April 30, 1871, 3.

154 *Harry was followed:* Boston city directories, various. George Wright and Charlie Gould started in 1871 at 18 Boylston ("cigars, tobacco, &c. and base ball goods"). Wright went solo in 1873; in 1874 relocated to 591 Washington. In 1875, store is at 39 Eliot, in 1878 at 790 Washington. Wright joined with Henry Ditson in 1879–80; first mention of "Wright & Ditson" in city directory is 1880, at 580 Washington. Harry Wright in 1879 formed Wright, Howland & Mahn sporting goods firm.

155 *Years later:* Albert G. Spalding, *America's National Game* (New York: American Sports Publishing, 1911), 199–200.

155 *Spalding, you've no business:* Ibid., 201–203.

156 *When word leaked: Worcester Spy,* 1875, per Gerald Astor, "Founding Fathers," *Baseball Hall of Fame 50th Anniversary Book* (New York: Prentice Hall Press, 1988).

156 *"Spalding," he said:* Spalding, *America's National Game,* 208.

156 *In "Interview":* "Sporting News: Base-Ball, An Interview with Mr. Spalding," Special Correspondence, *Chicago Tribune,* November 28, 1875, 13.

156 *After reviewing the prospects:* Ibid.

157 *The reporter added:* Ibid.

157 *Spalding then continued:* Ibid.

CHAPTER SEVEN: THE BIG IDEA

160 *He had been on his latest job:* "SPORTING, etc." *Chicago Daily Tribune,* October 24, 1875, 12. "Lewis Meacham," *Chicago Daily Tribune,* October 3, 1878, 8.

161 *After detailing a plan:* Ibid., 12.

161 *As Spalding later wrote:* "In the Field Papers," A. G. Spalding, *The Cosmopolitan; a Monthly Illustrated Magazine* (October 1889), 607.

162 *In another* Tribune *article:* "Sporting Notes; Some Further Account of the Formation of the National League, etc." *Chicago Daily Tribune,* February 7, 1876, 7.

163 *In an earlier day:* Harry Wright to Nick Young, May 12, 1873. Albert Spalding Baseball Collections. Harry Wright Papers, per David Quentin Voigt, *American Baseball: From Gentleman's Sport to the Commissioner System,* 42.

163 *Finally, to preempt:* "The Diamond Squared: And an Honest Base-Ball Association Born into the World," *Chicago Tribune,* February 4, 1876, 5.

163 *Chadwick's response:* Henry Chadwick, "National League of Professional Clubs: A Startling Coup d'Etat," *New York Clipper,* February 12, 1876.

164 *The Philadelphia White Stocking:* "Sports and Pastimes," *Brooklyn Daily Eagle,* February 15, 1876, 1. "Sports and Pastimes," *Brooklyn Daily Eagle,* March 4, 1876, 2. "Sports and Pastimes," *Brooklyn Eagle,* April 6, 1876, 1.

164 *The Mutuals:* Preston D. Orem, *Baseball 1845–1881* (Altadena, CA: self-published, 1961), 264–265.

165 *Louisville had endured:* "Cussed Crookedness," *Louisville Courier-Journal,* November 3, 1877, per Dean Sullivan, ed., *Early Innings: A Documentary History of Baseball 1825–1908* (Lincoln: University of Nebraska Press), 101–110.

166 *I wanted to get home:* "Devlin (from the *Chicago Tribune*)," *St. Louis Globe-Democrat,* November 12, 1876, 7.

166 *The* Louisville Courier-Journal. "Cussed Crookedness," 101–110.

TESTIMONY OF GEORGE HALL.

About three or four weeks after Al. Nichols joined the Louisville club, he made me a proposition to assist in throwing League games, and I said to him, "I'll have nothing to do with any League games." This proposition was made before the club went on its last Eastern trip. He never made the proposition about League games but once. In Pittsburgh he made me a proposition to throw the Allegheny game, and I agreed to it. He promised to divide with me what he received from his friend in New York, who was betting on the games. Nichols and I were to throw the game by playing poorly. While in Chicago, on the club's last Western trip, I received a telegram from Nichols, stating that he was $80 in the hole, and asking how he could get out. I told Chapman that this dispatch was from my brother-in-law who lived in Baltimore. I did not reply to the dispatch.

Devlin first made me a proposition in Columbus, Ohio, to throw the game in Cincinnati. He made the proposition either in the hotel or upon the street. We went to the telegraph office in Columbus and sent a dispatch to a man in New York by the name of McCloud, saying that we would lose the Cincinnati game. McCloud is a pool seller. The telegraph was signed "D. & H." We received no answer to this telegram. I did not know McCloud. Devlin knew him. McCloud sent Devlin $50 in a letter, and Devlin gave me $25. . . .

TESTIMONY OF JAMES A. DEVLIN.

Was introduced to a man named McCloud in New York, who said that when I wanted to make a little money to let him know. Was to use the word "sash" in telegraphing, and he would know what was meant. Hall first made the overture to me to throw games while in Columbus, Ohio. He wrote a letter to me and left it on the table in our room. In the letter he said, "Let us make some money." Can't remember what else was in it. Called Hall one side and asked him if he meant it, and he said "Yes." I proposed to telegraph to McCloud, and we did so. We made a contract to lose the Cincinnati game. McCloud sent me $100 in a letter, and I gave Hall $25 of it. Told him that McCloud only sent $50. Helped to throw a game in Indianapolis. Hall was with me in it. Received $100 from McCloud for it. Did not give any of this to Hall. Gave it to my wife. . . .

GEORGE HALL RECALLED.

Since last night I have thought of another game Nichols and I threw. It was with the Lowell Club, of Lowell, Massachusetts. He and I agreed to throw it. He did all the telegraphing. Never got a cent from Nichols for the games he and I threw. . . . I can't tell where it was that Nichols first approached me about throwing League games. When I told him that I would have nothing to do with League games, I meant that I would go in with him on outside games. I made the proposition about the Cincinnati game to Devlin. Last night I said he made it to me. . . .

JAMES DEVLIN RECALLED.

. . . Richard Tobin, who keeps the paper stand in Earle's Hotel, New York [239 Canal Street], introduced me to McCloud on our last trip East. Knew of McCloud, but never received any work from him before this. Tobin took me to McCloud's house, and it was there that I made the agreement with him. His address is 141 Broome Street, New York. He resides there with his family. It was on Sunday afternoon that I called on him. Never received but $300 from him. This was for one Cincinnati and two Indianapolis games. Was in one Indianapolis game by myself. Hall did not know it. Was in only one game at Cincinnati. Received all money from McCloud by mail. Hall sent telegraph to him about first Indianapolis game. The telegraph was sent from here. I told him to use the word "sash" [to denote that Louisville would lose]. I telegraphed him about second Indianapolis game. Nichols never spoke to me about games. Received money by telegraph from John J. Martin to amount of $100 for games won here. Got $25 for each game. This was when we were winning so many games on our own grounds. Signed my telegraphs to Martin "J. A. D." Never signed any telegraphs except "J. A. D." or "D. & H."

167 *Spalding, present:* Spalding, *America's National Game,* 228–229.

167 *Devlin also wrote:* Jim Devlin letter to Harry Wright, February 24, 1878. Albert Spalding Baseball Collections, Harry Wright Papers, personally consulted in 1983. This letter appears since to have been stolen.

168 *In 1872, the* New York Ledger: *New York Ledger,* November 30, 1872.

169 *David Pietrusza:* David Pietrusza, *Major Leagues* (Jefferson, NC: McFarland, 1991), 33.

169 *Of the fifty:* Henry Chadwick, *De Witt Base Ball Guide for 1878,* 38.

170 *Spalding described:* Spalding, *America's National Game,* 230–233.

172 *As the New York Giants':* John Ward, "Is the Base-Ball Player a Chattel?," *Lippincott's Magazine* (August 1887), 310.

173 *As late as 1911:* Sam Crane, "Fifty Greatest Ball Players in History," *New York Evening Journal.* The series commenced in November 1911; Crane stopped his enumeration at thirty.

173 *In 1874:* Orem, *Baseball 1845–1881,* 205.

173 *Yet Boston did not shrink:* Ibid.

174 *Even the financially challenged:* Ibid.

174 *Spalding took the reins:* Albert G. Spalding, *America's National Game,* 214.

178 *From his autobiography:* Mike Kelly, *Play Ball, Stories of the Diamond Ball Field* (Boston: Emery & Hughes, as reprinted by McFarland & Co. in 2006), 6.

178 *This last-named innovation:* "Games and Pastimes," *Chicago Daily Tribune,* March 12, 1876, 16.

178 *Baseball's kinship:* Chadwick, *De Witt Base Ball Guide for 1878.*

179 *Spalding's brainstorm:* Orem, *Baseball (1883) from the Newspaper Accounts* (Altadena, CA: self-published, 1967), 84.

CHAPTER EIGHT: UNION AND BROTHERHOOD

182 *Mark Twain had it right:* "New York Greets the Boys," *The Sun,* April 9, 1889, 1.

183 *The tremendous success:* James Charlton, *The Baseball Chronology: The Complete History of the Most Important Events in the Game of Baseball* (New York: Maxwell Macmillan International, 1991); also at: http://www.baseballlibrary.com/chronology/byyear.php?year=1882# October (October 28, 1882).

183 *In 1883, the Philadelphia Athletics:* Robert L. Tiemann, "Major League Attendance," in *Total Baseball,* multiple editions.

183 *As a whole:* Ibid.

184 *In 1881:* Ibid.

184 *The NL had:* The first AA victory came on October 4, 1882. Charlton, *Baseball Chronology* at http://www.baseballlibrary.com/chronology/byyear.php?year=1882# October.

184 *The 1883 Brooklyn team:* Philip J. Lowry, "Ballparks," in *Total Baseball,* multiple editions.

184 *The ball club's proprietors:* "The Brooklyn Club," *New York Clipper,* April 14, 1883.

184 *A somewhat less distant:* "Our National Game," *National Police Gazette,* October 20, 1883, 11.

184 *On March 14:* Charlton, *Baseball Chronology* at http://www.baseballlibrary.com/chronology/byyear.php?year=1883# March.

185 *That distinction:* W. Zachary Malinowski, "Who Was the First Black Man to Play in the Major Leagues?," *Providence Journal,* February 15, 2004; in modified form, his article also appeared in *Total Baseball*'s eighth edition.

185 *The* Providence Morning Star*:* Ibid.

186 *The White Sewing Machine manager:* "A Disabled Club," *Louisville Courier-Journal,* August 22, 1881, per Dean Sullivan, ed., *Early Innings: A Documentary History of Baseball 1825–1908* (Lincoln: University of Nebraska Press), 117–118.

186 *The Clevelands:* Ibid.

186 *Toledo manager Voltz:* Jerry Malloy, "Out at Home," *The National Pastime,* vol. 2 (Cooperstown: Society for American Baseball Research, 1983), 24–25; also Vern Luse, "PS," *The National Pastime,* vol. 4 (Cooperstown: Society for American Baseball Research, 1985). Luse wrote that the *Toledo Blade* of August 11, 1883, reported: "Walker has a very sore hand, and it had not been intended to play him in yesterday's game, and this was stated to the bearer of the announcement for the Chicagos. Not content with this, the visitors during their perambulations of the forenoon declared with the swagger for which they are noted, that they would play ball 'with no d—d nigger,' and when the Club arrived at the grounds Capt. Anson repeated the declaration to the Toledo management. . . . Anson hauled in his horns somewhat and 'consented' to play, remarking, 'we'll play this here game, but won't play never no more with the nigger in.' "

187 *Shortly before Walker's release:* Preston D. Orem, *Baseball (1884) from the Newspaper Accounts* (Altadena, CA: self-published, 1967), 124.

187 *He insisted:* Malloy, "Out at Home," 24–25.

188 *It became clear:* "Meeting of the National League in Baltimore," *New York Freeman,* March 28, 1887, per Dean Sullivan, ed., *Early Innings: A Documentary History of Baseball 1825–1908* (Lincoln: University of Nebraska Press), 146–148.

188 *James Weldon Johnson:* Per John Hope Franklin introduction to *Three Negro Classics* (New York: Avon, 1965), 15.

188 *Ned Williamson:* "Discovery of the Slide: The 'Feet-first' Slide Due to a Desire to Cripple Colored Players." *Sporting Life,* October 24, 1891, 3.

189 *On January 17:* "The Sporting World," *Cleveland Herald,* January 17, 1884, 3.

189 *In 1885, he would:* "A Good Opening," *Boston Globe,* June 24, 1885, 5 (picked up from *Cincinnati Enquirer*).

189 *And, in 1889:* Orem, *Baseball (1889) from the Newspaper Accounts,* 432–434.

189 *In distant times:* William A. Mann, "The Elysian Fields of Hoboken, New Jersey," *Base Ball* 1:1 (Spring 2007), 7–21.

190 *In addition to:* Jorge S. Figueredo, *Cuban Baseball: A Statistical History* (Jefferson, NC: McFarland, 2003), 7.

190 *In 1866, Annie Glidden:* Letter home by Vassar College student Anne Glidden; in Debra A. Shattuck, "Women in Baseball," *Total Baseball,* all editions.

191 *In 1868, in Peterboro:* Frank Luther Mott, *A History of American Magazines, 1865–1885,* vol. 3 (Cambridge: Harvard University Press, 1938), 44.

191 *The* Brooklyn Eagle: "Recent Events," *Brooklyn Eagle,* October 17, 1891, 4.

191 *In the* Sporting News: *Sporting News,* September 20, 1890.

193 *The* Kansas City Star: "A Dirty Rascal in Jail," *Kansas City Star,* August 17, 1891.

193 *On September 2, 1880:* David Pietrusza, *Lights On!* (Landham, MD: Scarecrow Press, 1997), 3–4.

193 *The experiment was repeated:* "Under the Midnight Sun," *Fort Wayne Gazette,* June 3, 1883, 8.

193 *In their practice-work:* "Chinese Base Ball," *Chicago Inter-Ocean,* September 1, 1888.

193 *The* Brooklyn Eagle: "The Chinese Are Getting Civilized," *Brooklyn Eagle,* September 20, 1888, 9.

193 *John Lang:* "A Chinese Base-Ball Club," *New York Times,* April 10, 1883, 1.

193 *In Chester, Pennsylvania: De Witt Base Ball Guide for 1884* (New York: Robert M. De Witt), 28.

194 *Fat men contested:* Ibid.

194 *Of the players:* Ibid.

194 *In 1885, two clubs:* Orem, *Baseball (1885) from the Newspaper Accounts,* 214.

194 *There were baseball novels:* William Everett, *Changing Base; or, What Edward Rice Learnt at School* (Boston: Lee and Shepard, 1868); Noah Brooks, *Our Base Ball Club and How It Won the Championship* (New York: E.P. Dutton and Co., 1884).

194 *There were baseball songs:* J. R. Blodgett, "The Baseball Polka" (Buffalo: Blodgett and Bradford, 1858). J. W. Kelly, "Slide, Kelly, Slide," copyright by F. Harding, 1889.

194 *There were numerous:* Francis Copeland Sebring, "Parlor Base-Ball," *Wilkes' Spirit of the Times,* November 24, 1866; also *Leslie's,* December 8, 1866. Patent application 74 154, February 4, 1868 (antedated January 23, 1868).

194 *The seeds of fantasy baseball:* "Advertisement 2—No Title," *The Youth's Companion,* March 26, 1885, 124. "A New Card Craze," *Duluth News-Tribune,* July 19, 1885. "Base Ball with Cards," *Boston Globe,* May 17, 1885; August 28, 1885; September 12, 1885.

194 *Played by four:* Orem, *Baseball (1883) from the Newspaper Accounts,* 97.

194 *Total prizes:* Ibid.

195 *As Harold and Dorothy Seymour:* Harold Seymour and Dorothy Seymour, *Baseball: The Early Years* (New York: Oxford University Press, 1960), 351.

196 *The latent promise: Sunday Mercury,* August 28, 1880.

196 *A. G. Mills observed:* John Ward, *Base-Ball: How to Become a Player* (Philadelphia: Athletic Publishing Company, 1888), 9.

197 *John Ward:* John Ward, "Is the Base-Ball Player a Chattel?," *Lippincott's Magazine* (August 1887), 315.

197 *Ward's August 1887:* Ibid., 312.

198 *Ward of the New York Giants:* Orem, *Baseball (1885) from the Newspaper Accounts,* 201.

198 *An article signed:* "The Salary Question," *Sporting Life,* September 2, 1885, 4.

200 *As he described:* Ward, *Base-Ball: How to Become a Player,* 9.

200 *The Brotherhood's initial:* "The Brotherhood and Its Work," *Players' National League Base Ball Guide* (Chicago: F. H. Brunnell, 1890), 7–10.

201 *This notion was reported:* "A Good Opening," *Boston Globe,* June 24, 1885, 5.

201 *His plan called:* Ibid.

201 *Although the date:* "The Baseball Conference; Rules Adopted that Will Surprise Players and the Public," *Macon Telegraph,* October 18, 1885.

201 *For 1886, the salary:* Amos Alonzo Stagg, *Touchdown!,* as told by Coach Amos Alonzo Stagg to Wesley Winans Stout (New York: Longmans, Green & Co., 1927), 195.

201 *Chicago announced:* Orem, *Baseball (1886) from the Newspaper Accounts,* 251.

202 *In right field:* Orem, *Baseball (1887) from the Newspaper Accounts,* 296.

202 *A newspaper report:* Ibid.

203 *In truth there:* Ibid., 262. Charlie Comiskey told the story differently, saying Welch did slide, though it was unnecessary. Gustaf W. Axelson, *"Commy": The Life Story of Charles A. Comiskey, the "Grand Old Roman" of Baseball, etc.* (Chicago: Reilly & Lee Co., 1919), 89–91.

203 *Von Der Ahe:* Orem, *Baseball (1887) from the Newspaper Accounts,* 296.

204 *Players were being treated:* Ward, "Is the Base-Ball Player a Chattel?," 313.

204 *In that year, an umpire:* Orem, *Baseball (1885) from the Newspaper Accounts,* 192.

205 *The* New York Times: "Helen Dauvray's Choice," *New York Times,* October 12, 1887, 1.

205 *The* Times *announcement:* Ibid.

CHAPTER NINE: SPORTING GOODS AND HIGHER THOUGHT

207 *A surviving ledger page:* Actually, the ledger does not survive but photos of selected pages came up for eBay auction on February 16, 2000, and were acquired by the author. The seller stated this provenance: "Photographs I have acquired with the Edward Faber Estate photographs that were taken by him in the 1950s. He would have been a product photographer for Spalding. . . . Lists notable associates such as George Wright (Wright & Ditson), Peck and Snyder, Reach & Johnson, capital stock, profit & loss, documentation from what I believe is their first year, it also documents the expenses (balls and bats etc.) of the Chicago BBC. . . . In April of 1998 I was in contact about the existance [sic] of this ledger [with] Consumer Relations rep Kelly Robbins from Spalding to find out if it still exists and her findings were that they now have no record of it."

207 *Despite the small scale:* Ibid.

207 *Harriet recalled:* Harriet I. Spalding, *Reminiscences of Harriet I. Spalding* (East Orange, NJ: privately printed, 1910), 97.

209 *The house of:* Horace S. Knapp, *History of the Maumee valley, commencing with its occupation by the French in 1680, etc.* (Toledo: Blade Mammoth Print. and Pub. House, 1872), 394.

209 *On April 25, 1876: Fort Wayne Daily News,* April 25, 1876, as reprinted in "What Happened During the Week of April 23 Forty, Thirty, and Fifteen Years Ago," *Fort Wayne Daily News,* April 22, 1916, 12.

209 *Dissolving the partnership: Fort Wayne City Directory,* 1878, 177.

209 *When it went bankrupt:* "This Morning's Dispatches Condensed," *Wisconsin State Journal,* February 22, 1884. "As Yet No Clue," *Fort Wayne World,* April 18, 1885, 1. "It's Fate—G. J. E. Mayer Goes to Denver, Col., with Mr. Nix's Million Behind Him," *Fort Wayne Sunday Gazette,* April 12, 1885, 5. *Fort Wayne Daily Gazette,* June 13, 1885.

210 *Apart from baseball:* Charles Warren Spalding, *The Spalding Memorial: A Genealogical History of Edward Spalding* (Chicago: American Publishers' Association, 1897).

211 *Turning his back:* "Temple & Related Lines in America," http://www.temple-genealogy.com/b2012.htm#P5576.

211 *In this popular book:* Walter Besant and James Rice, *The Seamy Side* (New York: Dodd Mead, 1888), 180–181.

212 *This day:* Charles Sturtevant, M.D., "Professional Etiquette and Medical Courtesy," *New England Medical Gazette of Homoeopathic Medicine,* vol. 34 (Boston: Otis Clapp & Son, 1899), 406.

212 *A hapless George: Fort Wayne Sentinel,* July 13, 1911 (reporting on events of twenty-five years ago). Also, "The Divorce Mill: Five Courts Grinding," *Chicago Inter-Ocean,* January 9, 1887, 6.

212 *Lizzie returned home:* "Personal Mention," *Fort Wayne Daily Gazette,* April 22, 1885, 7.

212 *On her visits:* Chicago City Directory, 1886, 264.

213 *By Lizzie's own account:* "Tributes to Helena Petrovna Blavatsky, etc.," in Katherine Augusta Westcott Tingley, *Helena Petrovna Blavatsky* (Point Loma, CA: Woman's International Theosophical League, 1921), 38.

213 *In 1889 she and George Jr.:* Fort Wayne City Directory, 1889. (Mrs. Lizzie C. Mayer, teacher, Ft. Wayne Conservatory of Music, boards at Hamilton House.)

213 *The Society, founded:* Henry Steel Olcott, *Old Diary Leaves, The True Story of the Theosophical Society* (New York: G. P. Putnam's Sons, 1895), 25*ff.*

213 *By 1888: Lucifer,* vol. 4 (London: Theosophical Publishing Society, 1889), 356.

214 *In their absence:* Olcott's "Foreign Order No. 1" in *The Theosophical Forum,* October 1939, 280–283.

214 *In a letter read:* Letter from Madame Blavatsky written in London, April 3, 1888, read to the convention April 22.

214 *At its beginning:* Michael Gomes, "Abner Doubleday and Theosophy in America: 1879–1884." *Sunrise* (Pasadena) 40, no. 4 (April–May 1991): 151–157 (Olcott to Doubleday, May 12, 1882, Doubleday Notebook 7, 10, per Gomes).

215 *While widely respected:* Donald S. Lopez Jr., *Prisoners of Shangri-La: Tibetan Buddhism and the West* (Chicago: University of Chicago Press, 1998), 41–44.

215 *Blavatsky fed this flame:* Letter from Mahatma Koot Hoomi to Miss Francesca Arundale, July 1884. A.P. Sinnett, *The Early Days of Theosophy in Europe* (London: Theosophical Publishing House, 1922), 58*ff.*

215 *When Lizzie Mayer:* "Chicagoans off for Europe," *Chicago Daily Tribune,* July 20, 1890, 11.

215 *In London, she studied:* "Local News," *Fort Wayne Sentinel,* October 1, 1890, 2.

215 *In 1921:* "Tributes to Helena Petrovna Blavatsky, etc.," in Tingley, *Helena Petrovna Blavatsky,* 38.

215 *Lizzie returned:* Passenger list for *City of New York,* 1890, 19, Arrival: *New York, United States;* microfilm serial *M237,* microfilm roll *M237_556,* Line *48,* List Number *1504.* Also "Local News," *Fort Wayne Sentinel,* October 9, 1890, 2.

215 *However, after resuming:* "Local News," *Fort Wayne Sentinel,* November 15, 1890, 2.

215 *A little more: Fort Wayne Sentinel,* November 29, 1890, 2.

215 *Once more:* "Local News," *Fort Wayne Weekly Gazette,* December 4, 1890, 5.

215 *Mrs. Mayer:* This fact may be deduced from what follows in the text, particularly the birth date and place of her son.

216 *Both the Mayer and Spalding:* Passenger list for *City of New York,* 1890, 16, Arrival: *New York, United States,* microfilm serial *M237,* microfilm roll *M237_556,* Line *35,* List Number *1504.*

216 *Somehow the near-penniless:* 1891 England Census, class *RG12,* piece *803,* folio 86, page 34, GSU roll *6095913.* For young Churchill's football exploits, "Durand Churchill, of the Olympian Games Committee," *Lowell Sun,* November 13, 1902, 8.

216 *In the United Kingdom census:* 1891 England Census.

216 *On June 14: 1891 England and Wales FreeBMD Index, 1837–1915* (database online), Provo, UT, USA: Ancestry.com Operations Inc., 2006. Quarter of Registration: Apr–May–Jun [1891]. District: Brighton. County: Sussex, East Sussex. District: Brighton. Volume: 2b. Page: 241.

216 *They raised:* "Family Receives Spalding Estate," *Los Angeles Times,* September 15, 1915, pg. II 7.

216 *The so-called widow Mrs. Mayer:* The boy who went to England with his mother in 1890 as George Mayer Jr. enrolled at M.I.T. in 1896 as Durand Mayer. "Asks Courts to Change Names," *Chicago Daily Tribune,* January 18, 1903.

216 *Although she continued:* Elizabeth Churchill Mayer was of course entitled to keep her married name whether she was widowed or divorced. By the standards of an earlier time, she might even have passed muster as a separated woman to label herself a widow, given the stigma of divorce. But in *Marital Status: 2000, Census 2000 Brief,* issued by the Census Bureau in October 2003, "the decennial census has asked about the marital status of the population since 1880. From 1880 through 1940, marital status was categorized as 'single,' married,' 'widowed,' or 'divorced.' 'Separated' was added as a category in 1950."

217 *He continued to dabble:* "The Chinese Are Getting Civilized," *Brooklyn Eagle,* September 20, 1888, 9.

217 *In 1899 he:* "Design for a Checker-Board. Specification forming part of Design No. 30,869, dated May 23, 1899. Application filed April 3, 1899. Serial No. 711,609."

217 *Yet she presented herself publicly:* "Tributes to Helena Petrovna Blavatsky, etc.," in Tingley, *Helena Petrovna Blavatsky,* 38.

218 *In 1853, she journeyed:* Rossiter Johnson, John Howard Brown, eds., *The Twentieth Century Biographical Dictionary of Notable Americans, vol. 1* (Boston: The Biographical Society, 1904), 326. Also, website of the Theosophical Society in Greece, http://www.theosophicalsociety.gr/english_site/biographies/blavatsky.html.

218 *A report of her life: New York Daily Graphic* (November 13, 1874). "More about Materialization," *Spiritual Scientist,* E. Gerry Brown, ed., Boston, volume I, November 19. (In the December 3, 1874, number of this weekly, Mme. Blavatsky is quoted thus: "Knowing this country to be the cradle of modern Spiritualism, I came over here from France with feelings not unlike those of a Mohammedan approaching the birthplace of his prophet. I had forgotten that 'no prophet is without honor save in his own country.' In the less than fourteen months that I am here, sad experience has but too well sustained the never-dying evidence of this immortal truth!")

218 *On September 22, 1874:* "Court Notes," *New York Times,* July 9, 1878.

218 *In her naturalization papers:* National Archives and Records Administration (NARA); Washington, DC; Soundex Index to Petitions for Naturalizations Filed in Federal, State, and Local Courts in New York City, 1792–1906 (M1674); Microfilm Serial: *M1674*; Microfilm Roll: *14*.

219 *In July she said:* "Citizen Helen P. Blavatsky: That Newly Naturalized Personage Explains Some Interesting Matters," *Daily Graphic,* July 9, 1878, 54.

219 *Five months later:* "H.P. Blavatsky's Adieux: The Ci-Devant Countess Ready to Depart for the East; Having Disposed of Strange Gods, She Ventilates Her Ideas—The Land of Freedom," *Daily Graphic,* December 10, 1878, 266.

219 *In her first year:* H. P. Blavatsky, "Marvellous Spirit Manifestations," *Daily Graphic,* October 30, 1874, and "About Spiritualism," *Daily Graphic,* November 13, 1874. Virginia Hanson, *H.P. Blavatsky and the Secret Doctrine* (Wheaton, IL: Theosophical Publishing House, 1971, 1988), 22–23.

220 *It was dubbed:* Henry Steel Olcott, *Old Diary Leaves, The True Story of the Theosophical Society* (New York: G. P. Putnam's Sons, 1895), 421–422.

220 *It was in her:* Mme. H. P. Blavatsky, *Isis Unveiled: A Master-Key to the Mysteries of Ancient and Modern Science and Theology* (New York: J. W. Bouton, 1877).

220 *In this book: The American Bookseller* III, no. 1 (May 15, 1877) (New York: American News Company), 298. "J. W. Bouton . . . has also in press, for immediate issue, a book on Magic, by Madame Blavatsky, of whose powers we have lately heard so much. It will be entitled *The Veil of Isis: a Skeleton Key to Mysterious Gates.*"

220 *With* The Secret Doctrine: H. P. Blavatsky, *The Secret Doctrine: The Synthesis of Science, Religion, and Philosophy, Vol. I—Cosmogenesis* (London: Theosophical Publishing Company, 1888). This was followed in the same year by *Vol. II, Anthropogenesis.* An unauthorized posthumous volume III was compiled from her unpublished manuscripts.

220 *On September 25, 1843:* David Block, *Baseball Before We Knew It,* 294–295.

221 *We may also understand:* Abner Doubleday letter to Ralph Waldo Emerson, sent to him not via the *Dial* but direct to "Concord, Middlesex County, Massachusetts," postmarked in Portland on August 18, 1845. From Houghton Library, Harvard College Library, Harvard University (MS Am 1280, 840).

223 *After leaving the Army:* Eliphas Levi, "*The Conjuration of the 4,*" translated from the French by Abner Doubleday (Holmes Pub Group LLC, 1991).

223 *He visited her:* H. P. Blavatsky, *The Diaries of H. P. Blavatsky,* 430. ("December 14. H.S.O. gone off early. Wimb. and Judge trying to help H.P.B. Today the trunks must go.—They do go—care of Hur. Chund, Bombay. So much the less. Tales feeling a sudden love for H.P.B. sends carriage and boy after her. Positive refusal.—Miss Potter came and wants to join Theosophical. Promises to send $5. Vediamo. Marble comes and—H.P.B. falls asleep. H.S.O. returns with phonograph weighing 100 pounds. General Doubleday came.—Went away as he came. . . .")

223 *On January 17, 1879:* Olcott's "Foreign Order No. 1" in *The Theosophical Forum,* October 1939, 280–283; letter in Library of Congress, per Michael Gomes, *The Dawning of the Theosophical Movement* (Wheaton, IL: Theosophical Publishing House, 1987), 233.

224 *Although his interim:* Abner Doubleday, Letter to the Editor, *Religio-Philosophical Journal* (April 28, 1888), 6.

224 *At his death, Doubleday:* Personal correspondence with David Wietersen, Archivist, Theosophical Society, Pasadena, May 2003.

225 *Before becoming president:* Obituary, *Sporting Life,* January 20, 1917, 7.

225 *In July 1889:* "New Incorporations," *New York Times,* July 4, 1889. ("The following certificates of incorporation have been filed in the Secretary of State's Office; The Theosophical Society and Universal Brotherhood form an association for 'literary, historical, and scientific purposes, and for their mutual improvement in religious knowledge and the furtherance of religious opinion by the distribution of literature, but not on sale, and by associating for the purpose of investigating science and religion.' ")

225 *Moving to Pittsburgh:* "American Branches Theosophical Society," *The Path* 5, no. 12 (March 1891). ("On Nov. 21st [1890] the General Secretary issued a Charter to the new "Vishnu T. S." of Pittsburg, Pa. There are 5 Charter Members. Its formation is to be credited to that beautiful type of gentle, genial manhood, lost to the Aryan T. S. but now diffusing through the provinces peace on earth and good will to men, Bro. Wm. C. Temple.")

225 *In 1893, the press:* classified ad, *Los Angeles Times,* September 15, 1893, 8.

225 *In the spring of 1902:* "New Baseball President; Spalding Resigns as Disputed Head of the National League; Temple Elected, Etc.," *New York Times,* April 3, 1902, 10.

CHAPTER TEN: THE GOSPEL OF BASEBALL

227 *The term was first applied:* The term *world championship* is said to have been applied to the 1884 postseason contest between the Providence Grays (NL) and New York Mets (AA). Certainly it was in use one year later: *Chicago Daily Tribune,* October 26, 1885, 2. The earliest use I have found of the precise phrasing *world series* is in "The Diamond," *Milwaukee Sentinel,* November 22, 1886, 8.

227 *Mildly worrisome:* "Ball Rules for 1889," *Washington Post,* November 23, 1888, 1.

228 *As* Sporting Life *noted: Sporting Life,* February 13, 1909, 6.

229 *Into the breach:* Donald Hall, "Casey at the Bat: A Ballad of the Republic," in *Total Baseball,* 3rd ed. (New York: Harper Perennial, 1993), 244–250.

230 *"Casey" proved:* Ernest Lawrence Thayer, "Casey at the Bat: A Ballad of the Republic, Sung in the Year 1888," *San Francisco Examiner,* June 3, 1888, 4.

230 *In his autobiography:* De Wolf Hopper, Wesley Winans Stout, *Once a Clown, Always a Clown: Reminiscences of De Wolf Hopper* (Boston: Little, Brown, 1927), 80.

230 *The good gray poet:* "City Intelligence: Brooklyn Young Men; Athletic Exercises," *Brooklyn Eagle,* July 23, 1846, 2.

230 *He had followed baseball: Brooklyn Daily Times,* June 18, 1858, per Walt Whitman, Emory Holloway, Vernolian Schwarz, *I Sit and Look Out: Editorials from the Brooklyn Daily Times* (New York: Columbia University Press, 1932), 106. Walt Whitman, *Leaves of Grass* (Brooklyn: self-published, 1855), 36.

231 *In his last years:* Horace Traubel, *With Walt Whitman in Camden,* vol. 4, Sculley Bradley, ed. (Philadelphia: University of Pennsylvania Press, 1953), 508.

231 *Long ere the second:* Walt Whitman, "Democratic Vistas," in *Two Rivulets* (Camden, NJ: author's edition, 1876), 60.

231 *In 1888, Ward:* John Ward, *Base-Ball: How to Become a Player* (Philadelphia: Athletic Publishing Company, 1888).

231 *Untroubled by the values:* James Charlton, *The Baseball Chronology: The Complete History of the Most Important Events in the Game of Baseball* (New York: Maxwell Macmillan International, 1991), also at: http://www.baseballlibrary.com/chronology/byyear.php?year=1888&previous=yes (June 7, 1888).

232 *In Omaha:* Adrian C. Anson, *A Ball Player's Career: Being the Personal Experiences and Reminiscences of Adrian C. Anson, Late Manager and Captain of the Chicago Base Ball Club* (Chicago: Era Publishing Co., 1900), 149–150.

232 *On November 11:* Harry Clay Palmer et al., "Scores of Games on the World's Tour," *Athletic Sports in America, England and Australia. Comprising History, Characteristics, Sketches of Famous Leaders, Organization and Great Contests of Baseball, Cricket, Football, La Crosse, Tennis, Rowing and Cycling. Also including the Famous "Around The World" Tour of American Baseball Teams, Their Enthusiastic Welcomes, Royal Receptions, Banquets, Great Games Played Before Notables of Foreign Nations, Humorous Incidents, Interesting Adventures, Etc., Etc.* (Philadelphia, Boston, Chicago, and St. Louis: Hubbard Brothers, 1889), 708–711.

232 *On November 22:* "Ball Rules for 1889," *Washington Post,* November 23, 1888, 1.

233 *Four months later:* "League Baseball Men; Cleveland Granted Admission to Take the Place of Detroit; Washington Still Get John Ward, Etc.," *Washington Post,* November 22, 1888, 2. "Pie for Washington; Reflections on the Schedule by Mr. Soden; No Decision on Manager or Captain Till John Ward's Return, Etc.," *Boston Daily Globe,* March 10, 1889, 7.

233 *A reporter:* Palmer et al., *Athletic Sports,* 333.

234 *To a visitor:* "A Policy for the South," *Washington Post,* April 5, 1889, 3.

234 *The world tour:* Anson, *A Ball Player's Career,* 284–285. Per Mark Lamster, *Spalding's World Tour: The Epic Adventure That Took Baseball Around the Globe—and Made It America's Game* (New York: Public Affairs, 2006), 35.

235 *The* New York Times: "Baseball at Delmonico's," *New York Times,* April 9, 1889, 5.

235 *He declared that the game:* Paraphrased in *New York Clipper,* April 13, 1889, 79. Also in the New York *Sun,* April 9, 1889, 1. Quoted precisely here, however, from recently discovered Mills notes for his speech, tucked into a menu from the banquet. A. G. Mills Papers, BA MSS 13.

235 *His words were met:* "New York Greets the Boys," *The Sun,* April 9, 1889, 1.

236 *Warming to the task:* Notes for A. G. Mills speech, previously unpublished but residing in A. G. Mills Papers, BA MSS 13.

236 *Digby Bell:* Palmer et al., *Athletic Sports,* 448–449.

236 *Teddy Roosevelt, too:* Mark Twain's speech was rendered in full in several newspapers, including the *Sun,* April 9, 1889, 1.

237 *Spalding, questioned: The New York World* in *Cleveland Leader,* May 12, 1889, per Harold Seymour, "The Rise of Major League Baseball to 1891," unpublished doctoral dissertation, Cornell University, 1956, 483, fn 70.

237 *As the rumbling:* "War to the Knife. The League Will Fight the Brotherhood Scheme," *Wheeling Register,* September 24, 1889, 1. Spalding invoked a well-known phrase that had been applied in print to Know Nothings in 1855 and to the Ku Klux Klan in 1871.

237 *There they drew:* Charlton, *The Baseball Chronology.*

237 *On November 4:* "Baseball War Declared," *New York Times,* November 5, 1889, 8.

238 *The phrasing of this vision:* "The Industrial System," *New York Times,* April 1, 1889, 5.

238 *The movement's statement:* Ibid.

238 *If this Nationalist Club credo:* H. P. Blavatsky, *The Key To Theosophy: Being a Clear Exposition, in the Form of Question and Answer, of the Ethics, Science, and Philosophy for the Study of Which the Theosophical Society Has Been Founded* (London: Theosophical Publishing Company, 1889), 44. ("Have not you heard of the Nationalist clubs and party which have sprung up in America since the publication of Bellamy's book? They are now coming prominently to the front, and will do

so more and more as time goes on. Well, these clubs and this party were started in the first instance by Theosophists. . . .") Also William Dwight Porter Bliss, ed., *The New Encyclopedia of Social Reform* (New York: Funk & Wagnalls, 1908), 107, 810–811, 1251.

239 *A sportsman and statistics enthusiast:* "A Point of Play: Messrs. Temple and Spalding Agree that the Pitcher Should be Exempt from Batting," *Sporting Life,* December 19, 1891, 1. "Pleased with Results," *Sporting Life,* March 12, 1892, 12.

239 *To the Brotherhood Manifesto:* A. G. Spalding, John B. Day, John I. Rogers, "Address of the League," *Daily Inter Ocean,* November 22, 1889, 2. (In the players' response to the owners, on this same page, they reminded the authors that at the "glorious start" of the league "Mr. Spalding deserted the Boston club, in which he was a player, to come to Chicago, and for no other reason than to better himself.")

239 *If the players would swaddle:* Ibid.

240 *But the King declined:* Spalding, *America's National Game,* 296–297. (Spalding: "Involuntarily I reached out my hand in congratulation of the great ball player on his loyalty.")

240 *Prior to the opening:* "Ward Wins His Fight," *New York Times,* January 29, 1890, 2.

240 *In the Giants' parallel case:* "Ewing Not Enjoined," *New York Times,* March 27, 1890, 8.

241 *Spalding reviewed:* Spalding, *America's National Game,* 288.

242 *Why did the Players' League:* Harold Seymour and Dorothy Seymour, *Baseball: The Early Years* (New York: Oxford University Press, 1960), 240.

242 *According to the* Sporting News: *Sporting News,* November 22, 1890, per Harold Seymour, "The Rise of Major League Baseball to 1891."

242 *By the terms of the decree:* "J. M. Ward May Remarry," *New-York Tribune,* September 18, 1903, 6.

242 *The Dauvray Cup:* "Boston Defeats All-America," *Morning Oregonian,* October 9, 1893, 2. ("Pittsburg Pencillings," *Sporting Life,* November 4, 1893, 4.) "Gastright's Return," *Sporting Life,* November 11, 1893, 3. This last reference is to the Dauvray Cup's exhibition in Cincinnati, its last known abode.

242 *Then, Spalding's Chicago club:* "Report of the Conference Committee," *New York Herald,* January 17, 1891, and *Cleveland Leader,* December 30, 1890, both per Harold Seymour, "The Rise of Major League Baseball to 1891."

242 *These ultimately were settled:* Charlton, *The Baseball Chronology.*

243 *In an informal meeting:* "Ward and Spalding: A Conference Between the Two Foremost Figures in the Base Ball World—What Was Said, Etc.," *Sporting Life,* December 20, 1890, 2.

243 *Spalding announced his retirement:* Anson, *Ball Player's Career,* 308.

244 *In that same year:* David Q. Voigt, "The History of Major League Baseball," in Thorn and Palmer, eds., *Total Baseball* (New York: Warner Books, 1989), 14.

245 *The Players' League:* John Holway and John Thorn, *The Pitcher* (New York: Prentice Hall Press, 1987), 301.

247 *The "Special Instructions":* By Order of the Committee, "Special Instructions to Players," undated from 1898, http://www.robertedwardauctions.com/auction/2008/1182.html#photos.

247 *A milestone event:* Eleanor Engle, "First Female Player?," in *Baseball Research Journal* (Cooperstown: Society for American Baseball Research, 1983), 159–161.

248 *Three weeks later:* "New Yorks Forfeit a Game," *New York Times,* July 26, 1898, 5. "Want Holmes Disciplined," *New York Times,* August 30, 1898, 5.

251 *As Johnson expected:* "Wants a New Agreement," *Chicago Daily Tribune,* November 19, 1900, 8. "War In Baseball Air," *Washington Post,* November 19, 1900, 8.

251 *"Turkey" Mike Donlin:* Charlton, *The Baseball Chronology,* www.baseballlibrary.com/chronology/byyear.php?year=1901.

251 *In preseason training:* "Two Interesting Sporting Characters," *Chicago Daily Tribune,* March 24, 1901, 19.

252 *If Muggsy [McGraw]: Cincinnati Enquirer,* March 11, 1901. "Baltimore Bulletin," *Sporting Life,* March 16, 1901, 5. "News and Comment," *Sporting Life,* March 23, 1901, 3. Robert Peterson, *Only the Ball Was White: A History of Legendary Black Players and All-Black Professional Teams* (New York: Oxford University Press, 1970), 54–57.

252 *This apotheosis lasted:* "New Baseball President; Spalding Resigns as Disputed Head of the National League; Temple Elected, Etc.," *New York Times,* April 3, 1902, 10.

253 *Unwilling or unable:* Fred Lieb, *The Baltimore Orioles* (New York: Putnam, 1955), 110.

253 *Let McGraw tell:* Ibid., 114.

253 *On July 16:* "Peace Is Farther Away," *Chicago Daily Tribune,* July 20, 1902, 11. "M'graw at Polo Grounds," *New York Times,* July 18, 1902, 6.

254 *In January 1903:* Lieb, *The Baltimore Orioles,* 120.

CHAPTER ELEVEN: THE WHITE CITY AND THE GOLDEN WEST

255 *Big-league attendance:* Robert L. Tiemann, "Major League Attendance," in *Total Baseball,* multiple editions.

256 *Alexander Joy Cartwright Jr.: Hawaiian Gazette,* July 19, 1892, per Nucciarone, *Alexander Cartwright.*

256 *Duncan F. Curry:* "Diamond Field Gossip," *New York Clipper,* April 28, 1894, 122. "The Obituary Record," *New York Times,* April 19, 1894, 2.

256 *Knickerbocker catcher:* Charles Schuyler DeBost died May 26, 1895, at Mohegan, Westchester County, buried at Green-Wood Cemetery in Brooklyn.

256 *For Harry Wright Day:* "Diamond Field Veterans," *New York Times,* April 12, 1896, 3. "Spalding Is a Jonah," *Chicago Daily Tribune,* April 14, 1896, 4. "Then and Now" (interview with Fred Cone), in *Sunday Blade,* August 15, 1896. "Harry Wright Day in Rockford," *Rockford Register-Gazette,* April 13–14, 1896.

256 *In 1899:* Adams died January 3, 1899. "The True Father of Baseball," first in *Elysian Fields Quarterly* 11, no. 1 (Winter 1992), 85–91, and then in several of

the eight editions of the encyclopedia *Total Baseball.* "Dr. D. L. Adams; Memoirs of the Father of Base Ball; He Resides in New Haven and Retains an Interest in the Game," *Sporting News,* February 29, 1896, 3. Also Harvard Medical School Library, Yale Alumni Records, and Connecticut State Library History & Genealogy Unit.

256 *A few years ago:* Auction conducted on eBay on May 24, 2005, by Global Garage Sales of Winooski, Vermont.

256 *The recipient's name:* The award was referenced in a report of the day's old-timers game. "The Knickerbocker Club: Baseball in the Olden Time," *New York Clipper,* October 9, 1875, 21. ("Then Mr. Taylor presented him with an elegant silver ball and two silver bats in morocco cases. The ball was inscribed. . . .")

257 *Drifting away:* "Poor Old Davis," *Rocky Mountain News,* October 6, 1875, from the *Sun.* ("Just as Davis drew back his hand to deliver the first ball, Mrs. McClinton, his daughter, stepped forward amid the cheers of the spectators and bound around his waist a belt of blue ribbon, on the front of which was embroidered in silver letters the name of the club, while from the left side depended two broad blue silk ribbons, on one of which were the words, 'To Poor Old Davis,' and on the other, 'For his 25th ball birthday.' "

257 *On the twenty-seventh of August:* Albert Spalding Baseball Collections, Knickerbocker Base Ball Club of New York, Club Books 1854–1868 at the New York Public Library.

257 *Designed by Davis:* Ibid. (entry for 1855 includes hand-drawn rendering of flag). "Poor Old Davis," *Rocky Mountain News,* October 6, 1875, from *Sun.*

257 *Davis entered:* New York City Directory for 1890 lists him at 332 East 17th Street.

258 *Too late:* Green-Wood Cemetery, burial search: http://www.green-wood.com/index.php/GWC/39.

258 *Like Cartwright:* "Death of a Pioneer: a 49'er Who Helped Make the History of the State," *San Jose Mercury News,* published as *Evening News,* September 14, 1888. "In Memoriam: Wm. R. Wheaton," *San Francisco Bulletin,* published as *Evening Bulletin,* September 27, 1888.

259 *Descending into solitude:* "Obituary," *Hartford Daily Times,* April 4, 1908.

261 *Unemployment peaked:* Stanley Lebergott, *Manpower in Economic Growth: The American Record Since 1800* (New York: McGraw-Hill, 1964), 522.

261 *When Swami Vivekananda:* Lewis Pyle Mercer, *Review of the World's Religious Congresses of the World's Congress Auxiliary of the World's Columbian Exposition, Chicago, 1893* (Chicago: Rand, McNally, 1893), 44. Swami Vivekananda, Dave DeLuca, *Pathways to Joy: The Master Vivekananda on the Four Yoga Paths to God* (Makawao, HI: Inner Ocean Publishing), 256–257.

261 *He continued:* Frank Tennyson Neely, ed., *Neely's History of the Parliament of Religions and Religious Congresses at the World's Columbian Exposition* (Chicago: F. T. Neely, 1893), 64.

261 *The* New York Herald: *New York Herald* (undated), per John Nichol Farquhar, *Modern Religious Movements in India* (New York: Macmillan, 1924), 202.

262 *Vivekananda later wrote:* Vivekananda, *The Complete Works of Swami Vivekananda*, vol. 4 (Calcutta: Advaita Ashrama, 1992), 317.

262 *William Emmette Coleman:* Vsevolod Sergyeevich Solovyoff, Vera Petrovna Zhelikhovskaia, William Emmette Coleman, *A Modern Priestess of Isis, Appendix C* (London: Longmans, Green, and Co., 1895), 358.

262 *Eventually, she wrote:* H. P. Blavatsky, *The Secret Doctrine: The Synthesis of Science, Religion, and Philosophy, Vol. II—Anthropogenesis* (London: Theosophical Publishing Company, 1888), 446.

263 *The vacuum of leadership:* Emmett A. Greenwalt, *The Point Loma Community in California* (Berkeley: University of California Press, 1955), 60.

263 *Elizabeth Mayer:* That she settled in New York by 1893 is demonstrated by "Religions of All Nations," *New York Times*, January 1, 1894, 9.

263 *Of the girl:* W. Michael Ashcraft, *The Dawn of the New Cycle: Point Loma Theosophists and American Culture* (Knoxville: University of Tennessee Press, 2002), 51. The story of the child's vision is also referenced in Iverson L. Harris, in an interview with Robert Wright, "Reminiscences of Lomaland: Madame Tingley and the Theosophical Institute in San Diego," *Journal of San Diego History* 20, no. 3 (Summer 1974).

263 *Mme. Blavatsky:* H. P. Blavatsky, *The Vahan: A Vehicle for the Interchange of Theosophical News and Opinion*, December 1890, 2.

264 *Krishna's death:* Ashcraft, *Dawn of the New Cycle*, 44.

264 *In April 1896:* "New Kind of College: Theosophy Will Be Taught in California Sumptuously," *Denver Evening Post*, December 29, 1896.

264 *As Doubleday:* "Third Annual Convention, T. S. A., First Day, Morning Session, April 25th," *The Theosophical Forum*, no. 1 (May 1897), 3–4.

264 *She and her cabinet:* "Leaders in Theosophy, Crusaders of the American Society in Denver," *Rocky Mountain News*, March 8, 1897, 2; "The Esoteric Culture Crusade," *New York Times*, March 22, 1897, 3; "Theosophy Is Split," *Milwaukee Sentinel*, February 20, 1898, 11.

264 *Though never losing:* "Temple Aggrieved," *Sporting Life*, October 16, 1897, 4. ("TEMPLE AGGRIEVED. . . . He declares that he will attend the League meeting and request that the cup be returned to its owner. 'I will also ask,' Mr. Temple says, 'that the League investigate the charges that the Baltimore and Boston players this year agreed to an equal division of the receipts in face of the League's explicit conditions about 60 per cent. to the winner and 40 per cent. to the loser. If these rumors are proven true I will ask that the offenders be blacklisted. The cup was offered to benefit the game generally, and to develop a fast series. This year's has not been such.' ")

264 *The future of this school:* "The Laying of the Corner Stone S. R. L. M. A. by the Founder-Directress, Katherine A. Tingley, at Point Loma, San Diego, California, February 23, 1897, Assisted by Mr. E. T. Hargrove, Mr. F. M. Pierce, and Others," *Theosophical Forum*, New Series 2:12 (April 1897), 191–192.

265 *In the period immediately:* Ashcraft, *Dawn of the New Cycle*, 156. ("Apparently no African Americans lived permanently on the site. [Ethel Wood Dunn] Lam-

bert told a Cuban official visiting Point Loma in 1908 that aside from Cuban 'colored' children, no other 'colored' children attended the Raja Yoga schools. A Point Loma official justified this fact by saying that 'We know the colored people in this country, and we know the colored people in this country are worse than the colored people in Cuba.' ")

265 *Mrs. Tingley intended:* Ashcraft, *Dawn of the New Cycle,* 93.

265 *Beginning in 1899:* "Training a Lotus Group," *Morning Oregonian,* July 9, 1899.

265 *It would not be long:* Iverson L. Harris, in an interview with Robert Wright, "Reminiscences of Lomaland: Madame Tingley and the Theosophical Institute in San Diego," *Journal of San Diego History* 20, no. 3 (Summer 1974).

266 *On the day:* "San Diego Brevities," *Los Angeles Times,* June 25, 1900, I, 11.

266 *On May 15, 1901:* Monmouth County Orphans Court in the State of New Jersey, May 15, 1901, obtained from Monmouth County Hall of Records, Office of the Surrogate, January 20, 2005.

266 *In his will:* Probate records obtained from Superior Court of California, County of San Diego, Central Records. "Decree of Distribution," July 26, 1918.

267 *The* Chicago Tribune: "Ask Courts to Change Names," *Chicago Daily Tribune,* January 18, 1903, 43.

267 *They had sold Meade Lawns: Rumson Borough Bulletin, Centennial Edition,* 2007, No. 2.

267 *As Upton Sinclair: The Profits of Religion: An Essay in Economic Interpretation* (Pasadena: self-published, 1918), 256.

268 *New York Giants:* "Spalding President of Baseball League," *New York Times,* December 14, 1901, 7. "Baseball Fight in Court; Injunction Restraining Spalding from Acting as President. Claim Election Was Illegal," *New York Times,* December 17, 1901, 7.

268 *In a February 1902:* "Baseball Officials Meet: A. G. Spalding's Resignation Not Accepted, Etc.," *New York Times,* February 23, 1902, 13.

268 *Spalding could not:* "New Baseball President: Spalding Resigns as Disputed Head of the National League," *New York Times,* April 3, 1902, 10.

269 *When Cap Anson heard:* "It's All in a Lifetime—Pitcher, Theosophist, Senator," *Chicago Daily Tribune,* October 23, 1910, G6.

269 *They were detained:* "Children from Cuba Held on Ellis Island," *New York Times,* November 2, 1902, 7.

269 *Her colony was called:* "Starved and Treated Like Convicts: Outrages at Point Loma; Exposed by an 'Escape' from Tingley. Startling Tales told in this City. Women and Children Starved and Treated Like Convicts. Thrilling Rescue," *Los Angeles Times,* October 28, 1901, per Evelyn A. Kirkley, "Starved and Treated Like Convicts: Images of Women in Point Loma Theosophy," *Journal of San Diego History* 43, no. 1 (Winter 1997). Also Richard F. Pourade, *The History of San Diego: Gold in the Sun, 1900–1919* (San Diego: Union Tribune Publishing Co., 1965), at http://www.sandiegohistory.org/books/pourade/gold/gold chapter2.htm.

270 *Gerry asked Albert Spalding: New York Journal,* November 5, 1902, per Emmett A. Greenwalt, *The Point Loma Community in California* (Berkeley: University of California Press, 1955), 59.
270 *According to the* New York Journal: Ibid.
270 *Spalding concluded:* Ibid.
270 *Spalding requested:* "Cuban Children to Be Sent Back," *New York Times,* November 8, 1902, 1.
270 *An Adyar Theosophist:* Greenwalt, *Point Loma Community in California,* 60–61.
270 *After soliciting: New York Herald,* November 8, 1902, per Greenwalt, *Point Loma Community in California,* 61.
271 *Ultimately, California:* " 'Lotus Buds' Admitted; Treasury Department Decides in Favor of Cuban Children," *New York Times,* December 7, 1902, 7.
271 *SPCC president:* " 'Lotus Buds' Start for California Home," *New York Times,* December 8, 1902, 3.
271 *As reported in:* "Spalding Likes Tingley Creed," *Fort Wayne Daily News,* March 30, 1903.
272 *The final straw:* Massimo Introvigne, "Who Is Irma Plavatsky? Theosophy, Rosicrucianism, and the Internationalization of Popular Culture from the Dime Novel to *The Da Vinci Code,*" presented at the annual CESNUR (Center for Study of New Religions) Conference, San Diego, 2006.
272 *Pursuing Dazaar:* Jess Nevins, "The Nick Carter Page," at http://www.oocities.com/jessnevins/carter.html. (One may wonder, seriously, whether Heinrich Himmler was a reader of Nick Carter and Dazaar serials, which were popular in several European countries including Germany.)

CHAPTER TWELVE: THE RELIGION OF BASEBALL

273 *His purpose in writing:* Victor Salvatore, "The Man Who Didn't Invent Baseball," *American Heritage* 34, no. 4 (June/July 1983):4.
273 *Overwhelmed by the need:* Letter from Mills to Spalding, November 5, 1904. Jack M. Doyle, Albert Spalding Scrapbooks, BA SCR 42.
274 *As Mills would:* Letter from Mills to Spalding, March 1, 1905. Jack M. Doyle, Albert Spalding Scrapbooks, BA SCR 42.
274 *As he elaborated:* Letter from Spalding to John Lowell, November 5, 1904. Jack M. Doyle, Albert Spalding Scrapbooks, BA SCR 42.
275 *Mills, in the aforementioned:* Letter from Mills to Spalding, March 1, 1905.
275 *In that form:* A. G. Spalding, "The Origin of the Game of Base Ball," *Akron Beacon Journal,* April 1, 1905. (This article begins oddly thus: "Nineteen hundred and five completes the 60th year of the life of base ball, for it dates its birth from the organization of the original Knickerbocker Base Ball Club of New York city, September 23, 1845. . . .")
275 *He sent this original:* Jack M. Doyle, Albert Spalding Scrapbooks, BA SCR 42.
275 *He also arranged:* "Abner Doubleday Invented Baseball: Abner Graves of Denver, Colorado, Tells How the Present National Game Had Its Origin," *Akron Beacon Journal,* April 4, 1905.

275 *I notice in saturdays:* Ibid. for printed version, manuscript in Jack M. Doyle, Albert Spalding Scrapbooks, BA SCR 42.

276 *Then he launched:* Ibid.

276 *Spalding's search: Freeman's Journal* (Cooperstown), March 5, 1924.

277 *The use of a starting pistol:* Nate DiMeo, "Olympic Sized Racism," *Slate,* August 21, 2008, http://www.slate.com/id/2197635/.

278 *Although he must soon:* "When Was Base Ball Organized," *Wilkes-Barre Times,* July 18, 1905.

278 *Yet, in the:* "Base Ball Origin," *Sporting Life,* August 12, 1905, 18.

278 *The* New Century Path: "Major-General Abner Doubleday," *New Century Path,* August 13, 1905.

278 *Furthermore, it is possible:* "Archaeology of Baseball," *The Sun,* May 2, 1905, 7.

279 *Following a financial embarrassment:* "Early Dow City History from 1851," *125 Years of Dow City—Arion History, 1869–1994* at the Crawford County, Iowa, GenWeb Project, http://freepages.genealogy.rootsweb.ancestry.com/~mykidsfamily/iacrawford.html. Horace J. Stevens, *The Copper Handbook: Manual of the Copper Industry of the World,* vol. 4 (Houghton, MI: Horace J. Stevens, 1904), 171. James A. Vlasich, *A Legend for the Legendary: The Origin of the Baseball Hall of Fame* (Bowling Green, OH: Bowling Green State University Popular Press, 1990), 21. F. W. Meyers, *History of Crawford County, Iowa: A Record of Settlement, Organization, Progress and Achievement,* vol. 1 (Chicago: S. J. Clarke Publishing Company, 1911), 197.

279 *In May 1895:* "Southern California News," *Los Angeles Times,* May 16, 1895, 13.

279 *In August:* Abner Graves, "Letters to the *Times,* Appreciates the Midsummer Number," *Los Angeles Times,* August 26, 1895, 6. "Tintic's Great Riches: Abner Graves Is Enthusiastic About Them," *Salt Lake Semi-Weekly Tribune,* July 19, 1898, 8.

279 *As Theosophical activity:* "Have Permanent Quarters," *Denver Evening Post,* June 9, 1896.

279 *Graves had also:* "Tintic's Great Riches: Abner Graves Is Enthusiastic About Them," *Salt Lake Semi-Weekly Tribune,* July 19, 1898, 8. Goodsprings Mining Co. (formerly Milford & Addison properties) advertisement, Display Ad 167—no title, *Los Angeles Times,* November 5, 1916, V12.

280 *As he wrote to Spalding:* Jack M. Doyle, Albert Spalding Scrapbooks, BA SCR 42.

281 *Upon release: New York World,* per *Freeman's Journal,* March 26, 1908, 1.

282 *Journalist Will Rankin wrote:* Alfred H. Spink, *The National Game,* 2nd ed. (St. Louis: National Game Publishing Co., 1911), 54. William M. Rankin, "Game's Pedigree: Alex Cartwright Was Father of Base Ball," *Sporting News,* April 2, 1908, 2.

282 *Referring to his father:* Letter to A. G. Spalding, March 22, 1909, quoted in part in *America's National Game,* 53.

283 *Smith's letter:* The letter was auctioned in 2006 by Robert Edward Auctions, http://www.robertedwardauctions.com/auction/2006/466.html.

284 *A. G. Mills' imagined:* "Baseball 77 Years Old," *New York Times,* February 6, 1916, S3.

285 *The Giants lost:* Charlton, *The Baseball Chronology.*

285 *The Giants played:* Robert L. Tiemann, "Major League Attendance," in *Total Baseball,* multiple editions.

285 *Who needed Theosophical:* Edgar Taft Stevenson, "Religion of Baseball," *Sporting Life,* May 28, 1910, 1.

288 *Baseball was:* Allen Sangree, "Fans and Their Frenzies: The Wholesome Madness of Baseball," *Everybody's Magazine,* August 1907, 387.

288 *Even after the carnage:* Morris R. Cohen, "Baseball," *The Dial* 67 (July 26, 1919), 57*ff.*

289 *Temple, however, again:* "Temple Will Be Guest of Champs," *Los Angeles Herald,* December 11, 1909.

289 *With the baseball public:* In full, in Spalding's inimitable florid style: *America's National Game: Historic Facts Concerning the Beginning, Evolution, Development and Popularity of Baseball with Personal Reminiscences of Its Vicissitudes, Its Victories and Its Votaries.*

290 *The Purple Mother:* "It's All in a Lifetime—Pitcher, Theosophist, Senator," *Chicago Daily Tribune,* October 23, 1910, G6.

290 *He stayed in touch:* "Jubilee Dinner Draws Notables," *New York Times,* February 2, 1926, 24. Abraham G. Mills papers, 1793–1929, bulk (1863–1929), New York Public Library, MssCol 2006.

290 *None at all:* Richard J. Tofel, "The Innocuous Conspiracy of Baseball's Birth," *Wall Street Journal,* July 19, 2001.

291 *Abner Graves, more dotty:* Abner Graves letter to the editor, *Freeman's Journal,* December 18, 1916. He says he will play in the game inaugurating Doubleday Field.

291 *Four years earlier:* "Denver Man Played First Baseball Game in History of Sport," *Denver Post,* May 9, 1912.

291 *Six months later:* Vlasich, *A Legend for the Legendary,* 21.

292 *In the following year:* "Hot Shot for 'Jim' Sullivan," *New York Times,* July 19, 1913, 5.

292 *Sullivan died suddenly:* The film was *Undine,* 1916, of which a reviewer wrote, "No one really cared much about the plot of *Undine:* It was enough that the sylphlike Ida Schnall showed up from time to time in various states of near-nudity."

292 *By the time:* "Spalding Heir Gives Reasons," *Los Angeles Times,* October 7, 1915, II 7.

292 *In his last will:* "Spalding Is Bitter Against Step-Mother, Former Local Woman," *Fort Wayne Journal-Gazette,* November 16, 1915, 12. (Keith Spalding's blistering and illuminating response to his stepmother's public statement regarding the estate and the circumstances of Albert Goodwill Spalding's funeral.)

293 *He further alleged:* Keith Spalding, "Opposition to Probate of Will," October 5, 1915, 7. Also, "Madame Tingley Demands Damages," *Los Angeles Times,* June 11, 1916, I 10.

293 *Mrs. Tingley was deposed:* "Spalding Will Contest Settled out of Court," *Los Angeles Times,* July 13, 1917, II 1.

293 *He alleged:* These claims were made before the court but had been expressed earlier in "Spalding Is Bitter Against Step-Mother, Former Local Woman," *Fort Wayne Journal-Gazette,* November 16, 1915, 12.

294 *His will:* "Writ of Mandate Issued in Spalding Case," *San Francisco Chronicle,* December 22, 1916, 10.

294 *Also during the contest:* "Spalding Heir Ruled Incompetent," *Oakland Tribune,* April 8, 1916, 1.

294 *On July 13, 1917:* "Spalding Will Contest Settled out of Court," *Los Angeles Times,* July 13, 1917, II 1.

294 *He went on:* "Plans Cruise On Own Vessel," *Los Angeles Times,* March 19, 1922, II 5. "Keith Spalding, Rancher, Was 83," *New York Times,* June 26, 1961, 31.

294 *Ten years after:* "$150,000 Is Sought in Spalding Estate," *Oakland Tribune,* October 13, 1936, 14. (Headline cites amount larger than that in the text of the article.)

294 *Lack of:* James Matthew Morris, Andrea L. Kross, *Historical Dictionary of Utopianism* (Lanham, MD: Scarecrow Press, 2004), 245.

295 *Their vision:* A memorably warped turn on Theosophical notions was the Heaven's Gate UFO cult headed by Marshall Herff Applewhite. Thirty-nine of its members, believing that California would sink into the sea, committed suicide in 1997 in order to attain a "level of existence above human" prior to boarding a spacecraft.

295 *In that same year:* Vlasich, *A Legend for the Legendary,* 34–35.

295 *Upon its display:* Ibid., 38.

296 *Cleland placed:* Ibid., 69–70.

296 *Beginning in 1934:* Ibid., 30.

[illegible] Spalding [illegible] 1912 [illegible]

[illegible] July 14, 1912 [illegible]

[illegible]

[illegible] April [illegible]

234 [illegible] Spalding [illegible] Will Convert [illegible] Times, June 13, 1912 [illegible]

244 [illegible] March 14, 1922 [illegible] Spalding [illegible] Times [illegible]

294 [illegible] $160,000 [illegible] Spalding [illegible]

[illegible] James Matthews [illegible] University Press, 2011 [illegible]

[illegible]

[illegible]

INDEX